The Politics of Distributing Social Transfers

The Politics of Distributing Social Transfers

State Capacity and Political Contestation in Sub-Saharan Africa and South Asia

Edited by

TOM LAVERS

OXFORD
UNIVERSITY PRESS

OXFORD
UNIVERSITY PRESS

Great Clarendon Street, Oxford, OX2 6DP,
United Kingdom

Oxford University Press is a department of the University of Oxford.
It furthers the University's objective of excellence in research, scholarship,
and education by publishing worldwide. Oxford is a registered trade mark of
Oxford University Press in the UK and in certain other countries

Impression: 1

Published in the United States of America by Oxford University Press
198 Madison Avenue, New York, NY 10016, United States of America

British Library Cataloguing in Publication Data
Data available

Library of Congress Control Number: 2021949603

ISBN 978–0–19–286252–5

DOI: 10.1093/oso/9780192862525.001.0001

Printed and bound by
CPI Group (UK) Ltd, Croydon, CR0 4YY

Acknowledgements

The project on which this book is based was conceived in the autumn of 2016 as part of the Effective States and Inclusive Development (ESID) research centre, based at the University of Manchester's Global Development Institute (GDI). Turning this original research idea into a research project and ultimately a book manuscript has been a long process and one that has required the considerable effort, input, support, and insight of an awful lot of people.

First, the project and book are particularly indebted to Sam Hickey, ESID's director of research. Sam has been truly exceptional as a supportive colleague who regularly goes out of his way to provide more junior researchers with opportunities, advice, and encouragement, both within GDI and beyond. I count myself as very fortunate to have worked with Sam and learned from him, and I hope that I will be able to pay forward some of that generosity in the future.

The project greatly benefited from the input of many participants from the ESID community at a series of project workshops to plan the research project and publication that took place in Manchester and Washington DC. In addition to the authors of the book chapters, these include: Armando Barrientos, David Booth, Julia Brunt, Sam Hickey, David Hulme, Mohammed Ibrahim, Tim Kelsall, Chris Lyon, Kate Pruce, and Kunal Sen. Furthermore, we received valuable comments and suggestions from participants at panels arranged to present early research findings at the annual meetings of the American Political Science Association (APSA) in Washington DC, the Development Studies Association (DSA) in Milton Keynes, and the ESID conference in Manchester.

The research would not have been possible without the time that our respondents generously contributed, as well as affiliations and collaborations by partner organizations. In particular, the support of the Organization for Social Science Research in Eastern and Southern Africa (OSSREA) in Ethiopia, the Institute of Research and Dialogue for Peace (IRDP) in Rwanda, and Social Science Baha (SSB) in Nepal was invaluable. Meanwhile, in Manchester, Julia Brunt, Kat Bethell, and Julie Rafferty all played vital roles in supporting the research project throughout.

In preparation of the manuscript, David Jackman and Kate Pruce both provided excellent research assistance with background literature reviews that contributed to the introductory and comparative chapters. Joseph Wong provided extremely insightful comment and critique on the majority of the papers in the volume. Adam Swallow at Oxford University Press expertly guided the book through the review process and was supportive and encouraging throughout. Kat Bethell supported the compilation of the final manuscript. The final stages of the book were completed while I was generously supported by a Leverhulme Research Fellowship.

Finally, my thanks to Arthur, Alice, and Shea who all accommodated absences and periods of intense workload, alongside the stresses and strains of life and Covid home-school, mostly with good humour.

Tom Lavers

Manchester, June 2021

This document is an output from a project funded by UK Aid from the UK Government for the benefit of developing countries. However, the views expressed and information contained in it are not necessarily those of, or endorsed by, the UK Government, which can accept no responsibility for such views or information, or for any reliance placed on them.

Contents

IV. UNIVERSALISTIC-INCLUSIVE CASES IN SOUTH ASIA

V. COMPARATIVE ANALYSIS

List of Figures

List of Tables

List of Abbreviations

ATM	Automated teller machine
CBT	Community-based targeting
CFSTF	Community Food Security Taskforce
CLIC	Community LEAP Implementation Committee
CSAC	Constituency Social Assistance Committee
CT-OVC	Cash Transfer for Orphans and Vulnerable Children
DA	Development agent
DLIC	District LEAP Implementation Committee
DoE	Department of Education
DPE	Directorate of Primary Education
EAWEP	Equal Access of Women to Education Project
EICV	Integrated Household Living Conditions Survey (Enquête Intégrale sur les Conditions de Vie des ménages)
EPRDF	Ethiopian Peoples' Revolutionary Democratic Front
ESID	Effective States and Inclusive Development research centre
FAR	Forces Armées Rwandaises
HDI	Human Development Index
HEW	Health extension worker
HSNP	Hunger Safety Net Programme
IEMIS	Integrated Educational Management Information System
IMF	International Monetary Fund
IRDP	Institute of Research and Dialogue for Peace
KAC	Kebele Appeals Committee
KANU	Kenya African National Union
KFSTF	Kebele Food Security Taskforce
KIHBS	Kenyan Integrated Household Budget Survey
LEAP	Livelihood Empowerment Against Poverty
LODA	Local Entities Development Agency
MGNREGA	Mahatma Gandhi National Rural Employment Guarantee Act
MINECOFIN	Ministry of Finance and Economic Planning
MINALOC	Ministry of Local Government
MIS	Management Information System
MP	Member of Parliament
NDC	National Democratic Congress
NGO	Non-governmental organization
NPP	New Patriotic Party
NPR	Nepalese rupee
OPCT	Older Persons Cash Transfer

OPDO	Oromiya People's Democratic Organization
OSSREA	Organization for Social Science Research in Eastern and Southern Africa
PDL-HIMO	Programme de Développement Local à Haute Intensité de Main d'Oeuvre
PESP	Primary Education Stipend Project
PMT	Proxy means test
PNC	People's National Convention
PSNP	Productive Safety Net Programme
PWSD-CT	Persons with Severe Disabilities Cash Transfer
RPF	Rwandan Patriotic Front
SACCO	Savings and Credit Cooperative Organization
SAU	Social Assistance Unit
SMC	School Managing Committees
SNNPR	Southern Nations, Nationalities and Peoples Region
TPLF	Tigrayan People's Liberation Front
TVET	Technical and vocational education and training
UNICEF	United Nations International Children's Emergency Fund
VUP	Vision 2020 Umurenge

Notes on Contributors

Edward Ampratwum is a Research Associate at the Global Development Institute (GDI), University of Manchester and a senior research fellow at the Center for Democratic Development, Ghana. His most recent research examines the politics of social protection implementation, with a focus on the intersectionality between political competition and power relations, state capacity and decentralized governance systems in Ghana. Other areas of his research include the politics of education and social accountability in urban service delivery. Edward holds a Ph.D. in Development Policy from the University of Manchester.

Jeevan Baniya is Assistant Director at Social Science Baha (SSB). His academic interests include public policy, democracy and development, state–society relations, governance, and gender and social inclusion (GESI). His research has been published in journals such as *Development and Change* and *Tribhuvan University Journal.*

Yangchen Gurung is an independent researcher, who was formerly a Research Associate with Social Science Baha (SSB). Her research interests include social inclusion, gender and minority rights, refugee rights, and environmental justice. She has co-written a chapter on Nepal's refugees in *South Asia State of Minorities Report 2019: Migrants, Refugees and the Stateless.*

Naomi Hossain is a political sociologist based at the Accountability Research Center at American University in Washington DC. She researches the politics of development, with a focus on understanding how people living with poverty and precarity get the public services they need. She has researched extensively across Bangladesh, and managed large comparative studies spanning another 20 countries in Asia, Africa, Latin America, and Europe. Recent books, edited or authored: *The Politics of Education in Developing Countries* (open access) (2019), *Food Riots, Food Rights, and the Politics of Provisions* (2017), and *The Aid Lab: Understanding Bangladesh's Unexpected Success* (2017).

Tom Lavers is a Senior Lecturer in Politics and Development at the University of Manchester's Global Development Institute. His research focuses on the politics of social policy, agrarian transformation, infrastructure, and state–society relations. He was one of the editors of the 2019 book, *The Politics of Social Protection in Eastern and Southern Africa.* He has previously published on the politics of social protection and other issues in leading journals, including *African Affairs, Development and Change, Geoforum, Journal of Agrarian Change, Journal of Peasant Studies, Social Science and Medicine*, and *World Development.*

Sanjay Mahato is an independent researcher, who was formerly a Research Associate with Social Science Baha (SSB). He is a visiting faculty at the Kathmandu University School of Management (KU SOM). His latest publications include articles in the *Journal of Southeast Asian Human Rights* and *The Politics of Change: Reflections on Contemporary Nepal.* His research interests include governance, political parties, elections, inclusion, big data, and survey research. He is also active in mainstream politics and international social democratic movements.

Eric Ndushabandi is Director of the Institute of Research and Dialogue for Peace (IRDP) in Rwanda. He holds a Ph.D. in Political Science from the Catholic University of Louvain in Belgium and is Senior Lecturer at the University of Rwanda, School of Governance and Political Science. Eric's research focuses primarily on transitional justice, memory and identity in post-conflict settings, democratization, and post-conflict peace building.

Sylvestre Nzahabwanayo (Ph.D.) is a Lecturer at the University of Rwanda College of Education (UR-CE) and Senior Researcher at the Institute of Research and Dialogue for Peace (IRDP) in Rwanda. His research involves the application of political philosophy to education, including issues such as citizenship, values, and peace education with a focus on youth in conflict-affected communities. He also specialized in social psychology with an emphasis on using Q-Methodology. Currently he is coordinating a Covid-19 response project, providing online psychosocial support through arts-based approaches.

Alesha Porisky is an Assistant Professor at Northern Illinois University in the Department of Political Science. She received her Ph.D. from the University of Toronto. Her research centres on social policies, cash transfers, state building and citizenship, with a particular focus on East Africa.

Uma Pradhan is Leverhulme Early Career Fellow (OSGA—South Asian Studies) and Junior Research Fellow (Wolfson College) at the University of Oxford. Her research examines the interconnection between state, society, and schooling. Her work has been published in journals such as *Nations and Nationalism*, *Compare: Journal of Comparative and International Education*, and *Oxford Research Encyclopedia of Education*.

Indrajit Roy is a Senior Lecturer—Global Development Politics at the Department of Politics, University of York. His research reflects on the growing role of the Global South in global development, with a specific focus on their underlying state–society complexes. His monograph *Politics of the Poor: Negotiating Democracy in Contemporary India* was published in 2018. He has published articles in *World Development*, *Journal of Peasant Studies*, *Journal of Development Studies*, *Economic and Political Weekly*, and *Journal of Asian Studies* among others.

Deepak Thapa is the Director of Social Science Baha. He writes regularly on Nepal's contemporary social and political issues, and is the author or editor of many publications including, most recently, editor of *The Politics of Change: Reflections on Contemporary Nepal* (2019). He has been a fortnightly columnist with *The Kathmandu Post* since 2009.

Timothy P. Williams is a Senior Associate at Proteknôn Consulting Group and an adjunct faculty member at Boston College School of Social Work. Previously he was an honorary research fellow with the Effective States and Inclusive Development programme at the University of Manchester. Timothy's research focuses on children's well-being, education, and protection, including a decade-long investigation into education and social policies in Rwanda. His work has received numerous awards, including the 2020 Dudley Seers Prize for best paper published in the *Journal of Development Studies* and the 2018 Joyce Cain Award from the Comparative and International Education Society of North America for his paper published in *World Development*.

PART I
RESEARCHING THE DISTRIBUTIONAL POLITICS OF SOCIAL TRANSFERS

1

The Global Spread of Social Transfers and the Challenge of Distribution

Tom Lavers

1. Introduction

Social protection has risen to a prominent position on the global development agenda since the turn of the millennium, with social transfers[1] in particular increasingly seen as the go-to response to poverty, inequality, and economic crises (Barrientos 2013). This trend has continued with the Covid-19 pandemic, with many countries expanding coverage and payments of existing programmes, and creating new programmes as part of the response to the economic fallout of lockdowns and lost earnings (Gentilini et al. 2020). The regions covered in this volume, sub-Saharan Africa and South Asia, have been among those where a significant increase in the number and scope of social transfer programmes has been apparent in recent decades.

Alongside the expansion of provision, the academic literature has likewise grown substantially in recent years. Within this burgeoning literature, however, there is a notable lack of research examining the political processes shaping the implementation of social transfer programmes. Yet, as so much social science research has highlighted (Lipsky 1980; Harriss 1988; Migdal 1988; Grindle and Thomas 1991), it is precisely between the policy pronouncements in a capital city and the delivery of programmes in towns and villages that the true nature of a policy becomes apparent. This is the analytical focus of this volume: the decisions made by state officials and politicians in administrative centres, towns, and villages; how these are shaped by social actors, including chiefs, clan leaders, landed elites, and civil society groups; and what this means for the distribution of social transfers. It is these interactions and power struggles—just as much as the social protection strategies and programme documents drafted by national policymakers, development partners, and international consultants—that define *the distributional politics of social transfers* and, in turn, shape the ability of social transfer programmes to deliver on their objectives.

Tom Lavers, *The Global Spread of Social Transfers and the Challenge of Distribution*.
In: *The Politics of Distributing Social Transfers*. Edited by Tom Lavers, Oxford University Press.
 DOI: 10.1093/oso/9780192862525.003.0001

The existing literature provides firm foundations from which to begin to explore the politics of distributing social transfers. Initial academic work on social transfers—much of it donor-funded and produced by an epistemic community of donor officials, consultants, and researchers keen to advance this agenda—focused largely on assessing programme impact and making the case for social transfers as means of reducing poverty and addressing all manner of social problems (see Barrientos and Hulme 2008; Hanlon et al. 2010, and numerous donor-commissioned impact evaluations). While these studies supported the case for the expansion of social transfers, they frequently also highlighted considerable variation in implementation effectiveness between and within countries: while some programmes largely deliver transfers on time to the categories of people identified in programme documents, in others, transfers end up in the hands of entirely different people to those intended and often well behind schedule (Coady et al. 2004; Watkins 2008; Handa et al. 2012; Berhane et al. 2013; Devereux et al. 2017).

Over the past decade, research has turned to understanding the deeply political global, regional, and national processes that have contributed to programme adoption and expansion. One key issue has been the competition between international organizations and bilateral agencies for prominence in global debates, with different organizations advancing divergent visions for social protection in the Global South (Deacon 2013; Von Gliszczynski 2015; Hickey and Seekings 2019). Another thread has been to analyse how international advocacy and sometimes donor conditionality intersect with national political dynamics related to electoral pressures, social mobilization, and regime ideology to shape policies and strategies in particular countries (Hickey 2008a; Seekings 2012; Koehler and Chopra 2014; Brooks 2015; Ouma and Adésínà 2018; Hickey et al. 2019; Abdulai 2020; Lavers and Hickey 2021). Whatever the origins of programmes, there are nonetheless clear signs that many national governments have come to see value in social transfers, evidenced by programmes' steadily expanding coverage as well as national governments taking increased responsibility for implementation and finance (Lavers and Hickey 2021).

This body of research, and specifically a recent edited volume which examined the intersection of international and national politics in the adoption and evolution of social protection (Hickey et al. 2019), provides the point of departure for this volume. The politics underpinning the design and expansion of particular programmes undoubtedly shapes the actual distribution of social transfers. Yet the influence of donor agencies—evident in the design of many programmes—declines exponentially as you move beyond the confines of ministries in capital cities into the provincial towns and rural villages where programmes are actually delivered. Likewise, while national governments shape implementation processes, their ability to implement a programme in line with their original objectives is contingent upon the history of state building and political relations between state agencies, political actors, and social organizations across the national territory.

Effective distribution of social transfers in line with programme guidelines and objectives cannot be assumed but is instead the outcome of an inherently political process involving negotiation, contention, and control. These complex processes shaping implementation are essential to understanding the distribution of social transfers and, ultimately, to assess the claims of these programmes as vital tools for poverty reduction and other purposes. The analytical focus in this volume is therefore on the processes by which people and communities are selected to enter and leave programmes, and how this relates to broader patterns of distribution within society.

In addition to the policy relevance of this focus, attempts to understand and explain patterns of variation in political processes also confront important debates within political science. First, the question arises as to whether such phenomena are best explained through historical legacies and path dependence—variously attributed to institutions or macro-sociological phenomena (Moore, Jr. 1967; Boone 2003; Pierson 2004; Acemoglu and Robinson 2012)—or contemporary political processes such as regime change, coalitions, and electoral politics (Poteete 2009; Van de Walle 2014; Brooks 2015). Second, the research raises questions about the appropriate unit of analysis for research. While research on comparative politics and the politics of development has heavily focused on the nation-state, this book joins a growing body of work that highlights the importance of sub-national comparisons given the considerable diversity within countries (Snyder 2001; Giraudy et al. 2019).

With respect to the distribution of social transfers, these debates arise in relation to the relative importance of historically embedded variation in state capacity and contemporary political dynamics. Implementation of social transfer programmes places particular burdens on state capacity. For example, states must be able to generate sufficiently accurate information with which to target programme participants (Ravallion 2015), whilst retaining autonomy from powerful local interests that might otherwise seek to capture programmes for their own benefit. Yet, state capacity is embedded in histories of state formation and varies enormously within countries (Mamdani 1996; Herbst 2000; Boone 2003; Singh 2015), with likely major implications for the distribution of social transfers. Indeed, a key challenge is that the poorest areas of countries, where social transfers are most important, are invariably where the state's presence and capacity is most limited. Meanwhile, one example of the ways in which contemporary political dynamics may shape the distribution of social transfers is through electoral competition. An important finding of existing research on the motivations of national governments in expanding social transfers is that politicians have sometimes sought to use social transfers as a means of securing votes and winning elections (Brooks 2015; Hickey et al. 2019; Lavers and Hickey 2021). While perhaps important for securing national political support, there is nonetheless a risk that the resulting distribution of social transfers is influenced by political criteria—rewarding political supporters—rather than protecting the most vulnerable (Mkandawire 2005; Van de Walle 2014; Hickey and Bukenya 2021). Moreover, the extent of these competitive pressures and thereby the incentives to manipulate distribution of social transfers are likely to vary considerably within countries.

It is with such questions regarding the politics of distributing social transfers that this book is concerned. The chapters in the volume present analysis of the distribution of social transfer programmes in Ethiopia, Ghana, Kenya, and Rwanda from sub-Saharan Africa, and Bangladesh and Nepal in South Asia. In addition to the between country and between region comparisons that this enables, each country case study emphasizes within country or sub-national variation in implementation. The central argument put forward in the book is that the distribution of social transfers is fundamentally shaped by a combination of the capacity and reach of the state across national territory—captured by Michael Mann's concept of infrastructural power (Mann 1984, 1986)—and the degree of national and local political contestation. A common aim within social protection debates has been to identify ways of de-politicizing the policy process or bypassing problematic local politics to avoid 'political capture' of programmes. Yet, these attempts ignore the fact that all processes of implementation and distribution—including those that are relatively effective and impartial—are necessarily shaped by politics. As such, not only is the distributional politics of social transfers a relatively unexplored area of academic interest, but it is also a topic that has important policy implications for the social protection agenda moving forward, including with respect to the future trajectory of programmes and the potential for social transfers to form part of a social contract.

Part I of the book provides the context for the case studies that follow. To do so, this first chapter discusses the global spread of social transfers and the distributional challenges that these programmes present. Chapter 2 then turns to the theoretical implications of this research focus, highlighting the importance of state capacity and political dynamics for the analysis of programme implementation and laying out the research design that guides the case studies presented in the book. The six country studies are divided into three parts, focusing in Part II on what are described as 'dominant-developmental' cases: Ethiopia and Rwanda; then in Part III on the 'competitive-distributive' cases of Ghana and Kenya; and, finally, in Part IV on the 'universalistic-inclusive' cases of Bangladesh and Nepal. Part V provides a comparative analysis of the cases, drawing out the empirical and theoretical implications of the studies.

Chapter 1 begins by discussing the spread of social transfers and how different types of programme have taken root in different parts of the world, including the two regions of direct interest: sub-Saharan Africa and South Asia. Next, the chapter reviews the literature on the distribution of social transfers, drawing on broader debates beyond these two regions. While the politics of implementation of social transfers and the distributional nature of this political contestation has been relatively neglected to date in much of sub-Saharan Africa and parts of South Asia, there is already a significant literature on Latin America, India, other parts of Asia, and the early period of today's welfare states on which to build. This chapter explores this existing literature with a view to highlighting key themes that inform the analytical approach pursued throughout the book. The discussion addresses, in turn: debates about targeting and graduation;[2] the mechanisms used to select programme participants in practice; and the productive ambitions of social transfer programmes.

2. The global spread of social transfers

Social transfer programmes have a long history in the developing world, going back at least as far as the early twentieth century in Africa and South Asia (Seekings 2011; Koehler and Chopra 2014). However, since the late 1990s there has been a rapid expansion in the number and scale of such programmes, with considerable diversity in the types of programme pursued in different countries (Barrientos 2013).

The common policy models for social transfer programmes were based on innovative programmes launched in Brazil, Mexico, and India, amongst others, in the 1990s. A process of diffusion, where countries have sought to learn from and mimic success stories, has taken place both regionally and globally (Sugiyama 2011; Brooks 2015; de Sardan 2018). However, the spread of these policy models has also clearly been influenced by the strong advocacy of social transfers by international organizations and bilateral donors who have framed particular policy instruments as the solution to poverty and, more speculatively, the basis of new social contracts between states and their citizens (Hickey 2011; Ferguson 2015; Von Gliszczynski 2015; de Sardan 2018; Hickey and Seekings 2019). Indeed, at times, this has gone beyond mere persuasion, with international actors using financial leverage and other political influence to press countries to adopt programmes (Ouma and Adésínà 2018; Abdulai 2019; Hickey and Bukenya 2021). While international advocacy has played an important role, donors are not all-powerful and cannot impose large-scale national programmes on governments. Rather, the expansion of programmes by national governments has been undertaken in response to assessments of domestic political dynamics and the potential for social transfers to contribute to elite political survival strategies (Garay 2016; Lavers and Hickey 2021). Diverse domestic political contexts have resulted in variation in the types of programme adopted and the degree of expansion.

In Latin America (Huber and Stephens 2012; Garay 2016), parts of South Asia (Koehler and Chopra 2014), and southern Africa (Ferguson 2015) the expansion of social transfers has been linked to processes of democratization, political mobilization, redistributive demands, and calls to expand social rights. In contrast, it is notable that the expansion of social transfers in most of sub-Saharan Africa has largely been a top-down process, based on the intersection of the interests and ideas of national governments and foreign donors, rather than the redistributive demands of empowered citizens. Indeed, several case studies highlight instances in which political elites have adopted programmes, expanded coverage or increased payments in anticipation of competitive elections, rather than in response to popular demands (Lavers and Hickey 2021), for example in Botswana (Seekings 2019), Ghana (Chapter 5; Abdulai 2019), Kenya (Chapter 6; Wanyama and McCord 2017), and Uganda (Hickey and Bukenya 2021).

However, electoral pressures are not the only driver of social transfers. Social protection, from its origins dating back some 2,000 years in Asia and Europe, has often been used as a means of securing political advantage and maintaining social order (Ravallion 2015). Indeed, low-cost social transfer programmes have been used by governments to maintain order in the context of high levels of inequality from the Poor Laws of nineteenth-century England to contemporary South Africa, Brazil, and China (Seekings and Nattrass 2005; Ngok 2013; Ravallion 2015; Saad-Filho 2015). Likewise, the Productive Safety Net Programme (PSNP) in Ethiopia and the Vision 2020 Umurenge Programme (VUP) in Rwanda (see Chapters 3 and 4) were both motivated by distributional crises considered a political threat to dominant party incumbent regimes (Lavers 2019a, 2019b).

Global advocacy of social transfers is linked, to a significant degree, to the post-structural adjustment 'New Poverty Agenda' manifest in the Millennium Development Goals and, consequently, great emphasis has been commonly placed on targeting the poorest (Mkandawire 2005, 2010; Barrientos and Hulme 2008; Ravallion 2015; Von Gliszczynski 2015). This emphasis has been reinforced by the International Monetary Fund (IMF) and World Bank's more recent embrace of poverty-targeted social transfers as a replacement for 'costly' and 'inefficient' food and fuel subsidies (Coady et al. 2015; Feltenstein 2017). Indeed, one of the main justifications for the expansion of social transfers has been that such programmes are a relatively inexpensive means of supporting the poorest without challenging market liberalism and existing patterns of wealth and accumulation (Mkandawire 2005; Saad-Filho 2015). The poverty focus is, in many cases, also supported by national political elites. In many African countries, political elites retain an idealized notion of the social support provided by communities and the agrarian economy, limiting state provision to those without support from other sources (Seekings 2012; Lavers 2019c). Likewise for Africa's self-styled 'developmentalist' governments, particularly Ethiopia and Rwanda, narrow targeting of social transfers is a means of promoting self-reliance and national development (Lavers 2019a, 2019b). As such, the ambitions of contemporary social transfer programmes fall well short of the key roles social policy has previously played within development including in production, redistribution, reproduction, social cohesion, and nation building (Oorschot 2002; Mkandawire 2004).

The narrative within which social transfers are framed differs in important ways in South Asia. Here, social protection has often been embedded within a language of social justice and constitutional rights to education, food, and work, with the state's responsibility to prevent famine and hunger of particular importance (Chapters 7 and 8; see also Koehler 2014; Hossain 2017). While these rights often go unfulfilled in practice, the result is that the objectives of many social transfer programmes are not limited to poverty reduction, but also include affirmative action and social inclusion, with women, girls, and discriminated social groups a particular focus (Koehler 2014; Hossain 2017). At the same time, however, donor influence remains important in several South Asian countries, including Bangladesh and Nepal, and the diffusion of poverty-targeted social transfers has also gained ground over the last two decades (Gazdar 2011; Drucza 2017; Hossain 2017).

A major focus of the social protection literature has been the remarkable rise of cash transfers conditioned on the use of social services, first in Latin America and then across the world, as shown in Fig. 1.1. While this diffusion has clearly been influenced by programmes in Brazil and Mexico, the idea of linking transfers to social conditions has roots in family allowances conditional on education attendance since at least the mid-twentieth century in Europe (Ravallion 2015). Other, apparently independent, early examples were Bangladesh's Food-For-Education programme established in 1993, which has since moved to cash payments (see Chapter 7) and education scholarships in Nepal that date to the 1970s (see Chapter 8). In contrast with many earlier European programmes, conditional cash transfers have usually been targeted to the poor.

Meanwhile, the expansion of social transfers in Africa has generally acknowledged the limited provision of education and health services, particularly in the poorest rural areas, as well as the inability of the state to monitor social conditions (Schubert and Slater 2006). As such, while conditional transfers exist on the continent (including in Ghana, the subject of Chapter 5) monitoring and enforcement of conditions has been limited, and unconditional cash transfers have been more common (see Fig. 1.1). While expansion has no doubt been inspired by the Latin American experience, unconditional cash transfers in South Africa and Mauritius also have a long history (Seekings and Nattrass 2005; Devereux 2007; Seekings 2011). In line with a focus on poverty, the majority of these programmes are targeted, though there are examples of 'universal' schemes where an entire target group is covered, notably social pensions in Lesotho, Namibia, and, most recently, Kenya (see Chapter 6).

Social transfer programmes have tended to focus on groups deemed to be particularly vulnerable and 'deserving', such as the elderly, children, and those with disabilities. In particular, working age adults are largely excluded in an attempt to avoid work disincentives, based on the assumption that adults should be self-reliant. This exclusion of working age adults ignores evidence that suggests that

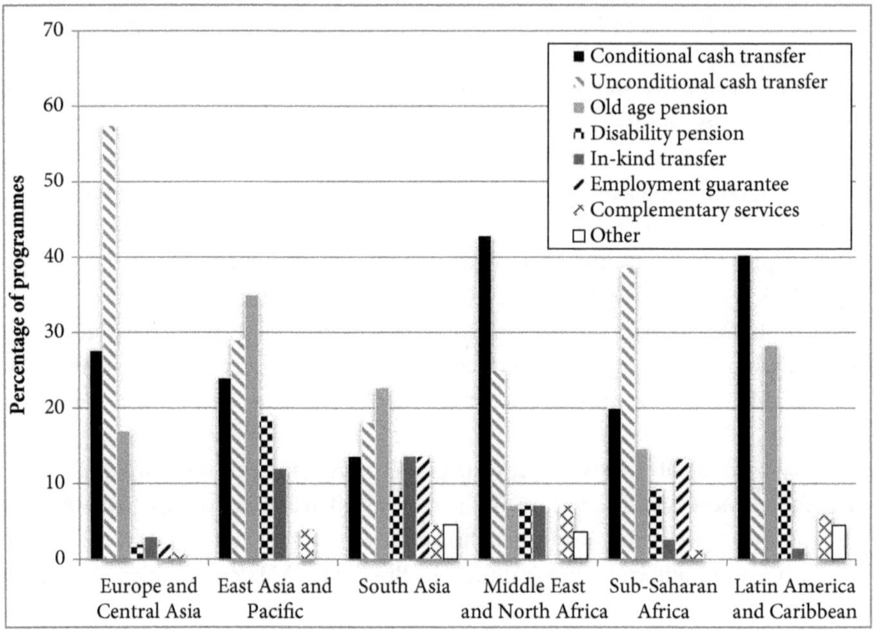

Fig. 1.1 Social transfer programmes by region
Source: Social Assistance Explorer for 2015

receipt of transfers does not provide a disincentive to work (Daidone et al. 2019) and disregards a frequent lack of employment opportunities. Where support is provided for working age adults, this often comes with stringent work requirements through public works or workfare schemes. As Fig. 1.1 shows, 'employment guarantee' schemes are almost exclusively pursued in sub-Saharan Africa and South Asia. Once again, such schemes have a long history that passes through the workhouses of England from the sixteenth century and the Famine Codes in colonial India from the late nineteenth century, before being popularized by Employment Guarantee Schemes first in Maharashtra and then across India (Ravallion 2015). In Africa, short-term public works have also long been used as a form of emergency relief (McCord 2012), while Ethiopia's Productive Safety Net Programme (see Chapter 3) and Rwanda's Vision 2020 Umurenge Programme (see Chapter 4) have significantly scaled up such past initiatives.

As such, while the expansion of social transfers has been common to many regions, the type of social transfer programme varies based on regional diffusion of particular models, the political motivations of elites, and the ideological preferences of national governments and donors. Vitally, different types of programme pose quite different implementation challenges depending on which groups they target, and whether states must monitor adherence to conditions, as discussed in the following sections.

3. Social transfers for whom? The targeting debate

Perhaps the key issue with respect to the distribution of social transfers is the process of selecting programme participants through targeting potential participants or exiting the programme through what has come to be known as 'graduation'. Other than a basic income grant, all social transfers are targeted in some way, whether based on means, demography, or geography. There is a huge literature on the theoretical, ethical, and practical strengths and limitations of targeting. In contrast, and somewhat surprisingly given the attention that targeting has received, there is relatively little research that examines the actual processes by which administrators apply targeting criteria and select participants, particularly in the countries covered in this book. Indeed, an important contribution of this volume is to provide a detailed analysis of the implementation process and the ways in which this is shaped by political factors.

Many contemporary debates about targeting essentially cover the same ground as those surrounding the nineteenth-century New Poor Laws in England, and related debates elsewhere, with relief seen as a disincentive to work and, based on Malthusian arguments, an incentive to high fertility and population growth (Dunkley 1981; Katz 2013; Ravallion 2015). As with their predecessors, contemporary social transfer programmes create a discontinuity between the poorest, who are targeted by social transfers, and the rest of the population. The central argument in favour of targeting is that in a context of scarce resources the impact of a programme will be maximized by selecting only those most in need and concentrating available resources on them (Coady et al. 2004; Slater 2011; Devereux 2016). Common concerns about the dangers of welfare dependency—whereby participants may come to rely on assistance and lose the incentive to work—reinforce the perceived need to target only those most in need. Based on these concerns, targeting has turned into a 'fetish' with an excessive focus on inclusion errors—whereby ineligible individuals are included in a programme when they should not be—rather than exclusion errors—where eligible households are excluded by the targeting process (Ravallion 2015). This emphasis is precisely the inverse of what would be required of a rights-based approach to social protection, which would prioritize the reduction of exclusion errors (Sepúlveda 2009).

Growing recent debates about graduation are motivated by the same underlying concerns as targeting: while targeting aims to select only eligible participants, graduation is concerned with removing the ineligible and reducing inclusion errors.[3] As such, graduation is likewise embedded within a narrow vision of social protection. In practice, graduation assumes that people graduate from a social transfer programme into self-sufficiency, rarely with any focus on building a social protection system that can provide protection, where needed, across the life-course (Samson 2015). For many programmes focused on vulnerable demographic groups the debate about graduation is limited—programme exit happens when children reach adulthood or when the elderly pass away. However, graduation and the need to promote self-sufficiency have become a major issue of concern for programmes for able-bodied adults, such as Ethiopia's PSNP and Rwanda's VUP, as well as BRAC's Targeting the Ultra Poor programme (Sabates-Wheeler and Devereux 2013).

There are a broad range of critiques of targeting (and graduation), which can be loosely grouped as political, ethical, and practical. The central political challenge to targeting is to question the claim that by targeting the poorest, programmes maximize redistribution. Ultimately this claim rests on the assumption that funding for social transfers is fixed and limited. In contrast, the experience of welfare states clearly highlights the 'paradox of redistribution'—that targeted programmes are actually far less redistributive than universal ones (Korpi and Palme 1988; Gelbach and Pritchett 2002). This paradox is explained by the cross-class solidarity and universalism required to maintain broad political support for generous social programmes, while narrow targeting tends to create a coalition in opposition to redistribution (Korpi and Palme 1988). The extent to which this paradox applies to contemporary developing countries, where patterns of class, taxation, aid, and social spending are very different, is under-researched.

Targeting is also frequently critiqued from an ethical perspective (Devereux 2016). One concern is that since any targeted programme inevitably has exclusion errors (as well as inclusion errors) 'it is the "tragedy of selectivity" that trying to target welfare to the truly needy inherently means that a part of them will not be reached' (Oorschot 2002, p. 182). Targeting of social transfers in effect knowingly deprives some of the poorest and most vulnerable people of support (Sen 1995). Moreover, targeting (often by design as a form of self-targeting, see Section 4) stigmatizes programme recipients and requires a loss of privacy and disclosure of personal information to access support that would not be accepted by the rest of the population (Sen 1995; Oorschot 2002; Standing 2007). Targeting often also has important gender implications. A common trend has been to target children as a group deserving of support. However, transfers are often made to mothers who are not seen as deserving in their own right, but who are thought more likely to act in the best interests of their children than men, despite a lack of strong evidence to support this claim (Akresh et al. 2016; Bastagli et al. 2016; Haushofer and Shapiro 2016).

These political and ethical critiques of targeting provide important context for the analysis in this book, but in our focus on implementation, it is the practical challenges that are most directly relevant to the analysis. A key question is whether targeted programmes are actually effective in reaching the poorest. The most commonly cited comparative study of targeting effectiveness assessed 122 targeted anti-poverty interventions in 48 countries, concluding that the median programme transfers 25 per cent more to the poorest than would otherwise be the case if random sampling had been used (Coady et al. 2004). Relatively pro-poor perhaps, but hardly a ringing endorsement of targeting efficacy. Furthermore, and in line with the aforementioned prioritization of inclusion errors over exclusion errors, the paper uses a measure of targeting effectiveness that focuses solely on inclusion errors, with no attention to eligible people excluded from the programmes (Coady et al. 2004, p. 25). More concerning still was the finding that one quarter of programmes were actually regressive: more likely to select non-poor people than random sampling (Coady et al. 2004). Of these, programmes in sub-Saharan Africa and South Asia were amongst the worst performers.[4] Subsequent assessments of graduation raise similar concerns regarding the difficulty of accurately assessing who should graduate from a programme (Sabates-Wheeler et al. 2015).

While it is commonly recognized that targeting is a challenge everywhere, the poorest countries are least well equipped to target support, with countries in Africa and South Asia often singled out for concern (Coady et al. 2004; Ravallion 2015). The challenges of targeting include the limited capacity of developing country states, particularly in rural and remote areas where poverty is most severe, and the dominance of the informal economy, which heightens the difficulty of generating sufficient information to assess who should and should not be included in a programme (Mkandawire 2005). Furthermore, in developing contexts where politics tends to be less institutionalized and resources are scarce, the discretionary powers afforded to state officials by targeted programmes can lead to politicization of distribution (Sen 1995; Mkandawire 2005). Indeed, a commonly expressed fear for social transfer programmes is the potential for targeting (though also graduation) to be shaped by clientelism (Devereux and White 2007; Abente Brun 2014).

While studies have raised concerns about the influence of clientelism on the distribution of social transfers in Africa (Wanyama and McCord 2017; Abdulai 2019; Hickey and Bukenya 2021; Pruce and Hickey 2019), as yet there is a lack of detailed research on implementation in these countries. More research is available for Latin America and South Asia. While several observers raised concerns that Brazil's Bolsa Família was susceptible to clientelism (Ansell and Mitchell 2011; Hall 2012); detailed research has concluded that the programme provided a boost in political support for President Lula and his Workers' Party on programmatic rather than clientelistic lines (Fried 2012; Sugiyama and Hunter 2013; Nichter 2014; Frey 2019). Mexico's main cash transfer programme[5] has similarly been subject to divergent assessments, representing continuity with past political clientelism (Ansell and Mitchell 2011) or a break from the past (De La O 2013). In India, research identifies clientelism as an important problem in Rajasthan, Uttar Pradesh, and West Bengal, though less so in Andhra Pradesh (Das 2015; Maiorano et al. 2018; Marcesse 2018; Das and Maiorano 2019). Similarly, in Bangladesh past studies argued that elite manipulation of targeting was common in the Food-For-Education programme (the predecessor of the programme covered in Chapter 7) (Galasso and Ravallion 2005). Likewise in Nepal, Dalit castes have frequently found it hard to access the transfers to which they are entitled without a powerful intermediary to approach the state on their behalf, entrenching existing patterns of clientelism (Drucza 2019).

Even were a programme able to identify its target group accurately at a particular point in time, major challenges remain. First, while some people suffer chronic poverty, research shows considerable variability in many people's circumstances within the year, from year to year and through the life-cycle (Krishna 2011). The result is that to hit a moving target of 'the poorest', targeting would need to be updated very regularly—something that rarely happens in practice (Kidd et al. 2017; Bah et al. 2019). Second, targeted programmes create perverse incentives for individuals to change their behaviour to be selected or to avoid graduating, resulting in poverty traps (Sen 1995; Oorschot 2002; Mkandawire 2005). Finally, the principle of targeting support at the poorest in society—if it can be achieved—raises difficult questions about social ordering. In many developing countries where the income distribution is relatively flat, there may be little difference in the incomes of the poorest 50 per cent of the population. By focusing on the poorest and providing a transfer sufficient to raise them out of poverty, a programme is likely to result in reordering of society, elevating the poorest above the near poor and often leading to social divisions and conflict in the process (Ellis 2012). The alternative is to reduce payments to such a minimal level as to preserve the existing social order, but have little impact on poverty (Ellis 2012; Hickey and Bukenya 2021).

The dominant focus on targeted social transfers therefore raises important questions regarding the political, ethical, and practical challenges of targeting. Of particular relevance for the present volume are questions about the state capacity required for effective distribution and the influence of politics on distribution as a result of the discretionary powers allocated to local officials. These themes are explored at length throughout the book.

4. The challenge of targeting

In the face of these challenges and in the context of the 'fetish' that targeting has become, a great amount of energy has been expended on developing targeting mechanisms that could address the informational challenge—the generation of accurate information on who should be included and excluded—in the context of the administrative challenge of limited state capacity and to overcome the risk of political interference in the selection process. Given that income or means tests are all but infeasible in informal and agricultural economies, social transfers tend to rely on a combination of alternative mechanisms, all of which, targeting advocates admit, are far from perfect (Coady et al. 2004; Grosh et al. 2008; Devereux et al. 2017).

The most common targeting mechanism across regions (see Fig. 1.2) is to select demographic groups, such as the elderly, children, or female-headed households. Compared to other targeting mechanisms, demographic targeting is

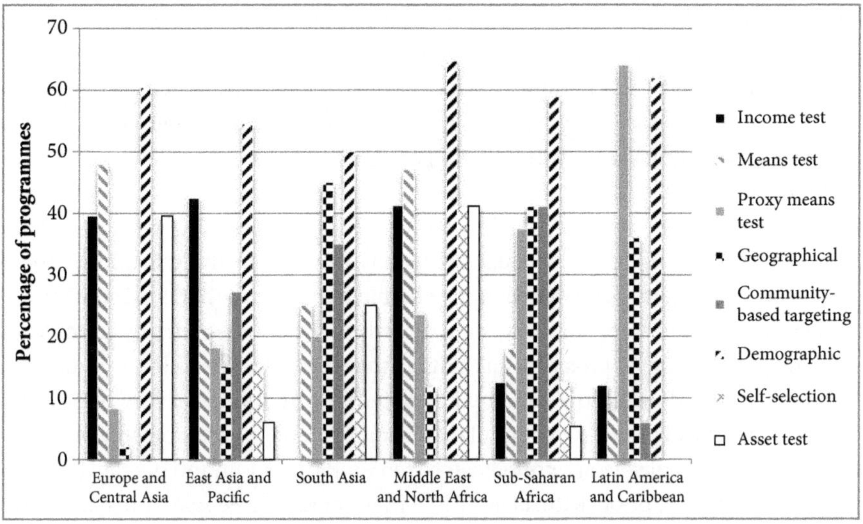

Fig. 1.2 Targeting mechanisms in social transfer programmes
Source: Social Assistance Explorer for 2015

administratively straightforward and the informational challenge is considerably lower, though the lack of comprehensive birth registration systems can pose barriers (Hunter and Sugiyama 2018). While 'deserving' demographic groups may well be considered worthy of support regardless, it should be noted that demographic criteria are not always closely related to poverty (Slater 2011). Where demographic criteria are the sole targeting mechanism, social transfers are effectively universal within a particular demographic group, as in the case of universal social pensions or child grants. Examples amongst the case studies in this book include Kenya (Chapter 6), Bangladesh (Chapter 7), and Nepal (Chapter 8). However, in most cases demographic criteria are used in tandem with other targeting mechanisms intended to identify individuals or households within these demographic groups.

The second most common targeting mechanism in sub-Saharan Africa and South Asia is geographical targeting to focus resources on the poorest regions within a country. Though detailed data on poverty incidence within countries are not always available, the informational challenge facing geographical targeting is considerably lower than that for targeting individuals. The key assumption underpinning geographical targeting is that poverty is spatially concentrated. In many countries this is the case to some degree, though inevitably poor individuals in relatively wealthy districts will be excluded as a result.

In addition to targeting particular demographic groups or geographical areas, a range of approaches have been employed to select individuals or households for inclusion in programmes. Proxy means tests aim to allocate social transfers based on need, but, in the absence of sufficient information, take proxies of poverty and hardship, such as demographics (e.g. female or elderly headed households), absence of productive resources (e.g. land, animals) or household characteristics (e.g. type of roof). The first programme to use a proxy means test was in Chile in 1980 (Coady et al. 2004) and proxy means tests have since spread widely across Latin America and the Caribbean, where they are used in 64 per cent of social transfer programmes. Proxy means tests are also common in sub-Saharan Africa, with 38 per cent of programmes employing them, likely as a result of World Bank enthusiasm for the supposedly 'objective' data that they provide (Grosh et al. 2008, p. 100). The spread of proxy means tests has resulted in the creation of social registries—vast databases of potentially eligible participants that tackle the impossible task of maintaining an up-to-date record of 'the poor'—in many countries.

A major critique of proxy means tests is that the accuracy of the econometric models used tends to be low. Moreover, conducting the survey on which the proxy means test relies is expensive and places a considerable burden on state capacity. The result is that surveys are not repeated frequently, providing an out-of-date view of who is and is not poor (Kidd et al. 2017). In order to stop people from gaming the system by adapting their behaviour or hiding assets, the criteria used in the proxy means test are often kept secret, leading to a lack of transparency regarding how selection is made (Brown et al. 2018). Moreover, the proxy means test requires a comprehensive initial selection of potentially eligible candidates, placing demands on the capacity and reach of the state to identify all those potentially eligible. Many of these practical challenges associated with proxy means tests are illustrated in the chapters on Rwanda (Chapter 4), Ghana (Chapter 5), and Kenya (Chapter 6).

In contrast, community-based targeting devolves responsibility for distribution, with community representatives or mass community meetings used to select programme participants. As a result, community-based targeting is relatively inexpensive for states to administer and attempts to address the informational challenge based on the assumption that communities have detailed knowledge of the circumstances of their members. Proponents, in line with the broader claims of the decentralization literature, claim that community-based targeting enables adaption of central targeting guidelines to local circumstances, providing greater community ownership over the programme, and has the potential for greater local state accountability to the population (Galasso and Ravallion 2005; Alatas et al. 2012). However, the use of community-based targeting is generally motivated by necessity 'where other options just do not seem feasible' (Coady et al. 2004, p. 61), primarily where state capacity to employ other mechanisms is limited. Unsurprisingly, community-based targeting is most common in sub-Saharan Africa, with 41 per cent of programmes, followed by South Asia, with 38 per cent. The main criticism of community-based targeting—in line with the literature on decentralization and participation in general—is regarding the tendency to ignore the power relations that shape any attempt to promote participation (Cooke and Kothari 2001; Hickey and Mohan 2004). The possibility of effective community-based targeting rests to a significant degree on the implausible assumption of community homogeneity (Galasso and Ravallion 2005). Yet, there is a very real danger that targeting may be influenced by powerful local actors, reinforcing existing class, gender, or ethnic divisions. Moreover, the programme's targeting rationale may clash with local values and understandings of distribution and deservingness, leading to significant local adaptation (Alatas et al. 2012; Sabates-Wheeler et al. 2013; de Sardan and Hamani 2018; Pruce 2019). In this volume, case studies on Ethiopia (Chapter 3), Rwanda (Chapter 4), Ghana (Chapter 5), and Kenya (Chapter 6) all examine community-based targeting processes.

The other main method employed to select individuals or households is self-selection. Self-targeting aims to make the receipt of transfers sufficiently undesirable, through labour requirements or social stigma, that only those most desperate for support will seek it out. Self-targeting, in practice, entails punishing the poor as a means of solving the informational challenge and limiting programme budgets. Self-targeting is particularly common in public works schemes in Africa and South Asia, and case examples here include Ethiopia (Chapter 3) and Rwanda (Chapter 4). Critiques—as with those of the workhouses of the past—tend to focus on the immorality of punishing poor people who seek support (Midgley 1984; Standing 2007), as well as questioning the effectiveness of self-targeting, which frequently leads to large exclusion errors as many eligible people do not take up support due to the costs involved (Mkandawire 2005).

Recent trends in targeting, given the limitations of each method, have been to combine multiple targeting approaches in an attempt to bypass weak state capacity and minimize opportunities for political interference. One common trend has been to combine community-based targeting and proxy means tests, with the proxy means test providing a supposedly 'objective' check on the subjective community assessment. Potentially eligible households are first identified through community-based targeting and these households are then surveyed, creating a social registry that enables centralized selection based on a proxy means test. In certain respects this approach mirrors the centralized selection of participants in Bolsa Família that is credited with avoiding problems with clientelism that have hampered the delivery of social programmes in the past. Here, the government created a new federal agency staffed by technocrats, which conducted regular audits of local registration processes, centralized control of the unified registry, and established direct payments to programme recipients through automated teller machine (ATM) cards (Fried 2012; Sugiyama and Hunter 2013; Nichter 2014). Similar arguments underpin De La O's (2013) claims that Mexico's Progresa has been delivered along programmatic lines, with strong centralized control bypassing powerful local intermediaries who have politicized programmes in the past. Once again, though, these are not mere technical reforms, but political processes. Bypassing local political influence over distribution must fit the political priorities of central government as illustrated by the divergent experiences of Rwanda (Chapter 4), Ghana (Chapter 5), and Kenya (Chapter 6).

Another trend has been donor promotion of social accountability mechanisms as means of holding state officials to account and improving service delivery (World Bank 2004). These initiatives aim to improve the transparency of targeting procedures and provide education to local communities about the objectives of the programmes and participants' rights, while independent grievance procedures provide an opportunity for those who feel they have been treated unfairly to appeal. Accountability mechanisms have achieved some apparent successes (Molyneux et al. 2016; Sugiyama 2016). However, once again, political context is key, with accountability mechanisms unlikely to gain much traction where political dynamics are not supportive (Cochrane and Tamiru 2016; Hickey and King 2016).

Whatever mechanisms are employed to select participants, it is clear from this discussion that they are highly imperfect, with important trade-offs between them. Moreover, targeting mechanisms are dependent, albeit to varying degrees, on the state's capacity to implement them, while they risk the possibility of political interference.

5. Productive ambitions for social transfers

Many social transfer programmes are not justified merely on their anti-poverty credentials but also based on the claim that they can have productive impacts. Indeed claims, and sometimes evidence, regarding the productive potential of social transfer programmes have often been important in securing political support and countering the preconception that social spending is just a drain on resources (Davis et al. 2016; Lavers 2019a, 2019b). More problematically, however, this productive focus resonates with the anti-poverty focus of many social transfer programmes, which frame the poor as a problem to be addressed, legitimating interventions to 'discipline and govern the poor' and transform them 'into better, more productive members of society' (Hickey 2008b, p. 353).

In some cases, productive claims rest on the social transfer itself—that by giving poor people money, they are better able to invest in productive activity and more likely to take the risks required to make productive investments. For the most part, however, claims rest on the conditions attached to social transfers. So, for conditional cash transfers, the expectation is that education and health conditions build human capital in the long term, producing healthier and better-qualified entrants into the workforce, as with programmes in Ghana (Chapter 5), Bangladesh (Chapter 7), and Nepal (Chapter 8). Yet evidence as to whether such conditional transfers have any more of an impact on education and health than unconditional ones is scarce (Slater 2011). Vitally, moreover, the economic impact of improved education and health is contingent on a dynamic economy that provides employment opportunities, something that is often not present in practice.

Programmes have also been critiqued based on the gendered assumptions embedded within them. Many programmes are specifically framed as tools to empower women, including by paying transfers to women in households and supporting the education of girls through education requirements. Indeed, there is some evidence that cash transfers can have such positive impacts (Hunter et al. 2020). Yet Mexico's Oportunidades and other conditional cash transfer programmes have been criticized for the significant obligations and additional work burden that they place on women, building on a legacy of maternalist social policies in Latin America that make support conditional on 'good motherhood' (Molyneux 2006; Cookson 2018; Piccoli and Gillespie 2018). Many social transfers are specifically paid to women based on social expectations regarding mothers' prioritization of their children.

Other programmes seek to mobilize social transfers more directly for productive purposes. Notably social transfers conditioned on public works participation aim to create infrastructure that can enhance productive activity including roads, terracing, and irrigation canals, as with those in Ethiopia and Rwanda. While the links between anti-poverty transfers and the Poor Laws have been noted, labour-intensive public works programmes are specifically reminiscent of the English workhouses that emerged in the sixteenth century but became the main form of support after the 1834 New Poor Laws. Just as with contemporary public works programmes, the turn to workhouses was motivated by the desire to reduce social spending and the assumption that poverty was ultimately the result of individual choice and bad behaviour (Mencher 1968; Hindle 2004). By making workhouses as unpleasant as possible, only the most desperate would seek support and those who did would learn discipline through the work regime within (Midgley 1984; Ravallion 2015). In doing so, the workhouse involved the exchange of limited relief for a loss of civic rights (Bahle et al. 2010, p. 450), with 'punishment by imprisonment' intended to provide 'corrective discipline' for the 'idle poor and vagabonds' (Jütte 1994, p. 169). There are undoubtedly parallels here with contemporary social transfer schemes based on public works. Self-targeting and concerns about dependency have long been central features of schemes in India, Ethiopia (Chapter 3), and Rwanda. And while none of the programmes goes as far as incarceration in the workhouse, Rwanda's VUP certainly raises questions about the loss of civic rights for programme participants (see Chapter 4). Moreover, Molyneux's gender critique of Oportunidades would largely apply also to the likes of Ethiopia's PSNP, which is explicitly gendered in its expectations of men and women's roles (see Chapter 3).

Public works schemes have often been criticized for the poor quality of the infrastructure created, resulting in questionable productive impacts (McCord 2012). Of more direct relevance to our focus on the distribution of social transfers are criticisms of the protective role of such public works and public employment schemes. The labour requirements of public works programmes necessarily exclude many of the most vulnerable who are unable to work—though many schemes now include unconditional support for the labour-constrained. Public works schemes also raise questions about the gendered division of labour and whether works requirements entrench or challenge existing gendered roles. Moreover, where schemes do not provide some form of employment guarantee, their credentials as a social protection programme are called into question (McCord 2012). This is an important distinction between Ethiopia's PSNP (see Chapter 3), which provides guaranteed employment for those enrolled, and Rwanda's VUP, where public works are dependent on the ability of local governments to organize projects (see Chapter 4).

Another increasingly common trend has been to link social transfers to a variety of credit, training, and agricultural extension programmes that seek to build participants' productive assets, frequently linked to the goal of graduation from support. Experience to date has been less than impressive, with modest improvements in livelihoods and limited success with graduation (Silvio et al. 2015; Daidone et al. 2019; Sabates-Wheeler et al. 2021). Beyond the questionable efficacy of these programmes, it is important to acknowledge the framing of such initiatives, with the implication that poverty is attributable in part to ignorance, with the social transfer programme used to teach participants the importance of self-reliance and hard work, ultimately leading to graduation. These rationales are infused within programmes in Ethiopia and Rwanda.

Here the key point is that while policy documents frame the productive role of social transfers as compatible with their protective role, this should not be taken for granted. One question addressed in subsequent case studies is how compatible the objectives are in practice and, where in tension, how officials administering programmes reconcile these competing programme objectives.

6. Conclusion

The global spread of social transfer programmes in recent decades has been remarkable, with programmes promoted and justified in terms of their potential to reduce poverty and vulnerability, address inequality and social injustice, and contribute to economic growth and social cohesion. Nonetheless, the motivation for adopting and expanding these programmes is not purely benign. Rather, programme expansion has been shaped by a range of political interests and ideological influences, with politicians often seeking to utilize programmes as a means of securing political advantage by winning votes or appeasing opponents; maintaining social order and projecting political authority; or placating the demands of social movements. Moreover, the combination of the global and regional diffusion of policy ideas and the influence of development partners, and domestic political processes has resulted in distinct patterns of policy adoption. In Africa, social transfers have tended to take the form of either unconditional, poverty-targeted transfers for vulnerable groups or labour-intensive public works programmes. In contrast, in South Asia there has been a stronger tendency towards universalistic programmes framed in terms of the need to address historical injustice.

The result then is that social transfer programmes are intertwined with political dynamics and that distinct forms of social transfer programme present particular challenges in terms of their implementation in practice. Despite regular concerns expressed in the literature regarding the challenge of implementing such programmes given the limited nature of state capacity in many developing countries and the dangers of the 'political capture' of programme implementation, very little research has been conducted on the actual process of implementing social transfer programmes in much of Africa and South Asia, and how this is shaped by political factors. This book makes a conceptual and empirical contribution to the literature by addressing this gap, theorizing the political factors shaping the implementation process in Chapter 2, highlighting the importance of attention to variation within countries, and analysing the distribution of social transfers in a set of six country studies.

The comparative findings of the volume, discussed in detail in Chapter 9, show that distinct combinations of state capacity and reach, and political dynamics combine in the case studies to produce significant inter- and intra-country variation in the distribution of social transfers. On the whole, high levels of state capacity or *infrastructural power* are associated with more impartial and effective programme implementation. However, state capacity alone is insufficient. Vitally, national and local political dynamics shape the ways in which this state capacity is deployed in programme implementation. Contrary to assumptions embedded in the good governance and accountability literature, none of the cases provides an example of political contestation driving increased effectiveness. In contrast, there are certainly instances where political competition—between parties locally or between national and local governments—provides incentives for politicians to intervene in the distribution of social transfers to try to secure political advantage. Meanwhile, for the most part, political dominance tends to be associated with relative impartiality in Bangladesh, Ethiopia, Ghana, and Rwanda. However, attempts to prioritize the productive objectives of social transfers in Ethiopia and Rwanda have undermined the programmes' protective function in spite of relatively strong capacity and impartial distribution.

Ultimately, the cases emphasize that effective implementation requires both state infrastructural power and its effective deployment through supportive power relations. Indeed, these two factors are key to understanding why, for example, targeting of the PSNP in Ethiopia's Afar and Somali regions has been so problematic, despite the fact that the programme in the rest of the country has been widely lauded as a model of effective implementation; why implementation of national guidelines varies sharply between electorally competitive and dominant districts in Ghana; or why the introduction of a universal scholarship in Bangladesh has sharply reduced confrontation between parents and teachers.

A strong tendency in the social protection literature has been to look for ways to de-politicize or to bypass problematic local politics based on the concern that social transfer programmes are vulnerable to political capture. The overwhelming conclusion of the case studies, however, is that removing politics from the implementation process is impossible and, moreover, that even relatively effective and impartial implementation is underpinned by political processes. Examples include Bangladesh, Ethiopia, and Rwanda, where the fusion of party and state provides vital capacity and direction for implementation, and Kenya, where the political sensitivity of inter-ethnic distribution has resulted in careful attention to ensure equitable and impartial allocation of social transfers.

Overall, the case studies highlight the many practical, political, and ethical challenges associated with the distribution of social transfers. In particular, governments' ability to distribute targeted social transfers effectively is heavily dependent on state infrastructural power and supportive political dynamics. In the many cases where such forms of capacity are lacking and political contestation risks undermining impartial implementation, universalistic policy designs offer considerable advantages.

Notes

1. The term 'social transfer' is used throughout this book for several reasons. First, this narrows the focus from social protection, which also includes social insurance and labour market regulation, and which are not covered here. Moreover, social transfer is a more accurate label for the programmes covered in this volume than social assistance. Social assistance is associated specifically with anti-poverty transfers (Bahle et al. 2010; Barrientos 2013), yet this book covers several programmes which are not specifically focused on poverty. Social transfers entail transfers—often of cash, but not exclusively—ranging from conditional cash transfers to social pensions to public works schemes.
2. Targeting refers to the process of selecting particular individuals or groups for inclusion in a programme—whether this is based on poverty, age, geography, or other characteristic. Graduation is the process by which individuals considered no longer to meet criteria for inclusion in a programme are selected for removal.
3. The related question of how to promote graduation through complementary programmes is discussed below.
4. The source material for the analysis was from 1985–2002, before the recent expansion of social transfers. Moreover, just five of the 122 programmes are social transfer programmes in sub-Saharan Africa and South Asia, the two regions of interest, and low-income African countries are entirely absent.
5. The programme was repeatedly rebranded by successive presidents from Progresa to Oportunidades to Prospera in an attempt to claim political credit for the programme (Niedzwiecki 2018).

References

Abdulai, A.-G., 2019. Rethinking elite commitment to social protection in Ghana: Insights from an adapted political settlements approach. *ESID Working Papers*, 112.

Abdulai, A.-G., 2020. Competitive clientelism, donors and the politics of social protection uptake in Ghana. *Critical Social Policy*, https://doi.org/10.1177/0261018320945605.

Abente Brun, D., 2014. Evaluating political clientelism. *In*: D. Abente Brun and L. Diamond, eds. *Clientelism, Social Policy and the Quality of Democracy*. Baltimore, MD

Acemoglu, D. and Robinson, J. A., 2012. *Why Nations Fail: The Origins of Power, Prosperity and Poverty*. London: Profile Books.

Akresh, R., De Walque, D., and Kazianga, H., 2016. *Evidence from a Randomized Evaluation of the Household Welfare Impacts of Conditional and Unconditional Cash Transfers Given to Mothers or Fathers*. Washington, DC: World Bank.

Alatas, V., Banerjee, A., Hanna, R., Olken, B. A., and Tobias, J., 2012. Targeting the poor: Evidence from a field experiment in Indonesia. *American Economic Review*, 102 (4), 1206–1240.

Ansell, A. and Mitchell, K., 2011. Models of clientelism and policy change: The case of conditional cash transfer programmes in Mexico and Brazil. *Bulletin of Latin American Research*, 30 (3), 298–312.

Bah, A., Bazzi, S., Sumarto, S., and Tobias, J., 2019. Finding the poor vs. measuring their poverty: Exploring the drivers of targeting effectiveness in Indonesia. *World Bank Economic Review*, 33 (3), 573–597.

Bahle, T., Pfeifer, M., and Wendt, C., 2010. Social assistance. *In*: F. G. Castles, S. Leibfried, J. Lewis, H. Obinger, and C. Pierson, eds. *The Oxford Handbook of the Welfare State*. Oxford: Oxford University Press, 448–461.

Barrientos, A., 2013. *Social Assistance in Developing Countries*. Cambridge: Cambridge University Press.

Barrientos, A. and Hulme, D., 2008. *Social Protection for the Poor and Poorest: Concepts, Policies and Politics*. London: Palgrave Macmillan.

Bastagli, F., Hagen-Zanker, J., Harman, L., Barca, V., Sturge, G., Schmidt, T., and Pellerano, L., 2016. *Cash Transfers: What Does the Evidence Say? A Rigorous Review of Programme Impact and of the Role of Design and Implementation Features*. London: Overseas Development Institute.

Berhane, G., Hoddinott, J., Kumar, N., Seyoum Taffesse, A., Tedla Diressie, M., Yohannes, Y., Sabates-Wheeler, R., Handino, M., Lind, J., Tefera, M., and Sima, F., 2013. *Evaluation of Ethiopia's Food Security Program: Documenting Progress in the Implementation of the Productive Safety Nets Programme and the Household Asset Building Programme*. Washington, DC: IFPRI.

Boone, C., 2003. *Political Topographies of the African State: Territorial Authority and Institutional Choice*. Cambridge: Cambridge University Press.

Brooks, S. M., 2015. Social protection for the poorest: The adoption of antipoverty cash transfer programs in the Global South. *Politics and Society*, 43 (4), 551–582.

Brown, C., Ravallion, M., and Van De Walle, D., 2018. A poor means test? Econometric targeting in Africa. *Journal of Development Economics*, 134, 109–124.

Coady, D., Grosh, M., and Hoddinott, J., 2004. *Targeting of Transfers in Developing Countries: Review of Lessons and Experience*. Washington, DC: World Bank.

Coady, D. P., Flamini, V., and Sears, L., 2015. The unequal benefits of fuel subsidies revisited: Evidence for developing countries. *IMF Working Papers*, 15 (250).

Cochrane, L. and Tamiru, Y., 2016. Ethiopia's productive safety net program: Power, politics and practice. *Journal of International Development*, 28 (5), 649–665.

Cooke, B. and Kothari, U., 2001. *Participation: The New Tyranny?* London: Zed Books.

Cookson, T. P., 2018. *Unjust Conditions: Women's Work and the Hidden Cost of Cash Transfer Programs*. Oakland, CA: University of California Press.

Daidone, S., Davis, B., Handa, S., and Winters, P., 2019. The household and individual-level productive impacts of cash transfer programs in sub-Saharan Africa. *American Journal of Agricultural Economics*, 101 (5), 1401–1431.

Das, U., 2015. Does political activism and affiliation affect allocation of benefits in the Rural Employment Guarantee Program: Evidence from West Bengal, India. *World Development*, 67, 202–217.

Das, U. and Maiorano, D., 2019. Post-clientelistic initiatives in a patronage democracy: The distributive politics of India's MGNREGA. *World Development*, 117, 239–252.

Davis, B., Handa, S., Hypher, N., Rossi, N.W., Winters, P., and Yablonski, J., 2016. *From Evidence to Action: The Story of Cash Transfers and Impact Evaluation in Sub-Saharan Africa*. Oxford: Oxford University Press.

De La O, A. L., 2013. Do conditional cash transfers affect electoral behavior? Evidence from a randomized experiment in Mexico. *American Journal of Political Science*, 57 (1), 1–14.

De Sardan, J.-P. O., 2018. Miracle mechanisms, traveling models, and the revenge of contexts: Cash transfer programs—a textbook case. *In*: J.-P. O. De Sardan and E. Piccoli, eds. *Cash Transfers in Context*. New York: Berghahn Books, 29–91.

De Sardan, J.-P. O. and Hamani, O., 2018. Cash transfers in rural Niger: Social targeting as a conflict of norms. *In*: J.-P. O. De Sardan and E. Piccoli, eds. *Cash Transfers in Context*. New York: Berghahn Books, 300–322.

Deacon, B., 2013. *Global Social Policy in the Making*. Bristol: Policy Press.

Devereux, S., 2007. Social pensions in southern Africa in the twentieth century. *Journal of Southern African Studies*, 33 (3), 539–560.

Devereux, S., 2016. Is targeting ethical? *Global Social Policy*, https://doi.org/10.1177/1468018116643849.

Devereux, S., Masset, E., Sabates-Wheeler, R., Samson, M., Rivas, A.-M., and Te Lintelo, D., 2017. The targeting effectiveness of social transfers. *Journal of Development Effectiveness*, 9 (2), 162–211.

Devereux, S. and White, P., 2007. Pilots, principles or patronage: What makes social protection succeed in southern Africa? Presented at the Social Protection and Ideologies of Welfare in Southern Africa Conference, Oxford University.

Drucza, K., 2017. The politics behind social protection in Nepal. *Asian Journal of Comparative Politics*, https://doi.org/10.1177/2057891117734652.

Drucza, K., 2019. 'At least the government is watching out for us now': Dalit perceptions and experiences of governance and cash transfers in three villages in Sarlahi, Nepal. *Modern Asian Studies*, 53 (6), 2041–2078.

Dunkley, P., 1981. Whigs and paupers: The reform of the English Poor Laws, 1830–1834. *Journal of British Studies*, 20 (2), 124–149.

Ellis, F., 2012. 'We are all poor here': Economic difference, social divisiveness and targeting cash transfers in sub-Saharan Africa. *Journal of Development Studies*, 48 (2), 201–214.

Feltenstein, A., 2017. Subsidy reforms and implications for social protection: An analysis of IMF advice on food and fuel subsidies. IEO Background Papers, *BP/17-01*, 2.

Ferguson, J., 2015. *Give a Man a Fish: Reflections on the New Politics of Distribution*. Durham, NC: Duke University Press.

Frey, A., 2019. Cash transfers, clientelism, and political enfranchisement: Evidence from Brazil. *Journal of Public Economics*, 176, 1–17.

Fried, B. J., 2012. Distributive politics and conditional cash transfers: The case of Brazil's Bolsa Família. *World Development*, 40 (5), 1042–1053.

Galasso, E. and Ravallion, M., 2005. Decentralized targeting of an antipoverty program. *Journal of Public Economics*, 89 (4), 705–727.

Garay, C., 2016. *Social Policy Expansion in Latin America*. Cambridge: Cambridge University Press.

Gazdar, H., 2011. Social protection in Pakistan: In the midst of a paradigm shift? *Economic and Political Weekly*, 46 (28), 59–66.

Gelbach, J. and Pritchett, L., 2002. Is more for the poor less for the poor? The politics of means-tested targeting. *Topics in Economic Analysis and Policy*, 2 (1), 1027.

Gentilini, U., Almenfi, M., Orton, I., and Dale, P., 2020. *Social Protection and Jobs Responses to COVID-19: A Real-Time Review of Country Measures*. Washington, DC: ILO, UNICEF, World Bank.

Giraudy, A., Moncada, E., and Snyder, R., 2019. *Inside Countries: Subnational Research in Comparative Politics*. Cambridge: Cambridge University Press.

Grindle, M. S. and Thomas, J., 1991. *Public Choices and Policy Change: The Political Economy of Reform in Developing Countries*. London: John Hopkins University Press.

Grosh, M., Del Ninno, C., Tesliuc, E., and Ouerghi, A., 2008. *For Protection and Promotion: The Design and Implementation of Effective Safety Nets*. Washington, DC: World Bank.

Hall, A., 2012. The last shall be first: Political dimensions of conditional cash transfers in Brazil. *Journal of Policy Practice*, 11 (1–2), 25–41.

Handa, S., Huang, C., Hypher, N., Teixeira, C., Soares, F. V., and Davis, B., 2012. Targeting effectiveness of social cash transfer programmes in three African countries. *Journal of Development Effectiveness*, 4 (1), 78–108.

Hanlon, J., Hulme, D., and Barrientos, A., 2010. *Just Give Money to the Poor: The Development Revolution from the Global South*. Sterling, VA: Kumarian Press.

Harriss, B., 1988. Policy is what it does: State trading in rural South India. *Public Administration and Development*, 8 (2), 151–160.

Haushofer, J. and Shapiro, J., 2016. The short-term impact of unconditional cash transfers to the poor: Experimental evidence from Kenya. *Quarterly Journal of Economics*, 131 (4), 1973–2042.

Herbst, J., 2000. *States and Power in Africa: Comparative Lessons in Authority and Control*. Princeton, NJ: Princeton University Press.

Hickey, S., 2008a. Conceptualising the politics of social protection in Africa. *In*: A. Barrientos and D. Hulme, eds. *Social Protection for the Poor and Poorest: Concepts, Policies and Politics*. London: Palgrave Macmillan, 247–263.

Hickey, S., 2008b. The return of politics in development studies I: Getting lost within the poverty agenda? *Progress in Development Studies*, 8 (4), 349–358.

Hickey, S., 2011. The politics of social protection: What do we get from a 'social contract' approach? *Canadian Journal of Development Studies*, 32 (4), 426–438.

Hickey, S. and Bukenya, B., 2021. The politics of promoting social cash transfers in Uganda: The potential and pitfalls of 'thinking and working politically'. *Development Policy Review*, 39 (S1), 1–20.

Hickey, S. and King, S., 2016. Understanding social accountability: Politics, power and building new social contracts. *Journal of Development Studies*, 52 (8), 1225–1240.

Hickey, S., Lavers, T., Niño-Zarazúa, M., and Seekings, J., eds., 2019. *The Politics of Social Protection in Eastern and Southern Africa*. Oxford: Oxford University Press.

Hickey, S. and Mohan, G., 2004. *Participation—From Tyranny to Transformation? Exploring New Approaches to Participation in Development*. London: Zed Books.

Hickey, S. and Seekings, J., 2019. Who should get what, how and why? DfID and the transnational politics of social cash transfers. *In*: S. Hickey, T. Lavers, M. Niño-Zarazúa, and J. Seekings, eds. *The Politics of Social Protection in Eastern and Southern Africa*. Oxford: Oxford University Press, 249–275.

Hindle, S., 2004. *On the Parish? The Micro-Politics of Poor Relief in Rural England c.1550–1750*. Oxford: Clarendon Press.

Hossain, N., 2017. *The Aid Lab: Understanding Bangladesh's Unexpected Success*. Oxford: Oxford University Press.

Huber, E. and Stephens, J. D., 2012. *Democracy and the Left: Social Policy and Inequality in Latin America*. Chicago, IL: University Of Chicago Press.

Hunter, W., Patel, L., and Sugiyama, N. B., 2020. How family and child cash transfers can empower women: Comparative lessons from Brazil and South Africa. *Global Social Policy*, https://doi.org/10.1177/1468018120981421.

Hunter, W. and Sugiyama, N. B., 2018. Making the newest citizens: Achieving universal birth registration in contemporary Brazil. *Journal of Development Studies*, 54 (3), 397–412.

Jütte, R., 1994. *Poverty and Deviance in Early Modern Europe*. Cambridge: Cambridge University Press.

Katz, M. B., 2013. *The Undeserving Poor: America's Enduring Confrontation with Poverty—Fully Updated and Revised*. Oxford: Oxford University Press.

Kidd, S., Gelders, B., and Bailey-Athias, D., 2017. Exclusion by design: An assessment of the effectiveness of the proxy means test poverty targeting mechanism. ESS Working Papers, 56.

Koehler, G., 2014. Approaching developmental welfare states: A 'welfare geography' of South Asia. *In*: G. Koehler and D. Chopra, eds. *Development and Welfare Policy in South Asia*. London: Routledge, 25–36.

Koehler, G. and Chopra, D., eds., 2014. *Development and Welfare Policy in South Asia*. London: Routledge.

Korpi, W. and Palme, J., 1988. The paradox of redistribution and strategies of equality: Welfare state institutions, inequality and poverty in the western countries. *American Sociological Review*, 63, 661–687.

Krishna, A., 2011. *One Illness Away: Why People Become Poor and How They Escape Poverty*. Oxford: Oxford University Press.

Lavers, T., 2019a. Social protection in an aspiring 'developmental state': The political drivers of Ethiopia's PSNP. *African Affairs*, 118 (473), 646–671.

Lavers, T., 2019b. Understanding elite commitment to social protection: Rwanda's Vision 2020 Umurenge Programme. *In*: S. Hickey, T. Lavers, M. Niño-Zarazúa, and J. Seekings, eds. *The Politics of Social Protection in Eastern and Southern Africa*. Oxford: Oxford University Press, 95–121.

Lavers, T., 2019c. Distributional concerns, the 'developmental state' and the agrarian origins of social assistance in Ethiopia. *In*: S. Hickey, T. Lavers, M. Niño-Zarazúa, and J. Seekings, eds. *The Politics of Social Protection in Eastern and Southern Africa*. Oxford: Oxford University Press, 68–94.

Lavers, T. and Hickey, S., 2021. Alternative routes to the institutionalisation of social transfers in sub-Saharan Africa: Political survival strategies and transnational policy coalitions. World Development, 146.
Lipsky, M., 1980. *Street-Level Bureaucracy: Dilemmas of the Individual in Public Services*. New York: Russell Sage Foundation.
Maiorano, D., Das, U., and Masiero, S., 2018. Decentralisation, clientelism and social protection programmes: A study of India's MGNREGA. *Oxford Development Studies*, 46 (4), 536–549.
Mamdani, M., 1996. *Citizen and Subject: Contemporary Africa and the Legacy of Late Colonialism*. Princeton, NJ: Princeton University Press.
Mann, M., 1984. The autonomous power of the state: Its origins, mechanisms and results. *European Journal of Sociology*, 25 (2), 185–213.
Mann, M., 1986. *The Sources of Social Power, Volume 1: A History of Power from the Beginning to AD 1760*. Cambridge: Cambridge University Press.
Marcesse, T., 2018. Public policy reform and informal institutions: The political articulation of the demand for work in rural India. *World Development*, 103, 284–296.
McCord, A., 2012. *Public Works and Social Protection in sub-Saharan Africa: Do Public Works Work for the Poor?* Tokyo, New York, Paris: United Nations University Press.
Mencher, S., 1968. *Poor Law to Poverty Program: Economic Security Policy in Britain and the United States*. Pittsburgh, PA: University of Pittsburgh Press.
Midgley, J., 1984. Poor Law principles and social assistance in the Third World: A study of the perpetuation of colonial welfare. *International Social Work*, 27 (1), 19–29.
Migdal, J. S., 1988. *Strong Societies and Weak States: State–Society Relations and State Capabilities in the Third World*. Princeton, NJ: Princeton University Press.
Mkandawire, T., ed., 2004. *Social Policy in a Development Context*. Basingstoke: Palgrave Macmillan/UNRISD.
Mkandawire, T., 2005. Targeting and universalism in poverty reduction. UNRISD Social Policy and Development Programme Papers, 23.
Mkandawire, T., 2010. How the new poverty agenda neglected social and employment policies in Africa. *Journal of Human Development and Capabilities*, 11 (1), 37–55.
Molyneux, M., 2006. Mothers at the service of the new poverty agenda: Progresa/Oportunidades, Mexico's conditional transfer programme. *Social Policy and Administration*, 40 (4), 425–449.
Molyneux, M., Jones, W. N., and Samuels, F., 2016. Can cash transfer programmes have 'transformative' effects? *Journal of Development Studies*, 52 (8), 1087–1098.
Moore, Jr., B., 1967. *Social Origins of Dictatorship and Democracy: Lord and Peasant in the Making of the Modern World*. Boston, MA: Beacon Press.
Ngok, K., 2013. The transition of social protection in China. *In*: J. Midgley and D. Piachaud, eds. *Social Protection, Economic Growth and Social Change*. Edward Elgar Publishing, 29–43.
Nichter, S., 2014. Political clientelism and social policy in Brazil. *In*: D. Abente Brun and L. Diamond, eds. *Clientelism, Social Policy and the Quality of Democracy*. Baltimore, MD: Johns Hopkins University Press, 130–151.
Niedzwiecki, S., 2018. *Uneven Social Policies: The Politics of Subnational Variation in Latin America*. Cambridge: Cambridge University Press.
Oorschot, W. J. H.van, 2002. Targeting welfare: On the functions and dysfunctions of means-testing in social policy. *In*: P. Townsend and D. Gorden, eds. *World Poverty: New Policies to Defeat an Old Enemy*. Bristol: Policy Press, 171–193.

Ouma, M. and Adésínà, J., 2018. Solutions, exclusion and influence: Exploring power relations in the adoption of social protection policies in Kenya. *Critical Social Policy*, https://doi.org/10.1177/0261018318817482.

Piccoli, E. and Gillespie, B., 2018. Making good mothers: Conditions, coercion, and local reactions in the Juntos Program in Peru. *In*: E. Piccoli and J.-P. O. De Sardan, eds. *Cash Transfers in Context*. New York: Berghahn Books, 184–201.

Pierson, P., 2004. *Politics in Time: History, Institutions, and Social Analysis*. Princeton, NJ: Princeton University Press.

Poteete, A. R., 2009. Is development path dependent or political? A reinterpretation of mineral-dependent development in Botswana. *Journal of Development Studies*, 45 (4), 544–571.

Pruce, K., 2019. Investigating the politics of global policy transfer: The case of social protection in Zambia. Ph.D. thesis. University of Manchester.

Pruce, K. and Hickey, S., 2019. The politics of promoting social cash transfers in Zambia. *In*: S. Hickey, T. Lavers, M. Niño-Zarazúa, and J. Seekings, eds. *The Politics of Social Protection in Eastern and Southern Africa*. Oxford: Oxford University Press, 176–201.

Ravallion, M., 2015. *The Economics of Poverty: History, Measurement, and Policy*. Oxford: Oxford University Press.

Saad-Filho, A., 2015. Social policy for neoliberalism: The Bolsa Família programme in Brazil. *Development and Change*, 46 (6), 1227–1252.

Sabates-Wheeler, R. and Devereux, S., 2013. Sustainable graduation from social protection programmes. *Development and Change*, 44 (4), 911–938.

Sabates-Wheeler, R., Lind, J., and Hoddinott, J., 2013. Implementing social protection in agro-pastoralist and pastoralist areas: How local distribution structures moderate PSNP outcomes in Ethiopia. *World Development*, 50, 1–12.

Sabates-Wheeler, R., Lind, J., Hoddinott, J., and Taye, M. T. 2021. Graduation after 10 years of Ethiopia's Productive Safety Net Programme: Surviving but still not thriving. *Development Policy Review*, 39 (4), 511–531.

Sabates-Wheeler, R., Yates, S., Wylde, E., and Gatsinzi, J., 2015. Challenges of measuring graduation in Rwanda. *IDS Bulletin*, 46 (2), 103–114.

Samson, M., 2015. Exit or developmental impact? The role of 'graduation' in social protection programmes. *IDS Bulletin*, 46 (2), 13–24.

Schubert, B. and Slater, R., 2006. Social cash transfers in low-income African countries: Conditional or unconditional? *Development Policy Review*, 24 (5), 571–578.

Seekings, J., 2011. British colonial policy, local politics, and the origins of the Mauritian welfare state, 1936–50. *Journal of African History*, 52 (2), 157–177.

Seekings, J., 2012. Pathways to redistribution: The emerging politics of social assistance across the Global 'South'. *Journal für Entwicklungspolitik*, 38 (1), pp. 14–34.

Seekings, J., 2019. Building a conservate welfare state in Botswana. *In*: S. Hickey, T. Lavers, M. Niño-Zarazúa, and J. Seekings, eds. *The Politics of Social Protection in Eastern and Southern Africa*. Oxford: Oxford University Press, 42–67.

Seekings, J. and Nattrass, N., 2005. *Class, Race, and Inequality in South Africa*. London: Yale University Press.

Sen, A., 1995. The political economy of targeting. *In*: D. Van De Walle and K. Nead, eds. *Public Spending and the Poor: Theory and Evidence*. Baltimore, MD: Johns Hopkins University Press, 11–24.

Sepúlveda, M., 2009. *Report of the Independent Expert on the Question of Human Rights and Extreme Poverty to the UN Human Rights Council*. New York: United Nations General Assembly.

Silvio, D., Pellerano, L., Handa, S., and Davis, B., 2015. Is graduation from social safety nets possible? Evidence from sub-Saharan Africa. *IDS Bulletin*, 46 (2), 93–102.
Singh, P., 2015. *How Solidarity Works for Welfare: Subnationalism and Social Development in India*. Cambridge: Cambridge University Press.
Slater, R., 2011. Cash transfers, social protection and poverty reduction. *International Journal of Social Welfare*, 20 (3), 250–259.
Snyder, R., 2001. Scaling down: The subnational comparative method. *Studies in Comparative International Development*, 36 (1), 93–110.
Standing, G., 2007. How cash transfers boost work and economic security. UNDESA Working Papers, 58.
Sugiyama, N. B., 2011. The diffusion of conditional cash transfer programs in the Americas. *Global Social Policy*, 11 (2–3), 250–278.
Sugiyama, N. B., 2016. Pathways to citizen accountability: Brazil's Bolsa Família. *Journal of Development Studies*, 52 (8), 1192–1206.
Sugiyama, N. B. and Hunter, W., 2013. Whither clientelism? Good governance and Brazil's 'Bolsa Família' program. *Comparative Politics*, 46 (1), 43–62.
Van De Walle, N., 2014. The democratization of clientelism in sub-Saharan Africa. *In*: D. Abente Brun and L. Diamond, eds. *Clientelism, Social Policy and the Quality of Democracy*. Baltimore, MD: Johns Hopkins University Press, 230–252.
Von Gliszczynski, M., 2015. *Cash Transfers and Basic Social Protection: Towards a Development Revolution?* New York: Springer.
Wanyama, F. O. and McCord, A., 2017. The politics of scaling up social protection in Kenya. ESID Working Papers, 87.
Watkins, B., 2008. *Alternative Methods for Targeting Social Assistance to Highly Vulnerable Groups*. Washington, DC: Kimetrica.
World Bank, 2004. *World Development Report 2004: Making Services Work for the Poor*. Washington, DC: Oxford University Press/World Bank.

2
The Politics of Distributing Social Transfers

Tom Lavers

1. Introduction

Chapter 1 showed that whilst social transfers have been framed as a means of addressing poverty, vulnerability, and inequality—and indeed can make important contributions in this regard—programme adoption, design, and implementation are all fundamentally political processes. Political leaders are often motivated as much by securing political advantage by winning votes, neutralizing opponents, and projecting authority, as they are by addressing a range of social ills. While a growing body of research examines the political drivers of the adoption and expansion of social transfer programmes, research on the political factors shaping implementation in Africa and South Asia is much more sparse.

Having outlined key debates in the social protection literature and highlighted the political nature of policy implementation in the introductory chapter, Chapter 2 develops the analytical framework employed in the six country cases in this volume, highlighting the importance of state capacity and political competition. In doing so, the discussion confronts important debates in the politics of development and political science that have relevance well beyond social protection. The first of these debates concerns the relative importance of historical legacies and contemporary political dynamics for explaining state performance and service delivery. On the one hand, a large body of literature highlights the path dependence of state capacity and the legacies of the history of state building within countries (Ertman 2005; Rueschemeyer 2005). The origins of capable states have been traced back over decades and even centuries to key foundational moments of war, state formation, social revolution, and colonialism (Skocpol 1979; Mann 1986, 2012; Tilly 1992; Acemoglu et al. 2000; Kohli 2004; Mahoney 2010; Slater 2010; Vu 2010; Fukuyama 2011). On the other hand, however, research highlights the important effects of more proximate factors such as regime change, coalition building, and electoral pressures that reshape development trajectories and policy outcomes, transforming people's lives in the process (Huber and Stephens 2001, 2012; Poteete 2009; Garay 2016; Khan 2018). To what degree, then, are countries' future prospects defined by their histories and under what

Tom Lavers, *The Politics of Distributing Social Transfers.* In: *The Politics of Distributing Social Transfers.*
Edited by Tom Lavers, Oxford University Press.
DOI: 10.1093/oso/9780192862525.003.0002

circumstances do contemporary political dynamics reshape these legacies? This chapter develops an analytical framework that highlights the intersection of these long-run and proximate factors, enabling their exploration in the cases studies that follow.

The second debate concerns the relevant unit of analysis in political research. Comparative politics and research on the politics of development have suffered from a considerable degree of 'methodological nationalism'. While undeniably important, national governments operate in a globalized context and are embedded within the societies of which they are a part. As such, the national level should not be automatically taken as the exclusive focus of analysis and, indeed, a focus on the national can obscure important dynamics taking place at other levels of analysis. This study, which focuses to a significant degree on the factors shaping policy implementation within countries, contributes to a growing literature described elsewhere as a 'sub-national turn' in comparative politics (Giraudy et al. 2019). While this emphasis on a recent turn to sub-national research risks minimizing the contribution of earlier sub-national comparative work (e.g. Hechter and Brustein 1980; Mamdani 1996; Boone 2003a), research on sub-national political processes is certainly resurgent at present. A sub-national focus is important given the great internal heterogeneity of politics, state capacity, and state–society relations within countries (Mamdani 1996; Herbst 2000; Boone 2003a, 2014; Giraudy 2015; Singh 2015; Soifer 2015), something that is so often assumed away in research focusing on country comparisons (Snyder 2001; Giraudy et al. 2019). From an analytical perspective, sub-national comparisons offer the advantage of multi-level theorization that encapsulates different levels of analysis from the international to national to local. Moreover, a sub-national approach offers the possibility of controlling for programme variation and a range of other political factors within countries as a means of carrying out more focused comparisons (Snyder 2001; Giraudy et al. 2019). Nonetheless, this sub-national variation has not yet formed a central focus of analysis of the politics of social protection in Africa and South Asia, other than in India.

Sections 2 and 3 of this chapter review key debates in the literatures on state capacity and the politics of implementation. Section 4 then outlines the analytical framework employed in the book, while Section 5 presents the research design and case selection.

2. State capacity and the distribution of social transfers

As discussed in Chapter 1, states seeking to implement social transfer programmes and distribute transfers to particular sections of their population require certain forms of state capacity. For the most part, the existing literature has tended to treat state capacity as a singular quality possessed to varying degrees by states. However, different tasks—from national security to industrial policy to service delivery—require quite different forms of state capacities (Centeno et al. 2017). Indeed,

> There is no reason to assume *a priori* that the pattern of strengths and weaknesses will be the same for all policies. One state may be unable to alter the structure of its medical system but be able to construct an efficient transportation network, while another can deal relatively easily with getting its citizens around but cannot get their illnesses cured.
>
> (Krasner 1978, p. 58)

What capacities are required to implement a social transfer programme effectively? The expansion of state capacity has regularly been highlighted as an essential step in the process of building welfare states (Kuhnle and Sander 2010). Meanwhile, one of the purported advantages of social transfer programmes is their administrative simplicity and the potential of new technology such as mobile money to overcome limits to state capacity (Hanlon et al. 2010; Ferguson 2015). Indeed, the rapid spread of social transfers led Seekings (2017) to note that developing countries have found it 'surprisingly easy' to establish programmes and deliver transfers to programme participants, albeit that there has been little research on the matter. Yet, the implementation and effective distribution of social transfers do place important demands on state capacity to identify participants, to deliver transfers, and to monitor performance (Barrientos 2009). The demands on state capacity only increase with programmes that entail complex targeting and graduation procedures, monitoring and enforcement of conditions, organization of public works, and links to livelihoods programmes (Joshi and Moore 2000). While all national programmes require some degree of central coordination, budgeting, and planning, the discussion in Chapter 1 suggests that the main challenge to state capacity is not necessarily the strength of the national agency tasked with overall responsibility for the programme. Instead, the main challenge is the ability of the local state offices to reach out across national territory—in particular to remote and marginal areas where many of the most vulnerable people reside—to work effectively with local communities and for central agencies to coordinate activities across this dispersed national network of officials to achieve the programme's objectives.

The starting point for many attempts to conceptualize state capacity is Max Weber's influential work (Gerth and Mills 2003), with numerous studies highlighting the importance of bureaucratic capacity or organizational competence. From this perspective, building a state staffed with competent, motivated, and well-organized officials is the route to enhancing capacity, which therefore requires training and education, meritocratic recruitment and predictable career paths, and an *esprit de corps* that promotes the pursuit of collective goals (Carpenter 2001; Gorski 2003; Evans et al. 2017). Having competent officials to implement a programme is, of course, important, not least in terms of the state's ability to post capable administrators to the least desirable posts in remote areas. Past research has highlighted a lack of staff and resources as a barrier to effective implementation of the Mahatma Gandhi National Rural Employment Guarantee Act (MGNREGA) in Rajasthan and Bihar in India (Chopra 2014, Dutta et al. 2014), the expansion of South Africa's social pension (Seekings 2017), and the extension of cash transfers in northern Kenya (Donovan 2015).

While important, the challenge of state capacity goes well beyond competence and resources, however. An important aspect of state capacity concerns intra-state relations. As Migdal (2001) argues, the state is often mistakenly presented as a monolithic, unitary actor, rather than the reality of a network of semi-autonomous organizations, each with its own interests and ideological orientation. Consequently, analysis of policy implementation must disaggregate the state to examine how different parts of the state—from national agencies to frontline officials—interact and coordinate their activities. Organizational coherence and effective implementation are the product of particular forms of intra-state relations, not an inherent feature of states. Local state officials have interests distinct from their superiors at other levels of the state, while they must also balance upward accountability to their superiors with downward accountability to the people living in their jurisdiction. As such, state coordination presents a principal–agent problem whereby higher-level officials—the principals—rely on the actions of lower-level officials—the agents—for effective implementation, but are never able to monitor their activities perfectly (Lipsky 1980; Soifer 2015; Ang 2016; Hassan 2020). The risk, therefore, is that lower-level officials diverge from guidelines set by their superiors, either based on their own personal interests or in response to pressure from local societal actors, undermining implementation in the process. The challenge of monitoring lower-level officials is only enhanced where communications and transport networks are limited, particularly in remote areas covered by many social transfer programmes.

As others have argued, rulers have pursued a range of diverse strategies—often varying within countries—in an attempt to address these challenges with a view to building state capacity and control (Boone 2003a; Soifer 2015; Hassan 2020). One such approach, often associated with new public management, has been to establish systems of performance assessment that strengthen top-down control through setting and monitoring progress toward centrally defined performance targets. The challenge, however, is that such forms of performance evaluation can easily lead agents to try to game the system by focusing on meeting targets rather than achieving actual programme objectives (Rasul and Rogger 2018; Hassan 2020). This is especially problematic where objectives of state policy are inherently hard to quantify and measure—as with aspects of social transfer programmes such as targeting. Moreover, attempts to control the activities of lower-level officials in this way can also be counterproductive by discouraging local innovation and adaptation of centrally defined objectives to local realities (Ang 2016). Indeed, Ang (2016) argues that a major factor in China's development successes in the last four decades was the system of performance assessment that rewarded innovation by local state officials, rather than attempting to control their activities. Others argue that strong political parties may offer an alternate means of monitoring and controlling the activities of state officials (Niedzwiecki 2018).

Research on implementation of social transfers indeed highlights the importance of intra-state relations. For example, Joshi and Moore (2000) highlight the challenges to implementation of the Maharashtra Employment Guarantee Scheme, the predecessor of India's MGNREGA, flowing from the coordination challenges between politicians and bureaucrats across different state agencies. These coordination challenges have been a factor in MGNREGA itself. One study attributes relatively effective implementation in Andhra Pradesh to the introduction of punishments for local programme officials in the form of salary deductions or even dismissal for those who fail to meet implementation targets (Maiorano et al. 2018). Furthermore, Niedzwiecki (2018) shows that variable implementation of social transfer programmes in Brazil and Argentina is partly the result of local government officials intentionally impeding implementation as a result of partisan affiliations.

Another important body of work highlights the importance of state–society relations to state capacity. States are often presented as independent from or floating above society. However, the disaggregated state is embedded in society through the connections of state officials and relations with powerful social actors (Migdal 1988, 2001; Hagmann and Péclard 2010). Ultimately the effective implementation of a social transfer programme is dependent on the state being able to identify programme participants within society, to mobilize communities to meet programme conditions, and to monitor delivery. State capacity therefore requires a delicate balance of both relative autonomy from societal influence and embeddedness within societal relations, as Peter Evans (1995) argued originally in relation to industrial policy, and, more recently, with respect to social policy (Evans et al. 2017). Autonomy of state officials is important since there is a very real danger that local officials become embedded in society and responsive to the demands of powerful societal actors, rather than the state hierarchy (Hassan 2020). With respect to social transfers, this could for example result in powerful landholding elites or chiefs exerting influence over distribution of programme resources, as described in Roy's (2019) account of MGNREGA in India. Similarly, other research on Latin America and South Asia highlights the potential for powerful local elites to influence programme selection and divert resources away from their intended recipients (Sugiyama and Hunter 2013, Maiorano et al. 2018). Where landed elites, chiefs or clan leaders mediate state–citizen relations, these powerful social actors are likely to impede state implementation capacity.

While some degree of insulation from societal influence is important to enable impartial implementation, states also depend on their ties to society for effective implementation, with state capacity enhanced by collaboration and coproduction with societal actors, and undermined by antagonistic relations (Cammett and MacLean 2014; Evans et al. 2017). A key factor shaping state–society relations in this regard is the issue of state legitimacy. Where people consider the state to be legitimate, they are much more likely to adhere to its requests and demands or even enter into collaborative relations (Buzan 1983; Gorski 2003; vom Hau 2008). Indeed, a central assumption of the good governance literature is that where local people are able to participate and hold local officials to account, this enhances the state's capacity to deliver (World Bank 2004). With respect to social transfers, this is potentially relevant to the widespread use of community-based targeting, which aims to draw on community knowledge to identify those most in need, as well as community mobilization for labour or behavioural conditionalities attached to many programmes. Moreover, decentralized delivery of social transfers is often associated with increased local ownership of programmes, compensating to a degree for the limited reach of the state through community mobilization (Plagerson et al. 2012; Sabates-Wheeler et al. 2020). In addition, the growing role of non-state actors such as private sector contractors and non-governmental organizations (NGOs) in the delivery of social transfers also highlights the importance of the state's relations with societal actors (Cammett and MacLean 2014; Donovan 2015; Seekings 2017; Ibrahim 2021). Where the state is able to regulate these actors effectively, collaboration with non-state actors can extend the reach of the state (Cammett and MacLean 2014).

Vitally, state capacity is likely to vary considerably across each of these three dimensions—competence and resources, intra-state relations, and state–society relations—within national territories. Not only is the state's reach shaped by its physical infrastructure of roads and communications, and its ability to post competent and motivated officials to remote districts, but the state's ability to monitor the activities of those officials and the ability of those officials to work with the communities under their jurisdiction also vary considerably. As such, state capacity has been an important theme of sub-national research (Giraudy et al. 2019), particularly in developing countries where variation in state capacity is particularly pronounced, for example in Latin America (Harbers 2015; Soifer 2015), South Asia (Singh 2015), and Africa (Mamdani 1996; Herbst 2000; Boone 2003a; Lund 2006; Boone 2014). This variation in the state's territorial reach is helpfully encapsulated in Michael Mann's (1984, p. 113) concept of *state infrastructural power*, namely 'the capacity of the state actually to penetrate civil society, and to implement logistically political decisions throughout the realm'. Infrastructural power highlights both the territorial and relational nature of state power. Indeed, a growing body of work has employed the concept of infrastructural power

(Soifer and vom Hau 2008; Levitsky and Way 2010; Slater 2010), including in analysis of social policy implementation in Latin America (Niedzwiecki 2018).

Research is fairly consistent in highlighting the deep historical roots of variation in state capacity. Where states have been able to build capacity in a short space of time, this has generally only been as a result of the high level of cohesion of political elites brought about by rare and severe shocks, such as war, social revolution or unmanageable social conflict (Skocpol 1979; Mann 1986; Tilly 1992; Kohli 2004; Slater 2010). These critical junctures, meanwhile, have had long-lasting impacts on state capacity. One commonly discussed factor is that of colonialism. Colonial indirect rule empowered chiefs and local leaders as a form of 'decentralized despotism' in much of Africa (Mamdani 1996; Lange 2009) and, to a degree, India (Kohli 2004), impeding state capacity post-independence. In contrast, direct rule provided the foundations of a civil service in parts of Africa (Lange 2009), while Kohli (2004) argues that Japanese colonialism established the bureaucratic foundations for subsequent developmental success in Korea. Others argue that colonial and post-colonial rulers have faced similar challenges in their attempts to project authority over territory and people as a result of variation in population density (Herbst 2000) and agrarian class structure (Boone 2003a, 2003b).

A more recent trend with important implications for state capacity is the decentralization of the state apparatus, which has been heavily promoted by the World Bank and other donors for several decades as part of good governance reforms. The stated aim of decentralization is to improve service delivery, popular participation, and state accountability by bringing the state closer to the people, providing citizens with opportunities to influence the policies that affect their lives (Crook and Manor 1998; Bardhan and Mookherjee 2006; Grindle 2007; Faguet and Pöschl 2015). As discussed in Chapter 1, decentralization is an important trend in relation to social transfers specifically, with local administrations tasked with key roles in programme administration, including participant selection, disbursement, and monitoring programme conditions. Meanwhile, social accountability measures aim to enhance popular participation and accountability of the local state.

Decentralization provides an additional challenge to state capacity, necessitating the recruitment and training of large numbers of officials to staff decentralized administrations, heightening the challenge of coordination between state agencies, and maintaining a balance between the autonomy and embeddedness of state officials. Despite the many claimed benefits of decentralization, research thus far has highlighted the extremely uneven outcomes of reforms, with proponents often ignoring the key role of power relations in shaping outcomes (Boone 2003a, 2003b; Jütting et al. 2005, Poteete and Ribot 2011). In authoritarian settings, central governments have often used administrative decentralization as a means of enhancing central control over people and territory (Chemouni 2014; Aalen and Muriaas 2017), while in others, powerful societal actors have exerted great influence over decentralized administrations (Crook and Manor 1998). In both instances, the expected benefits of decentralization in terms of accountability and participation are undermined.

Finally, while building state capacity is a long-run process and governments must, to a significant degree, work within the constraints of the legacy of past state building, it should be noted that implementation of social protection can be a means of building state capacity. Skocpol (1992), for example, shows how investment in the bureaucratic capacity required to deliver new programmes in the USA contributed to an expansion of state capacity, which could then be put to other purposes. Equally, research has highlighted the key role of social research and the creation of capacity to generate and manage statistical data as a key factor in the expansion of early welfare states (Landes 1972; Kuhnle 1996).[1] More recent research on social transfers also highlights comparable effects, albeit on a smaller scale, with the establishment of social transfer programmes in northern Kenya (Donovan 2015) and remote areas in Ghana serving to extend the reach of the state (Ibrahim 2021).

3. Social transfers as a political tool

One of the common limitations in the literature on state capacity has been to blur the lines between the capacity of the state and the purposes to which that capacity is directed, with outcomes of programme performance often taken as indicators of state capacity. Yet, as others have previously argued it is essential to distinguish between the capacities of a state and how this capacity is actually used in practice (Mann 1984; vom Hau 2012; Centeno et al. 2017). This section therefore considers the political factors that shape how state capacity is deployed. In doing so, as noted in the introduction to this chapter, the discussion raises the question of path dependence—to what extent are countries' development prospects—and, in this particular instance, the ability of states to implement social transfer programmes across their national territory—constrained by their history of state formation, or can particular forms of contemporary politics disrupt these pathways?

As argued in Chapter 1, social protection, as much as any other policy domain, is inherently political. While social protection is usually framed in technical or normative terms, the decision to adopt and expand social transfer programmes, and the decision to focus support on certain groups and not others is, ultimately, a political choice. Given the disaggregated nature of the state, as discussed in the previous section, these political dynamics shaping how state capacity is used play out across multiple levels from national governments to provincial administrative centres to frontline officials. In this way, politics shapes the distribution of social transfers and constitutes an important influence on implementation (Migdal 2001; Giraudy et al. 2019).

The common approach in policy circles has been to present political involvement in the implementation of social transfers as a problem to be avoided, since this risks the 'political capture' of programmes and the diversion of programme resources away from the intended recipients of support. As such, the assumption is often that de-politicized, technocratic implementation is both possible and desirable if only programmes can be designed in such a way as to bypass political actors. In contrast, the approach taken here is that all policy implementation is necessarily shaped by politics. Where impartial implementation takes place in line with programme guidelines, that in itself is a political outcome, just as much as the manipulation of a targeting process to direct resources to politically important constituencies. From this perspective, rather than asking how to avoid political capture, the challenge undertaken in this book is to better understand when political processes align with effective policy delivery.

National political dynamics exert an important, though inevitably constrained, influence on policy implementation. While national politicians are highly influential, they are constrained, as discussed in the previous section, by the principal–agent problem whereby they have limited ability to control the actions of local administrative officials. The ability of donors—heavily involved in policy design decisions in many countries—to shape implementation is even more limited. Donors can be highly influential in national ministries through control of finance, the introduction of policy ideas, and provision of technical assistance. But donors' ability to influence local implementation, other than through national governments, is all but non-existent in most cases. As discussed above, national governments may attempt to shape local implementation through a range of strategies including targets and performance evaluations for lower-level officials, the discursive framing of programmes and their objectives, or indirectly through political party hierarchies.

Existing research, discussed in Chapter 1, provides insights into the diverse motivations of national governments in pursuing social transfers and therefore the direction in which they are likely to influence lower-level officials implementing the programmes. In a number of countries, particularly in Latin America and South Asia, social transfers are increasingly framed in terms of social rights, with governments expanding programmes in response to political mobilization and redistributive demands (Huber and Stephens 2012; Koehler and Chopra 2014; Garay 2016). A rights-based framing—where underpinned by social mobilization—would seem most likely to drive programmatic implementation, with rights-bearing citizens mobilizing to demand effective service delivery from the state. In contrast, governments in a number of countries, particularly in Africa, have expanded social transfer programmes in response to competitive electoral pressures, but in the absence of significant bottom-up pressure for redistribution (Garay 2016; Wanyama and McCord 2017; Abdulai 2020; Lavers and Hickey 2021). Though an important driver of expansion, electoral pressures of this type potentially risk social transfer distribution focused on maximizing visibility in order to win votes or perhaps even direct attempts at vote buying. Finally, another distinct motivation for governments has been to use social transfers as a means of mobilizing resources—both programme costs and often participants' labour—to make productive investments in infrastructure development (Lavers 2019a, 2019b). Echoing the literature on 'productivist' social policy in East Asia (White and Goodman 1998; Holliday 2000; Gough 2004), such motivations are potentially compatible with programmatic implementation, but are likely to come with pressure to minimize state expenditure in order to maximize resources for development, potentially at the cost of protecting those in need.

While these national political motivations are likely to be important, national politicians must work through local state officials to actually deliver programmes. As such, the turn to sub-national comparisons is vital. Local political competition and partisan affiliation emerge here as potentially important factors shaping relations between key local actors, with implications for programme implementation (Ampratwum 2021). A common assumption by advocates of good governance reforms is that decentralization of programme implementation in the context of increased political competition and transparency of decision making will lead politicians seeking office to compete for votes based on their ability to deliver effectively the services required by voters. The result will therefore be the programmatic delivery of services. While certainly possible, this assumption neglects the reality of political competition in many developing countries, where informal institutions and power relations compete with formal rules and regulations (Migdal 2001; Khan 2018). In many settings, politicians' success in electorally competitive districts in actual fact relies on the support of party foot soldiers who enrol party members, mobilize them for party rallies, and bring them to polling stations. Consequently, these influential foot soldiers are often in a strong bargaining position from which to extract rents from local officials, such as jobs and services. The result is that research in Ghana has found that patronage is actually more prevalent in competitive than uncompetitive districts (Driscoll 2018; Ampratwum 2021). Indeed, this echoes research on Latin America that shows that partisanship and electoral competition can result in an increase in clientelism and vote buying (Schady 2000; Magaloni et al. 2007; Stokes et al. 2013).

The concept of clientelism has been criticized for the frequent imprecision of its definition and catch-all manner of its usage (Therkildsen 2005; Mkandawire 2015). Likewise in the social protection literature there is a tendency to attribute almost any political involvement to a vague notion of 'clientelism'. As such, it is important to proceed with a clear definition in mind. A working definition of political clientelism is: 'the selective distribution of goods and services by politicians to favored constituencies in exchange for their political loyalty' (Van de Walle 2014, p. 232). Where distribution of social transfers is clientelistic, participants would be selected or removed from a programme depending on the way in which they voted or based on other demonstrations of political loyalty.

There are several reasons why the distribution of social transfers is potentially vulnerable to clientelism. Vitally, clientelism requires that resources can be withheld from some section of the population and has consequently relied largely on private, excludable goods—such as targeted social transfers—rather than public goods (Hopkin 2006). Moreover, many have argued that clientelism is more common where poverty is widespread and inequality high, since patrons can more cheaply buy the support of the poor (Kitschelt 2007; Stokes 2007a; Sugiyama and Hunter 2013). In addition, clientelism may be more common in rural communities, where it is easier for politicians to assess how people vote and thereby enforce contingent exchanges (Sugiyama and Hunter 2013). The discretionary powers given to programme officials within targeted social transfer programmes, and their focus on the poor and, frequently, rural populations, therefore make social transfers a potentially valuable resource for clientelism (Sen 1995; Mkandawire 2005; Swamy 2016). Indeed, research has found that clientelism is an important factor shaping the distribution of social transfers in parts of India, in particular. In West Bengal clientelism is used to secure party political support (Das 2015), while in Uttar Pradesh clientelism has been used to consolidate the position of local elites (Marcesse 2018).

Yet such 'political capture' of social transfers is not a necessary outcome. Clientelism faces the inherent challenge of how to monitor and enforce the behaviour of the client and ensure that they adhere to the bargain (Kitschelt 2007). This is particularly acute in the context of secret ballots that limit patrons' ability to monitor clients' behaviour. Stokes (and others) has argued that it may be possible to compensate to some degree for the logistical challenge of secret ballots through large-scale machine politics—where political parties have sufficient numbers of foot soldiers to assess voter behaviour accurately based on their attendance at rallies, volunteering for party activities, and by 'looking voters in the eyes' as they come out of voting booths (Kitschelt 2007; Stokes 2007b). Where politicians lack the capacity to enforce the contingent exchange that is the core of clientelism, 'pork barrel politics' may be an alternative. Pork barrel politics involves the targeting of goods and services to particular geographical areas, usually based on the influence of a local politician hoping to build political support (Kitschelt 2007). Importantly, however, pork barrel politics does not imply a contingent exchange—there is no obligation on recipients of transfers to vote a particular way and there is no attempt to monitor or enforce recipients' behaviour.

Clientelism and pork barrel politics are by no means the only ways in which party politics is likely to influence implementation of social transfers, however. As Niedzwiecki's (2018) study in Argentina and Brazil shows, even where delivery is along programmatic lines, where programme delivery is decentralized, partisanship can still provide incentives for local politicians to support or impede implementation. She argues that local politicians' commitment to programme delivery is shaped by the attribution of credit for the programme in question. Where a programme is associated with a national government, as with Brazil's Bolsa Família, local governments either support implementation, as in Rio Grande do Sul where the government is run by the Workers' Party and thus aligned with the national government, or impede implementation, as in Goiás, where the opposition is in power (Niedzwiecki 2018).

In sum then, beyond the capacity of the state to implement a programme, contemporary political dynamics can exert an important influence on the distribution of social transfers. In particular, party politics can shape whether state capacity is mobilized towards the impartial and programmatic delivery of a programme, or whether local politicians seek to shape distribution away from the intended target population in order to secure political advantage.

4. Researching the politics of distributing social transfers

The preceding discussion serves to highlight some of the many factors shaping the distribution of social transfers. Building on this existing literature, this section outlines the analytical framework that is used in the remainder of the book to analyse case studies of policy implementation. The case studies examine which combinations of state capacity and political contestation underpin the effective distribution of social transfers. For the purposes of this study, implementation is considered to be effective when it is in line with state programme objectives and official guidelines, and therefore likely to reach target groups set by national policy. For example, the research asks, where state capacity is sufficient, what forms of politics lead to the effective deployment of this capacity and, where state capacity is limited, what political fixes can enable at least a minimal level of performance in spite of these limitations?

Rather than a unitary actor, the state is conceptualized as a network of distinct organizations, each of which has its own organizational interests and incentives (Migdal 2001). These state organizations are involved in a continuous struggle for domination with a range of societal organizations over the ability to set and enforce rules within society. Following Migdal (2001, p. 48), societal organizations include 'informal and formal organizations, ranging from families and neighbourhood groups to mammoth foreign-owned companies, [that] use a variety of sanctions, rewards, and symbols to induce people to behave according to the rules of the game'. Meanwhile, domination may comprise a full range of interactions from violence and coercion to the establishment of legitimate authority and the acceptance of an authority's right to rule. For this purpose, states employ diverse strategies of engagement with sub-national elites in their quest to control and administer territory and people (Boone 2003a). These struggles—based on both competing interests and ideas—play out across numerous arenas from the national government to community meetings in villages (Migdal 2001; Hagmann and Péclard 2010). That said, however, there is no clear dividing line between the state and society. Rather, state officials are embedded in society through their membership of families, clans, businesses or clubs, ties which are not necessarily abandoned as soon as state officials arrive at work.

Viewed from this perspective, the process of policy implementation is not simply an impartial application of formal rules and laws by bureaucrats, but rather a *negotiated* and *contested* process that takes place across the multiple arenas of state–society interactions (Grindle and Thomas 1991; Migdal 2001; Hagmann and Péclard 2010). In this process, formal and informal institutions, and ideas all have the potential to influence decision making with the result that implementation on the ground may well vary considerably from the intentions of higher levels of government. Meanwhile, policy implementation forms part of the ongoing struggle for domination between state and societal actors and in the process of this negotiation and/or contestation, both state and society are themselves transformed. Building on this basic conceptualization of the state and policy implementation, the preceding discussion highlighted two broad factors shaping the distribution of social transfers: state infrastructural power and political contestation.

Mann's far-reaching analysis of the history of human civilization leads him to identify many aspects of state infrastructural power, ranging from logistical capacity, organizational forms, and transportation to the generation and storage of information about its citizens and ability to assess and deduct taxes (Mann 1986, 2012). For our present purposes, however, it is necessary to highlight more precisely the dimensions of state infrastructural power required to distribute social transfers across a territory. Here we build on Mann, as well as recent work by Soifer and vom Hau (Soifer and vom Hau 2008; vom Hau 2012; Soifer 2015) that develops the concept of infrastructural power.[2] Three dimensions are highlighted. First is the physical, financial, and human resources, and competence of the state. For the state to reach the intended recipients of social transfer programmes, it must have some minimum of trained officials at its disposal, as well as the transport and communications infrastructure needed to reach them. The second dimension is the relations within a state, between its component parts (Migdal 1988; Soifer 2015). The competence of state officials is important but insufficient on its own. In addition, it is necessary for higher-level state officials to be able to exert influence over the activities of lower-level officials, directing them to the pursuit of state objectives. Third, state infrastructural power also depends upon the relations between the disaggregated state and society (Migdal 1988; Soifer and vom Hau 2008). Infrastructural power is perhaps likely to be strongest where state intervention is widely seen as legitimate within society and, consequently, infrastructural power is enhanced by the support of societal actors (Soifer and vom Hau 2008; vom Hau 2008). This may entail the mobilization of non-state actors—chiefs, community leaders, elders, and private companies—to support the activities of the state. If necessary, however, it may be that where the state is strong in comparison with social actors, states can impose their wishes on their societies, resulting in relatively effective implementation.

The starting assumption is that a social transfer programme is likely to be implemented effectively where: the state has sufficient human and physical resources to carry out its tasks; where higher levels of the state are able to monitor and evaluate effectively the activities of lower-level officials; and where the state is seen as legitimate by society, or, failing that, is sufficiently powerful to be able to impose its wishes on society. Each of these aspects of state infrastructural power—resources and competence, intra-state relations, and state–society relations—has the potential to vary within national territories. Moreover, the evolution of state infrastructural power is historically contingent (Centeno et al. 2017). As such, each case study takes history seriously—within the necessary space constraints—highlighting how historical processes of state formation have shaped contemporary variation in state infrastructural power. This historical focus, meanwhile, is complemented with attention to the more recent initiatives undertaken by national governments to extend state infrastructural power within their territory. In particular, high levels of elite cohesion and perceived vulnerability to internal or external threats has often been required for governments to invest in building the capacity and reach of the state (Slater 2010).

While state infrastructural power is important, the preceding review highlights a range of political factors that also shape distribution. In line with Centeno et al. (2017), while variations in state infrastructural power are historically contingent and evolve over time, politics shapes the degree and purposes to which state infrastructural power is deployed at any one point in time. While Centeno et al.'s (2017) concern is primarily in terms of national politics and how political leadership, coalitions, and parties shape the deployment of state capacity, our focus here on the distribution of social transfers requires consideration of the political forces shaping the deployment of state infrastructural power across multiple state arenas from the national to the local (Migdal 2001; Hagmann and Péclard 2010). A central theme throughout the cases in the chapters that follow concerns this intersection between the infrastructural powers of the state and political contestation that shapes the state's distribution of social transfers.

Of these political dynamics, an important influence is certainly the stated and unstated priorities of the national government. As discussed at length in Chapter 1, national governments adopt and expand social transfer programmes for a wide variety of reasons from seeking electoral advantage through the distribution of transfers, to appeasing potential opponents, responding to the demands of social movements or mobilizing resources for national development. These priorities are passed down to local-level officials through systems of performance assessment and the discursive framing of policies and target groups. Yet the ability of national governments to realize these ambitions depends ultimately on their compatibility with the multiple dimensions of state infrastructural power and other local political dynamics that constrain the actions of state officials across a country's territory. While many social transfer programmes are modest in terms of national expenditure, they usually constitute a significant inflow of resources at local government level. As such, they can become an important focus of contestation at local levels between state officials, political parties, and societal actors.

The political fault-lines in a particular locality vary considerably across the diversity of the countries covered in the volume. The case studies that follow consider a range of issues, depending on the particular contexts they address. However, a prominent concern is the degree of competition and contestation of party politics at national and local level. Electoral competition may provide politicians with the incentive to deliver social transfers effectively and impartially as a means of securing popular support. On other occasions, however, electoral competition is instead driven by the desire to secure votes through the distribution of patronage, potentially motivating politicians to intervene in the distribution of social transfers to secure support. The starting assumption, therefore, is that political contestation is likely to undermine implementation, since it provides incentives for contending groups to implement the distribution of social transfers to their advantage. Likewise, implementation is likely to be disrupted where there is a lack of alignment between national and local politicians, providing incentives for local political actors to impede implementation to limit national politicians' ability to claim credit.

The case studies that follow therefore apply this broad framework, examining the intersection between state infrastructural power and political contestation in the distribution of social transfers.

5. Research strategy

The chapters in this volume pursue a shared research strategy based on a comparative case-based approach (Gerring 2006; Yin 2008; Bevan 2009). From this perspective, cases are seen as 'configurations of aspects' (Ragin 2000) with an emphasis on understanding cases as complex wholes rather than a collection of variables. As such, the focus of the case studies that follow is to examine how multiple causal mechanisms interact in complex ways in particular cases. Such an approach and the diversity of the cases involved necessarily places limits on the comparative analysis that is possible between cases. While recognizing this causal complexity, the comparative analysis in the concluding chapter draws out common patterns of contingent causal conjunctions, aiming for what has been described as 'mid-range theory' (George and Bennett 2004).

In terms of data generation techniques, the research is primarily qualitative. Our emphasis here is to understand processes—how decisions are made and the contestation involved in the distribution of social transfers. Such complex, and often politically sensitive, processes are difficult to research at the best of times, but the decision was made that qualitative techniques such as key informant interviews, focus group discussions, and participant observation offered the best prospects of unpicking this complexity. The studies, nonetheless, complement qualitative research with quantitative evidence from evaluations of particular programmes, official statistics, and, in some cases, also survey work. Country chapters provide further details on the methodological approach employed in each case.

The research focuses on six countries—two from South Asia and four from sub-Saharan Africa. The intention of this selection was to contrast two different regions, as well as different types of programme and political rationale driving programme design. Part II of the book considers two dominant party systems—Ethiopia and Rwanda—that have sought to use social transfers conditioned on participation in labour-intensive public works as part of a project of national development and state building, combining protective and productive objectives. These cases are labelled *dominant-developmental.* In contrast, two of the countries—Ghana and Kenya—have highly competitive political systems where poverty-targeted unconditional cash transfers were expanded with the aim of maximizing the visible distribution of social transfers. These countries are referred to as *competitive-distributive* cases and are considered in Part III. Finally, Part IV presents two *universalistic-inclusive* cases—Bangladesh and Nepal—where transfers are paid to students based on school attendance with increasingly universalistic coverage framed as an attempt to promote social inclusion.

Each country case examines between two and four sub-national cases reflecting variation of state infrastructural power and the degree of political contestation within the country.[3] Sub-national case selection is discussed in detail in the relevant chapters and summarized briefly here. In four of the countries covered—Ethiopia, Ghana, and Kenya in Africa, and Nepal in South Asia—there is clear variation in state infrastructural power between a centre where the state is relatively strong and a periphery where it is much weaker. As such, sub-national cases were selected specifically to explore this variation, focusing on cases with high and low levels of infrastructural power. In Rwanda and Bangladesh, while sub-national cases were selected with a view to exploring variation, state-building projects over recent decades have resulted in relative homogeneity in the reach and capacity of the state across its territory. Here, while major variation in infrastructural power was not expected, case selection nonetheless focused on 'most likely' cases for variation, based on the assumption that if variation was not found between those cases, it would be unlikely elsewhere in the country. In each country a pair of cases was selected to explore the variation between the centre and a relatively remote rural or peripheral site.

Table 2.1 Sub-national case selection

Role for social transfers	Politics	Infrastructural power	
		Low	High
Dominant-developmental	**Contested**	Ab'ala, Gala'elu (Eth.)	Kuyyu, Merti (Eth.)
	Dominant	Rubavu (Rw.)	Ahferom, Wajirat (Eth.) Huye (Rw.)
Competitive-distributive	**Contested**	Sissala East (Gh.) Marsabit (Ken.)	Gomoa West (Gh.) Nakuru (Ken.)
	Dominant	Wa West (Gh.) Homa Bay (Ken.)	Assin South (Gh.) Nyeri (Ken.)
Universalistic-inclusive	**Contested**	Saptari (Nep.)	Ilam (Nep.) Araihazar (Bang.)
	Dominant	Jumla (Nep.) Haluaghat (Bang.)	Lalitpur (Nep.)

Case selection also aimed to highlight variation in political contestation. Three of the countries—Ghana, Kenya, and Nepal—have relatively competitive political systems, while three—Ethiopia,[4] Rwanda, and Bangladesh[5]—are governed by dominant parties with little prospect of losing power through electoral means. However, this national picture masks considerable variation within countries. While Kenyan and Ghanaian politics is highly competitive at a national level, the districts selected for detailed examination in each country are a mixture of competitive and dominant districts, chosen to highlight the impact of competitive pressures on distribution of social transfers. In Nepal, cases were selected to illustrate variation in the degree to which sub-altern groups had mobilized politically given the importance of such mobilization to recent political developments and the fluidity of party political affiliations. In Ethiopia, though the ruling party was electorally dominant throughout its territory, the relationship between the party and society and the legitimacy of the ruling party varied markedly across the country, with cases selected to illustrate this contestation.

Table 2.1 presents a summary of this sub-national case selection. It should be noted that the comparison of high vs low infrastructural power and dominant vs contested politics is in relation to comparisons between sub-national cases *within* rather than between countries. For example, the table shows that state infrastructural power was initially expected to be higher in Huye than in Rubavu among the Rwandan sites, not necessarily that infrastructural power was expected to be higher in Ahferom, Ethiopia than in Rubavu, Rwanda.

Our initial expectations were that high levels of infrastructural power and dominant political settings were more likely to favour the effective distribution of social transfers. Here, to reiterate, distribution is considered 'effective' where it is in line with the stated objectives and guidelines of the programme in question, albeit that these objectives are themselves open to critique. The importance of state infrastructural power should be obvious—where the state has the ability to reach all its people and territory with sufficient, well-trained staff who act on their directions from above and are insulated from attempts by social elites to influence decision making unduly, we would expect distribution in line with programme guidelines. There are also, however, good reasons to expect that the incentive to politicize distribution may vary based on the degree of political contestation. Broadly speaking, competitive electoral settings are likely to provide stronger incentives to politicize distribution in order to secure short-term political advantage than where a leader or party is dominant.

Table 2.2 briefly summarizes some of the key features of the social transfer programmes examined in each country. Two countries—Ghana and Kenya—employ social transfer schemes that are targeted to the poorest amongst vulnerable social groups, principally the elderly, children, and those living with disabilities. In Ghana, there are also weakly enforced conditions requiring use of social services. The case studies of Bangladesh and Nepal focus on school stipends, essentially education-conditioned social transfers. Until recently both programmes were also targeted, focusing on 'poor and meritorious' students as well as girls and historically disadvantaged caste groups. In 2016, Bangladesh made the stipend available to all students in public schools. The last two programmes—in Ethiopia and Rwanda—differ in that social transfers for most participants are conditional on participation in public works. The public works focus is the result of the programme's coverage of able-bodied adults in addition to unconditional transfers for those deemed unable to work. Each programme is targeted at the poorest, with some prioritization for the most vulnerable. Combined, these cases cover the full range of targeting mechanisms discussed in Chapter 1, with most programmes combining multiple targeting mechanisms.

Though this diversity of programme design undoubtedly places limits on the direct comparability of the programmes, countries nonetheless confront similar challenges in the distribution of social transfers related to state capacity and political contestation. Notably, all programmes confront the informational challenge—how to generate sufficiently accurate and legitimate information with which to distinguish between eligible and ineligible participants. For this reason, those tasked with implementation face delicate and complex trade-offs between the competing demands placed on them. From above, such officials are often under pressure from higher-level government officials, who may require them, for example, to expand provision in an attempt to secure mass political support, or to limit provision to meet ambitious graduation targets. From below, state

Table 2.2 Programme characteristics

	Ethiopia	Ghana	Kenya		Rwanda	Bangladesh	Nepal
Programme name(s)	Productive Safety Net Programme (PSNP)	Livelihood Empowerment Against Poverty (LEAP)	Cash Transfer for Orphans and Vulnerable Children (CT-OVC)	Older Persons Cash Transfer (OPCT)	Vision 2020 Umurenge Programme (VUP)[6]	Primary Education Stipend Project (PESP)[7]	Scholarship Programme[8]
Date of adoption	2005	2008	2004	2006	2008	2002	2011
Targeting mechanisms	Geographical, CBT, and self-targeting	Demographic, geographical, CBT, and PMT	Demographic, CBT, PMT	Demographic, geographical, means test	Geographical, CBT, PMT, and self-targeting	Demographic, geographical, asset test	Demographic, geographical, means test
Conditions	Labour-intensive public works[9]	School attendance and health check-ups	No	No	Labour-intensive public works	School attendance	School attendance
Graduation/ exit strategy	Yes	No	No	No	Yes	No	No
Coverage including all household members (% of total population)	7,640,000 (8%)	618,001 (2.2%)	1,326,000 (2.8%)	1,275,346 (2.7%)	362,722 (3%)	34,762,500 (22%)	13,800,000 (48%)

Source: Social Assistance Explorer (http://www.social-assistance.manchester.ac.uk) for 2015, World Development Indicators (http://wdi.worldbank.org) (2015) for population figures.

officials are subject to demands from their community members and powerful social elites to include particular groups within the selection, frequently at odds with both the programme guidelines and the wishes of higher-level officials (which are not always the same). Moreover, the tensions between these competing pressures must be resolved in the context of highly variable resource availability and political contestation, which shape state infrastructural power and frequently severely constrain their options.

The remainder of the book explores these country examples and compares the findings across countries: Part II focuses first on what Table 2.1 describes as the 'dominant-developmental' cases of Ethiopia and Rwanda; Part III then turns to the 'competitive-distributive' cases of Ghana and Kenya; and Part IV examines the 'universalistic-inclusive' cases of Bangladesh and Nepal. Finally, Part V provides a comparative analysis of the cases that links back to the theoretical and policy debates raised in these first two chapters.

Notes

1. The sensitive data requirements of social protection, including access to identity documents, the turn to biometric technology, and data storage, raises big questions about the potential for abuse and misuse of such systems (Donovan 2015; Hunter and Sugiyama 2018; Khan and Roy 2019; Sepúlveda 2019), as well as the role of such data in expanding the control and reach of the state (Scott 1998).
2. Vom Hau's (2012) excellent summary of the literature takes a slightly different approach to this study. Here, I argue that competence and resources, intra-state relations, and state–society relations all have the potential to vary across national territory and these jointly constitute state infrastructural power. Vom Hau, in contrast, views territorial reach or infrastructural power as a distinct dimension of state capacity, alongside organizational competence and embeddedness.
3. The unit of analysis is, of course, important for between country comparisons. Case selection focuses on districts, though inevitably there are limitations to the comparability of these district administrations between countries where factors such as territory, population, and the powers of decentralised administrations vary considerably (Snyder 2001; Soifer 2019).
4. The ruling party in Ethiopia dominated politics for nearly three decades. Since 2018 the country has been undergoing a political transition entailing some degree of opening up. The outcome of this transition and implications for political competition are highly uncertain at the time of writing.
5. The growing dominance of the Awami League over the last decade has effectively transformed the previously highly competitive nature of Bangladeshi politics (Jackman and Maitrot 2019).
6. Social Assistance Explorer includes only the direct support component of the VUP, excluding the public works and financial services elements since the VUP public works do not provide guarantee of employment but are instead supply driven. While this is

not an unreasonable decision, the public works element is the central focus of the VUP as a whole and is covered in the case study in Chapter 3. As a result, the details in this column regarding targeting approach, exit strategy, and coverage diverge from Social Assistance Explorer for Rwanda.

7. The latest available year in the Social Assistance Explorer is for 2015 when the programme was still targeted on the rural poor. Since 2016, PESP has covered all children in public schools.
8. Nepal's Scholarship Programme is not included in the Social Assistance Explorer. Data on the number of children in receipt of transfers are taken from Chapter 8. Based on an average household size of 4.6, programme reach of 3 million children gives coverage of 13,800,000.
9. Behavioural conditions were introduced to the direct support component of the PSNP in 2015, though implementation of these has been inconsistent to date.

References

Aalen, L. and Muriaas, R. L., 2017. *Manipulating Political Decentralisation: Africa's Inclusive Autocrats*. New York: Routledge.

Abdulai, A.-G., 2020. Competitive clientelism, donors and the politics of social protection uptake in Ghana. *Critical Social Policy*, https://doi.org/10.1177/0261018320945605.

Acemoglu, D., Johnson, S., and Robinson, J. A., 2000. The colonial origins of comparative development: an empirical investigation. *National Bureau of Economic Research Working Papers*, 7771.

Ampratwum, E., 2021. The politics of social protection implementation in Ghana: Tracing pathways to uneven effectiveness. Ph.D. thesis. University of Manchester.

Ang, Y. Y., 2016. *How China Escaped the Poverty Trap*. Ithaca, NY: Cornell University Press.

Bardhan, P. K. and Mookherjee, D., 2006. *Decentralization and Local Governance in Developing Countries: A Comparative Perspective*. Cambridge, MA: MIT Press.

Barrientos, A., 2009. Introducing basic social protection in low-income countries: Lessons from existing programmes. *In*: P. Townsend, ed. *Building Decent Societies: Rethinking the Role of Social Security in Development*. New York: Springer, 253–273.

Bevan, P., 2009. Working with cases in development contexts: Some insights from an outlier. *In*: D. Byrne and C. C. Ragin, eds. *The SAGE Handbook of Case-Based Methods*. London, Thousand Oaks, New Delhi: Sage Publications, 467–493.

Boone, C., 2003a. *Political Topographies of the African State: Territorial Authority and Institutional Choice*. Cambridge: Cambridge University Press.

Boone, C., 2003b. Decentralization as political strategy in West Africa. *Comparative Political Studies*, 36 (4), 355–380.

Boone, C., 2014. *Property and Political Order in Africa: Land Rights and the Structure of Conflict*. Cambridge: Cambridge University Press.

Buzan, B., 1983. *People, States, and Fear: The National Security Problem in International Relations*. Brighton: Wheatsheaf.

Cammett, M. and MacLean, L. M., 2014. *The Politics of Non-state Social Welfare*. Ithaca, NY: Cornell University Press.

Carpenter, D. P., 2001. *The Forging of Bureaucratic Autonomy: Reputations, Networks, and Policy Innovation in Executive Agencies, 1862–1928*. Princeton, NJ: Princeton University Press.

Centeno, M., Kohli, A., and Yashar, D. J., 2017. Unpacking states in the developing world: Capacity, performance and politics. *In*: M. Centeno, A. Kohli, and D. J. Yashar, eds. *States in the Developing World*. Cambridge: Cambridge University Press, 363–379.

Chemouni, B., 2014. Explaining the design of the Rwandan decentralization: Elite vulnerability and the territorial repartition of power. *Journal of Eastern African Studies*, 8 (2), 246–262.

Chopra, D., 2014. 'They don't want to work' versus 'They don't want to provide work': Seeking explanations for the decline of MGNREGA in Rajasthan. ESID Working Papers, 31.

Crook, R. C. and Manor, J., 1998. *Democracy and Decentralisation in South Asia and West Africa: Participation, Accountability and Performance*. Cambridge: Cambridge University Press.

Das, U., 2015. Does political activism and affiliation affect allocation of benefits in the Rural Employment Guarantee Program: Evidence from West Bengal, India. *World Development*, 67, 202–217.

Donovan, K. P., 2015. Infrastructuring aid: Materializing humanitarianism in northern Kenya. *Environment and Planning D: Society and Space*, 33 (4), 732–748.

Driscoll, B., 2018. Why political competition can increase patronage. *Studies in Comparative International Development*, 53 (4), 404–427.

Dutta, P., Murgai, R., Ravallion, M., and Van De Walle, D., 2014. *Right to Work? Assessing India's Employment Guarantee Scheme in Bihar*. Washington, DC: World Bank.

Ertman, T., 2005. Building states—Inherently a long-term process? An argument from comparative history. *In*: M. Lange and D. Rueschemeyer, eds. *States and Development*. New York: Springer, 165–182.

Evans, P., Huber, E., and Stephens, J., 2017. The political foundations of state effectiveness. *In*: M. Centeno, A. Kohli, and D. J. Yashar, eds. *States in the Developing World*. New York: Cambridge University Press, 380–408.

Evans, P. B., 1995. *Embedded Autonomy: States and Industrial Transformation*. Princeton, NJ: Princeton University Press.

Faguet, J.-P. and Pöschl, C., 2015. *Is Decentralization Good for Development? Perspectives from Academics and Policy Makers*. Oxford: Oxford University Press.

Ferguson, J., 2015. *Give a Man a Fish: Reflections on the New Politics of Distribution*. Durham, NC: Duke University Press.

Fukuyama, F., 2011. *The Origins of Political Order: From Prehuman Times to the French Revolution*. London: Profile Books.

Garay, C., 2016. *Social Policy Expansion in Latin America*. Cambridge: Cambridge University Press.

George, A. L. and Bennett, A., 2004. *Case Studies and Theory Development in the Social Sciences*. Cambridge, MA; London: MIT Press.

Gerring, J., 2006. *Case Study Research: Principles and Practice*. Cambridge: Cambridge University Press.

Gerth, H. H. and Mills, C. W., 2003. *From Max Weber: Essays in Sociology*. London: Routledge.

Giraudy, A., 2015. *Democrats and Autocrats: Pathways of Subnational Undemocratic Regime Continuity within Democratic Countries*. Oxford: Oxford University Press.

Giraudy, A., Moncada, E., and Snyder, R., 2019. Subnational research in comparative politics. *In*: A. Giraudy, E. Moncada, and R. Snyder, eds. *Inside Countries: Subnational Research in Comparative Politics*. Cambridge: Cambridge University Press, 3–54.

Gorski, P. S., 2003. *The Disciplinary Revolution: Calvinism and the Rise of the State in Early Modern Europe*. Chicago, IL: University of Chicago Press.

Gough, I., 2004. East Asia: The limits of productivist regimes. *In*: I. Gough and G. Wood, eds. *Insecurity and Welfare Regimes in Asia, Africa and Latin America: Social Policy in Development Contexts*. Cambridge: Cambridge University Press, 169–201.

Grindle, M. S., 2007. *Going Local: Decentralization and the Promise of Good Governance*. Princeton, NJ: Princeton University Press.

Grindle, M. S. and Thomas, J., 1991. *Public Choices and Policy Change: The Political Economy of Reform in Developing Countries*. London: John Hopkins University Press.

Hagmann, T. and Péclard, D., 2010. Negotiating statehood: Dynamics of power and domination in Africa. *Development and Change*, 41 (4), 539–562.

Hanlon, J., Hulme, D., and Barrientos, A., 2010. *Just Give Money to the Poor: The Development Revolution from the Global South*. Sterling, VA: Kumarian Press.

Harbers, I., 2015. Taxation and the unequal reach of the state: Mapping state capacity in Ecuador. *Governance*, 28 (3), 373–391.

Hassan, M., 2020. *Regime Threats and State Solutions: Bureaucratic Loyalty and Embeddedness in Kenya*. Cambridge: Cambridge University Press.

Hechter, M. and Brustein, W., 1980. Regional modes of production and patterns of state formation in western Europe. *American Journal of Sociology*, 85 (5), 1061–1094.

Herbst, J., 2000. *States and Power in Africa: Comparative Lessons in Authority and Control*. Princeton, NJ: Princeton University Press.

Holliday, I., 2000. Productivist welfare capitalism: Social policy in East Asia. *Political Studies*, 48 (4), 706–723.

Hopkin, J., 2006. Conceptualizing political clientelism: Political exchange and democratic theory. Paper prepared for the APSA annual meeting, Philadelphia, 31 August–6 September.

Huber, E. and Stephens, J. D., 2001. *Development and Crisis of the Welfare State: Parties and Policies in Global Markets*. Chicago, IL: University of Chicago Press.

Huber, E. and Stephens, J. D., 2012. *Democracy and the Left: Social Policy and Inequality in Latin America*. Chicago, IL: University of Chicago Press.

Hunter, W. and Sugiyama, N. B., 2018. Making the newest citizens: Achieving universal birth registration in contemporary Brazil. *Journal of Development Studies*, 54 (3), 397–412.

Ibrahim, M., 2021. Social protection, state capacity and citizenship building in Ghana: Do quasi-universal insurance and targeted social assistance policies generate different feedback effects? Ph.D. thesis. University of Manchester.

Jackman, D. and Maitrot, M., 2019. Managing coercion and striving for dominance in Bangladesh. ESID Working Papers, 129.

Joshi, A. and Moore, M., 2000. Enabling environments: Do anti-poverty programmes mobilise the poor? *Journal of Development Studies*, 37 (1), 25–56.

Jütting, J., Corsi, E., Kauffmann, C., Mcdonnell, I., Osterrieder, H., Pinaud, N., and Wegner, L., 2005. What makes decentralisation in developing countries pro-poor? *European Journal of Development Research*, 17 (4), 626–648.

Khan, M. and Roy, P., 2019. Digital identities: A political settlements analysis of asymmetric power and information. *SOAS Working Papers*, 15.

Khan, M. H., 2018. Power, pacts and political settlements: A reply to Tim Kelsall. *African Affairs*, 117(469): 670–694.

Kitschelt, H., 2007. Citizen–politician linkages: An introduction. *In*: H. Kitschelt and S. Wilkinson, eds. *Patrons, Clients and Policies: Patterns of Democratic Accountability and Political Competition*. Cambridge: Cambridge University Press, 1–49.

Koehler, G. and Chopra, D., eds., 2014. *Development and Welfare Policy in South Asia*. London: Routledge.

Kohli, A., 2004. *State-Directed Development: Political Power and Industrialization in the Global Periphery*. Cambridge: Cambridge University Press.

Krasner, S., 1978. *Defending the National Interest*. Princeton, NJ: Princeton University Press.

Kuhnle, S., 1996. International modeling, states, and statistics: Scandinavian social security solutions in the 1890s. *In*: D. Rueschemeyer and T. Skocpol, eds. *States, Social Knowledge, and the Origins of Modern Social Policies*. Princeton, NJ: Princeton University Press, 233–263.

Kuhnle, S. and Sander, A., 2010. The emergence of the western welfare state. *In*: F. G. Castles, S. Leibfried, J. Lewis, H. Obinger, and C. Pierson, eds. *The Oxford Handbook of the Welfare State*. Oxford: Oxford University Press, 61–80.

Landes, D. S., 1972. Statistics as a source for the history of economic development in western Europe. *In*: V. R. Lorwin and J. M. Price, eds. *The Dimensions of the Past: Materials, Problems, and Opportunities for Quantitative Work in History*. New Haven, CT: Yale University Press, 53–91.

Lange, M., 2009. *Lineages of Despotism and Development: British Colonialism and State Power*. Chicago, IL: University of Chicago Press.

Lavers, T., 2019a. Social protection in an aspiring 'developmental state': The political drivers of Ethiopia's PSNP. *African Affairs*, 118 (473), 646–671.

Lavers, T., 2019b. Understanding elite commitment to social protection: Rwanda's Vision 2020 Umurenge Programme. *In*: S. Hickey, T. Lavers, M. Niño-Zarazúa, and J. Seekings, eds. *The Politics of Social Protection in Eastern and Southern Africa*. Oxford: Oxford University Press, 95–121.

Lavers, T. and Hickey, S., 2021. Alternative routes to the institutionalisation of social transfers in sub-Saharan Africa: Political survival strategies and transnational policy coalitions. *World Development*, 146, 000–000

Levitsky, S. and Way, L. A., 2010. *Competitive Authoritarianism: Hybrid Regimes after the Cold War*. Cambridge: Cambridge University Press.

Lipsky, M., 1980. *Street-Level Bureaucracy: Dilemmas of the Individual in Public Services*. New York: Russell Sage Foundation.

Lund, C., 2006. Twilight institutions: Public authority and local politics in Africa. *Development and Change*, 37 (4), 685–705.

Magaloni, B., Diaz-Cayeros, A., and Estévez, F., 2007. Clientelism and portfolio diversification: A model of electoral investment with applications to Mexico. *In:* H. Kitschelt and S. I. Wilkinson, eds. *Patrons, Clients, and Policies: Patterns of Democratic Accountability and Political Competition*. Cambridge: Cambridge University Press, 182–205.

Mahoney, J., 2010. *Colonialism and Postcolonial Development: Spanish America in Comparative Perspective*. Cambridge: Cambridge University Press.

Maiorano, D., Das, U., and Masiero, S., 2018. Decentralisation, clientelism and social protection programmes: A study of India's MGNREGA. *Oxford Development Studies*, 46 (4), 536–549.

Mamdani, M., 1996. *Citizen and Subject: Contemporary Africa and the Legacy of Late Colonialism*. Princeton, NJ: Princeton University Press.

Mann, M., 1984. The autonomous power of the state: Its origins, mechanisms and results. *European Journal of Sociology*, 25 (2), 185–213.

Mann, M., 1986. *The Sources of Social Power, Volume 1: A History of Power from the Beginning to AD 1760*. Cambridge: Cambridge University Press.

Mann, M., 2012. *The Sources of Social Power, Volume 2: The Rise of Classes and Nation-States, 1760–1914*. Cambridge: Cambridge University Press.

Marcesse, T., 2018. Public policy reform and informal institutions: The political articulation of the demand for work in rural India. *World Development*, 103, 284–296.

Migdal, J. S., 1988. *Strong Societies and Weak States: State–Society Relations and State Capabilities in the Third World*. Princeton, NJ: Princeton University Press.

Migdal, J. S., 2001. *State in Society: Studying How States and Societies Transform and Constitute One Another*. Cambridge: Cambridge University Press.

Mkandawire, T., 2005. Targeting and universalism in poverty reduction. UNRISD Social Policy and Development Programme Papers, 23.

Mkandawire, T., 2015. Neopatrimonialism and the political economy of economic performance in Africa: Critical reflections. *World Politics*, 67 (3), 563–612.

Niedzwiecki, S., 2018. *Uneven Social Policies: The Politics of Subnational Variation in Latin America*. Cambridge: Cambridge University Press.

Plagerson, S., Harpham, T., and Kielmann, K., 2012. Cash transfers and citizenship: Evidence from South Africa. *Journal of Development Studies*, 48 (7), 969–982.

Poteete, A. R., 2009. Is development path dependent or political? A reinterpretation of mineral-dependent development in Botswana. *Journal of Development Studies*, 45 (4), 544–571.

Poteete, A. R. and Ribot, J. C., 2011. Repertoires of domination: Decentralization as process in Botswana and Senegal. *World Development*, 39 (3), 439–449.

Ragin, C. C., 2000. *Fuzzy-Set Social Science*. Chicago, IL: University of Chicago Press.

Rasul, I. and Rogger, D., 2018. Management of bureaucrats and public service delivery: Evidence from the Nigerian civil service. *Economic Journal*, 128 (608), 413–446.

Roy, I., 2019. Class politics and social protection: A comparative analysis of local governments in India. *Journal of South Asian Development*, 14 (2), 121–150.

Rueschemeyer, D., 2005. Building states—inherently a long-term process? An argument from theory. *In*: M. Lange and D. Rueschemeyer, eds. *States and Development*. New York: Springer, 143–164.

Sabates-Wheeler, R., Wilmink, N., Abdulai, A.-G., De Groot, R., and Spadafora, T., 2020. Linking social rights to active citizenship for the most vulnerable: The role of rights and accountability in the 'making'and 'shaping'of social protection. *European Journal of Development Research*, 32 (1), 129–151.

Schady, N. R., 2000. The Political Economy of Expenditures by the Peruvian Social Fund (FONCODES), 1991–95. *American Political Science Review*, 94 (2), 289–304.

Scott, J. C., 1998. *Seeing Like a State: How Certain Schemes to Improve the Human Condition Have Failed*. London: Yale University Press.

Seekings, J., 2017. State capacity and the construction of pro-poor welfare states in the 'developing' world. *In*: M. Centeno, A. Kohli, and D. J. Yashar, eds. *States in the Developing World*. Cambridge: Cambridge University Press, 363–379.

Sen, A., 1995. The political economy of targeting. *In*: D. Van De Walle and K. Nead, eds. *Public Spending and the Poor: Theory and Evidence*. Baltimore, MD: Johns Hopkins University Press, 11–24.

Sepúlveda, M., 2019. Biometric technology and beneficiary rights in social protection programmes. *International Social Security Review*, 72 (4), 3–28.

Singh, P., 2015. *How Solidarity Works for Welfare: Subnationalism and Social Development in India*. Cambridge: Cambridge University Press.

Skocpol, T., 1979. *States and Social Revolutions: A Comparative Analysis of France, Russia and China*. Cambridge: Cambridge University Press.

Skocpol, T., 1992. *Protecting Soldiers and Mothers: The Political Origins of Social Policy in the United States*. Cambridge, MA: Harvard University Press.

Slater, D., 2010. *Ordering Power: Contentious Politics and Authoritarian Leviathans in Southeast Asia*. Cambridge: Cambridge University Press.

Snyder, R., 2001. Scaling down: The subnational comparative method. *Studies in Comparative International Development*, 36 (1), 93–110.

Soifer, H., 2015. *State Building in Latin America*. Cambridge: Cambridge University Press.

Soifer, H., 2019. Units of analysis in subnational research. *In*: A. Giraudy, E. Moncada, and R. Snyder, eds. *Inside Countries: Subnational Research in Comparative Politics*. Cambridge: Cambridge University Press, 92–112.

Soifer, H. and Vom Hau, M., 2008. Unpacking the strength of the state: The utility of state infrastructural power. *Studies in Comparative International Development*, 43 (3–4), 219.

Stokes, S.C., 2007a. Is vote buying undemocratic? *In*: F. Schaffer, ed. *Elections for Sale: The Causes and Consequences of Vote Buying*. Boulder, CO: Lynne Rienner, 81–99.

Stokes, S.C., 2007b. Political clientelism. The Oxford Handbook of Comparative Politics Boix, C. and Stokes, S. (eds). Oxford: Oxford University Press.

Stokes, S. C., Dunning, T., Nazareno, M., and Brusco, V., 2013. *Brokers, Voters, and Clientelism: The Puzzle of Distributive Politics*. Cambridge: Cambridge University Press.

Sugiyama, N. B. and Hunter, W., 2013. Whither clientelism? Good governance and Brazil's 'Bolsa Família' program. *Comparative Politics*, 46 (1), 43–62.

Swamy, A. R., 2016. Can social protection weaken clientelism? Considering conditional cash transfers as political reform in the Philippines. *Journal of Current Southeast Asian Affairs*, 35 (1), 59–90.

Therkildsen, O., 2005. Understanding public management through neo-patrimonialism: A paradigm for all African seasons? *In*: G. R. Olsen and U. Engel, eds. *Understanding the African Exception*. Aldershot: Ashgate, 35–52.

Tilly, C., 1992. *Coercion, Capital, and European States, AD 990–1992*. Cambridge, MA and Oxford: Blackwell.

Van De Walle, N., 2014. The democratization of clientelism in sub-Saharan Africa. *In*: D. Abente Brun and L. Diamond, eds. *Clientelism, Social Policy and the Quality of Democracy*. Baltimore, MD: Johns Hopkins University Press, 230–252.

Vom Hau, M., 2008. State infrastructural power and nationalism: Comparative lessons from Mexico and Argentina. *Studies in Comparative International Development*, 43 (3–4), 334.

Vom Hau, M., 2012. State capacity and inclusive development: New challenges and directions. ESID Working Papers, 2.

Vu, T., 2010. *Paths to Development in Asia: South Korea, Vietnam, China, and Indonesia*. Cambridge: Cambridge University Press.

Wanyama, F. O. and McCord, A., 2017. The politics of scaling up social protection in Kenya. ESID Working Papers, 87.

White, G. and Goodman, R., 1998. Welfare Orientalism and the search for an East Asian welfare model. *In*: R. Goodman, H.-J. Kwon, and G. White, eds. *The East Asian Welfare Model: Welfare Orientalism and the State*. London: Routledge, 3–24.

World Bank, 2004. *World Development Report 2004: Making Services Work for the Poor*. Washington, DC: Oxford University Press/World Bank.

Yin, R. K., 2008. *Case Study Research: Design and Methods*, 4th edition. London: Sage Publications.

PART II

DOMINANT-DEVELOPMENTAL CASES IN AFRICA

3

State Infrastructural Power and Social Transfers

The Local Politics of Distribution and Delivering 'Progress' in Ethiopia

Tom Lavers

1. Introduction

Ethiopia's Productive Safety Net Programme (PSNP) is a large and complex programme that provides transfers in cash and food in exchange for public works from most participants, and unconditional direct support for a minority considered unable to work.[1] Support is targeted both geographically and to individual households. The PSNP was originally introduced in response to a major food crisis in 2002–3. However, from its launch in 2005, the government viewed the provision of support as a temporary measure. In line with the leadership's focus on rapid development and its embarrassment at recurrent food crises, the PSNP's ultimate aim was to promote mass graduation and thereby remove the need for the programme's existence (Lavers 2019). As such, the PSNP aims to make a productive contribution through public works to build community infrastructure and linked livelihoods initiatives to raise household productivity. The assumption is that by focusing transfers on the poorest and supporting productive activity through these initiatives, most PSNP participants will be able to graduate from support.

This chapter analyses the distributive aspects of PSNP implementation at local level—namely the *wereda* (districts) and *kebele* (sub-districts)—focusing on two main issues.[2] The first is how local authorities resolve the 'informational challenge' to state infrastructural power faced by any targeted programme, namely how to generate sufficiently detailed information with which to select households, while limiting undue influence of powerful local actors who might otherwise influence distribution for their own benefit. For this purpose, the PSNP relies on community-based targeting, whereby basic guidelines are provided to elected community committees, which then draw on their 'local knowledge' to select those

Tom Lavers, *State Infrastructural Power and Social Transfers.* In: *The Politics of Distributing Social Transfers.* Edited by Tom Lavers, Oxford University Press. © Oxford University Press (2022).
DOI: 10.1093/oso/9780192862525.003.0003

most in need. The second is the tension between the programme's productive ambitions to promote graduation consistent with the focus on delivering national development and the key role of supporting the poorest.

The PSNP is targeted to particular geographic areas and households within those. Analysis has shown that geographical targeting excludes large numbers of poor and vulnerable people who live outside PSNP *wereda* (Vargas Hill and Porter 2013). Nonetheless, extensive biannual evaluations of *household targeting* underpin the conclusion that from

> an international perspective, the PSNP is well targeted ... the PSNP is better targeted than any of the African safety net programs reported by Coady, Grosh, and Hoddinott (2004). There is little evidence of elite capture throughout the regions where the PSNP is being operated.
>
> (Coll-Black et al. 2012, p. 317)[3]

It should be noted here that the international standard to which the PSNP is compared is not high—the targeting of social transfers in developing countries is often very poor (Coady et al. 2004). Moreover, evaluations are not uniformly positive. While household targeting in the highland regions—the historical centre of the Ethiopian state, which contributes the majority of programme participants—is considered relatively effective, targeting in lowland regions of Afar and Somali—the historic periphery—is problematic. One recent study compared PSNP participation with livestock ownership—important in areas in which pastoralism continues to play a significant role—concluding that the lowest two deciles were *least likely* to receive the PSNP (Sabates-Wheeler et al. 2013). This analysis underpins the federal government's acknowledgment that access 'to PSNP transfers in Afar and Somali is in effect not targeted' (MoA 2014a, p. 13). Within the highlands, evaluations also show variation (Berhane et al. 2015). Targeting in Tigray is more effective, with the lowest income quintile considerably more likely to participate. In Oromiya and SNNPR, while the lowest income quintile is more likely to be included in the programme, many differences between income quintiles are not statistically significant.

The existing literature on the PSNP is dominated by impact evaluations, which are useful in assessing programme effectiveness, but provide limited insights into the dynamics that shape distribution and the evident variation that exists. A few papers have considered the politics of PSNP implementation (Lavers 2013; Cochrane and Tamiru 2016), but are limited to single case studies. This chapter employs a comparative research design, examining six sites in three Ethiopian regions: Afar, Oromiya, and Tigray. In so doing, the chapter highlights two key ways in which state infrastructural power and politics shape PSNP distribution. First, the distribution process is dependent on the particular configurations of party, state, and societal power relations in different sites. A key factor is the ability of the local party-state to mobilize local communities and address the informational challenge through either the party-state machinery or, where the party-state is lacking, clan structures. Rather than political party involvement undermining effective implementation, as might be expected, effective implementation in Ethiopia is actually dependent on the infrastructural power of the fused party-state. Second, state infrastructural power is also key to understanding the resolution to the recurrent tension within the programme between its developmental ambitions and core protective function. A central political priority for government is to demonstrate progress with respect to food insecurity, through graduation and a reduction of PSNP participants at the national level (Lavers 2019). The result is that party-state infrastructural power is brought to bear to meet graduation targets, regardless of household food security, in order to fit a national narrative of 'progress'.

The chapter begins by analysing the distinct historical pattern of state building in Ethiopia and the attempts by the Ethiopian Peoples' Revolutionary Democratic Front (EPRDF) to expand state infrastructural power. The chapter then outlines the study's methodology and case selection. The case studies themselves are discussed in two main sections: the first analyses state infrastructural power in each site and how this is embedded within state–society relations; and the second examines PSNP distribution, focusing on targeting and graduation.

2. Building the state and party in Ethiopia and the varying legacy for infrastructural power

State infrastructural power is conceptualized in terms of the resources available to the state, the relations between state agencies, and those between state and society. Consequently, infrastructural power is shaped by contemporary political processes, but also has deep historical roots. The discussion therefore begins with a brief overview of the long-run pattern of state formation in Ethiopia, before focusing on the expansion of the party-state undertaken under the EPRDF.

The Ethiopian polity has a history of several thousand years, with its origins in contemporary Tigray, Amhara, and neighbouring Eritrea (see Fig. 3.1). However, much of the west, south, and east of the country was only incorporated into Ethiopia through conquest in the late nineteenth century. A push for modernization in the final decades of Haile Selassie's (1930–74) reign led to the gradual replacement of rule through nobility with bureaucratic structures (Zewde 1991). Moreover, under the *Derg* (1974–91), uniform state structures were established down to the village level, with peasant associations created across the highlands. The Derg initiated a 'project of *encadrement*, or incorporation into structures of control, which was pursued with remarkable speed and ruthlessness' (Clapham 2002, p. 14). Encadrement utilized land reform and, subsequently,

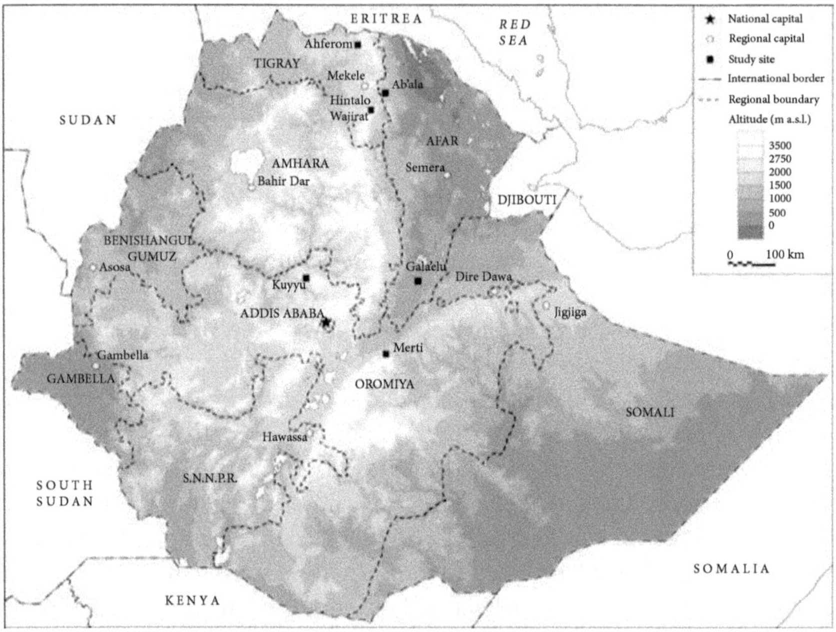

Fig. 3.1 Map of the Ethiopian research sites and federal boundaries
Note: In 2019 Sidama voted for statehood and separation from SNNPR.
Source: Author.

resettlement, villagization, and collectivization of agriculture, as the means to secure the '"capture" of the peasantry in a way that subjected them increasingly to state control' (Clapham 2002, p. 15).

In the lowland periphery, in contrast, the state's presence remained limited. The dominant highland perception was that these areas were economically and culturally backward, with mobile livelihoods, such as pastoralism, shifting cultivation, and flood-retreat agriculture, considered inferior to settled agriculture. Even Derg era *encadrement* was only partially successful, with 'pastoralist associations' bringing the state into greater proximity, but struggling to establish direct state control (Wolde 2002). Markakis (2011) summarizes Ethiopian state formation by distinguishing three parts of the country: the historic centre, the *highland core*, comprising Tigray and Amhara; the *highland periphery*, comprising much of Oromiya and northern parts of the Southern Nations, Nationalities and Peoples Region (SNNPR); and the *lowland periphery*, comprising Afar, Benishangul-Gumuz, Gambella, Somali, and southern Oromiya and SNNPR.

The EPRDF, which came to power in 1991, originated in the Tigrayan People's Liberation Front (TPLF), which mobilized the Tigrayan peasantry based on an ethno-nationalist message. The TPLF formed the EPRDF coalition to represent Ethiopia's ethnic groups and the EPRDF consciously framed its state-building efforts in opposition to the history of northern-led state building and exploitation. The EPRDF adopted a federal system, in an attempt to provide ethnic self-determination. Significant powers were formally devolved to ethno-regional administrations, each of which was controlled by an ethnically defined member or affiliate of the EPRDF. Nonetheless, in practice, the federal government retained massive influence over regions, not least through parallel party structures. Furthermore, the EPRDF struggled to shake the perception that it was a creation of and dominated by the TPLF. Many EPRDF parties and, notably, the Oromiya People's Democratic Organization (OPDO) were long perceived by their own ethnic constituencies as artificial creations of the TPLF (Clapham 2009). Moreover, the historical marginalization and exploitation of the lowland periphery was not reversed by federalism. Parties running lowland regions were only affiliates, not full members, of the EPRDF and lacked voting rights within the coalition. Meanwhile, the priorities of federal development strategies frequently overrode regional autonomy (Lavers 2012).

The EPRDF prioritized the pursuit of rapid, state-led development above all else. This shaped the government's approach to food security, which was framed as the 'real source of our national humiliation' (MoI 2002, pp. 10–11), leading to the productive aspirations of the PSNP and the focus on graduation. These developmental ambitions also resulted in the extension and intensification of *encadrement*, expanding the infrastructural power of a fused party-state. A central focus was to extend the party-state beyond the *kebele* (equivalent to the Derg's peasant associations) down to the household level. From 2011, this involved creation of sub-*kebele* administrations or *kushet*[4] to oversee villages within a *kebele*, and the division of men, women, and youth into *development teams* (sometimes referred to as development armies) of 25–30 households and *one-to-five networks* covering five to six households, each with its own leadership structure and reporting requirements to higher levels. Meanwhile, in areas populated by pastoralists and shifting cultivators, a central focus of government activity was a policy of villagization intended to address the supposedly unsustainable livelihoods of pastoralists and bring them in line with settled farmers elsewhere in the country (MoFA 2008).

Sub-*kebele* structures played several roles. First, these structures were used for service delivery, providing information about government initiatives and mobilizing communities to contribute to national campaigns. These structures were gendered, with male development teams focusing on agriculture, while women—associated with the domestic sphere—worked on health and sanitation. Second, the model farmers and households who led development teams and one-to-fives were expected to demonstrate exemplary behaviour to their teams through adherence to government initiatives. Third, model farmers and development team leaders were enrolled en masse as party members, with development teams used to disseminate party political, as well as developmental, messages. Fourth, development teams constituted an important means of generating information about the community, in a context in which the lowest formal tier of the state—the *kebele*—was responsible for a large and dispersed population. This included providing information to the *kebele* administration on: early identification of pregnant women, so that the health extension workers (HEWs) could conduct antenatal checks; monitoring and enforcing efforts to stop female genital mutilation; and monitoring school attendance. As shown below, this infrastructural power of the development teams and one-to-fives was also exploited for the PSNP.

Alongside these structures of control, there was a coherent attempt to establish mechanisms to make state officials accountable to superiors and, in principle, to the population that they serve. The system of *gim gema*—whereby officials regularly self-critiqued their performance in front of their superiors and those that they serve and were then subject to withering critique by others—was extended from its use by the TPLF throughout the civil war with the Derg to the entire party-state apparatus. In principle, these systems of performance evaluation applied also to the sub-*kebele* structures of *kushet*, development teams, and one-to-fives. Moreover, national development targets were systematically cascaded into performance targets for officials in lower levels of the state.

The result is that the Ethiopian government for some time possessed an unusual capacity—compared to others in Africa—to implement federal policy initiatives. As Prime Minister Meles once argued,

> Unlike all previous governments our writ runs in every village. That has never happened in the history of Ethiopia. The state was distant, irrelevant ... Now we have a formally structured state, there is a school in every village and clinics in every village, roads, infrastructure.
>
> (Meles, cited in Dowden 2012)

The reality, however, was that the party-state's infrastructural power varied markedly within Ethiopia, based on the particular pattern of state formation described above and sharply contrasting relations between the ruling party and society in the different regional states. While Meles was right that the government's writ did run large across the country, it ran much larger in some places than others.

Before proceeding, it is necessary to discuss the political changes in the years leading up to fieldwork, which was conducted in 2018. From 2014, a wave of unprecedented protests took place across Oromiya, sparked by plans for the expansion of Addis Ababa, but fuelled by widespread landlessness and unemployment, growing Oromo nationalism, the illegitimacy of the OPDO, and the heavy-handed response of the military and police to initially peaceful protests (Davison 2016). The protests led to the replacement of the OPDO leadership in 2016, with the reform-minded Lemma Megersa installed as regional president and Abiy Ahmed as deputy. This new leadership achieved a remarkable turnaround by aligning themselves with the protestors and occasionally against the federal government.

Following Prime Minister Hailemariam Dessalegn's resignation in early 2018, Abiy Ahmed of the resurgent OPDO was selected as the new prime minister. These events were influential with respect to state infrastructural power, unleashing a counter-process resisting state *encadrement*. Centrifugal forces strengthened, leading to growing regional autonomy from federal control, while past systems of top-down control were increasingly contested. However, the OPDO leadership temporarily achieved newfound legitimacy in Oromiya, while a reform process of 'Deep Renewal'—originally launched under Hailemariam but seized upon by the new leadership—attempted to revitalize party-state structures down to the grass roots. The result was that the fieldwork period in the first half of 2018 was marked by considerable fluidity in the pattern described above, particularly in Oromiya.

After fieldwork concluded, the EPRDF coalition parties and affiliates, with the exception of the TPLF, merged to form the Prosperity Party. Tensions between the federal government and the TPLF, which retained power in Tigray, grew over time until military conflict broke out in late 2020. The TPLF was removed from office by a combination of Ethiopian and Eritrean armed forces, and Amhara militias, and commenced a rural insurgency that was ongoing at the time of writing. These events took place some time after fieldwork was completed and are not covered in the main analytical sections. However, the conclusion briefly reflects on the implications of these changes for state infrastructural power.

3. Methodology

Fieldwork entailed application of the same research protocols across six sites in three regions between March and July 2018. Fieldwork in each site was conducted in two phases, with workshops in between fieldwork periods used to compare and contrast findings between the sites and to identify common research themes. In each site, data generation involved approximately 25–30 key informant interviews with officials from *wereda*, *kebele*, and *kushet* administrations, social elites and individual residents, as well as ten focus group discussions—comprising men or women—regarding people's experiences with the programme. Details of interviews and focus groups can be found in the annex to this chapter. Primary data generation was supplemented with documentary sources and official statistics. Fieldwork in each region was conducted by a male and a female researcher with fluency in local languages, with the female researcher conducting interviews with women wherever possible. The exception is Afar, where two male researchers were paired, due to the difficulty of identifying a female researcher.

An important limitation is the influence of social desirability bias. Given the efforts of the dominant party-state to shape norms regarding 'good' behaviour and to enforce these, it is challenging to get respondents to talk openly about their experiences and opinions (Østebø et al. 2018). This is even more challenging when gender and class relations are overlaid on political sensitivities. Women in conservative rural communities have historically played a limited role in social and political life, and social norms mean that many women find it difficult to speak out. To a degree, we were able to address this by pairing male and female researchers. Nonetheless, whatever reassurances are provided, the expectation is that outsiders probably have ties to party-state or donor agencies. Respondents therefore tend to report what they believe to be the official position, rather than what actually happens in practice. To a degree, such limitations can be addressed by gaining respondents' trust, spending an extended period in the community or through triangulation. However, these strategies are imperfect and, particularly, in a time-bound and resource-constrained study such as this, some limitations are inevitable.

Case selection draws on Markakis' threefold typology, selecting one region from each of his categories. Within these categories, an attempt was made to highlight the extremes of party-state building, with Tigray, home to the TPLF and origin of the EPRDF, chosen from the highland core; Oromiya, where OPDO/EPRDF legitimacy is perhaps most contested, chosen from the highland periphery; and Afar, one of the poorest regions where state building has advanced the least, from the lowland periphery. Within regions, two *wereda* and two *kebele* were selected from different parts of the region in question. These are: Ende Mariam *kebele*, Ahferom *wereda* and Tsehafti *kebele*, Hintalo Wajirat *wereda*, both in Tigray; Ad-kelu keble, Ab'ala *wereda* and Dabal *kebele*, Gala'elu *wereda*, both in Afar; and Halelo Cerri *kebele*, Kuyyu *wereda* and Shamo Gado *kebele*, Merti *wereda*, in Oromiya.

While the study cannot generalize from a mere two sites to what are very large regions, where similar findings are identified in two quite different sites, it does provide some indication that the phenomena are not limited to that specific location. The *wereda* are marked on Fig. 3.1.[5] Fig. 3.2 shows the coverage of the PSNP in each *kebele*, which broadly reflects the regional distribution of the PSNP. Afar is the only region in which the PSNP operates in every single *wereda*, and also has the highest proportion of its population covered by the programme, as in the research sites. Tigray is the highland region with the highest proportion of its population covered by the PSNP. Finally, the PSNP covers a much smaller proportion of the Oromo population in general and the research sites in question.

Finally, it should be noted that the PSNP in Afar takes a slightly different form to that in the other two regions. The PSNP in Afar involves in-kind food transfers, rather than a mixture of cash and food elsewhere. More directly relevant to the present chapter, there has never been an attempt to promote graduation in Afar. This is not to say that the government has willingly accepted long-term provision of social transfers in the region. Rather, for the government, the key to regional transformation is villagization, which is believed to offer the possibility of greater food security.

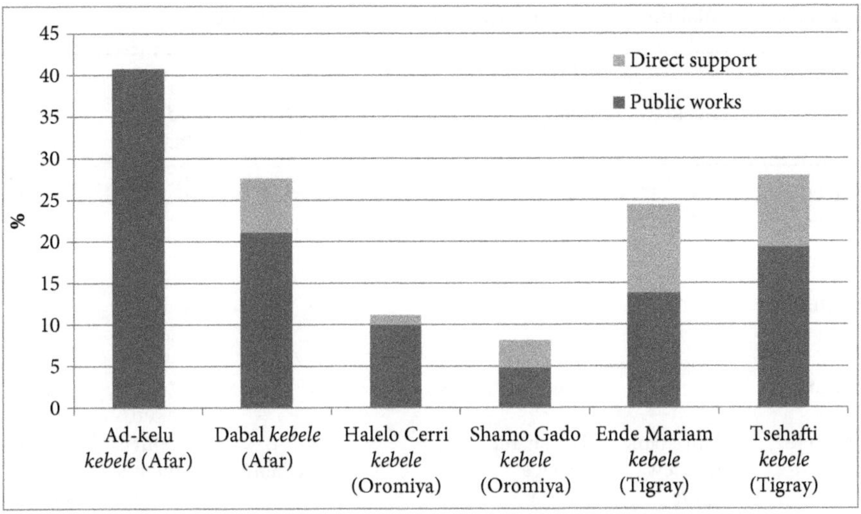

Fig. 3.2 PSNP coverage as a percentage of *kebele* population in 2018

4. Variations in party-state infrastructural power

This section focuses on party-state infrastructural power in the six research sites, situating this within the broad pattern of variation highlighted above. The following section then examines how infrastructural power shapes PSNP distribution.

The first element of state infrastructural power is the resources available to the state. In terms of physical infrastructure within the *kebele* in question, the differences were not enormous (see Table 3.1). The Tigray and Oromiya sites undoubtedly enjoyed better external transport links to urban centres, where services such as grid connections, mobile coverage, and internet were readily available, than those in Afar. However, within the sites themselves, there were only modest differences. One site in each of Oromiya and Tigray had electricity access in the *kebele* centre, though not the majority of the *kebele*. There was no grid connection in the other four sites. Roads within each *kebele* were very limited, reaching only parts of the *kebele*, and *kebele* administrations lacked any form of transportation, with the partial exception of Enda Mariam *kebele*, where there was a broken motorbike. Mobile coverage was patchy and inconsistent everywhere.

There were clearer differences in staffing and staff qualifications (see Table 3.2). Development agents (DAs) are responsible for agricultural policies, including the PSNP. However, all officials sit on PSNP committees and thereby contribute to implementation. In terms of staffing and qualifications, Oromiya and Tigray were comparable, with elected officials reaching at least an intermediate level of secondary education, while employees all had post-secondary qualifications. Afar fell short, with elected officials lacking any formal education, while *kebele* employees

Table 3.1 Availability of basic infrastructure in the research sites

	Afar		Oromiya		Tigray	
	Ad-kelu	**Dabala**	**Halelo Cerri**	**Shamo Gado**	**Enda Mariam**	**Tsehafti**
Electricity access	No	No	No	Limited, excludes *kebele* centre	No	Yes, in *kebele* centre
Computer	No	No	No	No	No	One in *kebele* office
Transport	No	No	No	No	Motorbike (broken)	No
Mobile network	Unreliable in a few spots	Unreliable service in some places	No	Yes, but unreliable	Yes, but unreliable	In two of four *kushet*

were both short on numbers and inferior in qualifications compared to Oromiya and Tigray. Afar was clearly at a disadvantage in terms of the resources available to the *kebele* administration compared to Oromiya and Tigray. However, this resource constraint was further exacerbated by other aspects of infrastructural power, namely intra-state and state–society relations.

The operation of the sub-*kebele* administrative structures was unsurprisingly imperfect everywhere. However, the TPLF—building on a long history of centralized state control, the absence of significant neo-customary authorities, and the legacy of close relations between the Front and the peasantry during the armed struggle—came closest to this 'ideal' in Tigray. The development team structure in Tigray provided a formidable basis for service delivery, a means of mobilizing the population for developmental activities, and a strong normative steer as to what it meant to be a good citizen in the EPRDF's Ethiopia. The analysis therefore begins with Tigray, before turning to Oromiya and Afar to highlight marked differences.

In the two Tigray sites, the system of *kushet*, development teams, and one-to-fives was well established and working fairly effectively. Team meetings were held regularly and well attended. The one-to-fives were expected to meet weekly to discuss activities and plans, as well as messages passed down from higher levels, while the development team leaders should meet fortnightly. In principle, attendance was monitored and compulsory. While this undoubtedly varied in practice, numerous respondents in Tsehafti *kebele* noted that failure to participate in one-to-fives resulted in denial of government services and material penalties, including deductions from PSNP transfers:

Table 3.2 Qualifications of *kebele* officials in study sites

	Afar		Oromiya		Tigray	
	Ad-kelu	**Dabala**	**Halelo Cerri**	**Shamo Gado**	**Enda Mariam**	**Tsehafti**
Chair	None	None	11th grade	9th grade	10th grade	7th grade
Deputy	None	None	7th grade	Diploma	N/A	N/A
Manager	10th grade	Diploma	TVET	UG degree	Studying towards UG degree	UG degree
DA1	None	Diploma	UG degree	UG degree	UG degree	TVET
DA2	N/A	Diploma	Studying towards UG degree	UG degree	UG degree	TVET
DA3	N/A	N/A	Diploma	Diploma	UG degree	TVET
DA4	N/A	N/A	N/A	N/A	UG degree	N/A
HEW1	7th grade	Diploma	Diploma	Diploma	Diploma	TVET
HEW2	10th grade	10th grade	Diploma	N/A	Diploma	TVET
HEW3	10th grade	8th grade	N/A	N/A	N/A	N/A
Social worker	N/A	N/A	N/A	N/A	UG degree	N/A

TVET: technical and vocational education and training
UG: undergraduate
Source: Case studies.

> If members are not attending meetings and not participating in activities by development teams and networks, they will be punished by deducting from the PSNP support and emergency relief they get from the government.[6]

Respondents nonetheless admitted that the development team structures were less effective in remote parts of the *kebele*, where administrative oversight was more limited. Moreover, male development teams were more effective than the female ones, with attendance and enthusiasm among women dropping over time. The main reasons noted were that women struggled to combine one-to-fives with domestic responsibilities and that the focus of women's teams on a consistent set of health extension packages over many years had resulted in a loss of interest.

Providing guidance to this party-state structure, annual performance targets were cascaded down through tiers of party-state administration for state officials and sub-*kebele* structures, and progress was regularly evaluated through *gim gema*. Respondents emphasized that *gim gema* was taken very seriously, with criticism of an official's performance seen as a great source of embarrassment. The response of one *kushet* leader was typical:

> Being severely criticized in *gim gema* in the community is considered as disgrace or disrespecting the community who elects you. Leaders who are severely criticized must either resign or the community will dismiss them.[7]

The government used these evaluations to rank the performance of administrations and officials regionally and locally, as well as to allocate promotions, training opportunities, and, sometimes, modest material rewards. The result was that, in Tigray, the party-state certainly met Mann's definition of infrastructural power in terms of the state's ability to 'penetrate civil society' (Mann 1984, p. 189). In the two sites, the party-state had not merely penetrated civil society, but subsumed it, with no truly independent societal organization present.

In Oromiya, the same structures were unable to establish the tight control and oversight evident in Tigray. Beneath the *kebele*, *kushet* administrations were established in both sites. While this functioned in Shamo Gado *kebele*, *kebele* officials in Halelo Cerri readily admitted that the *kushet* only ever existed on paper.[8] Likewise, while development teams and one-to-fives had been established, their performance was highly variable and well below that in Tigray. As one official in Kuyyu *wereda* admitted, 'it cannot be said that it [the development team structure] is active and is doing well, it is more theoretical'.[9] Some development team leaders and members reported that they had not had any meetings for at least a year.[10] Indeed, development teams and one-to-fives were increasingly seen as voluntary.[11]

Several respondents noted a reduction in the functioning of development teams during the Oromo protests in the years prior to fieldwork.[12] However, others argue that the structures were never really effective. For example, one male focus group respondent reported that

> We know we are in the one-to-five team but we never had a meeting ... the one-to-five is just there in name but not active.[13]

Oromiya state officials repeatedly highlighted the importance of development teams and the limitations presented by their current dysfunction. As the DA in Halelo Cerri put it, 'All *kebele* administration related works and also community development work is done using these arrangements.'[14] Consequently, the regional government's view was that

> we must rebuild them ... they are essential for everything. Before we just assumed that things worked by themselves, but when these [development teams] disappear you realize how important they are.[15]

Performance targets were cascaded down from national plans to local state officials in Oromiya also. In theory, these performance assessments were the basis for allocating promotions and training opportunities, as in Tigray. However, several respondents were sceptical about this, suggesting that personal ties were actually more influential.[16] Furthermore, *kebele* officials in Oromiya were unanimous that the regularity of performance evaluations and the pressure to meet performance targets had also declined. Most respondents noted that evaluation was strong up to the 2015 elections and the end of the national development plan in 2015, but fell away afterwards.[17] Beneath the *kebele*, performance assessment was more sporadic still, with dysfunctional development teams no longer assessed. At the individual level, the population had not been evaluated as model households or farmers since 2012–13.[18] The result was that party-state infrastructural power in Oromiya—in terms of the capacity to mobilize the population, disseminate information, draw on local knowledge and provide a normative model of exemplary behaviour—was severely curtailed.

The Afar sites provide a further contrast. The *kebele* in each Afar site was divided into *kushet*.[19] However, rather than a de facto additional tier of the state, as in Tigray, the *kushet* was a forum in which a *kushet* leader engaged with powerful clan leaders regarding the administration of the area. As one *kushet* leader noted,

> We don't have formal government recognized structure to administer this *makafta* [*kushet*]. We use the customary laws to lead our people and manage the resources of the land. The clan leaders are the key people who jointly govern the community with me.[20]

The development team structure, meanwhile, only existed on paper and most respondents in the communities had never even heard of them. The party-state in Afar has never had the infrastructural power to organize the local population or to control household affairs to this degree. Efforts at establishing performance evaluations were likewise limited. The regional food security office admitted that

> Our office is a coordination office, we have no mandate to punish them [*wereda* officials]. We recommend, but the implementation is up to them.[21]

Similarly, while the *wereda* did set targets for *kebele* officials, there was little meaningful evaluation and no pressure or reward to raise performance in either site.[22] As reported in Gala'elu,

> There are no penalties for failing to meet our target. Nobody asks about our achievement or failure. We do as much as we can perform and leave the rest of the work.[23]

In the two Afar sites, as across the region, the clan was central to local governance. Party-state structures compensate for their limited capacity and legitimacy by building on the comparatively stronger and more legitimate clan. In Ad-kelu, the party-state structure was fused with the clan, with dominant clan leaders taking key positions in the local party-state. In Dabal *kebele*, clan leaders did not have formal *kebele* positions, but were widely acknowledged as the key authority figures and had party roles at zonal and regional level.[24] Moreover, *kebele* officials were subordinate members of the same clans and deferred decision making to clan leaders in recognition of their authority in the local community. As one *kebele* official acknowledged,

> The two systems are complementary to each other. To make a state run without customary laws is like to ask a person walk with only one foot.[25]

Clan leaders themselves went further:

> I don't think the state will be able to function on its own without our support. We have supported them in a lot of ways as the community has much trust in us and want to be served by us too.[26]

In sum, it is clear that the three regions present sharply contrasting relations between party, state, and society, with important implications for party-state infrastructural power. Moreover, strong similarities between the two research sites in each of the three regions suggest that these patterns go beyond the isolated experience of any one *kebele*. In Tigray, the party-state had effectively penetrated society, establishing close top-down control down to the household level and embedding performance evaluation that provided a strong normative steer as to desired behaviour of community residents. The result was a comparatively high degree of party-state infrastructural power. The same strategy had been pursued in the Oromo sites, with some success. However, party-state infrastructural power was more limited, even prior to the last few years, with many acquiescing to the initiatives of a coercive state, despite the illegitimacy of the local party-state. The unrest of recent years meant a collapse in this infrastructural power. Finally, the Afar sites represent a quite different configuration, with a weak party-state founded on and working through clan structures. Here, party-state infrastructural power was severely constrained, and forced to depend upon clan authorities to achieve developmental and political objectives.

5. State infrastructural power and the local politics of distributing the PSNP

The analysis now examines how this variation in party-state infrastructural power influences PSNP distribution through household targeting and graduation. The discussion begins by examining variation in the configuration of actors involved in PSNP implementation across the research sites. The section then goes on to highlight two main findings. First, that variation in party-state infrastructural power shapes how the state addresses the informational challenge presented by targeting. Second, party-state infrastructural power, in the form of performance evaluations, is used to impose graduation from the PSNP in line with the national focus on demonstrating developmental progress, but ignoring the reality of local food insecurity.

Party-state infrastructural power and PSNP administration

PSNP implementation at the *kebele* level, according to programme guidelines, is to be carried out by three committees, with the DAs taking particular responsibility, and overseen by the *kebele* cabinet. The Kebele Food Security Taskforce (KFSTF) is responsible for the overall operation of the programme and should comprise the *kebele* chair and manager, the DAs, HEWs, school teacher, and representatives of women's and youth associations (MoA 2014b, pp. 18–8). The Community Food Security Taskforce (CFSTF) operates at the *kushet* level and is responsible for household targeting, identification of graduates from the programme and general monitoring of implementation. This Community Taskforce is expected to have broad representation from the community, including elected representatives of women, men, youth, and elderly, as well as a representative of the *kebele* taskforce, a DA, and HEW (MoA 2014b, pp. 18–6). Finally, the Kebele Appeals Committee is responsible for hearing and adjudicating complaints about programme implementation. The appeals committee is required to have no overlap in membership with the other committees and should comprise a member of the *kebele* council, a DA, HEW, and male and female elders (MoA 2014b, pp. 18–9). The rationale underpinning this structure is to ensure breadth of participation, to ensure that all community groups can feed into selection, and to divide responsibilities between committees to limit the possibility of any one group manipulating the programme to their own advantage. Nonetheless, programme guidelines ignore the power relations between the party-state and society, and pay only limited attention to gender relations, limiting their scope to ensuring that women are represented on committees.

PSNP committees in the research sites adhered to programme guidelines to varying degrees (Table 3.3). In every committee there was some female representation, albeit less than 50 per cent of committee members. For the most part, the committees in Tigray were properly constituted, while there were more significant problems in the two Oromo cases and, to a degree, those in Afar. In Oromiya, committees operated, if at all, at the beginning of a PSNP phase, rather than playing a continuous role in programme administration. According to the chair of the Shamo Gado *kebele*, the Kebele Food Security Taskforce's role was 'nominal. Their work is covered by development agents.'[27] Meanwhile, a selection committee comprising the *kebele* cabinet and women's league representative was formed every five years to conduct selection and then disbanded afterwards. In Halelo Cerri, there had never been a Community Food Security Taskforce, with the Kebele Food Security Taskforce conducting selection instead.[28] Moreover, the membership of the Kebele Appeals Committee in Halelo Cerri was a subset of the membership of the *kebele* taskforce, preventing any possibility of independent appeals, as envisaged in programme guidelines. Overlap between committee membership and independence of the appeals process also arose as an issue in the Afar sites. However, here the problem may not be so much a failure to follow guidelines, but the shortage of *kebele* staff. Each committee requires the membership of DAs and HEWs. Where the *kebele* is understaffed, those who are in place have to fill in across multiple committees, undermining the independence of the committees.

The capacity of these structures to administer the PSNP is also shaped by the training that staff receive, on what is a large and complex programme. Here again, there was a clear difference between the two highland regions—where the *kebele* chair, manager, and DAs received annual training—and Afar, where the chair of Dabal *kebele* was the only official across two sites who had ever received PSNP training.

These committees were by no means the only actors involved in distributing the PSNP, however. PSNP distribution was adapted to local contexts and the specific configuration of party-state–society relations discussed above. Depending on the region, party structures, development teams, one-to-five networks, and clans, all entirely absent from implementation guidelines, actually constituted key actors in implementation. As noted above, the state was fused with party structures, with the result that the party inevitably played a role in implementation also. Across the sites, the vast majority of the members of the Kebele Food Security Taskforce—not just the *kebele* chair and deputy, but also the headteacher and extension agents—were local party leaders. Moreover, the positions of women and youth representatives on the taskforce were routinely allocated to the heads of the party-affiliated women's and youth leagues in all the research sites. The role of the development teams—also party-political structures—varied between sites, depending on their effectiveness. In Tigray, development teams were centrally involved in all aspects of the programme, from targeting to graduation to organization of public works. This was not just limited to the particular *kebele* studied by the project, but respondents at federal, regional, and *wereda* level all acknowledged the importance of the development teams. As noted by the Tigray regional food security office, the development teams are

> not only for the PSNP but for any development activity ... [development teams] are in every *wereda*, every *kushet*, both women and men.[29]

Table 3.3 Constitution of PSNP committees and access to PSNP training in the study sites

	Afar		Oromiya		Tigray	
	Ad-kelu	**Dabala**	**Halelo Cerri**	**Shamo Gado**	**Enda Mariam**	**Tsehafti**
KFSTF	Mostly correct, but no elders' representative and no HEW.	Correct	Mostly cor-rect, but no DA or elders' representative.	Mostly correct when it was operational, but no HEW. Dysfunctional for last four years.	Correct	Correct
CFSTF	Mostly correct, but no DA or HEW.	Mostly correct, but no DA.	Incorrect: No CFSTF has been formed.	Incorrect: Only operated briefly at beginning of programme.	Mostly correct, but no HEW.	Mostly correct, but no DA or HEW.
KAC	Mostly correct, but missing a DA.	Incorrect: two individuals overlap with KFSTF and missing a DA.	Incorrect: Com-plete overlap with KFSTF.	Correct	Mostly correct, but missing a HEW.	Mostly correct, but missing a DA and HEW.
Training	None	Chair once	Annual training	Annual training	Annual training	Annual training

In Tigray, elected community representatives for men, women, and youth required in the community taskforce were, in practice, leaders of development teams, who were included in the committee 'by default'.[30] As a result, the size of the taskforce varied, depending on the number of development teams in the *kushet*. While the programme guidelines aim to ensure breadth of participation in the PSNP committees, the reality in Tigray is that virtually all committee positions are taken by individuals incorporated in various ways into hierarchical party-state structures.

In Oromiya, development teams were also central to PSNP implementation, playing a key role in targeting, graduation, and organization of public works. However, development team leaders were never integrated into what are dysfunctional community taskforces in Oromiya, as in Tigray, but were expected to work with these committees. The marked deterioration of the development teams in Oromiya raises questions about their future role in the programme.

In Afar, development teams had never been functional and consequently played no role in the PSNP, highlighting an important gap in the infrastructural power of the party-state. To fill the gap, the party-state drew on the clan for PSNP implementation, replicating the general approach to governance described above. Clan and lineage leaders were called on to play key roles in the selection of participants and managing appeals, in particular.

Mobilizing state infrastructural power to target the PSNP

Variation in the party-state and its relationship with society emerged as a central source of variation in the selection of households for inclusion in the PSNP. On receiving a quota of PSNP places from the federal government, *wereda* then allocate PSNP places to the *kebele* under their authority, based on past experience of food insecurity and recent needs. The Kebele Food Security Taskforce in turn distributes PSNP places to the Community Food Security Taskforces at the *kushet* level. The Community Food Security Taskforce then selects households for inclusion in the programme, based on the programme guidelines, which establish basic criteria. Households should be community members who have faced food shortages of at least three months every year for three years, or who have faced a severe recent loss of productive assets (MoA 2014b, pp. 3–7). Preference is given to vulnerable groups, such as female-headed households, those with chronic illness, elderly caring for orphans, and poor pregnant and lactating women. These criteria are, however, only a guide, with *wereda* food security offices able to adapt criteria to local settings.

The task facing the Community Food Security Taskforce is significant. In the 1990s, community-based targeting of food aid was conducted at the *kebele* level. However, following reviews of procedures, new targeting guidelines concluded that *kebele* were 'too large to carry out identification of beneficiaries', and so 'smaller community groups such as Kushet … are best placed to select beneficiaries', due to the close social ties between members of these communities (DPPC 2000, p. 37). While numbers are more manageable at *kushet* level, a taskforce of about 10–12 people is still expected to classify the income and assets of the entire population of their *kushet*, which in the study sites varied between 1,000 and 3,000 people. As such, these committees still faced a significant challenge in generating information with which to make the selection.

In Tigray, this informational challenge was resolved by mobilizing the infrastructural power of the party-state, with the development teams and one-to-fives centrally involved in targeting.[31] The development teams were used, since 'they know each other's livelihood condition'.[32] The size of *kushet* made it very difficult for a community taskforce to assess the assets and relative poverty of every household. The development teams therefore offered the advantage of mobilizing local knowledge for household selection. In some instances, development team leaders provided the committee with a list of those most in need from their teams and the taskforce reconciled these lists. In some cases in both sites, however, taskforce members and development team leaders reported that the quota allocated to the *kushet* was further sub-divided between development teams and even one-to-fives with PSNP places allocated between members of these groups.[33] One taskforce member reported,

> After the responsibilities and quotas are distributed to development teams by *kushet* clusters, the quotas are again disseminated to [one-to-five] network leaders for targeting the poorest in their networks.[34]

In Tigray, male and female development teams were involved in selection, producing separate lists that were combined by the committee. However, some respondents admitted that 'women development teams are passive. It is the males who most often participate in this process.'[35]

Respondents in Oromiya at all levels, from the region to *wereda* and *kebele*, similarly emphasized the importance of the development teams for targeting. As noted by the Merti *wereda* agriculture officer,

> the process of beneficiary selection starts at the one-to-five team level … they [development teams] are the sources for the beneficiary section process.[36]

The stated rationale was that these structures provided detailed local knowledge, to which the formal structures of the state did not have access. According to the DA in Halelo Cerri, 'as we cannot differentiate the poor from the rich, the process of screening has been conducted by them [development teams]'.[37] As in Tigray, exact practices varied between *kushet*. In some cases, development team leaders provided recommendations to the taskforce,[38] while in others a quota was allocated to each development team and one-to-five.[39] The collapse of development teams in Oromiya therefore raises questions about PSNP implementation going forward. It is unclear whether it would be possible at present to mobilize development teams to conduct another wealth ranking exercise, given their current dysfunction.

Selection in Oromiya was also gendered. In Tigray, male and female development teams should have been involved in the selection process, although, as noted, male teams were more active. In Oromiya, however, selection was conducted by male teams alone.[40] This may be partly related to the gendered nature of the agricultural extension system, with agricultural activities—including the PSNP—falling within the remit of male development teams. In theory, in Oromiya, female-headed households should be included in the men's (agriculture-focused), as well as women's (health-focused), development teams. Consequently, even if the selection process was dominated by men, the development teams would include all households, whether female- or male-headed. However, in reality, participation of female-headed households in male teams was very limited, not least as a result of the burden of productive and reproductive responsibilities that they face, as acknowledged by one team leader:

> They [women] are caught up by domestic chores and most of them are not that interested so the selection is done by the male development team.[41]

The challenge regarding how to generate sufficiently detailed (and ideally accurate) information with which to select participants is therefore addressed in Tigray and Oromiya by mobilizing party-state infrastructural power through development teams and one-to-fives. In Afar, this option was not available and the informational challenge was tackled by working with the clan structure. In Dabal *kebele*, PSNP quotas were allocated to *kushet*, based on negotiation between state officials and clan leaders.[42] Moreover, the *kushet* leaders used the clan structures to substitute for the absence of development teams. Of particular importance is the *dhalla* (literally a compound in Afar-Af), a lineage-based group that live together and trace their origins back three to five generations. The leader is known as the *Dhalla Aba*. These *dhalla* were used to replicate the role of the one-to-fives in PSNP distribution, with *wereda* officials even referring to these as 'traditional one-to-fives', albeit that they lie outside the authority of the party-state:

> The only one-to-fives we use in implementation of PSNP are the traditional ones [*dhalla*] ... So, in PSNP, we use the *dhalla* leaders to communicate with the beneficiaries living in one *dhalla* and the leaders are very helpful in this regard.[43]

A local clan leader in Dabal *kebele* highlighted the importance of these *dhalla* in mobilizing knowledge of the economic status of individuals and their role in allocating PSNP support:

> *Dhalla aba* are the key players to provide specific information and economic status of each community member living in their *makafta* [*kushet*] ... PSNP quotas within the *dhalla* are distributed by the *dhalla aba*.[44]

In Ad-kelu, the targeting process and outcome was markedly different from that in Dabal. Here the selection took place solely through consultation between the *kushet* leader and other clan leaders.[45] Moreover, the *wereda* and *kebele* leadership claimed to have completely misunderstood the rationale of the PSNP, with the result that they only selected able-bodied individuals capable of carrying out labour-intensive public works and there was no direct support in the *wereda* (see Fig. 3.2), excluding many of the most vulnerable people. In the absence of oversight of programme implementation or pressure for performance from above, there had been no attempt to correct this. The *kebele* administration insisted that they followed the instruction they received from the *wereda* and their belief that this was the design of the PSNP nationwide.[46] Yet, other *kebele* officials were well aware that this selection process was incorrect, with the HEW particularly vociferous in his criticism of the *kebele* administration.[47] While the original error might plausibly have been made out of ignorance, no action was taken to address it, despite acknowledgement of the problem.

The Afar cases illustrate not only the limits of party-state infrastructural power in the region, but also the dangers of devolving responsibility to clan structures, over which the state has little control. In Gala'elu, where clan leaders distribute PSNP places through the *dhalla*, focus groups and individual interviews suggest that both PSNP participants and those excluded have high regard for clan leaders and consider the process to be fair, given the limited resources available.[48] In contrast, the process was opaque in Ab'ala, conducted by *kebele*/clan and *kushet* leaders, with little public involvement. Indeed, respondents were largely unaware what the selection process was and why they were included or not.[49]

In summary, then, the case studies highlight sharply contrasting ways in which the local state sought to address the informational challenge associated with targeting, depending on the particular history of party-state expansion and infrastructural power in that location. Where the EPRDF's project of *encadrement* had advanced furthest—in Tigray—the development team and one-to-five networks were mobilized to this end. The aim of the local state was to create a similar system in Oromiya. However, the party-state had never been entirely successful here, and the collapse of party-state infrastructural power raises important questions for implementation of the PSNP and other services going forward. In Afar, in contrast, the local state had to rely on the clan structure and its greater territorial reach to identify recipients of support. In doing so, the lack of state oversight of the clan structures brings particular risks.

Delivering 'progress' through graduation

In line with ruling party ideology and its focus on national development, the government had always conceived the PSNP as a means of promoting self-reliance as well as providing support. As such, mass graduation and the reduction of the number of food-insecure people requiring PSNP support had long been a key political objective (Lavers 2019). Party-state infrastructural power is also an important factor shaping graduation. Of particular importance here is the relationship between levels of the state administration and the system of performance evaluations. This section focuses on Tigray and Oromiya, since concerns over programme implementation and the relevance of the livelihoods programme to pastoralist settings meant that graduation has not yet been attempted in Afar, where the main priority for livelihoods is the ongoing villagization programme (see Lavers, Mohammed et al. 2020).

In principle, graduation should be a bottom-up, evidence-based process using similar systems to that for targeting. According to programme guidelines,

> A household has graduated when, in the absence of receiving PSNP transfers, it can meet its food needs for all 12 months and is able to withstand modest shocks.
> (MoARD 2010, p. 21)

The Community Food Security Taskforce is expected to compare a number of proxy indicators, including livestock holdings, landholdings, and education status to asset benchmarks 'to determine food security status' (MoARD 2010, p. 21).

The federal government made large-scale graduation a central PSNP priority after its adoption in 2005. Progress with graduation was modest in the early phases of the programme, but a national target to graduate 80 per cent of PSNP participants by 2015 focused attention on graduation (Lavers 2019). The result was the mobilization of party-state infrastructural power in the pursuit of graduation, with federal graduation targets cascaded down as performance targets for state officials, as acknowledged by officials at all levels. A Tigray regional government respondent noted,

> They [local state officials] have the responsibility to support graduation. I am assessed also. It is the same for all regional, *tabiya* [*kebele*], and *kushet* staff.[50]

The result was that leaders of *kebele*, *kushet*, development teams, and even sometimes one-to-fives were set graduation targets and were expected to produce annual lists of graduates.[51] Rather than an evidence-based assessment, the reality was a top-down process imposed through quotas, with officials held accountable for failure to meet graduation targets. Respondents in *wereda* and *kebele* across the Tigray and Oromiya sites readily admitted that in the period 2010–15 people were forced to graduate, regardless of their readiness to do so. In Tigray, the regional quota was reduced to roughly half between 2010 and 2015, before a slight increase in 2016, with a new phase of the PSNP. The result was that many participants were graduated in order to meet performance targets, but were subsequently brought back into the programme after 2015, given their inability to support themselves, or were instead shifted to receipt of emergency assistance.[52] As one official in Ahferom *wereda* admitted,

> Whether participants reach the minimum requirements for graduation or not, it is a must to graduate from the programme in its fifth year, since that is the end of the programme ... There are even others who were part of PSNP3 [2010–15] and currently not part of PSNP4 [2015–20], though they are still chronically food insecure.[53]

Similar pressures were evident in Oromiya. While Oromiya made little progress with graduation in the early years, from 2014 the regional administration came under strong pressure from the federal government. As one regional official highlighted, 'We frequently get questions from the federal level—where is your progress on graduation?'[54] The result was that large-scale graduation was enforced through quotas issued to lower-level officials. As the DA in Shamo Gado *kebele* noted,

> Every year we are asked to make targets of graduation. Even though we know that people are less likely to improve and graduate out of the support, we give the *wereda* agriculture bureau a certain number because it is a must to make targets.[55]

Pressure for graduation was particularly intense in Merti *wereda*. For reasons that were not entirely clear, the federal government sharply reduced the *wereda*'s PSNP allocation. The response of the wereda agricultural bureau was typical of many:

> We graduated 60 per cent of the beneficiaries by 2006 [Ethiopian Calendar, 2014 in Gregorian Calendar], because the government and higher officials of the programme forced us ... we just selected 60 per cent of our beneficiaries without considering their status ... most of the graduates were not self-sufficient.[56]

Kebele officials in Merti *wereda* were well aware that large-scale, arbitrary graduation posed significant risks to vulnerable households. Consequently, rather than remove households from the programme entirely, the decision was made to reduce the amount provided to each household, ensuring that most households continued to get something. According to the DA,

> rather than excluding households, we used a strategy of reducing the number of beneficiary individuals from each household ... If we exclude a household, they will be in danger. So, we managed the number in such a way.[57]

The result is that the imposition of graduation targets not only creates an inaccurate perception of progress, but also undermines the narrowly targeted rationale of the programme. Narrow targeting is the result of the government's concerns about the dangers of welfare dependency and the donor focus on poverty reduction (Lavers 2019). However, focusing resources on the poorest is also a key requirement of the PSNP's graduation model, enabling participant households to build up resources and become self-reliant. What actually took place, in contrast, was mass graduation driven primarily by a federal target, intended to maintain the perception of progress towards food security and national development. It is impossible to say for sure how many people were truly self-sufficient at this time, but respondents suggested that it was a relatively small proportion of graduates. In most cases, in both Oromiya and Tigray, graduation was staged to meet performance targets.

PSNP4 (2015–20) brought about a change in approach. Rather than ending the PSNP through mass graduation, the PSNP was expected to maintain a steady caseload of 8–10 million people, with new participants enrolled as others graduate out. This did not, however, mean that pressure for graduation disappeared. The federal government again set a target of 80 per cent graduation as a contingency, should there be insufficient funding to continue the PSNP for a fifth phase and with a view to demonstrating progress in tackling food insecurity. The initial years of PSNP4 coincided with a particularly severe El Niño and food crisis that prevented graduation. Nonetheless, in 2018, pressure for graduation re-emerged.

Importantly, however, the political context had changed significantly since 2015, when the federal government was able to impose large-scale graduation through party-state infrastructural power. Political fragmentation since 2015 had resulted in greater regional autonomy, erosion of performance evaluation, and, with it, decline in infrastructural power. As a result, many local governments were increasingly resistant to new demands. As an Oromiya regional government official highlighted,

> This year we have been set a target of 11,140 households for graduation, but there is no tangible progress ... There is resistance from the *wereda* level. They say that the people are not ready, they need more time and we don't want to insist.[58]

A similar reaction was evident in Tigray, where respondents reported that they were set annual targets of 10 per cent graduation during PSNP4. In 2017–18, these targets were met in Enda Mariam *kebele*, though in Tsehafti, the *kebele* considered that no one had made sufficient progress to graduate and missed the target.

The arbitrary graduation of PSNP participants to create the perception of progress is perhaps the most problematic illustration of the tensions between the PSNP's protective role and its developmental ambitions. This graduation process depends on strong party-state infrastructural power and, particularly, the system of performance evaluation, by which federal and regional governments direct the activities of lower-level officials.

6. Conclusions

This chapter examined the ways in which party politics and state infrastructural power shaped the distribution of social transfers in Ethiopia. The chapter highlights several main findings. First, long-run histories of state formation and more recent political party mobilization gave rise to sharp variations in the infrastructural power of the fused party-state in different parts of Ethiopia, and this had important implications for service delivery, including PSNP distribution. In Tigray, where evaluations suggest that the programme was relatively effectively delivered (Berhane et al. 2015), party-state *encadrement* had subsumed civil society, exerting close control over the local population and using party-state structures to mobilize the population for the purposes of targeting. Comparison with other regions highlights the importance of these structures. In Oromiya, the long-run weakness and recent collapse of development teams and party-state infrastructural power undermined delivery of the PSNP. Meanwhile, in Afar, a severely limited party-state works through powerful clan structures, deferring significant authority over selection to clan leaders. Past evaluations in Afar show that targeting has been highly problematic as a result (Sabates-Wheeler et al. 2013). A common concern in the targeting literature is that involvement of party-political actors in programme implementation may lead to politicization of distribution and the use of social transfers to secure party support. However, in Ethiopia, in a context in which the ruling party dominated formal politics and was easily able to organize electoral victories, there was very little evidence of such practices. Rather, relatively effective implementation actually relied upon the infrastructural power provided by a fused party-state.

Second, the strength of party-state infrastructural power—until relatively recently—was used to impose federal targets for graduation through the system of performance evaluation. This pursuit of graduation was used to maintain a narrative of 'progress', frequently disregarding the actual circumstances of food-insecure households in the process. This highlights the more problematic side of high levels of party-state infrastructural power in Ethiopia and the top-down system of accountability on which it rested. As such, the study also raises questions about performance evaluation and how political leaders might best direct the activity of lower-level officials. The case study showed that, even where infrastructural power is high, the system of target setting and evaluation does not always lead to good outcomes. Yuen Yuen Ang (2016) draws a useful distinction here between the ability to *influence* the priorities of local officials and attempts to *control* their activities. In her work, she argues that governments should aim to influence priorities, since their lack of information and the need to be adaptive to local contexts mean that attempts at control are frequently counterproductive. The Ethiopian government's attempts to promote graduation can be seen as an attempt at control that backfired. While the objective of improving food security is laudable, the attempt to assess this through graduation rates inevitably led to a narrow focus on the target rather than the outcome and, ultimately, contributed to the forced graduation of many food-insecure households. As Chapter 4 shows, Rwanda's Vision 2020 Umurenge Programme, which drew inspiration from the PSNP for its original design, has faced comparable challenges in reconciling the productive and protective roles of social transfer programmes contingent on participation in public works and livelihood programmes to promote graduation.

Finally, it is important to note that the situation observed during fieldwork in 2018 has changed markedly in subsequent years as Ethiopia's political crisis has deepened. Indeed, the fusion of party and state has meant that political crisis has quickly translated into a crisis of state infrastructural power. Early signs of this were apparent in Oromiya in 2018, with the collapse of development teams and considerable uncertainty within local government. Since then the situation in parts of western Oromiya has further disintegrated with a growing insurgency by the Oromo Liberation Army. The military conflict in Tigray from November 2020 and the removal of the TPLF from office, meanwhile, has led to the collapse of state infrastructural power in what was the region with the strongest presence of the party-state. Among the many challenges faced by the federal government is that the previous system of state administration and service delivery, which was dependent on the EPRDF, has disintegrated. To the extent that Ethiopia's PSNP was a success story, as has been claimed by past evaluations, this status must be in doubt given these ongoing political challenges.

Annex: List of respondents

Regional governments

AR1, Expert, Afar Disaster Prevention and Food Security Programme Coordination Office, Semera, July 2018

OR1, Head of PSNP, Bureau of Agriculture, Addis Ababa, January 2018, June 2018, June 2019

TR1, Food security team leader, Bureau of Agriculture, Mekele, April 2018

Kuyyu *wereda*, Oromiya

OKK3, Female Kebele Food Security Taskforce member, Halelo Cerri *kebele*, March 2018
OKK4, Development agent, Halelo Cerri *kebele*, March and July 2018
OKK6, Manager, Halelo Cerri *kebele*, July 2018
OKZ1, Development team leader, Halelo Cerri *kebele*, July 2018
OKI1, Male resident, Halelo Cerri *kebele*, July 2018

Merti *wereda*, Oromiya

OMW4, Food security desk, Merti *wereda*, Abomsa, May 2018
OMW5, Health extension coordinator, Merti *wereda*, Abomsa, May 2018
OMK1, Development agent, Shamo Gado *kebele*, May and June 2018
OMK3, Chair and manager, Shamo Gado *kebele*, May 2018
OMK4, Health extension workers, Shamo Gado *kebele*, May and 20 June 2018
OMZ1, Male development team leaders, Shamo Gado *kebele*, 9 May 2018
OMF1, Focus group with male residents, Shamo Gado *kebele*, May 2018
OMF2, Focus group with male residents, Shamo Gado *kebele*, May 2018
OMF8, Focus group with male PSNP non-participants, Shamo Gado *kebele*, 10 May 2018

Ab'ala *wereda*, Afar

AAK1, Health extension worker, Ad-Kelu *kebele*, May 2018
AAK2, Kebele chairman and manager, Ad-Kelu *kebele*, May and June 2018
AAZ1, *Makafta* leader, Ad-Kelu kebele, May 2018
AAF1, Focus group discussion with female PSNP participants, Ad-Kelu *kebele*, May 2018
AAF2, Focus group discussion with male PSNP participants, Ad-Kelu *kebele*, May 2018
AAF3, Focus group discussion with male PSNP non-participants, Ad-Kelu *kebele*, May 2018
AAF4, Focus group discussion with female PSNP non-participants, Ad-Kelu *kebele*, May 2018

Gala'elu *wereda*, Afar

AGW2, Expert, food security desk, Gala'elu *wereda*, March 2018
AGK1, Kebele chair and manager, Dabal *kebele*, March and June 2018
AGC1, Customary leaders, Dabal kebele, March and June 2018
AGF2, Focus group discussion with male PSNP participants, Dabal *kebele*, March 2018
AGF3, Focus group discussion with male PSNP non-participants, Dabal *kebele*, March 2018
AGF4, Focus group discussion with female PSNP participants, Dabal *kebele*, March 2018
AGF5, Focus group discussion with female PSNP non-participants, Dabal *kebele*, March 2018

Hintalo Wajirat *wereda*, Tigray

THW2, Food security coordinator, Hintalo Wajirat *wereda*, May 2018
THK3, Development agents, Tsehafti *kebele*, April 2018, June 2018
THZ1, *Kushet* leader, Tsehafti *kebele*, April 2018
THZ2, Female Community Food Security Taskforce member, Tsehafti *kebele*, April 2018
THZ6, Male Community Food Security Taskforce member, Tsehafti *kebele*, June 2018
THF5, Focus group with male PSNP non-participants, Tsehafti *kebele*, April 2018

Ahferom *wereda*, Tigray

TAW3, Food security coordinator, Ahferom *wereda*, March 2018
TAK4, Development agents, Ende Mariam *kebele*, March 2018, June 2018
TAZ4, Female Community Food Security Taskforce member, Ende Mariam *kebele*, March 2018, June 2018

Notes

1. Local level fieldwork was conducted by Moges Belay and Senait Abrha in Tigray; Dunyat Haile and Yerosan Mesfin in Oromiya; and Bisrat Woldeselassie and Dawud Mohammed in Afar. The Organization for Social Science Research in Eastern and Southern Africa (OSSREA) provided an affiliation and support for the research. Nick Scarle of the Manchester Cartographic Unit produced the map.
2. Ethiopia's administrative structures are organized as follows: federal; regional; zones; *wereda* (districts); *kebele* (or *tabiya* in Tigray—sub-districts); *kushet* (in Tigray, with other names used in other regions).
3. A 2010 Human Rights Watch report claimed that the PSNP and emergency relief was denied to opposition supporters through household targeting (Human Rights Watch 2010). Though plausible, the evidence presented was anecdotal. Other studies have found no evidence of systematic manipulation of targeting.
4. *Kushet* is the name used in Tigray. For simplicity in this chapter, the term is used across all sites, rather than the equivalent terms: zones in Oromiya or *makafta* in Afar.
5. More detailed findings for each site are presented elsewhere (Lavers, Haile, et al. 2020, Lavers, Mohammed, et al. 2020).
6. Interview respondent THF5.
7. Interview respondent THZ1.
8. Interview respondent OKK6.
9. Interview respondent OMW5.
10. Interview respondents OMF1.
11. Interview respondent OKI1.
12. Interview respondents OMF1, OMZ1.
13. Interview respondent OMF2.
14. Interview respondent OMK1.
15. Interview respondent OR1.
16. Interview respondent OMK1.

17. Interview respondents OMK1, OKK6.
18. Interview respondent OMK4, OKK6.
19. An existing term for a local meeting place, *makafta*, has been taken as the name of these sub-*kebele* units.
20. Interview respondent AAZ1
21. Interview respondent AR1.
22. Interview respondent AAK1.
23. Interview respondent AGK1.
24. Interview respondent AGC1.
25. Interview respondent AGK1.
26. Interview respondent AGC1.
27. Interview respondent OMK3.
28. Interview respondents OKK3, OKK6.
29. Interview respondent TR1.
30. Interview respondents THZ1, THZ2.
31. The claim that people know the wealth of their neighbours is open to question. The issue is resolved in the sense that it provides a mechanism by which the programme can function and the approach enjoys considerable local legitimacy.
32. Interview respondent TAW3.
33. Interview respondents TAZ4, THZ6.
34. Interview respondent TAZ4.
35. Interview respondent THZ6.
36. Interview respondent OMW4.
37. Interview respondent OKK4.
38. Interview respondents OKK3, OKZ1.
39. Interview respondent OKK4.
40. Interview respondents OMK1, OKK4, OKK6.
41. Interview respondent OKZ1.
42. Interview respondent AGC1.
43. Interview respondent AGW2.
44. Interview respondent AGC1.
45. Interview respondent AAZ1.
46. Interview respondent AAK2.
47. Interview respondent AAK1.
48. Interview respondents AGF2, AGF3, AGF4, AGF5.
49. Interview respondents AAF1, AAF2, AAF3, AAF4.
50. Interview respondent TR1.
51. Interview respondents TR1, THK3, THW2, TAK4, TAZ4, OKK4, OKZ1, OMF8.
52. Interview respondent TAK4, THW2, THK3, THZ2.
53. Interview respondent TAW3.
54. Interview respondent OR1.
55. Interview respondent OMK1.
56. Interview respondent OMW4.
57. Interview respondent OMK1.
58. Interview respondent OR1.

References

Ang, Y. Y., 2016. *How China Escaped the Poverty Trap*. Ithaca, NY: Cornell University Press.

Berhane, G., Hirvonen, K., Hoddinott, J., Kumar, N., Seyoum Taffesse, A., Yohannes, Y., Sabates-Wheeler, R., Strickland, A., Lind, J., Tefera, M., and Nishan, B., 2015. *The Implementation of the Productive Safety Nets Programme in the Ethiopian Highlands, 2014: Program Performance Report*. Washington, DC: IFPRI.

Clapham, C., 2002. Controlling space in Ethiopia. *In*: W. James, D. L. Donham, E. Kurimoto, and A. Triulzi, eds. *Remapping Ethiopia: Socialism and After*. London: James Currey, 9–32.

Clapham, C., 2009. Post-war Ethiopia: The trajectories of crisis. *Review of African Political Economy*, 36, 181–192.

Coady, D., Grosh, M., and Hoddinott, J., 2004. *Targeting of Transfers in Developing Countries: Review of Lessons and Experience*. Washington, DC: World Bank.

Cochrane, L. and Tamiru, Y., 2016. Ethiopia's Productive Safety Net Program: Power, politics and practice. *Journal of International Development*, 28 (5), 649–665.

Coll-Black, S., Gilligan, D. O., Hoddinott, J., Kumar, N., Taffesse, A. S., and Wiseman, W., 2012. Targeting food security interventions in Ethiopia: The Productive Safety Net Programme. *In*: P. Dorosh and S. Rashid, eds. *Food and Agriculture in Ethiopia: Progress and Policy Challenges*. Philadelphia, PA: University of Pennsylvania Press, 280–317.

Davison, W., 2016. In Ethiopia, anger over corruption and farmland development runs deep. *The Guardian*, 18 January.

Dowden, R., 2012. Meles Zenawi interview excerpts: 'Unlike all previous governments our writ runs in every village' [online]. African Arguments. Available from: https://africanarguments.org/2012/05/unlike-all-previous-governments-our-writ-runs-in-every-village-excerpts-from-an-interview-with-meles-zenawi-by-richard-dowden/ (accessed 3 November 2014).

DPPC, 2000. *National Food Aid Targeting Guidelines*. Addis Ababa: Disaster Preparedness and Prevention Commission.

Human Rights Watch, 2010. *'One Hundred Ways of Putting Pressure': Violations of Freedom of Expression and Association in Ethiopia*. New York: Human Rights Watch.

Lavers, T., 2012. 'Land grab' as development strategy? The political economy of agricultural investment in Ethiopia. *Journal of Peasant Studies*, 39 (1), 105–132.

Lavers, T., 2013. Food security and social protection in highland Ethiopia: Linking the Productive Safety Net to the land question. *Journal of Modern African Studies*, 51 (3), 459–485.

Lavers, T., 2019. Social protection in an aspiring 'developmental state': The political drivers of Ethiopia's PSNP. *African Affairs*, 118 (473), 646–671.

Lavers, T., Haile, D., and Mesfin, Y., 2020. The politics of distributing social transfers in Oromiya, Ethiopia: Encadrement, disengagement and the fluctuation of state infrastructural power. ESID Working Papers, 142.

Lavers, T., Mohammed, D., and Wolde Selassie, B., 2020. The politics of distributing social transfers in Afar, Ethiopia: The intertwining of party, state and clan in the periphery. ESID Working Papers, 141.

Mann, M., 1984. The autonomous power of the state: Its origins, mechanisms and results. *European Journal of Sociology*, 25 (2), 185–213.

Markakis, J., 2011. *Ethiopia: The Last Two Frontiers*. Oxford: James Currey.

MoA, 2014a. *Productive Safety Net Programme 4: Design Document.* Addis Ababa: Ministry of Agriculture.

MoA, 2014b. *Productive Safety Net Programme Phase IV: Programme Implementation Manual.* Addis Ababa: Ministry of Agriculture.

MoARD, 2010. *Productive Safety Net Programme: Programme Implementation Manual (Revised).* Addis Ababa: Ministry of Agriculture and Rural Development.

MoFA, 2008. *Draft Policy Statement for the Sustainable Development of Pastoral and Agro Pastoral Areas of Ethiopia.* Addis Ababa: Ministry of Federal Affairs.

MoI, 2002. *Foreign Affairs and National Security Policy and Strategy.* Addis Ababa: Ministry of Information.

Østebø, M. T., Cogburn, M. D., and Mandani, A. S., 2018. The silencing of political context in health research in Ethiopia: Why it should be a concern. *Health Policy and Planning,* 33 (2), 258–270.

Sabates-Wheeler, R., Lind, J., and Hoddinott, J., 2013. Implementing social protection in agro-pastoralist and pastoralist areas: How local distribution structures moderate PSNP outcomes in Ethiopia. *World Development,* 50, 1–12.

Vargas Hill, R. and Porter, C., 2013. *PSNP/HABP Formulation Process: Vulnerability Study to Assist with Assessment of Potential Caseload for Next Generation of PSNP & HABP.* Mimeo.

Wolde, T., 2002. Evading the revolutionary state: The Hor under the Derg. *In*: W. James, D. L. Donham, E. Kurimoto, and A. Triulzi, eds. *Remapping Ethiopia: Socialism and After.* London: James Currey, 37–59.

Zewde, B., 1991. *A History of Modern Ethiopia, 1855–1974.* London: James Currey.

4

Distributing Social Transfers in Rwanda

The Case of the Vision 2020 Umurenge Programme (VUP)

Timothy P. Williams, Sylvestre Nzahabwanayo, Tom Lavers, and Eric Ndushabandi

1. Introduction

The Rwandan government introduced the Vision 2020 Umurenge Programme (VUP) in 2008.[1] To qualify for support, most programme participants are required to engage in public works, with unconditional Direct Support reserved for a minority of households without able-bodied adults. Public works are divided between Public Works Classic, in which participants provide manual labour for construction of infrastructure such as feeder roads and terraces, and Public Works Expanded, introduced more recently for individuals with some labour capacity but who have caretaking responsibilities that would prevent them from traveling to distant worksites (LODA 2017). Public Works Expanded entails work like sweeping nearby roads and caring for communal gardens. Public works opportunities are based on the capacity of local government to organize projects and there is no guarantee of work for programme participants.

Participants are selected through community-based targeting, with a proxy means test introduced in 2016 to verify the initial selection. A central aim of the VUP is to ensure that the programme not only provides protection for some of the poorest people, but also makes a productive contribution to households and communities. As such, public works are intended to create community infrastructure, while the VUP also contains a Financial Services component intended to improve livelihoods and 'promote graduation from extreme poverty among labour-endowed households', through the distribution of group and individual loans (LODA 2017, p. 20).[2] The VUP has been gradually rolled out across Rwanda since 2008. By 2019, the programme had reached 244 of 416 sectors and 133,000 households with Public Works Classic; 150 sectors and 23,000 households with Public Works Expanded; and 107,000 households with Direct Support (World Bank 2019).

Timothy P. Williams et al., *Distributing Social Transfers in Rwanda.* In: *The Politics of Distributing Social Transfers.*
Edited by Tom Lavers, Oxford University Press.
DOI: 10.1093/oso/9780192862525.003.0004

Most existing research on the VUP comprises donor- and government-linked evaluations of different aspects of the programme (Ashley and Kyanga 2013; Gahamanyi and Kettlewell 2015; Sabates-Wheeler et al. 2015). Lavers (2019) focuses specifically on the political economy drivers of adoption and design of the VUP. This study showed that the government's motivation for introducing the VUP was what the government perceived to be a distributional crisis after evaluations of the national development strategy in 2007 showed high growth rates, rising income, and inter-regional inequality, as well as stagnating rates of poverty reduction. Since coming to power following the genocide against the Tutsis in 1994, the Rwandan Patriotic Front (RPF) has legitimized its rule by marking a clean break from the regional and ethnic divisions of the past, instead promoting a narrative of national unity, seeking to provide all Rwandan citizens with a stake in the country's future and taking care to maintain impartiality in policy implementation development (Golooba-Mutebi 2013; Williams 2017). Rising inequality and the struggle to reduce poverty threatened this narrative, leading to strong political pressure to come up with an ambitious programme that would quickly address these problems. The VUP was also shaped by RPF ideology, notably a long-standing focus on individual and national self-reliance (Behuria 2016; Chemouni and Mugiraneza 2020), and the need for all available resources to be directed towards national development. The result of these factors was a programme that sought to combine protective and productive objectives, alongside an ambitious pace to expand the programme to reduce poverty and inequality (GoR 2007). These ambitious initial targets were important in securing political support for the programme (Lavers 2019).

The chapter is based on fieldwork in two districts selected to test whether historical legacies of state formation shaped distribution of the VUP. We draw on data from 94 interviews and focus group discussions across two districts. Key informant interviews were conducted with state officials at different administrative levels, participants and non-participants in the programme, and donor representatives. Mixed-gender focus group discussions were also held with participants and non-participants of the programme.[3] Transcripts were coded thematically in a way that was consistent with the research questions and concepts that were central to this study, while attending to similarities and differences observed between districts.

This chapter advances two main findings. First, despite historical variation in state–society relations in different parts of Rwanda, there is no clear evidence that this shaped distribution of social transfers in the study sites. While there are differences in implementation between the sites, these cannot be fully explained through variation in state infrastructural power. These findings are consistent with the Rwandan government's stated commitment to regional equality in policy implementation. Second, and despite the relatively uniform implementation across sites, the VUP has struggled to balance productive and protective objectives in one programme. In particular, state infrastructural power in the form of top-down performance evaluations often prioritizes productive objectives over protective ones. As a result, the chapter suggests ongoing challenges regarding the distribution of social transfers, and the ability of the VUP to reach its intended target group: Rwanda's poorest. Past studies have raised doubts about the efficacy of targeting in the VUP (Sabates-Wheeler et al. 2015). This chapter suggests that attempts to address these problems through the introduction of a proxy means test have not resolved these issues. The selection resulting from these combined processes is widely perceived as arbitrary, with the proxy means test undermining community influence over distribution. And yet, this classification is then rigidly enforced, with those classified as amongst the poorest experiencing a loss of rights, reminiscent of a long and problematic history of poverty targeting globally.

The rest of this chapter is organized as follows. Section 2 examines the historical and political context of state formation and the ways that this has shaped state infrastructural power, providing the justification for case study selection. Section 3 examines how state infrastructural power manifests in the study sites and particularly in relation to the VUP. Section 4 focuses on the tension between the productive and protective roles of the VUP, and how this delicate balance is shaped by state infrastructural power. Section 5 specifically looks at the mechanisms for distributing VUP resources, namely targeting and graduation. Section 6 provides a conclusion in which we locate study findings within a broad discussion of state-building in Rwanda.

2. Rwandan state formation: regional and ethnic antagonisms and the promotion of national unity

This section provides a brief overview of the history of state formation in Rwanda, the legacy this provided in terms of regional antagonisms, ethnic tensions, and variation in state infrastructural power, and the strategy pursued under the RPF that has explicitly sought to overcome past inter-regional imbalances. This discussion provides context for the analysis that follows and provides the justification for case selection in the final part of the section.

The historical record unequivocally shows that the people who first inhabited what would become Rwanda shared the same religion and the same language (Vansina 2004). But this literature also suggests that patterns of usurpation were a key point of contention throughout the pre-colonial and colonial eras (Newbury 1988; Newbury and Newbury 2000; Pottier 2002; Vansina 2004). While Rwanda's central and southern regions were the heart of the kingdom, inhabitants of north-west Rwanda resisted incorporation by the royal court (Newbury and Newbury 2000). By the time of German occupation at the turn of the twentieth century, 'The north in particular was very unruly, and Musinga's [the Rwandan king] authority there was only nominal' (Reyntjens 2004, p. 517). Indeed, German and Belgian colonists supported efforts of the kingdom to subdue what is now the northwest of Rwanda and bring it under central authority in the 1920s (Pottier 2002). Particularly in the latter of half of the colonial era, Rwanda's royal court, comprised of Tutsi elites, collaborated with the colonial authorities. Through a policy of indirect rule, the Europeans sought to accomplish their aims 'without altering existing patterns of authority' (Newbury 1988, p. 59). Over time, however, the court did gradually expand its control by replacing local chiefly authority with accountability mechanisms to state authorities, as part of a process of bureaucratization of structures of authority.

A Hutu solidarity movement coincided with the lead-up to European withdrawal in 1961 (Birmingham 1995), uniting the Hutu elite against Tutsis and other power holders. Waves of protest and violence targeted Tutsis, and many were either killed or fled the country (Des Forges 1999). The new republic's democratic elections enabled Hutu-led parties to win a majority of votes (Newbury 1988). Having removed the king and chieftaincy, the new regime recreated structures of authority with many of the same characteristics, namely a high degree of centralization of power in the president, in place of the king, and mayors, governors, and party leaders who filled the void left by chiefs (Reyntjens 2004). Rwanda's first elected president, Gregoire Kayibanda, was a southerner who favoured Hutus from his home area (Prunier 1995). Whereas before independence, northern and southern Hutus united in opposition to the monarchy, this shared enemy was gone. The northwest still held a grievance against being ruled by the south and actively resisted southern efforts to gain more control (Pottier 2002).

The second republic began after a bloodless coup by the northern-dominated military in 1973, and General Juvenal Habyarimana took power. The regional antagonisms that had festered during the first republic came to a head during this time. 'It was clear who would benefit from his regime', noted Verwimp (2013, p. 197). During the second republic, southern Hutus and Tutsis were not promoted to senior posts. Introducing a regional element to official administrative criteria was a strategy Habyarimana used to favour his *akazu*, or 'little house', a reference to 'a special circle within the larger network of personal connections' and home region that supported Habyarimana (Des Forges 1999, p. 40). Habyarimana had no interest in helping the south. For example, during that time, Gitarama and Butare, two southern prefectures, had about 20 per cent of the country's population but received just 1 per cent of government funding (Verwimp 2000). When a famine struck the south in the 1980s, rather than redirect resources to help, Habyarimana passively allowed people in the south to starve (Newbury and Newbury 1994, Verwimp 2013). Underpinned by strong economic performance in the first decade of Habyarimana's rule, the reach of the state expanded considerably during this period, aided by the major expansion of roads and communications infrastructure, along with state and party structures that could control the population (Prunier 1995).

Fluctuating prices for coffee and other commodities in the 1980s put the country on the verge of economic collapse by the time the RPF invaded on 1 October 1990. The RPF consisted of Tutsi refugees who had fled Rwanda to Uganda to escape the violence that had been directed at them during the two republics. The following year, Habyarimana's government initiated a series of reforms to introduce multiparty elections. However, this move brought to the surface long-standing tensions between northern and southern Hutus. Southerners resented the dominance of Hutus from the north, while northern Hutus considered themselves to be 'purer ethnically, and historically less subservient to the Batutsi than the predominantly "mixed" southerners' (Hintjens 1999, p. 259).

On 6 April 1994, Habyarimana was killed when his plane was shot down. Targeted killings of political rivals and all Tutsis quickly began. At least 800,000 Tutsis and moderate Hutus were killed between April and July (Prunier 1995; Des Forges 1999). By the time the RPF ended the genocide in July 1994, 1.8 million people were internally displaced and over 2 million, primarily Hutus, fled to neighbouring countries such as the Democratic Republic of Congo, Tanzania, and Burundi (Des Forges 1999). In terms of state infrastructural power, the result of the genocide was the almost complete destruction of infrastructure and the absence of a civil service, which had fled the country en masse (Golooba-Mutebi 2008). The destruction of human life and infrastructure was particularly concentrated in the south (Pottier 2002).

Following the genocide, the Government of National Unity and subsequent RPF-dominated government rebuilt the state to a degree that has impressed even its strongest critics.

> The Rwandan Leviathan is highly centralised and hierarchical, and it reaches every inch of the territory and every citizen ... a mere two years after the extreme human and material destruction of 1994, the state had been rebuilt. Rwanda was again administered from top to bottom.
>
> (Reyntjens 2004, p. 209)

Notably, for the RPF a key priority has been to overcome the ethnic and regional divisions that characterized Rwanda in the past. If the government were to realize peace and prosperity, all regions of the country would need to be included in its state-building project. As such, the northwest, the part of the country in which state infrastructural power was weakest up to the colonial era, has been a particular focus for state-building since the genocide, given ongoing security threats from remnants of the Forces Armées Rwandaises (FAR) in the Democratic Republic of Congo (Golooba-Mutebi 2008).

Between 1998 and 1999, former President Bizimungu led a series of meetings, known as *Urugwiro Village*, in order to re-establish and re-envision the social and economic trajectory of the country (RoR 1999). Subsequently, the government embarked on a social and economic re-engineering project that sought to distance itself from a legacy marked by ethnic divisionism, regional antagonism, and conflicts over scarce natural resources (RoR 2000). A key element of this developmental and political project has been the massive decentralization of the state since the early 2000s. Decentralization has further extended the reach of the state, through the creation of a new tier of the state, the *umudugudu* or village, and the reorganization and expansion of the capacities of each of the six tiers of the Rwandan state, as follows:

National → Province (4) → District (30) → Sector → Cell → Village[4]

This process has been conducted with the intention of increasing local implementation capacity, while extending the power of the central state to direct frontline officials (Chemouni, 2014). This expansion of the state has taken place at a time of RPF dominance in politics, with the result that the distinction between the party and the state is frequently unclear.

Rationale for case selection

In line with the rest of this volume, the Rwandan case study examined how historical legacies of state infrastructural power shape the current distribution of social transfers. In Rwanda, our hypothesis was that the state-building project pursued by the RPF in recent decades would have largely removed past variation in the state's infrastructural power and its capacity to distribute social transfers. To test this, the study selected 'most likely' cases for variation, since an absence of variation in these cases would suggest an absence of variation elsewhere (Eckstein 2000). As such, the study sites are (see Fig. 4.1):

- Huye District in the Southern Province, which has been central to Rwanda since pre-colonial times and would therefore be expected to exhibit a particularly high degree of state infrastructural power. Nonetheless, the area was severely affected by the genocide, with many Tutsis and moderate Hutus massacred. Since 1994, the area has been amongst the poorest parts of Rwanda, compounded by the out-migration of many of those with means.
- Rubavu District in Rwanda's Western Province, which was incorporated into the Rwandan polity relatively late on during the colonial era and, of anywhere, might be expected to have a lower degree of state infrastructural power.

We conducted research within the highest- and lowest-performing sectors in each district, as indicated on performance contracts, with a view to capturing a range of experiences within each district. Additional inclusion criteria were that each

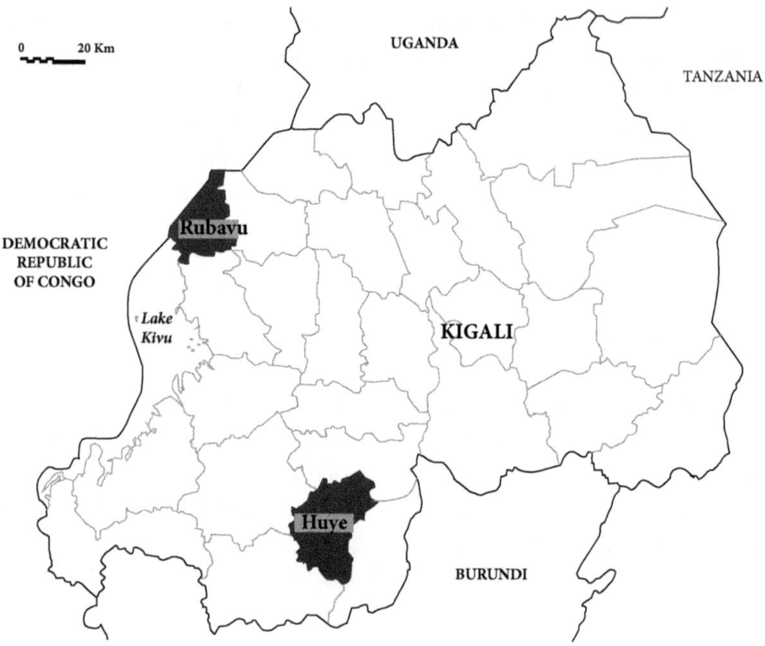

Fig. 4.1 Map of the Rwandan research sites
Source: Authors.

sector needed to also be rural and offer the Public Works Classic component of VUP. Within each sector, we selected the middle-performing cell, a strategy which allowed us to identify a fairly 'typical' cell within the high-performing and low-performing sectors of each district, respectively.

3. Infrastructural power and the implementation of the VUP

This section analyses state infrastructural power according to the three components highlighted in the framework introduced in Chapter 2: state resources; intra-state relations; and state–society relations. The discussion highlights the importance of these dimensions for the specific challenge of implementing the VUP. Infrastructural power is characterized by a shortage of human resources to implement the VUP across the tiers of Rwanda's governance system. However, a well-established system of performance evaluation and the dominance of the ruling party provide clear lines of accountability between tiers of the state, enabling relatively strong top-down control of the activities of local officials. Importantly, there is relatively little variation in these three dimensions between the two research sites.

State resources

Responsibility for VUP implementation is distributed across the six tiers of Rwanda's decentralized state administration. The national agency responsible for the VUP is the Local Entities Development Agency (LODA), an agency under the Ministry of Local Government (MINALOC). LODA focuses on planning and design of policy and working with local state officials to implement these policies and evaluate impact (LODA 2016b). Dedicated VUP staff are based at the district level—the main local state entity—with pre-existing officials at the sector level, who have other primary duties, taking responsibility for aspects of VUP implementation. Payment of VUP transfers and the financial services component is sub-contracted by the district to Savings and Credit Cooperative Organizations (SACCOs) (LODA 2016b). Targeting, meanwhile, is based on the Ubudehe programme, discussed further in Section 5. Ubudehe classification takes place at the village level—not a formal administrative tier of the state, but a creation of the decentralization process used as 'a channel of grassroots mobilization and information diffusion' (Chemouni, 2014, p. 248). Ubudehe entails an initial classification at a community meeting that places all community members in one of four Ubudehe categories, under the supervision of the village leader and a village Ubudehe committee. This community-based targeting is then verified using a household survey coordinated by the village leader. The initial selection is checked by higher administrative levels at the cell and district, before being finalized at the national level. VUP participation is reserved for the poorest, placed in category 1.

Despite the ambitious scale of the programme, the VUP has limited human resources to carry out its work. At the national level, LODA has few qualified staff members who focus on the VUP and these are supplemented with several foreign and donor-funded technical assistance posts. The shortage of staff makes it difficult for LODA to evaluate the quality or financial status of the reports it receives from districts (LODA 2016b). At the sub-national level, the number of dedicated staff members working on the VUP is limited. The original VUP rollout hired two administrators for each sector to which the programme was extended. However, this approach was dropped in 2012, due to the cost, with a smaller number of district VUP staff taking responsibility for the sectors under their control (Lavers 2019). By 2016, there were, on average, 0.4 dedicated VUP staff members per sector. The result is that responsibility for key VUP components falls to sector officials with other primary responsibilities. For example, public works may fall under the purview of the land manager for the sector; direct support under a social affairs officer; and financial services is managed through SACCOs. LODA itself has questioned whether it has 'the capacity to implement the VUP [effectively] without the provision of supplementary staffing' (LODA 2016b, p. 28).

Intra-state relations

A key aspect of state infrastructural power concerns the ability of the central state to influence the activities of lower-level officials, ensuring that policy implementation is consistent with the intended policy. A key means by which this is achieved is the system of *imihigo* or performance contracts. Rwandan governance places great emphasis on *imihigo*, which are used to identify priorities for state officials. Quantitative, measurable targets are set on an annual basis, with officials required to sign the *imihigo* and commit to its realization. In the case of district mayors, this solemn signing ceremony is undertaken in the presence of the president himself (Chemouni 2014). Furthermore, districts are assessed and ranked based on their success in reaching these targets. To summarize the sentiments of many officials we spoke with, *if an activity is on the performance contract, local officials will make it a priority. If it is not on the performance contract, it won't be prioritized with the same sense of urgency.*

For the VUP, *imihigo* targets relate to quantifiable aspects of programme implementation, including the number of work days allocated to Public Works Classic participants, loan recovery, and infrastructure creation (e.g., LODA 2016a). Indeed, the pressure on officials to improve their own *imihigo* performance has led some local officials in Huye to introduce strict accountability measures for VUP Public Works Classic participants. Officials drafted performance contracts for VUP Public Works Classic participants to track how they used their transfers. For example, participants could state they would use their funds to clean their latrine, buy a mattress, or purchase livestock. The village chief reviewed the plans and if their proposal was not approved, participants would not receive their payment. As one sector official noted,

> We had them to go home and write down things, which they plan to do from the money that they will be paid. Then we said that at the end of a certain period 'we will come to your homes and evaluate whether these people had managed to accomplish their goal.' … I can tell you, now we have got a number of good testimonies from people who come and say, 'I really thank you for the good mentorship you have given me, now I have been able to buy my own land' or 'I have been able to buy my own animal', like that, like that … we have got even two families which have requested to be moved up from Ubudehe category 1. They themselves have decided that in the next year they want to be in category 2.[5]

However, as discussed above, the VUP is only one of several responsibilities within the *imihigo* for most of the officials responsible for its implementation. As such, the VUP competes to some degree with other priorities for officials' attention. In some cases, this has led officials to reallocate funds from the VUP to other projects.

For example, in Huye, officials redirected funds from Direct Support participants to fund income-generating activities, including the construction of a small hostel, much to the frustration of VUP participants. Further instances of this tension between competing *imihigo* targets are discussed in Section 4.

State–society relations

Effective distribution of the VUP also depends on relations between state and society, and, in particular, the state's ability to mobilize the population for targeting and work requirements placed on programme participants. The reconstruction and extension of the Rwandan state following the genocide has taken place at a time of almost complete RPF dominance of politics. Perhaps unsurprisingly, therefore, fieldwork respondents made little distinction between the RPF and the state. An example is provided by a cell chief in Huye, who noted that as chief he is the de facto chairperson of the party for his village.

> They [the RPF and state] are like one and the same. After seeing that the governmental programmes are there to improve the lives of the population, that we are all members of the RPF family and that we know that the RPF is the one that plans, supports, and give us those activities, we consider them as both activities of the RPF and also as governmental activities.[6]

Across the study sites, participants attributed the VUP to the central government. To them, the VUP offered tangible evidence that the national government, ruling party, and president had their best interests in mind and that the poor and vulnerable had not been forgotten. Local people often described national officials, and the president in particular, in terms such as 'the parent' who looks after his children (see also Benda and Pells 2020). Many described specific VUP activities, such as Direct Support, as the practice of 'giving soap' to people through the fulfilment of basic material needs. The VUP was cited as evidence of how the leaders today seek to differentiate from leaders in the pre-genocide era, especially under the divisive rule of the former regime. This came out prominently in Rubavu. Local people said that the VUP shows poor people that the government loves them; that it 'doesn't want to kill them', like prior divisive regimes did.

When asked what, if anything, was expected from VUP recipients in exchange for receiving VUP support, a common response was that people are compelled to 'love' the government. In addition to using VUP benefits wisely, loving the government could manifest through activities like: participating in *umuganda* (unpaid community work); achieving targets in their household performance contract; and offering testimonials of what the RPF-led government had done for people; as well as paying financial contributions to the RPF, known as a payment 'to the family' (*umuryango*). The latter was an expected contribution of all citizens, regardless of whether they were a member of the ruling party or not. In a focus group for Public Works Expanded participants in Nyamyumba Sector, Rubavu, one informant noted, 'If they say give money to "the family" (*Ifaranga ry'umuryango*) I contribute for it, because they give me support. I have to help, too, as a citizen.'

Similarly, in a focus group discussion, Direct Support participants in Nyamyumba Sector, Rubavu, commented:

> Respondent 1: 'I think that the government doesn't have any expectation from us except to elect them and to dance for them.'
>
> Respondent 2: 'Yeah, just singing and clapping for them. Like now there are ongoing elections, which are coming very soon.'

The adherence to government initiatives was also frequently linked to the developmental ambitions of the country and the specific productive objectives of the VUP. A participant in a focus group in Huye noted,

> When you have nothing and don't have hope of getting anything, you don't feel happy. You don't love the authorities. But when you get an opportunity to do something to help you improve your situation and move forward, you feel good. You feel like they didn't abandon you and that they are there for you.[7]

Programme participants at all levels said that the VUP is proof that the widows and elderly had not been forgotten. The fact that the elderly were looked after was seen as a testament that the RPF cared for those citizens on the margins, even if their household may not be that vital to the country's development. However, even those included in Direct Support are expected to make a productive contribution, by encouraging their children and grandchildren:

> I am getting old, so the government is not expecting big things from me. But they expect big things from my child. Imagine if I had a young child who was not clean, who was hungry. But the government realizes that my child needs to study. … After he finishes senior six, he will join the army and he will serve the country.[8]

Indeed, in apparent contradiction to the dominant VUP narrative of the importance of self-reliance and concerns about dependency, during election campaigns local RPF officials would actively encourage recipients of support to provide testimonials regarding the benevolent acts of the party. This included the participants in the VUP but also recipients of other support provided to individuals and households, whether by giving a cow to a widow, providing a loan for a sewing machine, or health insurance that saved lives.

Despite the association of the VUP with the central government, the numerous challenges with implementation, as discussed below, were instead attributed by respondents to the failings of local government to fulfil its performance contracts, rather than any problem with the programme or central government.

> If the leaders were leading like the president does, we would have been rich by now … If they can lead as he does, it would be good, because he sends cows to give to vulnerable. Officials here give cows to the people who already have cows.[9]

In summary, the fieldwork provided little evidence of systematic variation in the three dimensions of state infrastructural power between the two sites. Despite the contrasting experiences of the two sites in the pre-colonial and colonial eras, variation in state infrastructural power appears similar in the two sites. Indeed, if anything, the state has a stronger presence in the northwestern sites than the south—a testament, it would seem, to the catastrophic impact of the genocide there. Overall, state infrastructural power in the field sites is characterized by strong top-down control by the central state over local state officials through the *imihigo* system and dominance of the fused party-state locally, with local people expressing a willingness to acquiesce to central government initiatives. That said, however, state infrastructural power, particularly in relation to the VUP, is constrained by the shortage of staff. Local officials have to juggle the VUP with other responsibilities and are frequently stretched as a result.

4. Productive ambitions and the challenges for social protection

One of the VUP's key functions and indeed one of the key selling points of the original proposal that secured central government support is to combine the protective role of the VUP with productive investments in the local economy. While potentially complementary, the reality is that the complementarity between providing support to those in need and mobilizing labour to expand infrastructure has often been hard to achieve. Here we focus on two areas of tension between the productive and protective functions of the programme: the labour requirements of VUP public works; and the financial services package, which aims to improve livelihoods and promote graduation. The high degree of state infrastructural power—and particularly the top-down control afforded by *imihigo*—is key here, with performance targets frequently focusing attention on productive goals to the detriment of the programme's protective functions.

Past studies highlighted a long-standing labour-intensive public infrastructure programme (Programme de Développement Local à Haute Intensité de Main d'Oeuvre, PDL-HIMO) as one of the main influences on the VUP design (Lavers 2019). Indeed, the primary focus of this former programme on infrastructure creation, rather than social protection, continues to be of relevance. A consistent challenge with VUP has been the capital-intensive nature of the infrastructure created, reducing the proportion of the budget available for public works and therefore the availability of sufficient employment opportunities for programme participants (Lavers 2019). The fieldwork highlighted these issues. One central tension was the question of whether people should be selected for work based on their need for support or on the labour requirements of a particular project, which might necessitate hiring comparatively better-off, able-bodied people in order to build roads quickly. The link between labour capacity and poverty classification is not discussed in VUP design documents, but is a recurrent challenge for local officials administering the programme.

Local officials in both sites are confronted with challenging *imihigo* targets, in particular relating to infrastructure development. At the same time, however, one of the main resources at their disposal to realize infrastructure development—the VUP—comes with strict instructions from LODA to limit Public Works Classic to Ubudehe category 1. Officials reported concerns that these guidelines overlooked the realities of each district, with those in category 1 often physically unable to carry out the tasks expected of them. The result is that the focus on infrastructure development in the *imihigo* can lead to the recruitment of those outside category 1, undermining the protective role of the programme. As one sector official overseeing Public Works Classic noted,

> We get some people from the second category to do things that require more energy, like carrying rocks. The others do road works. Every person has to work according to their age and capacity.[10]

Given the large number of people living in poverty, particularly in Huye, a social development officer suggested that there is a need to open Public Works Classic to other poor people who are able-bodied and ready to work. Indeed, in Rubavu, some officials had taken this upon themselves, hiring more able-bodied workers in category 2 and category 3 to break down large rocks to construct roads. Officials said that people in category 3 were occasionally hired if they had a specific skillset. For instance, sector land managers mentioned they would pay those in category 3 a higher wage to break up volcanic rocks to build roads. Although this meant the inclusion of the non-poor, as classified by Ubudehe, officials said this was a necessary expenditure for the sector's infrastructure-related goals. According to a VUP Public Works Classic recipient in category 3,

> Yes, we are paid by VUP but we are considered like casual employees. We don't get the low payment like those in the first category. When a task is given to us, we immediately get paid after we finish it.[11]

The tension between the VUP's productive ambitions and its protective function was also evident with respect to the Financial Services component. The rationale of Financial Services is to provide micro-credit to individuals and groups to enable them to invest in improved livelihoods, ultimately leading to their graduation from the VUP. Once again, this productive function was a key selling point of the original design process and integral to the VUP's ambition to promote graduation out of poverty (Lavers 2019). These productive objectives are integrated into the *imihigo* for local officials, with specific targets relating to both money disbursed and repayment rates, translating into pressure on officials to give out money and to recoup loans. A local official in Rubavu summarized how he thinks about the VUP in relation to achieving *imihigo* targets:

> Tomorrow I will wake up at 4 a.m. and go to look for those people who are going to repay me [for Financial Services]. Then I will put that money in the bank for accounting while waiting for someone else to present a project for getting a loan. If I was supposed to get paid back an amount of 4,500,000 Frw[12] and I only collected 1,500,000 Frw, you can calculate the rate or the percentage of achievement of my *imihigo*. It is the same for public works and for those people working in the roads. We commit ourselves to giving a job to these people through the VUP public works programme.[13]

The Financial Services programme has faced several challenges regarding the loan procurement and distribution processes. Those wanting to take out loans must provide a business plan approved by SACCO officials. However, many borrowers originally understood the programme as a gift, similar to the unconditional transfers provided through Direct Support. The loans were initially provided at low interest rates (2 per cent per year), and officials said many recipients did not bother paying back their loan. But when the government raised interest rates to 11 per cent in 2014, authorities were placed under additional pressure to recoup loans by chasing down borrowers. One of the challenges for officials is that they should recoup loans without formal and legal recourse. Group loans were seen as one way to minimize the risk.

The situation concerning loans was particularly fraught in Huye. According to officials, eligible households, in what is a poor district, were not taking out loans because they were worried that they would not be able to repay the loan and would thus be subject to punishment. As a result, a lot of money intended for financial services went unused. Most of the projects were in the areas of agriculture and animal husbandry. But if crops failed or animals died, households had no way to pay back the loans, putting them in bad standing with local officials.

> When we tell them that they can request for loans and make a small business ... they are afraid of it [because of the past experience], and they say no. In brief, we are encouraging them to take a risk and take loans.[14]

The reluctance of local people to participate in the Financial Services programme put Huye officials in a difficult position since they were under pressure to deliver on the VUP's productive objectives through their *imihigo* targets for disbursing loans. Officials therefore responded in various ways: disbursing loans to households without strong business plans, so that officials could reach their disbursement targets; reallocating funds earmarked for financial services to other activities in the sector; giving loans to households in category 3 who were seen as more creditworthy than those in category 1 or 2; or returning unused money to the district. Officials in Huye acknowledged that the situation is not working in the way it was intended:

> It is like local government is pushing people to take these loans, because it is something that they need for their performance contracts. To achieve their objectives, they have to force people to take these loans, so that they can be able to report it as an accomplishment. In this sector, for example, they have set an objective of giving loans to 50 projects this year. But then you find local government doesn't have time to make follow up with these people to ensure they're using the loans well.[15]

Rubavu provides an example of the more extreme measures taken by local officials to enforce loan repayment and meet *imihigo* targets. There were some reports of local officials placing those who fail to repay loans in jail as a temporary measure to convey that these loans are serious. Since VUP is a social programme, authorities do not typically work through the legal system to get loans back, so some took other measures to show VUP recipients they were serious about repayment. For instance, during a meeting between fieldworkers and the executive secretary of a sector, the secretary was on a phone call with a woman who was complaining that her husband had been sent to jail. According to the official, the woman was the president of a Financial Services savings group. When the group defaulted on their loan, the local officers went looking for the woman. However, when the loan officers could not find the leader of the group, they decided to put her husband in jail instead. 'We had to arrest somebody', the executive secretary explained. This is despite the executive secretary's admission that there is no formal recourse for failure to repay Financial Services loans. Nonetheless, she felt that punishment needed to be enacted, to show that the sector was serious about loan repayment. Indeed, this punishment also ignored the specific circumstances of the case. The man and woman in question had land on which they grew potatoes in a nearby forest called Giswati. In 2010, however, as part of a conservation effort, the government relocated families out of the forest, in the process affecting the livelihoods of many households in the area. The executive secretary admitted that this 'negatively impacted the Financial Services section of VUP programme, due to the farmers' inability to repay their loans. Even worse, this increased the number of people enrolled in the first Ubudehe category.' Nonetheless, this did not stop the local administration from imprisoning people for defaulting on loans.

Clearly, therefore, the protective and productive objectives of the VUP—while complementary in principle—are frequently in tension in practice. Moreover, state infrastructural power and, in particular, the high degree of top-down control afforded by *imihigo* has led to the prioritization of quantifiable targets and, often, the productive ambitions of the programme, to the detriment of the protective functions. Key examples are the inclusion of households beyond those classified in Ubudehe as the poorest, in order to meet the labour requirements of infrastructure projects, as well as pressure to disburse loans regardless of the creditworthiness of borrowers and to take sometimes drastic and arbitrary measures to enforce repayment of non-performing loans.

5. Distributing the VUP

This section turns specifically to the distributional function of the programme, looking at the Ubudehe programme used to classify households and the promotion of graduation from the VUP.[16] State infrastructural power is again important, shaping the government's response to the challenge faced by any targeted programme regarding how to generate information with which to distinguish between those who do and do not meet criteria for inclusion.

Ubudehe and the distribution of social transfers

The government launched Ubudehe in 2001 with the aim of providing small grants to support community-led projects. As part of this process, all households in a community were classified by their own members into one of what were then six categories, from the poorest to the wealthiest. Ubudehe's aim was to 'increase the level of institutional problem solving capacity at the local level by citizens and local government by putting into operation the principles of citizen participation through collective action' (MINECOFIN 2003, p. 4). Yet, over time, Ubudehe has effectively become a distributional mechanism for allocating support to those considered most in need, as more and more programmes used Ubudehe's wealth classification to distribute resources. Those placed in the lowest Ubudehe categories qualify not only for the VUP, but also for free or discounted health insurance, and their children can qualify for university scholarships.[17]

Ubudehe as a form of community-based targeting represents one solution to the challenge faced by any targeted social transfer programme—the need to produce sufficiently detailed information with which to distinguish those who meet programme criteria from those who do not. Indeed, Ubudehe utilizes the infrastructural power inherent in Rwanda's decentralized administrative structure to reach out into communities and mobilize them and the knowledge that they have of their members. Classification takes place in community meetings held at the village level—the lowest tier of state administration—organized by the village leader and overseen by an Ubudehe committee. This preliminary list is taken to a cell committee, which reviews and passes the list up to higher levels of local government. Once district and national authorities have vetted the list, it is returned to the villages (Sentama 2014).[18]

However, the accuracy of Ubudehe's classification is widely questioned and, as one might anticipate, the process presents numerous challenges. While advocates claim that community-based targeting draws on the detailed local knowledge of community members, it is also an inherently subjective process. Indeed, past research has shown that the Ubudehe categories are applied very differently across the country (Sabates-Wheeler et al. 2015). The result is that a poor household in a wealthy district may live in very different conditions to a poor household in a poor area, yet be included in the same category (Sentama, 2009; Hasselskog and Schierenbeck 2015; Sabates-Wheeler et al. 2015; IRDP 2018). Moreover, as more programmes use Ubudehe to identify those in need, there are strong financial motivations for households to try to ensure their classification amongst the poorest households. In addition to the challenges facing Ubudehe in general, as discussed in the previous section, the productive ambitions of the VUP also provide strong incentives for local officials to extend the programme beyond category 1. The result is that past research has questioned the targeting effectiveness of Ubudehe. For instance, a 2015 study found that 62 per cent of households from the poorest consumption quintile, based on the nationally representative Integrated Household Living Conditions Survey (EICV), were not included in the poorest two of the six (at the time) Ubudehe categories (Sabates-Wheeler et al. 2015).

The government's response to these concerns has been to modify the Ubudehe process in several ways. This included the 2016 reduction in the number of categories from six to four and the addition of a short household survey, introduced in the hope of adding an 'objective' element to the process. A copy of this survey (translated from Kinyarwanda to English) is located in Table 4.1. The use of a rudimentary proxy means test to verify community-based targeting is therefore an attempt to strengthen central control over programme selection. Yet, this also raises questions as to how these very different methodologies are combined to produce a selection of participants and what this implies for the participatory element of the programme. Nonetheless, it is worth noting that, despite the willingness to revisit the methodology for classifying households, there does not seem to be strong pressure on local officials to improve implementation of Ubudehe. Despite a strong narrative of self-reliance and concerns about dependency used to justify the targeted nature of the programme, there has not been an attempt to include an assessment of the accuracy of targeting in *imihigo*, for example. The result, as discussed above, is that strong incentives for local government officials to include those outside category 1, in order to meet productive targets, remain.

Table 4.1 Criteria for Ubudehe categorization

Category name	Criteria/*Ibikiranga*	Remarks and examples
Extremely Poor (category 1)	a) No house or ability to rent one. b) Very often struggles to get food.	One of these criteria is enough to qualify a household for this category.
Poor (category 2)	a) Owns a house or rents one. b) Often works. c) Often gets food. d) Struggles to get basic items such as soap.	Inability to work is not enough to disqualify one from this category.
Self-Sustaining (category 3)	a) With an employee in public or private sector. b) With a member self-employed with business. c) Farmers with surplus for market. d) With a member who is a small trader.	Any of these is enough to qualify a household in this category. For households in this category who may be having varying levels of welfare (e.g., not all public servants have same income), they are further separated by their businesses and their level of asset accumulation, as in category 4.
Rich (category 4)	a) With a big trader (may be producing locally, or in import and export trade). b) With a member who has (an) industry(ies). c) With a member who owns tracks, commercial building, in big cities, petrol station, etc.	Some farmers, traders and employees in public and private sector might find a way into this category, as a result of their investment levels/asset acquisition levels.

Distributing the VUP in practice

Fieldwork revealed that the process by which the survey was administered was inconsistent across our study sites. In some villages, leaders administered the survey before the community-based selection, while in other villages it was administered afterwards. Indeed, a village leader in Rubavu told us that he does not hold a community meeting at all, opting instead to let the survey determine Ubudehe categories entirely. In Huye, a district officer said that the community selection has little influence on the categorization process now and that the survey is used to verify the true conditions of households:

> The community doesn't know that the completed form is actually the one that will determine which categories they deserve. If they knew this, most of them would have lied.[19]

Indeed, the use of the household survey to alter the results of the community classification was the object of considerable frustration from several respondents, who felt that community involvement was being undermined. Regardless of the accuracy of community-based targeting versus proxy means tests (both of which have significant limitations, as discussed in Chapter 1), it appears that many view the community process as more legitimate.

> Community members sit together and put people in their respected Ubudehe categories and send it to Kigali. And once they put that info in a computer, the category changed. That is the common problem in my village and even the whole Nyamyumba.[20]

The survey did, though, provide a means of depersonalizing any criticism of the classification system, with targeting problems often framed as a problem 'with the machine' or a computer malfunction, thereby avoiding criticism of the government.

While there are clearly financial incentives for households to be included in Ubudehe category 1, fieldwork also highlighted several major deterrents. First, while inclusion in category 1 offers some assurance that the government will look after households, this came at a price of restriction of freedom of movement and assets, and even limitations of citizenship. Those in category 1 considered themselves to be, as many focus group participants put it, 'children of the government'. Many said they were perceived (and often perceived themselves) as destitute and unable to care for themselves, thus depending on the government for help. This dependency came as the cost of some restrictions of freedoms and, in particular, restrictions on movement. As noted above, officials in parts of Huye district took it upon themselves to draft performance contracts for VUP participants as a means of ensuring they used their transfers effectively, but, in the process, this limited individuals' freedom over how they spent their money. Furthermore, some local people and officials across both districts said that those in category 1 are not allowed to get a passport or other travel documents. The explanations for this varied. For example, some suggested the government does not want poor people leaving the country because it gives Rwanda a bad image. Other local officials said that if a household is in category 1, it would not be able to afford a passport anyway. When we asked district-level officials about these travel restrictions, most said this was not happening. But this contradicted nearly all other respondents, who brought this theme up repeatedly and without prompt from the field research team and who insisted that this practice was in effect.[21]

The constraints on mobility were mentioned more often in Rubavu, due to the proximity of the Congolese border and because many people in Rubavu relied on the Democratic Republic of Congo for economic activities like trade. Thus, despite the material benefits associated with category 1, many people in Rubavu said they preferred not to be classified in the first category because of the inability to pass freely across the border for commerce and trade.

> The reason that people want to move from the first category to the second is that sometimes they aren't allowed to cross the border to Congo. People here always want to cross the border for job opportunities, like working as porters or farming. People here in Nyamyumba would want to move to the second category despite the fact that they would lose some opportunities, so that they can get more opportunities when they cross border, which they can't do if they're in the first category. That's what the people really want.[22]

Second, beyond restrictions of freedoms, participants also described a lack of dignity, a sense of stigma, and shame associated with category 1. The original Ubudehe six-fold classification had not just numbers, but also labels for the categories. Though the category 1 label is directly translated as 'those in abject poverty', as Sabates-Wheeler et al. explain,

> The English translation does not do justice to the metaphorical nature of some of the characteristics. For example, for households in category 1, umutindi nyakujya, the literal translation of the characteristics captures the misery of extreme poverty; for instance, 'doesn't even have nails to scratch himself with' and 'death would be a relief'.
>
> (Sabates-Wheeler et al. 2015, p. 105)

While the categories were subsequently reformed to provide just a numerical classification, the stigma and shame associated with the lowest Ubudehe category appear to remain. Indeed, some respondents worried that the government would use their destitute status as a reason to deepen control over their lives. In Rubavu, there was a rumour that those in the first category would be forced to get some type of mark, like a marking or an earring, to signify their invalid status. In Huye, some said that one day the government would round up and relocate all of those in category 1 to another area so that they can receive proper monitoring and guidance.

> We are afraid. I have to be honest. There was a rumour that said the government will mark people in category 1 by giving them earrings. I didn't hear this in any meeting but the rumour was around here circulating. Then I was asking myself, how will I keep being in Ubudehe category 1? If I get that earring, everyone will know that I'm in category 1. It is a shame. It is embarrassing. Some people in category 1 are not happy for this reason.[23]

As far as we are aware, these rumours do not have merit. Nonetheless, the rumours certainly circulated in communities, shaping how local people understood the social significance of their categorization and also shaping state–society relations. In short, if the VUP produced narratives around empowerment, opportunity, and self-reliance, so too were there narratives around paternalism, top-down control, and restriction of freedoms. The result is that by restricting the freedom of those included in category 1 and stigmatizing such classification, the programme risked undermining its protective objectives, since such negative aspects of the programme risk some of the poorest and most vulnerable people intentionally excluding themselves from participation.

The VUP has always had a strong focus on graduation from poverty. The assumption is that the VUP should not become a permanent mechanism of support, except for the most vulnerable Direct Support participants. For the majority of VUP participants the effective use of social transfers and loans from the Financial Services component should provide opportunities to invest in improved livelihoods and graduate from the programme. The initial VUP design was hugely optimistic regarding graduation, anticipating that most households would graduate after just six months of support (GoR 2007). While the VUP has become more realistic regarding graduation over time, there remains pressure within government to ensure that participants do graduate. In particular, the Ministry of Finance and Economic Planning, while drafting the national development strategy, the Economic Second Development and Poverty Reduction (2013–18), pushed MINALOC to increase graduation from the VUP. Lavers cites one senior MINECOFIN respondent as follows:

> You cannot have people receiving support for three to five years, it is too much … a person who is 30–40 years old who is not disabled, they cannot be in a social protection programme for five years. A success story is when after three years someone graduates from poverty and we do not need to support them any more.
>
> (MINECOFIN official, cited in Lavers 2019)

In spite of this apparent pressure at high levels of government, local officials did not often identify graduation and pressure to reduce numbers in the VUP as a defining issue. Indeed, it would seem that state infrastructural power has not been mobilized to enforce graduation through performance targets in the way that it has done in Ethiopia (see Chapter 3). Nonetheless, local people, particularly in Huye, suggested that they felt local leaders were under pressure to offer a positive image of the area. Officials also felt pressure to show improvements in their region, even if it came at the expense of advocating for the needs of their constituency. For example, local people as well as some officials felt the number of poor people was underestimated by officials, which, in turn, worsened their economic situation, because they did not receive the support for which they might have been eligible. The process of targeting placed local officials in a challenging situation when it came to accountability. Some officials suggested there was a tension: upwards to the government that they serve, or to their constituents, to whom they deliver services on behalf of the government. This could lead to tension between local leaders and community members.

> I think there could be some tension in the situation because the leader wants just to preserve his appearance as someone who is having many rich people in [their] community and that will make them to continue to go down in poverty due to things they are not getting while they should.[24]

Nearly all officials we asked said that they did not receive a quota that limits the availability of VUP places. However, one local official in Huye challenged this, indicating that he is required to align Ubudehe categories for the area under their jurisdiction with EICV data and the poverty rates that this identifies.

> When you are going to classify them in categories, they tell you what percentage that you are not allowed to go below … Someone from LODA one time came by and told us, 'EICV4 [consumption poverty measure] is not wrong … The indicator of development and wellness was shown to be more than 71 per cent in the EICV4; so why are you showing [on Ubudehe] that it is less than 60 per cent? You have to take it to the level of the country' … The reality on the ground is not the same found in EICV4.[25]

The fieldwork suggests therefore an inconsistent and sometimes contradictory approach to targeting in the VUP. The VUP has always had a strong narrative in favour of self-reliance and concern about the dangers of welfare dependency. Yet programme design and the mobilization of state infrastructural power inconsistently prioritize these concerns. While classification in category 1 is stigmatized and provides the rationale for the state to increase monitoring of participants, problems with Ubudehe classification abound and it is not clear that there is great pressure to rectify these problems. For example, there has not been any attempt to include a measure of targeting accuracy in the all-important *imihigo*. Likewise, despite the narrative of the VUP as a means of solving poverty and promoting graduation, there appears to be inconsistent pressure on local officials to ensure graduation.

6. Conclusions

This chapter analyses the distribution of Rwanda's VUP using the lens of state infrastructural power and how this intersects with party politics. In doing so, the chapter shows that the Rwandan state and ruling party possesses relatively high levels of infrastructural power as a result of the decentralized administrative structures of the party-state, which reach into society in every part of the country, and the top-down mechanisms—notably *imihigo*—which provide central government with significant control over the activities of lower-level officials. This analytical focus highlights three main findings.

First, and in contrast to the three other African countries covered in this volume, the legacy of state formation in Rwanda has not contributed to significant variation in the infrastructural power required to deliver social transfers. As expected, in Rwanda the comparison of two 'most likely' cases for variation in infrastructural power failed to identify clear variation. Both sites are characterized by a high degree of top-down control by the central government over local state officials and by the party-state over society. Rwanda therefore represents a case in which past historical variation in state infrastructural power has been significantly overcome—with respect to the delivery of social transfers at least. This would appear to be the result of a rather unique combination of factors specific to Rwanda, namely: the catastrophic impact of the genocide, the dominance of the RPF in what is a small territory, and the government's particular approach to state-building that has explicitly sought to overcome past regional divisions.

Second, the Rwandan case provides useful insights into the links between party politics and distribution of social transfers. The Rwanda case study found no clear evidence that RPF involvement in VUP implementation had led to 'political capture' of distribution—a common concern for social transfer programmes in general. Instead, the fused nature of the party-state suggests that state infrastructural power, including the capacity to deliver programmes such as the VUP, depends to a significant degree on the strength of the party, as much as that of the state. Despite common concerns about the dangers of political capture in social transfer programmes, the VUP suggests that party involvement in implementation is not necessarily problematic and can play an important role in service delivery. In this respect, the findings share considerable similarities with the role of the fused party-state in Ethiopia, and particularly in Tigray, where the strength of the party was a key factor underpinning the relatively effective delivery of the Productive Safety Net Programme (see Chapter 3).

Third, despite high levels of state infrastructural power, the case study did highlight major limitations in the distribution of the VUP, particularly in relation to the objectives for which infrastructural power was deployed. While *imihigo* is an important tool and a key element of the infrastructural power of the Rwandan state, any system of performance evaluation is necessarily limited. In particular, systems of performance evaluation are suited to assessing progress towards clear and quantifiable objectives, but much less able to capture the full complexity of programme delivery. Regarding the VUP, the limitations of the *imihigo* are clear, with targets focusing on assessments of the disbursement and repayment of loans, and creation of infrastructure, for example, but no attempt to assess the more complex challenge of accurate targeting. Such debates echo those raised by Ang (2016) in relation to performance assessment in China. Rather than attempting to control the activities of local government officials through detailed top-down assessments—as is the case with *imihigo*—Ang argues that national governments are better off attempting to influence their activities. The latter involves setting broad objectives but leaving space for local officials, who have a better understanding of the communities in which they work, to adapt initiatives to local contexts.

Clearly, as the VUP highlights, even where states possess high levels of infrastructural power, this is insufficient for effective implementation. Ultimately, it makes a difference to what end infrastructural power is deployed. Since its inception, the VUP has struggled to reconcile its protective and productive objectives. While the state possesses significant infrastructural power, the top-down control provided by *imihigo* frequently led to the prioritization of targets linked to the productive function of the programme, to the detriment of its protective role. This included the necessity for local officials to push people who were concerned about their ability to repay into taking out loans and then taking coercive measures to enforce repayment of those loans subsequently. Similarly, the aim of using VUP public works to create public infrastructure also led local officials to divert resources away from those classified as the poorest to those classified as relatively better off because of their superior labour power. This tension between the protective and productive aspects of the programme again mirrors comparable challenges with Ethiopia's PSNP.

The pressure to meet productive targets therefore clearly has an impact on the distribution of the programme. However, this distributional process—comprising both targeting and graduation—exhibits apparently contradictory characteristics. On the one hand, the programme is cast within a strong narrative of self-reliance and concerns about welfare dependency that focus attention on strict poverty targeting and pressure to graduate from the programme. Perhaps unsurprisingly, as a result, there is a considerable sense of stigma amongst programme recipients and certain restrictions on their freedoms. At the same time, however, recurrent problems with Ubudehe classification and the prioritization of productive objectives over the effectiveness of targeting appear to suggest some ambivalence regarding the importance of targeting accuracy. Likewise, fieldwork did not identify strong pressure to push graduation in practice. Though the government is keen to avoid welfare dependency and contributes to the stigma attached to VUP participation, the RPF has actively sought to use the VUP as a means of demonstrating its benevolence and as a sign of its support for the rural population. The programme is celebrated by the party, the government, and participants, even as there are strong sanctions and coercive mechanisms placed against those in lower Ubudehe categories.

Notes

1. This study was carried out through a partnership between the Effective States Inclusive Development (ESID) programme at the University of Manchester and the Institute of Research and Dialogue for Peace (IRDP) based in Kigali. Rwanda's Ministry of Local Government (MINALOC) provided written permission for this study. This chapter benefited from feedback at an early stage validation meeting held at IRDP in Kigali in December 2019, as well as feedback provided by two anonymous reviewers. This feedback strengthened the conceptual arguments made in the study. The authors wish to thank Juventine Mujawase and Jeanine Balezi, who led the fieldwork, and Samantha Lakin, who provided technical and administrative support.
2. The original design of the VUP was influenced in important ways by a study tour to Ethiopia's Productive Safety Net Programme (PSNP) (Lavers 2019). As such, the programme design of the two programmes remains similar in many respects (see Lavers, this volume).
3. All fieldwork was carried out by a team of three Rwandan researchers under the supervision of the lead researcher (Tim Williams). Each field researcher had extensive previous experience conducting qualitative research.
4. An additional tier of administration called the *Isibo*—a grouping of 10–15 households—was added in August 2018, shortly after the completion of fieldwork.
5. Land Officer, Simbi Sector, Huye District.
6. Village Leader, Simbi Sector, Huye District.
7. FGD Public Works Classic, Simbi Sector, Huye District.
8. FGD Public Works Classic, Simbi Sector, Huye District.
9. FGD Public Works Classic, Simbi Sector, Huye District.
10. Land Manager, Nyamyumba Sector, Rubavu District.
11. Public Works Classic participant, Kanzenze Sector, Rubavu District.
12. There were approximately 1,200 Rwandan francs (Frw) to the British pound at the time of fieldwork in 2018.
13. Cell Executive Secretary, Nyamyumba Sector, Rubavu District.
14. MPG Caseworker, Karama Sector, Huye District
15. SACCO Manager, Simbi Sector, Huye District.

16. The VUP entails both geographical and household targeting. Geographical targeting, by which EICV consumption data are used to identify the poorest regions of the country (LODA, 2017), is not considered here.
17. At the end of 2019, the government removed Ubudehe categorization as a criterion for university scholarships.
18. In late June 2020, the Ubudehe categorization underwent another reform with reports suggesting that the government intends to use the newly created *Isibo* structures of 10–15 households in Ubudehe classification, reinforcing the important role of state infrastructural power in meeting the challenge of identifying programme participants.
19. Social Development Officer, Huye District.
20. Village Leader, Nyamyumba Sector, Rubavu District.
21. The withholding of passports from Rwanda's poorest was a finding also reported in a research study by Transparency International Rwanda. A summary of findings has been reported in local media. See: https://www.chronicles.rw/2019/08/14/poorest-rwandans-refused-passports-claims-new-research/
22. Local official, Nyambyuma Sector, Rubavu District.
23. FGD Public Works Expanded, Kanzenze Sector, Rubavu District.
24. FGD non-participants, Simbi Sector, Huye District.
25. This statement hints at the impact of the previously cited study by Sabates-Wheeler et al. (2015), which compared Ubudehe categories and EICV consumption data. While their research highlighted the challenge of distributing resources using a subjective community assessment and monitoring progress using a household survey, the result may be that government officials have come under pressure to align Ubudehe categories with EICV results in a rather blunt, top-down manner.

References

Ang, Y. Y., 2016. *How China Escaped the Poverty Trap*. Ithaca, NY: Cornell University Press.

Ashley, S. and Kyanga, A., 2013. *Rwanda: Vision 2020 Umurenge (VUP)—Project Completion Review 2013 Final Report*. Bristol: IDL Group.

Behuria, P., 2016. Countering threats, stabilising politics and selling hope: Examining the Agaciro concept as a response to a critical juncture in Rwanda. *Journal of Eastern African Studies*, 10 (3), 434–451.

Benda, R. and Pells, K., 2020. The state-as-parent: Reframing parent–child relations in Rwanda. *Families, Relationships and Societies*, 9 (1), 41–57.

Birmingham, D., 1995. *The Decolonization of Africa*. London: UCL Press.

Chemouni, B., 2014. Explaining the design of the Rwandan decentralization: Elite vulnerability and the territorial repartition of power'. *Journal of Eastern African Studies*, 8 (2), 246–262.

Chemouni, B. and Mugiraneza, A., 2020. Ideology and interests in the Rwandan patriotic front: Singing the struggle in pre-genocide Rwanda. *African Affairs*, 119 (474), 115–140.

Des Forges, A. L., 1999. *Leave None to Tell the Story: Genocide in Rwanda*. New York: Human Rights Watch; International Federation of Human Rights.

Eckstein, H., 2000. Case study and theory in political science. *In*: R. Gomm, M. Hammersley, and P. Foster, eds. *Case Study Method*. London: Sage, 119–164.

Gahamanyi, V. and Kettlewell, A., 2015. Evaluating graduation: Insights from the Vision 2020 Umurenge Programme in Rwanda. *IDS Bulletin*, 46 (2), 48–63.

Golooba-Mutebi, F., 2008. Collapse, war and reconstruction in Rwanda: An analytical narrative on state-making. *Crisis States Research Centre Working Papers*, 28 (series 2).

Golooba-Mutebi, F., 2013. Politics, political settlements and social change in post-colonial Rwanda. *ESID Working Papers*, 24.

GoR, 2007. *Vision 2020 Umurenge: An Integrated Local Development Program to Accelerate Poverty Eradication, Rural Growth, and Social Protection*. Kigali: Government of Rwanda.

Hasselskog, M. and Schierenbeck, I., 2015. National policy in local practice: The case of Rwanda. *Third World Quarterly*, 36 (5), 950–966.

Hintjens, H., 1999. Explaining the 1994 genocide in Rwanda. *Journal of Modern African Studies*, 37 (2), 241–286.

IRDP, 2018. *A Perception Study on Vision 2020 Umurenge Program (VUP) as a Poverty Reduction Strategy for the Poorest Households in Rwanda*. Kigali: Institute of Research and Dialogue for Peace.

Lavers, T., 2019. Understanding elite commitment to social protection: Rwanda's Vision 2020 Umurenge Programme. *In*: S. Hickey, T. Lavers, M. Niño-Zarazúa, and J. Seekings, eds. *The Politics of Social Protection in Eastern and Southern Africa*. Oxford: Oxford University Press, 95–121.

LODA, 2016a. Huye Disrict imihigo 2016–2017. Retrieved from https://www.huye.gov.rw (accessed 15 October 2020).

LODA, 2016b. *Vision Umurenge 2020 Programme: Accelating Sustainable Graduation from Extreme Poverty and Fostering Inclusive National Development*. Kigali: Local Administrative Entities Development Agency.

LODA, 2017. *Annual Activity Progress Report: Fiscal Year 2016/2017*. Kigali: Local Administrative Entities Development Agency.

MINECOFIN, 2003. Ubudehe mu Kurwanya Ubukene, Ubudehe to Fight Poverty, Concept Note, Government of Rwanda. Kigali: Ministry of Economics and Finance.

Newbury, C., 1988. *The Cohesion of Oppression: Clientship and Ethnicity in Rwanda, 1860–1960*. New York: Columbia University Press.

Newbury, D. and Newbury, C., 1994. Rwanda: The politics of turmoil. *Journal of the International Institute*, 1 (2), 1–2.

Newbury, D. and Newbury, C., 2000. Bringing the peasants back in: Agrarian themes in the construction and corrosion of statist historiography in Rwanda. *American Historical Review*, 105 (3), 832–877.

Pottier, J., 2002. *Re-imagining Rwanda: Conflict, Survival and Disinformation in the Late Twentieth Century* (Vol. 102). Cambridge: Cambridge University Press.

Prunier, G., 1995. *The Rwanda Crisis: History of a Genocide*. New York: Columbia University Press.

Reyntjens, F., 2004. Rwanda, ten years on: From genocide to dictatorship. *African Affairs*, 103 (411), 177–210.

RoR, 1999. *Report on the Reflection Meetings Held in the Office of the President of the Republic from May 1998 to March 1999*. Retrieved from: https://repositories.lib.utexas.edu/bitstream/handle/2152/4907/2378.pdf?sequence=1 (accessed 24 September 2021).

RoR, 2000. *Rwanda Vision 2020*. Retrieved from Kigali: https://repositories.lib.utexas.edu/bitstream/handle/2152/5071/4164.pdf (accessed 24 September 2021).

Sabates-Wheeler, R., Yates, S., Wylde, E., and Gatsinzi, J., 2015. Challenges of measuring graduation in Rwanda. *IDS Bulletin*, 46 (2), 103–114.

Sentama, E., 2009. Peacebuilding in post-genocide Rwanda: The role of cooperatives in the restoration of interpersonal relationships. Ph.D. thesis. Gothenburg University.

Sentama, E., 2014. *Ubudehe Categorization and Its Impact on Citizens' Living Conditions in Rwanda*. Kigali: Rwanda Civil Society Platform.

Vansina, J., 2004. *Antecedents to Modern Rwanda: The Nyiginya Kingdom*. Madison, WI: University of Wisconsin Press.

Verwimp, P., 2000. Peasant ideology and genocide in Rwanda under Habyarimana. *Yale University Genocide Studies Working Papers*, 19. Retrieved from https://gsp.yale.edu/node/312 (accessed 24 September).

Verwimp, P., 2013. *Peasants in Power: The Political Economy of Development and Genocide in Rwanda*. New York: Springer.

Williams, T. P., 2017. The political economy of primary education: Lessons from Rwanda. *World Development*, 96, 550–561.

World Bank, 2019. Reducing vulnerability and strengthening inclusion in Rwanda through rural development and enhancing social protection. Results Brief, 29 October. Washington, DC: World Bank. Retrieved from https://www.worldbank.org/en/results/2019/10/29/reducing-vulnerability-and-strengthening-inclusion-in-rwanda-through-rural-development-and-enhancing-social-protection (accessed 24 September 2021).

PART III

COMPETITIVE-DISTRIBUTIVE CASES IN AFRICA

5

Uneven Targeting of Cash Transfers

Local Party-Political Competition and State Infrastructural Power in the Implementation of Social Protection in Ghana

Edward Ampratwum

1. Introduction

The Livelihood Empowerment Against Poverty (LEAP) is a social transfer programme that provides cash and social services such as health insurance and school fee waivers to households in extreme poverty (MMYE 2007; Osei 2011). For most households, the transfers are unconditional. However, those with orphans of school-going age, and pregnant and nursing mothers, must attend school, antenatal services, and birth registration. LEAP transfers are distributed using a combination of geographical and community-based targeting procedures, and a proxy means test. LEAP currently covers more than 200,000 households across all regions and districts in the country (World Bank 2016, 2018; Hamel and Flowers 2018). This translates into more than 1.1 million individuals, equivalent to 43 per cent of the country's extremely poor population (Ablo 2018; Hamel and Flowers 2018; World Bank 2018). The expansion and rollout of LEAP have been closely shaped by electoral politics, with major expansions announced prior to elections in 2008, 2012, and 2016, and incumbents directing programme resources to their strongholds in an attempt to reward their base (Abdulai 2020). The three northern regions, which have higher poverty rates, encompass 55 per cent of LEAP coverage despite constituting only 17 per cent of the Ghanaian population (Hamel and Flowers 2018). Nonetheless, districts with the lowest poverty rates have the highest coverage as a percentage of the poor. This reflects both the population concentration in Ghana (poor regions have fewer people) as well as the political need to secure national coverage in the programme (World Bank 2018; Abdulai 2020).

LEAP evaluations have generally highlighted positive impacts including a marginal reduction in poverty incidence, an improvement in food consumption,

Edward Ampratwum, *Uneven Targeting of Cash Transfers.* In: *The Politics of Distributing Social Transfers.* Edited by Tom Lavers, Oxford University Press. © Oxford University Press (2022).
DOI: 10.1093/oso/9780192862525.003.0005

an increase in school enrolment and attendance, and a rise in health insurance enrolment (De Groot et al. 2015; Angeles et al. 2017). Despite these positive outcomes, there is evidence of considerable variation in implementation effectiveness across districts (Wodon 2012; Niyuni 2016). For instance, Gbedemah et al. (2010) report that the imbalance of administrative officials across districts and communities undermines the ability of some districts to establish oversight committees to administer the programme. This chapter focuses on explaining variation in implementation. To do so, the analysis draws on detailed case studies of four districts from northern and southern Ghana, selected to highlight variation in state infrastructural power and political competition. These case studies are based on some 260 key informant interviews, 24 focus group discussions, and observations conducted over a period of eight months (February–October 2018). This primary material is supplemented by documentary sources and official statistics.

Drawing on the existing literature, there are good reasons to expect that implementation of Ghana's LEAP would be affected by both the highly competitive nature of electoral politics and variation in state infrastructural power between the relatively strong state in the south of the country and the weaker state in the north. Analysis of the four case studies found that party-political competition—within as well as between parties—has exerted the main influence on distribution of LEAP transfers. In politically competitive sites, the need to mobilize all available resources to secure political loyalty and votes led local politicians to intervene in supposedly technical processes by which communities and households were selected for inclusion in the programme. While implementation in politically dominant districts was far from perfect, the absence of such political pressures meant that targeting processes remained primarily technical exercises. Lower levels of physical infrastructure and staffing in the northern sites posed a challenge to implementation and required officials to devolve greater responsibilities to community-level actors and party officials, sometimes fuelling local patronage networks. However, the impact of clear differences in state infrastructural power between northern and southern Ghana pales in comparison to that exerted by political dynamics.

The next section begins by highlighting variation in state infrastructural power and political competition within Ghana, before analysing the variation in these factors of interest across the study sites in the Upper West and Central regions. The chapter then outlines the decentralized administrative structures used in the LEAP targeting process and how the operation of these structures is shaped by variation in state infrastructural power. The following sections focus on the LEAP implementation process, analysing the influence of political competition on geographical and household targeting. The final section concludes.

2. State infrastructural power and the consolidation of competitive politics in Ghana

This section analyses the historical trajectory of state formation in Ghana, showing how this has resulted in variation in state infrastructural power within the country, while a highly competitive electoral system has developed since the 1990s. This variation in infrastructural power and electoral competition was used as the basis of case selection for the four research sites.

Research on state formation in Ghana has underscored the role of powerful social organizations in the formation of pre-colonial states. In the southern and middle belts of the country, the necessity to protect the economic interests of traditional authorities, by securing the trans-Saharan trading routes, formed the basis for expansionist policies (Hymer 1970; Clark 1990). The arrival of European traders on the southern coastline changed the direction of the trade from the inland towards the coast. However, this reinforced the accumulation of resources, deployment of commercial centres, and concentration of population in the southern belt of the country (Hymer 1970; Clark 1990). In the colonial era, British colonialists' capitalist accumulation further tended to develop the south and 'under-develop' the north (Ladouceur 1973; Plange 1984, p. 30). The legacy of the early and long contact with European traders, missionaries, and colonizers led to the concentration of state infrastructure such as road and rail networks, educational institutions, and churches in the south (Hymer 1970; Atiemo 2015). In contrast, in the north of the territory, 'only the feeblest of efforts were made to promote the economic development' (Ladouceur 1973, p. 66). The colonial state invested in basic resources rather than long-term infrastructure projects due to the cost and difficulties of mobilizing revenues and administering taxes in the vast northern territories (Ladouceur 1973; Lentz 2006).

Post-colonial authorities failed to address this north–south imbalance in infrastructure distribution. For instance, though the Nkrumah regime proposed to bridge disparities through the Seven-Year Development Plan (1963–70), most of the proposed industrial projects and public investment in physical and financial infrastructure remained in the south (Konadu-Agyemang 2000; Shepherd et al. 2004). State policies in the 1980s and 1990s further exacerbated social and economic inequalities (Shepherd et al. 2004; Vanderpuye-Orgle 2004). In the Fourth Republic (1993 to present), despite considerable donor and non-governmental organization investments in secondary and primary schools, and healthcare infrastructure, the northern part of the country remains disadvantaged in the provision of quality health and education facilities, and personnel (Mohan 2002; Shepherd et al. 2004; UNDP 2018).

Under the Fourth Republic, Ghana has adopted an elaborate non-partisan decentralized system. District Assemblies act as implementing entities and have primary responsibility for planning, financing, and delivering services to local people (Alam and Koranteng 2011; Zakaria 2013; World Bank 2018). Beneath the districts are the Area Councils and Unit Committees. District Chief Executives are the leaders of the District Assemblies and these key officials are appointed by the central government, ensuring that only loyal cadres are sent to head local administrations. According to the Local Government Act of 1994, 70 per cent of local councillors are elected on non-partisan platforms, while the remaining 30 per cent are appointed by the President in consultation with a host of local influential actors including executives of the ruling party and foot soldiers of the ruling party. These appointees are sometimes posted to critical committees in the District Assemblies to entrench the hold of the national ruling party (Crook 1999; Crawford 2004; Awortwi 2010; Debrah 2016). Unit committees are elected to liaise with local communities and the Assembly councillors.

The return of multiparty elections in 1992 resulted in the consolidation of a highly competitive two-party political system, with elections frequently won with very slim margins and regular turnover of power (Gyimah-Boadi 2009; Bob-Milliar and Paller 2018). The two main parties, the National Democratic Congress (NDC) and the New Patriotic Party (NPP) can trace their roots to antecedents in the decade preceding independence (Jockers et al. 2010; Oduro et al. 2014; Abdulai and Hickey 2016). The NDC has used a narrative of solidarity with the poor and social democracy, and strong ethno-regional linkages to consolidate its political hold in the Volta and northern regions (Morrison 2004; Jockers et al. 2010; Abdulai and Hickey 2016). In contrast, the NPP's strongholds are in the southern part of the country, especially urban centres, while the party has maintained particularly strong alliances with traditional leaders of the southern and middle belts (Morrison 2004). The intense competition for political power has also highlighted the 'high tendency for inter- and intra-elite factionalism'(Oduro et al. 2014, p. 7; Whitfield 2011; Bob-Milliar 2012). Indeed, the fact that these two political parties have required significant organizational capacity at the local level to succeed in closely fought elections has enhanced the power and influence of intra-party factions (Bob-Milliar 2014). Moreover, intense political competition has incentivized visible social policies and provisioning in order that parties show their concerns for local constituencies in an attempt to win votes (Carbone 2011), while public investment is focused on short-term electoral pay-offs rather than long-run investments (Prempeh and Kroon 2012). Reflecting the intensely competitive political system at the national level, operating a non-partisan local government in Ghana has proven challenging. Research shows that the result has often been the politicization of local administration, tensions around control over district public facilities, and excessive control of the national ruling party over District Assembly leadership (Ofei-Aboagye 2018).

Drawing on these insights, the study selected four district research sites representing differing levels of state infrastructural power and local political competition. Two cases were drawn from the Central region, located in the south of Ghana where state infrastructural power is relatively strong. Gomoa West is located on the coast (see Fig. 5.1) and has a number of urban centres. In contrast, Assin South is located in the hinterland of the Central region, with no urban centres. An additional two cases were selected from the Upper West region, which typifies the systematic underdevelopment of the northern part of the country. Wa West district is located in the south of Upper West region and has no urban centres. Sissala East is located in the northeast with few urban localities (see Fig. 5.2). As shown in Table 5.1, poverty rates are considerably higher in the sites in the Upper West region and, in particular, Wa West.

Regarding the state of political competition, the Central region is politically competitive as a whole, but exhibits variation in competitiveness at the district level. Within the Central region, Assin South is an example of a politically dominant district, where the NPP has won the last five presidential elections with an average of 59 per cent of the vote (see Fig. 5.3). In Gomoa West, on the other hand, no party has dominated politics since 2000. Importantly, the NPP and NDC canvassed core supporters from different localities within Gomoa West, with the majority of NDC supporters in the forest inland and the NPP in the coastal lowlands.[1] Though the Upper West is a political stronghold for the NDC, there is also sub-regional variation in competition (see Fig. 5.4). In Wa West, the NDC has won

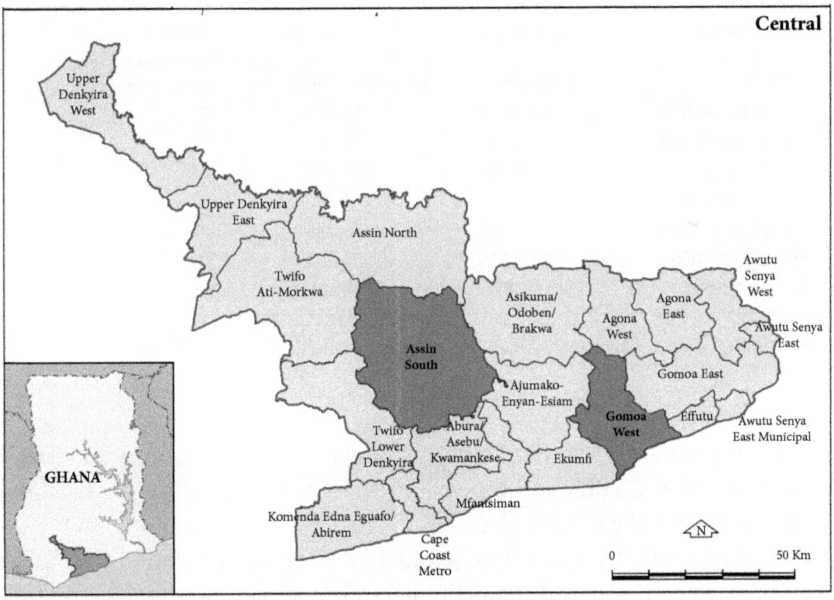

Fig. 5.1 Map of the research sites in Central Region
Source: University of Manchester Cartographic Unit.

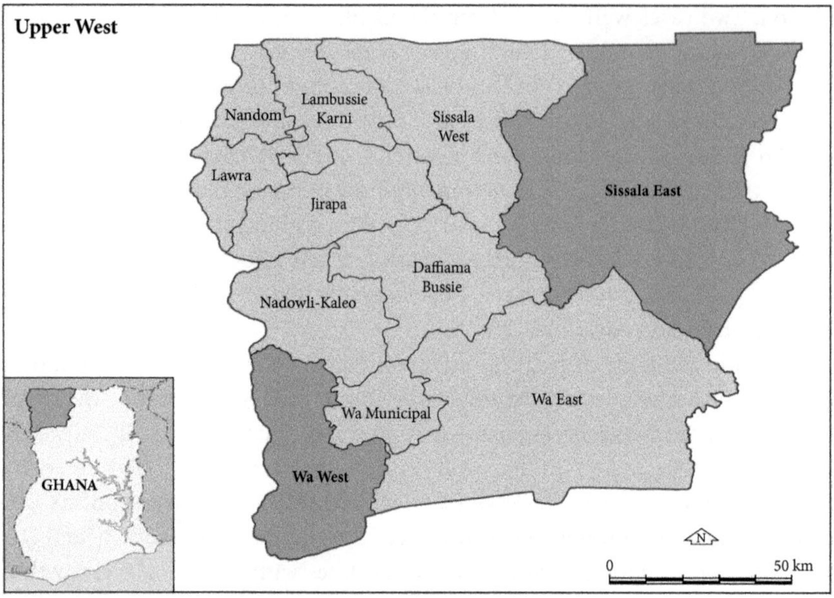

Fig. 5.2 Map of the research sites in Upper West Region
Source: University of Manchester Cartographic Unit.

Table 5.1 Poverty indicators for the research sites

Category	Population	Poor persons	Poverty incidence (%)
Gomoa West	132,833	29,967	23
Assin South	102,069	24,066	24
Central	2,113,763	415,143	**20**
Wa West	80,382	74,297	92
Sissala East	55,764	26,399	47
Upper West	688,328	477,631	**70**
National	**24,658,823**	**6,800,000**	**23**

Source: Author's field data (2018).

the last five presidential elections with an average of 63 per cent. In Sissala East, in contrast, the NDC, NPP, and People's National Convention (PNC) have all won the district vote in the last five elections.

The research sites were therefore selected to illustrate variation in state infrastructural power and political competition, as summarized in Table 5.2. The initial expectation was that stronger infrastructural power in the Central region would result in better LEAP performance compared to the Upper West region. However, within each region the level of political competition is expected to influence

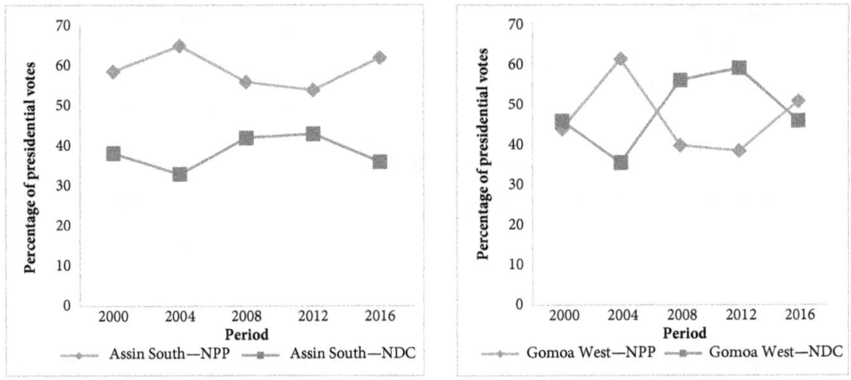

Fig. 5.3 Presidential vote shares in the research sites in Central Region
Source: EC Ghana (2018).

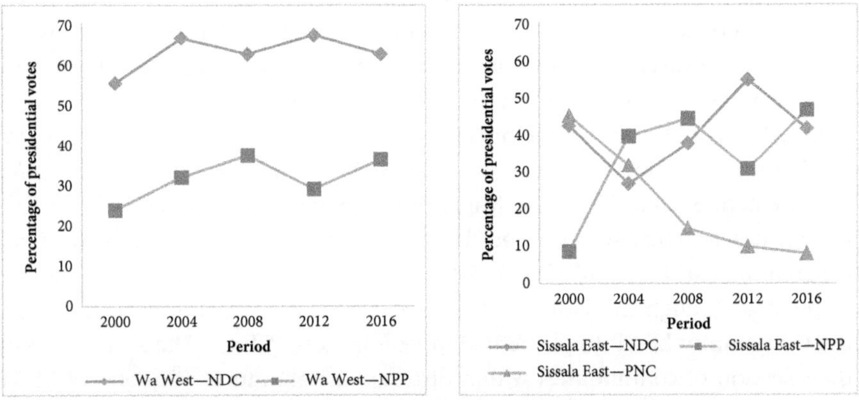

Fig. 5.4 Presidential vote shares in the research sites in Upper West Region
Source: EC Ghana (2018).

the mobilization of state capacity for implementation, with competitive settings providing the incentive for party-political actors to influence programme implementation as a means of securing short-run political advantage to the detriment of impartial implementation. In contrast, in dominant settings, local administrations have the possibility of setting aside short-term political interests to focus on impartial implementation. The result is that impartial and effective implementation is most likely in Assin South, where the state possesses strong infrastructural power that is likely to be mobilized in a dominant political setting. Sissala East, in contrast, has the least advantageous combination in that competitive politics are likely to undermine the deployment of already limited infrastructural capacity.

Table 5.2 Infrastructural power and political competition across the study sites

		Electoral competition	
		Dominant	**Competitive**
Infrastructural power	**High**	Assin South	Gomoa West
	Low	Wa West	Sissala East

3. Targeting LEAP and the challenge of state infrastructural power

This section provides an overview of the administrative structures used for LEAP implementation and, in particular, the involvement of these in the targeting of LEAP. This targeting comprises, in turn: geographical targeting, community-based targeting, a proxy means test, and community verification. Finally, the discussion examines how variation in state infrastructural power shapes the ability of these administrative structures to carry out their responsibilities.

LEAP is centrally driven but implemented through decentralized structures involving state and societal actors (see Fig. 5.5). At the national level, the LEAP Management Secretariat in the Ministry of Gender, Children, and Social Protection has responsibility for coordination, management, and oversight of the programme (MMYE 2007; MoGCSP 2015). LEAP targeting was originally implemented through the District LEAP Implementation Committee (DLIC) and the Community LEAP Implementation Committees (CLIC). The DLIC oversaw the selection of communities within districts, the allocation of quotas of LEAP places to these communities, and the recruitment of enumerators and community volunteers responsible for household targeting. The centrally appointed District Chief Executive chaired the DLIC while membership included district officials and non-state actors including representatives of faith-based organizations and a non-governmental organization (MMYE 2007; MoGCSP 2015). Importantly, neither traditional authorities nor the local Member of Parliament (MP) had any official role in the LEAP implementation. The CLIC, meanwhile, was responsible for community-based targeting and assisting with appeals (MMYE 2007). The CLIC was a body of 8–10 people from the local elite, chosen based on their in-depth knowledge of household poverty and vulnerability in their community (MMYE, 2007). Once an initial selection of potential participants had been made by the CLIC, their eligibility was verified based on a survey and proxy means test carried out by locally recruited enumerators. The intention of this decentralized administration was to ensure greater local ownership, participation, and accountability. Yet, as with other forms of decentralized service provision in Ghana, the existence of implementation structures involving state and non-state actors often resulted

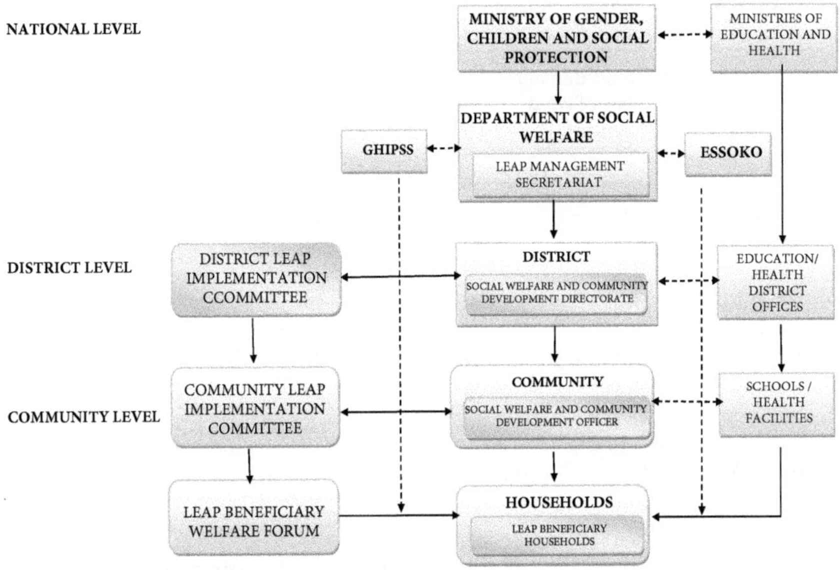

Fig. 5.5 The structure of the decentralized LEAP implementation
Source: Author's adaptations of Ayala (2010).

in entwining the programme in power relations between influential local actors, leading to variable application of programme guidelines (Gbedemah et al. 2010; Wodon 2012; Niyuni 2016).

Internal and external evaluations raised concerns about the influence of political and influential social actors on the targeting process. As a result, the LEAP Management Secretariat, with support and guidance from the World Bank, Department for International Development. and the United Nations International Children's Emergency Fund (UNICEF), introduced a series of reforms in 2015 intended to improve targeting accuracy and ensure that LEAP benefits the poorest households (World Bank 2016, 2018). One key aspect of the reforms was to replace the politically appointed District Chief Executives with non-political District Coordinating Directors as chairpersons of the DLICs. The reform also sought to replace CLICs, many of which had become inactive, with Community Focal Persons, who were mainly local education bureaucrats or health volunteers.[2] Furthermore, donor-sponsored reforms aimed to re-centralize control over the targeting process. For this purpose, the LEAP Management Secretariat, in collaboration with the Ghana Statistical Service, was to use district poverty maps in the selection of LEAP communities, with the role of districts reduced to confirming centralized selection. The proxy means test, in contrast, was to be centrally administered and contracted to a private company, ESOKO. The company recruits and appoints enumerators independent of the district administration. These enumerators evaluate

Table 5.3 Availability of basic infrastructure in the research sites

	Road density (km of road per km^2)	Dwellings using electricity (%)	Persons aged 12+ owning mobile phone (%)	Persons aged 12+ accessing internet (%)
Gomoa West	4.0	70	36	2
Assin South	2.7	42	31	2
Central	**3.2**	**66**	**45**	**7**
Wa West	3.2	10	10	1
Sissala East	1.0	36	21	1
Upper West	**1.7**	**31**	**22**	**3**
National	**3.2**	**64**	**48**	**8**

Sources: Ghana Statistical Service (2014c, 2014d, 2014a, 2014b), ASDA (2018), GWDA (2018), WWDA (2016) and SEDA (2018).

potential participants in real time using tablets. Finally, ESOKO enrols participants and passes this list to the LEAP Management Secretariat and the districts for community announcement to proceed.

Variation in state infrastructural power provides an important influence on these administrative structures and their ability to carry out their tasks as outlined in LEAP guidelines. Implementation challenges have been exacerbated in areas of low infrastructural power with the turn to increasingly technology-intensive implementation since 2015. Table 5.3 illustrates the legacy of uneven state formation on contemporary infrastructure. Research sites in Central region have greater road density, access to electricity, and telecommunications than those in the Upper West. The result is that bureaucrats in Assin South and Gomoa West in the Central region travel shorter distances to reach communities and can deliver electronic-based services in almost all communities.[3] The lack of physical infrastructure in sites in the Upper West region, on the other hand, presents challenges for bureaucrats, who must travel long distances on motorbike or on foot to reach communities.[4] In addition, delivery of services requiring electricity can take place in only a few communities.

Similar variations are evident in the deployment of social welfare personnel in the districts, with greater staff availability in the Central than the Upper West region (see Table 5.4). In some districts in the Central region, for instance, District Social Welfare Directorates were overstaffed as bureaucrats refused less-sought-after postings elsewhere,[5] while districts in the Upper West were clearly understaffed and under-qualified,[6] with bureaucrats often refusing postings to this under-resourced region.

In the Central region, the better coverage of transport and communication infrastructure supported the targeting process. In Assin South and Gomoa West,

Table 5.4 Social welfare staff deployed in research sites

	Staff per 1,000 poor population	**Staff per 1,000 LEAP participants**	**Staff per 1,000 LEAP households**
Gomoa West	0.3	2.1	8.5
Assin South	0.4	2.2	8.7
Central	**0.4**	**3.8**	**15.0**
Wa West	0.1	0.3	1.2
Sissala East	0.2	0.3	1.3
Upper West	**0.2**	**0.8**	**3.1**
National	**0.4**	**1.8**	**11.9**

Sources: GSS (2018).

bureaucrats confirmed that most roads, except those around the forest reserves, were in good condition and easily accessible by car and motorbike, while there are short distances between communities. As such, LEAP officials could freely select all eligible communities without concerns about access, while Social Welfare officials could easily monitor enrolment.[7] This ensured that potential participants were assessed and enrolled in their own communities without incurring financial and temporal travel costs.[8] Likewise, physical infrastructure enabled enumerators to centrally target and enrol households relatively easily in most of the Central region, with good telecommunication coverage enabling rapid assessment of potential households using the centrally controlled proxy means test. The main exception here was in communities bordering the forest reserves in Assin South, where access to telecommunication and the electric grid was relatively poor. As such, there were a few instances in which Social Welfare officials required community members to travel to adjourning communities to enrol due to technological constraints.[9] Importantly, the adequate availability of local Social Welfare staff in Assin South and Gomoa West enabled the Social Welfare Directorate to oversee household targeting.[10]

In contrast, officials in the Upper West region faced the challenge of much more limited physical infrastructure in the form of roads, electricity, and communications to support LEAP targeting. In Wa West and Sissala East, inadequate road networks hampered selection of poor communities located in inaccessible parts of the district. As a result, bureaucrats selected most LEAP communities from the more accessible parts of the districts along major roads.[11] In addition, limited access to the electricity grid and weak telecommunications coverage prevented the local Social Welfare officials from setting up targeting and enrolment points in many communities.[12] In both Wa West and Sissala East, a lack of internet access in most LEAP communities meant Social Welfare officials had to set up cluster enrolment points in communities with better internet access.[13] As a result, many people had to travel long distances to enrol on LEAP, while these enrolment points often became congested, requiring people to wait for long periods.[14] Meanwhile, in Sissala East, Social Welfare officials were forced to rely on politically aligned Assembly Members and ruling party executives to relay information on LEAP to communities, given the limited communications infrastructure. As the senior local Social Welfare bureaucrat revealed,

> one key challenge is the poor communication network. So sometimes, we rely on the Assembly Members and the LEAP committee members to mobilize the selected households ahead of the enumeration.
>
> (Int. respondent SSBT02)

Importantly, insufficient numbers of local Social Welfare officials in Sissala East further undermined bureaucrats' ability to monitor the targeting and enumeration process.[15] As such, this reliance on party foot soldiers and politically aligned Assembly Members to compensate for insufficient staffing, provided an important entry point for these political actors to exert influence on the process, as discussed further in the next section.

In summary, in the two districts in the Central region, stronger state infrastructural power in the form of physical resources, competences, and oversight supported the targeting of communities and households, regardless of their geographical locations. In the Upper West region sites, on the other hand, weak state infrastructural power in the form of insufficient physical infrastructure and staffing presented a major challenge for the targeting process. Bureaucrats were forced to rely on the involvement of local political actors to compensate for the lack of physical infrastructure, therefore opening space for political influence on the programme. The remaining two sections examine how variation in political competition shaped LEAP administrative structures and thereby the targeting process. Section 4 focuses on geographical targeting which involves the selection of communities, and Section 5 examines household targeting within LEAP communities.

4. Political competition and geographical targeting

Before 2015, DLICs were tasked with the identification and selection of deprived communities within their district using a set of indicators including: high incidence of guinea worm, Buruli ulcer, and HIV/AIDS; enrolment in the National Health Insurance Scheme; access to quality basic social services; child labour or child trafficking; and the degree of geographical isolation (MMYE 2007a, p. 29). Following the 2015 reform, this community selection was partially re-centralized. Fieldwork traced the constitution of LEAP committees and the process of targeting

LEAP in the research sites as well as the impact of the 2015 reforms. This analysis reveals that the DLIC and CLIC remain interlocked in the local configuration of power, varying within, rather than between, regions despite reforms introduced to undercut the influence of local political elites.

The politically dominant Assin South and Wa West districts

In the politically dominant Assin South and Wa West districts, the limited degree of political competition resulted in the relatively technocratic constitution of the DLIC, ensuring that selection of LEAP communities largely conformed to the indicators outlined in the LEAP manual.

In the politically dominant Assin South in Central region, the DLIC was constituted according to the guidelines and avoided inclusion of political figures. Committee members included heads of the decentralized directorates of Planning, Information, Education, Health, and Social Welfare, as well as the representative of a local non-governmental organization.[16] Interviews with bureaucrats showed that whereas the NDC-appointed District Chief Executive occasionally participated in the deliberations of the DLIC, the NPP MP was not directly consulted.[17] NPP electoral dominance meant there was relatively little incentive to intervene in the community targeting process and, as a result, the poverty indicators outlined in the LEAP manual featured strongly in community selection. According to the senior planning bureaucrat who also served on the DLIC,

> we looked at the vulnerability of these communities. We used the poverty profiles of communities in the district and selected communities that had history of vulnerability with more aged people who were taking care of orphans and those with more persons with disability in their households.
>
> (Int. respondent ASBT04, male, 6 years at District Assembly)

Indeed, respondents identified the lack of political competition as a key factor in this process. Significantly, NPP dominance ensured strong presence of NPP Members in the District Assembly, enabling these Assembly Members to hold the District Chief Executive and other political officials appointed by the NDC national government to account. As the planning officer indicated,

> NDC [District] Chief Executives desisted from manipulating the DLIC because of the dominance of the NPP in the district ... most of the Assembly Members held NPP executive positions and they could accuse the [District] Chief Executives of political bias.
>
> (Int. respondent ASBT04, male, 6 years at District Assembly)

In contrast in 2015, when a centralized system for geographical targeting was introduced, the NDC Chief Executive used his national political connections to change some of the centrally selected communities. This was done ostensibly to ensure balanced coverage of the territories of the two main traditional authorities in the district. Nevertheless, interviews established that the Chief Executive's main motive was to direct the selection to communities that favoured his political ambitions in internal party primaries at the time. Thus, in Assin South, though political dominance generally resulted in community selection following the LEAP guidelines, after 2015, political actors were able to intervene in community selection at times.

A similar situation where political dominance enabled a relatively technocratic composition and functioning of the DLIC was reported in the Wa West district of the Upper West region. Here, the DLIC was mainly made up of departmental heads of various units of the District Assembly, such as planning, health, education, and health insurance.[18] Notwithstanding the presence of technocrats on the committee, the District Chief Executive chaired the committee, while the Social Welfare Director served as the secretary. The MP retained strong influence over the mandate of the committee, although he did not directly serve on the DLIC. As such, geographic targeting progressed from an initially rather opaque process in the initial 2008 selection, to a more transparent and inclusive one by the 2016 programme expansion. In 2008, selection focused on communities along the major trunk roads in the district, without the involvement of the DLIC. However, interviews indicated that in 2016,

> poverty rankings of the communities in the district, rather than political considerations, formed the basis for the selection of LEAP communities. Communities with higher poverty scales were targeted for LEAP.
>
> (Int. respondent WWAM10, male, 12 years as elected political leader)

Further interviews with political elites confirmed the dominance of technocratic considerations. The District Chief Executive and local bureaucrats largely prevented local NDC officials and Assembly Members from intervening in the selection of LEAP communities. Key bureaucrats confirmed the District Chief Executive, who had ambitions of succeeding the four-term NDC MP, wanted to be seen as 'a father for all' and so decided to promote a fairer selection of the communities.[19] The Chief Executive tasked the DLIC to propose a list of potential communities, ensuring that as much as possible, the poor would benefit from LEAP.[20] The former leader of the General Assembly of the District Assembly, confirmed the more technocratic selection in 2016 and revealed that

> we found out later that some of the communities the DLIC selected had never voted for the ruling NDC party. Yet we had to maintain them [these communities] and include them on the list of LEAP communities. Some party officials

> requested that the 'NPP' communities had to be changed and replaced with other communities known for voting for the NDC in previous elections. But the Chief Executive insisted that as much as possible, constituency party executives should stay off the LEAP community targeting process.
>
> (Int. respondent WWAM10, male, 12 years as elected political leader)

As such, the constitution and operation of the DLIC in these two politically dominant districts was relatively technocratic, in line with programme guidelines. Nevertheless, NDC control of the central government at the time of fieldwork and locally through the NDC MP in Wa West enabled the MP to retain some influence over the District Assembly, the District Chief Executive, and the DLIC. This is in contrast to the NPP-dominated Assin South where the NPP MP was sidelined by the NDC-appointed District Chief Executive.

The politically competitive Gomoa West and Sissala East districts

In contrast, in Gomoa West and Sissala East districts, intense political competition among key political and social actors provided incentives for political involvement in the DLIC and an extremely partial selection of LEAP communities, diverging from the guidelines set out in the LEAP manual.

In the Gomoa West district, Central region, the committee of technocrats outlined in the LEAP manual did not and never had existed.[21] Rather, key political actors such as the District Chief Executive, ruling party executives, and elected Assembly Members aligned with the ruling party had responsibility for managing LEAP.[22] The result was that competitive pressures within and between parties strongly shaped community selection, with influential persons within the then ruling NDC, rather than technocrats, seizing control of the process.[23] Interviews with a senior Social Welfare bureaucrat revealed that

> the NDC Chief Executive, NDC Member of Parliament, and NDC constituency party executives targeted communities that mainly favoured the NDC and had previously voted NDC rather than the NPP.
>
> (Int. respondent GWBT02, female, 10 years as SWCDO official)

Importantly, even after the central application of geographic targeting from 2015, the intensity of local political competition ahead of the parliamentary primaries resulted in local party figures utilizing their national networks to alter the centrally selected LEAP communities. The primary was contested by the incumbent NDC MP, the NDC District Chief Executive, and a ruling NDC party financier. Interviews with local Social Welfare officials showed that the then District Chief Executive, who drew much of his support from the coastal belt of the district, attempted—unsuccessfully—to direct LEAP to communities that supported his parliamentary candidacy by using his control of resources to court influential Assembly Members to his faction.[24] Meanwhile, the NDC MP was more successful in altering the centrally selected LEAP communities to those that favoured his re-election by enlisting the support of the Minister of Gender, Children, and Social Protection.[25] According to the senior Social Welfare bureaucrat,

> the NDC Member of Parliament went to the extent of visiting the then Social Protection Minister. The Minister had to call me [Social Welfare official] at one point … to go ahead and work in the communities that the Member of Parliament was agitating to add to the LEAP communities in the district.
>
> (Int. respondent GWBT01, male, 6 years in SWCDO)

Reflecting the intensity of competition surrounding geographical targeting, the former District Chief Executive admitted that

> the choice of LEAP communities and other social services always brings confusion between the Member of Parliament and the District Chief Executive … the Member of Parliament wants the communities to go one way or the other, District Chief Executive wants others to go this way, leading to divisions and conflicts in the district.
>
> (Int. respondent GWAM02, male, 8 years as political leader)

Thus, in Gomoa West, political involvement in the district LEAP committee and the politicized application of community targeting procedures resulted in greater partiality, despite the introduction of reforms to centralize control.

Equally, in the competitive Sissala East district in Upper West, the nature of political competition shaped the formation of the DLIC and greater partiality in geographic selection, contrary to the LEAP manual. According to one Social Welfare official,

> political actors at the district rather than technocrats dominated the DLIC … the District Chief Executive and few politically connected members of the District Assembly, and constituency executives of the ruling NDC party associated with the District Chief Executive's faction made decisions about LEAP.
>
> (Int. respondent SSBT01, male, 12 years as SWCDO official)

Interviews with top bureaucrats[26] and social elites[27] indicated that prior to the 2015 reforms, the then ruling NDC District Chief Executive, along with party officials, dominated geographic targeting, excluding local Social Welfare bureaucrats.[28] As an Assembly Member affirmed,

> once the political head decides on LEAP communities, it is captured at the Social Welfare office and at the General Assembly and it is extremely difficult for anyone to change the names of communities once the list is made public.
>
> (Int. respondent SSAM09)

The result of this political prioritization was that many of the poorest communities were excluded from LEAP.[29] An interview with a senior Social Welfare official affirmed that

> LEAP was given to communities that provided 100 per cent to the ruling NDC party and party candidates in internal party primaries.
>
> (Int. respondent SSBT04, female, 6 years at District Assembly)

Even after 2015, local party officials in Sissala East maintained control of the geographic targeting process. Rather than working with the list of communities selected by the national LEAP Management Secretariat, local party officials composed a list that was sent to the Secretariat by the influential NDC MP, who was formerly the District Chief Executive. Senior ruling party functionaries in the district reported that the selection of LEAP communities reignited a conflict within the ruling NDC between the District Chief Executive, MP, and constituency party chairperson.[30] The then District Chief Executive who wanted to contest the internal party parliamentary primaries attempted to use allocation of LEAP and other social services to secure the support of communities. This put the District Chief Executive in conflict with the incumbent MP who contended that LEAP allocations to the district had resulted from her lobbying efforts at the national level.[31] The result was that internal party competition spawned conflicts over distribution of resources, including LEAP, undermining the impartiality of geographic targeting.

In sum, the nature of local political competition across the four districts was an important factor shaping the degree of political involvement in administrative structures and, consequently, the geographical targeting of LEAP communities. In Gomoa West and Sissala East, intense electoral competition led politicians to insert themselves into what are formally technocratic decision-making processes, leading to the allocation of LEAP places as a means of rewarding loyal communities and vehicles to reward party loyalists. Indeed, in the two competitive districts, the ties and personal connections of local political officials with influential national government 'godfathers' were sufficient to circumvent the 2015 reforms which aimed to centralize technocratic control over geographic targeting. In contrast, in the dominant districts of Wa West and Assin South, the lack of political competition meant that there was limited incentive for local politicians to use LEAP in this way and LEAP administration remained relatively technocratic.

5. Political competition and household targeting

Targeting of LEAP households within communities follows a two-step process: community-based targeting and a proxy means test. In the first step, potentially eligible households are identified by members of the CLIC or Community Focal Persons based on indicators such as the presence of extremely poor members who are elderly (over 65 years old), disabled, or caring for orphans and vulnerable children. In the second step, enumerators administer a standard questionnaire to all initially selected households, verifying their eligibility using a proxy means test (MMYE, 2007). The 2015 reforms sought to re-centralize the enumeration process and proxy means test, which were contracted to a private company, bypassing the district administration.[32] As with geographic targeting, the degree of local political competition was an important influence on the degree of impartiality in this selection process.

The politically dominant Assin South and Wa West districts

In the NPP-dominant Assin South in Central region, despite the largely technocratic geographic targeting process at district level, household targeting within communities was more influenced by political factors. Before 2015, the CLIC was made up of unit committee members, representatives of traditional authorities, and local ruling party leaders. The prominence of these political actors was a clear departure from the initially more technocratic arrangement at the district level.[33] Interviews with various community actors revealed that before 2015, CLIC members selected LEAP households following two steps. First, households had to meet the basic poverty indicators set out by the LEAP Management Secretariat.[34] Second, eligible households had to prove their strong association with local traditional leadership, a member of the CLIC's family or the NDC at local level.[35] As a senior Social Welfare bureaucrat affirmed,

> CLICs selected their family members and households that were close to them though they were poor households ... They also overlooked other poor eligible households due to their personal problems with those households.
>
> (Int. respondent ASBT04, male, 6 years at District Assembly)

Beyond the desire of CLIC members to enrol their family and or party members, traditional leaders also clamoured to enrol their close family relations. Interviews with traditional leaders showed enrolling family members relieved them of the burden of having to provide for them.[36] Hence, in the pre-reform period in Assin South, though LEAP households met the minimum programme criteria, they were also required to tick the box of being associated with members of the CLICs, traditional leaders, or NDC party executives.

After 2015, these powerful local actors were able to maintain their influence over the targeting, despite the objectives of the revised process. The newly appointed Community Focal Persons (who were mainly representatives of traditional leaders or local NDC party executives), working together with some former CLIC members, continued to compose their own lists of eligible households and presented these individuals for assessment. By taking this initiative, the former CLICs and the Community Focal Persons bypassed the constraints of the new centralized process by ensuring that only favoured households were presented for assessment by the independent enumerators.[37] According to a senior Social Welfare bureaucrat,

> during the sensitization on the LEAP instead of the CLICs or focal persons letting everybody come around, you see that some few people will come around and the few people coming are all from one [the ruling] party ... the community focal persons try to ascertain the political affiliation of all persons that present themselves for enumeration.
>
> (Int. respondent ASBT01, male, 10 years as SWCDO official)

Local committee members in Assin South therefore intervened to restrict access to the proxy means test to persons associated with members of the CLICs, traditional leaders or ruling party executives. This circumvented the 2015 reforms and maintained local political influence over household targeting.

In the NDC-dominant Wa West in Upper West, household targeting at the time of fieldwork was more consistent with LEAP guidelines. In the initial 2008 selection, however, household targeting had been quite problematic. This was largely the result of misalignment between the NPP government at national level, which launched the LEAP programme in 2008, and the dominance of the NDC in the district. In this context, local representatives of the NPP central government attempted to use the programme to reward its weak political support base in the district.[38] Interviews revealed that

> in the 2008 household targeting, majority of the beneficiaries were widows and widowers in the NPP communities ... they were subsequently enrolled on the programme without any assessment.
>
> (Int. respondent WWCL21, male, former CLIC member)

At the time of fieldwork, when there was alignment between the national NDC government and NDC dominance in the district, discussions with senior Social Welfare bureaucrats indicated that the DLIC had picked local bureaucrats such as health volunteers and school inspectors to serve as Community Focal Persons in each community, replacing non-performing CLIC members.[39] The Community Focal Persons in each community worked with volunteers drawn from a variety of ethnic groups in order to avoid dominance by any one, in addition to representatives of faith-based organizations who assisted in the implementation of LEAP protocols.[40] The result was that in the 2016 expansion of LEAP, the NDC political figures in the district—the MP, District Chief Executive, local community executives, and Assembly Members—collaborated to ensure that Community Focal Persons and local Social Welfare bureaucrats followed LEAP targeting guidelines with minimal interference from the party's foot soldiers. The support of the District Chief Executive and MP for impartial application of the guidelines enabled bureaucrats to stand up to local party foot soldiers who sought to influence the selection process. Consequently, whenever footsoldiers or party executives complained to the District Chief Executive or MP about bureaucrats' unwillingness to grant preferential access for party members, they were scolded and told to leave bureaucrats to focus on their work.[41]

The politically competitive Gomoa West and Sissala East districts

As with the geographic targeting process, intense political competition in Gomoa West and Sissala East undermined the impartiality of household targeting. In Gomoa West in the Central region, just as the DLIC was heavily politicized, at the community level, CLICs acted as an extension of the NDC party.[42] Consequently, local party executives including chairpersons, secretaries, and women organizers automatically became members of the CLIC.[43] Assembly Members and traditional leaders aligned to the NDC also appointed persons favourable to the interest of the NDC party as members of CLICs.[44]

The result was that before 2015, CLIC members, who were mainly NDC party foot soldiers aligned to the District Chief Executive, enrolled old and vulnerable party members on LEAP. This was done to demonstrate the 'caring' nature of the ruling party for its loyal party members.[45] An Assembly Member reported that

> in this district LEAP is political, and we channelled the LEAP through the party people.
>
> (Int. respondent GWAM15, male, 8 years as Assembly Member)

Subsequently, local ruling party executives often required evidence of commitment of either the household in question or persons associated with that household to the party before they would be considered for targeting. In addition, traditional authorities aligned to the ruling party jostled with their Assembly Member counterparts to promote the inclusion of their dependants on the programme. Discussions with bureaucrats indicated that these local traditional leaders sought to enrol their close family to reduce their dependency on these leaders.[46]

Even after the 2015 reforms, local party officials went to the selected LEAP communities and noted the voter identity card numbers and party card numbers of the potential households prior to the arrival of the independent enumerators.[47]

Party foot soldiers indicated that this pre-registration constituted a critical 'sieving' process,[48] with the result that non-party persons who felt they were eligible could not avail themselves at the community LEAP assessment centres.[49] Moreover, NDC actors in the CLICs and NDC-affiliated Assembly Members undertook extensive coaching of persons and household heads prior to the enumeration and proxy means test. As the former NDC District Chief Executive suggested,

> with these poor people if you do not coach them, they will give responses that will lead to their disadvantage [disqualification], so you always have to be coaching them on the best responses to qualify them for the programme.
>
> (Int. respondent GWAM02, male, 8 years as appointed political leader)

It was thus not surprising when the ruling party aligned Assembly Member concluded that

> those who were strong and connected got the LEAP. The poor persons did not qualify for LEAP. Those who were most vulnerable could not be assessed for LEAP.
>
> (Int. respondent GWAM17, male, 12 years as Assembly Member)

Likewise, in the competitive Sissala East district in Upper West, politically connected actors heavily influenced household targeting. Discussions with various community leaders revealed that CLICs were made up of political actors in LEAP communities rather than the health and education service workers and volunteers, as required by the LEAP manual.[50] Most of these individuals held various party political positions at the polling station level.[51] NDC constituency executives and foot soldiers, who doubled as CLIC members, ensured that their preferred households got enrolled.[52] Discussions with local community actors revealed that before 2015, the District Chief Executive visited communities and directly participated in household targeting. Bureaucrats and Assembly Members reported that the District Chief Executive personally promised to facilitate increases in the local coverage of LEAP once she was elected MP in 2012.[53] An Assembly Member affirmed that

> the ruling party District Chief Executive handpicked beneficiary households based on her perception of their political influence in society. If they realized that you are an influential party member and that you have the capacity to influence people to do the voting, they will come and select you. This led to the vulnerable persons losing out in the selection of the programme.
>
> (Int. respondent SSAM04, male, 12 years as Assembly Member and political leader)

Even after the 2015 reforms, senior bureaucrats showed that the targeting process followed a similar pattern to before. An Assembly Member affirmed that

> CLIC members selected potential beneficiaries from only registered NDC party members and unqualified persons.
>
> (Int. respondent SSBT02; SSAM12; SSTA02)

In addition, bureaucrats revealed that locally appointed enumerators rather than field officers of the independently appointed enumeration company were used, further undermining the targeting process.[54] Instead of assessing whole households for eligibility, they assessed more than one person from the same household. This resulted in the over-sampling of participants from some favoured communities to the neglect of other poorer localities. As an Assembly Member affirmed,

> in Bendei and Vamboi, for instance, husbands, wives, and their dependent children were assessed and registered separately. So, each person could receive LEAP individually, leaving other vulnerable households within the selected LEAP communities grossly under-represented.
>
> (Int. respondent SSAM04, male, 12 years at District Assembly and also political leader)

Moreover, local enumerators, in collaboration with local NDC party executives, coached party members on the best responses to the assessment questionnaires.[55] Interviews with a Social Welfare bureaucrat suggested that

> the party leaders coached the selected members to ensure that their responses portrayed them as ultra-poor and vulnerable members and eligible for LEAP. For the most part these persons were traders in the market and others also had their own farms. So, they prepared them on the best responses to qualify them for the programme.
>
> (Int. respondent SSBT02, female, 4 years at District Assembly)

Thus, though political involvement in household targeting was present to some degree in all four sites, there was a greater degree of manipulation in the politically competitive Gomoa West and Sissala East districts than the politically dominant ones. In the politically dominant Wa West district, local politicians used their political influence to create a buffer for bureaucrats to conduct household targeting for the 2016 expansion of the programme based on the established guidelines. The link between political dominance and impartial targeting was less clear in Assin South, however. Here, while the NPP is locally dominant, NDC representatives of the national government interfered in household targeting to ensure that participants not only met LEAP criteria but were also connected to CLIC members, traditional leaders or the NDC party.

6. Conclusion

This chapter has shown that, broadly in line with initial expectations, the distribution of LEAP in Ghana is shaped by sub-national variation in both state infrastructural power and political competition. The division between a relatively strong state in southern Ghana and comparatively weak infrastructural power in the north of the country has roots in the colonial era, while successive post-independence governments have reinforced this division. The analysis above shows that this legacy of past processes of state formation has enduring impacts on the distribution of LEAP, with the lack of physical infrastructure and human resources in the Upper West region posing challenges to effective targeting of the programme. These limits to state infrastructural power have only been exacerbated with the introduction of increasingly technology-intensive targeting and disbursement systems that expose the weakness in transport and telecommunications infrastructure. Consequently, vulnerable people in remote communities are excluded from the programme.

While important, the impact of state infrastructural power on targeting pales into insignificance compared with the influence of political competition. As shown in the preceding analysis, there are clear differences in the application of geographic and household targeting processes between politically dominant and competitive districts. The implementation of LEAP and other social programmes using decentralized state structures has ignited competing pressures among local state officials and societal actors. In politically competitive districts, between party and, often, also within party competition has led political actors to infiltrate LEAP committees and to seek to influence the distribution of transfers with a view to using the programme as a means of building their own political support. While the implementation process was not entirely insulated from political influence in the politically dominant cases, for the most part geographic and, to a degree, household targeting largely conformed to programme guidelines. Where there were problems with targeting in dominant districts, this can be attributed, in part, to misalignment between national and local politics. This was the case in Wa West during the initial rollout of LEAP in 2008 and in Assin South in more recent expansions in 2016, where the locally dominant party was in opposition to the national incumbent. The result was political divisions between the local party and centrally appointed district officials, which led the national ruling party—NPP in Wa West and NDC in Assin South—to seek to influence selection in favour of their weak political base in the districts.

The government, under the guidance of donors, launched a reform of the LEAP targeting process in 2015 with a view to limiting the influence of local political actors by recentralizing control over geographic and household targeting. In many respects, these reforms mirror similar steps taken in Kenya (see Chapter 6). However, unlike in Kenya, the reforms to Ghana's LEAP have done little to insulate the programme from political influence. Regarding geographic targeting, local political leaders in competitive districts exploited connections with powerful national politicians to circumvent central controls on the process. Likewise, local party officials have maintained influence on household targeting, limiting those submitted for evaluation by enumerators to those with political connections and coaching favoured participants on how to answer the survey questions. These findings raise wider questions pertaining to how social transfer programmes and decentralized social services in general might best confront entrenched local political dynamics and whether it is possible to 'reach around' influential local political and social actors. The failure to insulate LEAP from local politics underscores that technical fixes can succeed only where they are aligned with political dynamics.

Notes

1. Int. respondent GWAM11; GWAM06.
2. Int. respondent LMS02; LMS04.
3. Int. respondent ASBT01; ASBT04; GWBT01; GWBT04.
4. Int. respondent WWAM05; SSBT01.
5. Int. respondent ASBT02; ASBT04; ASBT05; GWBT01; GWBT03.
6. Int. respondent WWBT17; WWBT13; WWAM07; SSAM12; SSAM05; SSBT04; SSBT05.
7. Int. respondent ASBT02; ASBT05.
8. Int. respondent ASAM15.
9. Int. respondent ASBT01.
10. Int. respondent GWAM17; GWAM02; GWAM01; GWBT03.
11. Int. respondent WWBT12; WWAM07; SSBT04.
12. Int. respondent WWBT12; WWCL19.
13. Int. respondent SSBT01; WWBT12.
14. Int. respondent SSBT02; WWAM27; WWCL29; WWAM5; WWBT12.
15. Int. respondent WWBT12.
16. Int. respondent ASBT01.
17. Int. respondent ASBT01; ASAM08; ASAM04; ASAM15.
18. Int. respondent WWBT12; WWBT13; WWAM12.
19. Int. respondent WWBT12.
20. Int. respondent WWAM27; WWAM10.
21. Int. respondent GWBT01; GWBT02.

22. Int. respondent GWBT01; GWBT04.
23. Int. respondent GWBT01; GWAM02.
24. Int. respondent GWBT01; GWAM17.
25. Hon. Arthur, MP for Gomoa West served on the following committees during his first term in Parliament (2009–12): Finance, Local Government, and Employment, Social Welfare and State Enterprises. In his second term in Parliament (2012–16), he served on the following committees: Standing Orders Committee and Public Accounts Committee.
26. Int. respondent SSBT01; SSBT02; SSBT04.
27. Int. respondent SSAM14.
28. Int. respondent SSBT04; SSCL05; SSAM02; SSAM05; SSAM12; SSAM04; SSTA01.
29. Int. respondent SSBT04; SSAM14.
30. Alijata had not succeeded in facilitating the appointment of an NDC District Chief Executive allied to her interests against that of the faction of Halutie, the former NDC MP and Minister of State under the NDC administration from 2009 to 2012 (SSBT02; SSBT05; SSAM05).
31. Int. respondent SSAM01; SSAM09; SSAM12.
32. Int. respondent LMS01; LMS02.
33. Int. respondent ASAM04; ASAM08; ASAM07; ASBT02; ASBT01.
34. Int. respondent ASBT01.
35. Int. respondent ASBT01.
36. Int. respondent ASBT04.
37. Int. respondent ASBT01.
38. Int. respondent WWCL21; WWAM10; WWFGD02; WWCL13.
39. Int. respondent WWBT12.
40. Int. respondent WWBT13.
41. Int. respondent WWCL23.
42. Int. respondent GWCL08; GWCL09.
43. Int. respondent GWAM12.
44. Int. respondent GWBT01; GWAM14.
45. Int. respondent GWBT01; GWAM02.
46. Int. respondent GWTA03; GWTA01.
47. Int. respondent GWAM13; GWBT01.
48. Int. respondent GWFGD01; GWFGD03.
49. Int. respondent GWAM18; GWAM17; GWCL08; GWAM15; GWFGD01; GWFGD03.
50. Int. respondent SSCL05; SSCL06; SSCL03; SSCL04.
51. Int. respondent SSAM10; SSAM09; SSAM13; SSAM02; SSAM12.
52. Int. respondent SSAM06; SSAM10; SSAM12; SSAM14.
53. Int. respondent SSAM02; SSAM06; SSAM12; SSBT02.
54. Local language challenges in the Sissala area undermined the ability of independent enumerators to undertake the assessment of potential LEAP households (Int. respondent SSBT02; SSBT01).
55. Int. respondent SSBT02; SSBT01.

References

Abdulai, A.-G., 2020. Competitive clientelism, donors and the politics of social protection uptake in Ghana. *Critical Social Policy*, https://doi.org/10.1177/0261018320945605

Abdulai, A.-G. and Hickey, S., 2016. The politics of development under competitive clientelism: Insights from Ghana's education sector. *African Affairs*, 115 (458), 44–72. https://doi.org/10.1093/afraf/adv071

Ablo, M., 2018. *Policy, Legislation and Coordination in Social Protection*. Retrieved from https://spc.socialprotection.or.ke/images/downloads/presentations/Mawutor-Ablo-Policy-Legislation-and-Coordination-in-Social-Protection.pdf(accessed 2019-01-25).

Alam, M. and Koranteng, R., 2011. *Decentralisation in Ghana: Papers Presented at Workshops Held at GIMPA, Ghana from 2007–2010*. London: Commonwealth Secretariat.

Angeles, G., Chakrabarti, A., Handa, S., Spektor, G., Osei, R. D., Osei-Akoto, I., and De Groot, R., 2017. *Livelihood Empowerment Against Poverty Programme Endline Impact Evaluation Report*.

ASDA. 2018a. *Assin South District Assembly: Annual Progress Report 2017*. Accra.

Atiemo, A. O., 2015. Religion and custom are not the same: Sacred traditional states and religious human rights in contemporary Ghana. *Law and Religion in Africa: The Quest for the Common Good in Pluralistic Societies*, 35 (4), 157–172.

Awortwi, N., 2010. The past, present, and future of decentralisation in Africa: A comparative case study of local government development trajectories of Ghana and Uganda. *International Journal of Public Administration*, 33 (12), 620–634. https://doi.org/10.1080/01900692.2010.514451

Ayala, F., 2010. For Protection and Promotion: The Design and Implementation of Effective Social Safety Nets. Retrieved from http://siteresources.worldbank.org/SAFETYNETSANDTRANSFERS/Resources/281945-1131468287118/1876750-1282583453267/Ayala_Ghana_case_2nd-Session_12-9-2010.pdf (accessed 29-11-2016).

Bob-Milliar, G. M., 2012. Party factions and power blocs in Ghana: A case study of power politics in the National Democratic Congress. *Journal of Modern African Studies*, 50 (4), 573–601. https://doi.org/10.1017/S0022278X12000481

Bob-Milliar, G. M., 2014. Party youth activists and low-intensity electoral violence in Ghana: A qualitative study of party foot soldiers' activism. *African Studies Quarterly*, 15 (1). https://doi.org/10.1191/1478088706qp063oa

Bob-Milliar, G. M. and Paller, J. W., 2018. Democratic ruptures and electoral outcomes in Africa: Ghana's 2016 election. *Africa Spectrum*, 53 (1), 5–35. https://doi.org/10.1177/000203971805300102

Carbone, G., 2011. Democratic demands and social policies: The politics of health reform in Ghana. *Journal of Modern African Studies*, 49 (3), 381–408. https://doi.org/10.1017/S0022278X11000255

Clark, G. 1990. Class Alliance and Class Fractions in Ghanaian Trading and State Formation. *Review of African Political Economy, Democracy* (49), 73–82.

Crawford, G., 2004. Democratic decentralisation in Ghana: Issues and prospects. *POLIS Working Papers*, 9 (9), 1–23.

Crook, R., 1999. 'No-party' politics and local democracy in Africa: Rawlings' Ghana in the 1990s and the 'Ugandan model'. *Democratization*, 6 (4), 114–138. https://doi.org/10.1080/13510349908403635

De Groot, R., Handa, S., Park, M., Osei Darko, R., Osei-Akoto, I., Bhalla, G., and Ragno, L. P., 2015. Heterogeneous Impacts of an Unconditional Cash Transfer Programme on Schooling: Evidence from the Ghana LEAP Programme *(No. 10)*. Retrieved from https://www.unicef-irc.org/publications/pdf/iwp_2015_10.pdf (accessed 2016-12-27).

Debrah, E., 2016. Decentralization, District Chief Executives, and District Assemblies in Ghana's Fourth Republic. *Politics and Policy*, 44 (1), 135–164. https://doi.org/10.1111/polp.12146

Gbedemah, C., Jones, N., and Pereznieto, P. 2010. Gendered risks, poverty and vulnerability in Ghana: Is the LEAP cash transfer programme making a difference? *ODI Project Briefings*, 52.

Ghana Statistical Service. 2018. *Poverty Trends in Ghana (2005–2017)*. Accra.

Ghana Statistical Service, 2014a. *Assin South Report: District Analytical Report*. Accra.

Ghana Statistical Service, 2014b. *Gomoa West Report: District Analytical Report*. Accra.

Ghana Statistical Service, 2014c. *Sissala East: District Analytical Report*. Accra.

Ghana Statistical Service, 2014d. *Wa West: District Analytical Report*. Accra.

GWDA. 2018. *Gomoa West District Assembly Report*. Accra

Gyimah-Boadi, E., 2009. Another Step Forward for Ghana. *Journal of Democracy*, 20 (2), 138–152. https://doi.org/10.1353/jod.0.0065

Hamel, R. and Flowers, K., 2018. Lessons from Ghana: A Role for Social Protection Investments to Support Food and Nutrition Security. Retrieved from www.csis.org (accessed 2019-01-25).

Hymer, S. H., 1970. Economic forms in pre-colonial Ghana. *Journal of Economic History*, 30 (1), 33–50. https://doi.org/10.1017/S0022050700078578

Jockers, H., Kohnert, D., and Nugent, P., 2010. The successful Ghana election of 2008: A convenient myth? *Journal of Modern African Studies*, 48 (1), 95–115. https://doi.org/10.1017/S0022278X09990231

Konadu-Agyemang, K., 2000. The best of times and the worst of times: Structural adjustment programs and uneven development in Africa—The case of Ghana. *Professional Geographer*, 52 (3), 469–483. https://doi.org/10.1111/0033-0124.00239

Ladouceur, P. A., 1973. Regionalism and Political Development in Northern Ghana: A Study of the Political Effects of Social and Economic Disparities (University of Sussex). https://doi.org/10.1017/CBO9781107415324.004 (accessed 2020-07-19).

Lentz, C., 2006. *Ethnicity and the Making of history in Northern Ghana*. Edinburgh: Edinburgh University Press.

MMYE, 2007. *Livelihood Empowerment against Poverty (LEAP) Social Grants Pilot Implementation Design*. Accra: Ministry of Manpower, Youth and Employment.

MoGCSP, 2015. *National Social Protection Policy Final Draft*. Accra: Ministry of Gender, Children and Social Protection.

Mohan, G., 2002. The disappointments of civil society: The politics of NGO intervention in northern Ghana. *Political Geography*, 21 (1), 125–154. https://doi.org/10.1016/S0962-6298(01)00072-5

Morrison, M. K. C., 2004. Political parties in Ghana through four republics: A path to democratic consolidation. *Comparative Politics*, 36 (4), 421–442. https://doi.org/10.2307/4150169

Niyuni, W., 2016. Linking Social Protection Programmes in Ghana: The Case of the LEAP Cash Transfer Programme. Retrieved from https://www.h-brs.de/files/paper9_niyuni_web.pdf (accessed 2016-12-27).

Oduro, F., Awal, M., and Ashon, M., 2014. *A dynamic mapping of the political settlement in Ghana*. Retrieved from https://papers.ssrn.com/sol3/papers.cfm?abstract_id=2386788 (accessed 2017-10-19).

Ofei-Aboagye, E., 2018. Emerging Issues in Decentralization and Local Governance. Accra: Unpublished work.

Osei, R. D., 2011. Reducing Poverty through *a* Social Grants Program: The Case of Ghana. Retrieved from https://web.worldbank.org/archive/website01589/WEB/IMAGES/PARALLE_.PDF (accessed 2016-12-16).

Plange, N. K., 1984. The colonial state in northern Ghana: The political economy of pacification. *Review of African Political Economy*, 11 (31), 29–43. https://doi.org/10.1080/03056248408703598

Prempeh, H. K. and Kroon, C., 2012. *The Political Economy Analysis of the Oil and Gas Sector in Ghana: The Implications for STAR-Ghana*. Accra: STAR-Ghana.

SEDA. 2018. *Sissala East District Assembly: Composite Budget For 2017–2019 Programme Based Budget Estimates*. Accra

Shepherd, A., Gyimah-boadi, E., Gariba, S., Plagerson, S., and Musa, A. W., 2004. Bridging the north south divide in Ghana: Draft Summary. In *Equity and Development: World Development Report 2006*. Washington, DC: World Bank.

UNDP, Ghana, 2018. *Northern Ghana Human Development Report 2018*. Accra: United Nations Development Programme, Ghana. (accessed 2020-12-16).

Vanderpuye-Orgle, J., 2004. Poverty, spatial inequality and polarization: A multi-faceted analysis of the impact of economic reform in Ghana. Master of Science thesis. Cornell University.

WWDA. 2016. *Wa West District Assembly: Annual Progress Report 2016*. Wa.

Whitfield, L., 2011. Competitive clientelism, easy financing and weak capitalists: The contemporary political settlement in Ghana. DIIS Working Papers, 27.

Wodon, Q., 2012. *Improving the Targeting of Social Programs in Ghana*. The World Bank. Washington DC.

World Bank, 2016. *Ghana: Social Protection Assessment and Public Expenditure Review*. Retrieved from http://documents.worldbank.org/curated/en/776791491300371576/pdf/114004-revised-Ghana-SP-report-Draft-for-public-disclosure.pdf (accessed 2018-12-18).

World Bank, 2018. *Ghana Priorities for Ending Poverty and Boosting Shared Prosperity*. The World Bank, Washington DC. https://doi.org/10.1596/30974 (accessed 2019-01-25).

Zakaria, H. B., 2013. *Looking Back, Moving Forward: Towards Improving Local Governments' Performance in Ghana*. Retrieved from http://www.austlii.edu.au/au/journals/ComJlLocGov/2013/14.pdf (accessed 2017-10-04).

6

The Distributional Politics of Social Transfers in Kenya

Alesha Porisky

1. Introduction

Kenya was a relatively early adopter of social transfers in Africa, with its first pilot programme—the Cash Transfer for Orphans and Vulnerable Children (CT-OVC)—introduced by the United Nations International Children's Emergency Fund (UNICEF) and the government in 2004.[1] The CT-OVC was followed by government-funded and implemented social transfer programmes for vulnerable Older Persons (OPCT) and Persons with Severe Disabilities (PWSD-CT). These programmes all provide targeted bimonthly unconditional monetary transfers to vulnerable populations and operate nationwide, while a fourth targeted programme, the Hunger Safety Net Programme (HSNP), operates only in the northern counties. In Kenya's highly competitive electoral environment, the government has focused on the broad expansion of these social transfer programmes as a highly visible means of distribution (Porisky *n.d.*). The latest government initiative takes these efforts a step further with the adoption of the Inua Jamii pension in 2017/18 that provides unconditional transfers to everyone aged 70 and above not receiving a pension or another social transfer.

Observers have raised concerns that social transfers implemented in competitive electoral environments may be prone to politicization, as political actors seek to distribute social transfers in ways that build popular support (Driscoll 2018). Indeed, the involvement of Members of Parliament (MPs) in Constituency Social Assistance Committees has led some scholars to argue that social transfers in Kenya have been 'successfully co-opted' by MPs to serve as a 'constituency-level patronage resource' (Wanyama and McCord 2017, p. 22; see also Wanyama and Nyambedha 2017). In contrast, studies from other world regions have demonstrated that it is possible to limit the political manipulation of social transfers, even in countries with long histories of patronage politics, if there is 'solid ministerial commitment, thoughtful policy design and strong technocratic capacity'

Alesha Porisky, *The Distributional Politics of Social Transfers in Kenya.* In: *The Politics of Distributing Social Transfers.* Edited by Tom Lavers, Oxford University Press. © Oxford University Press (2022).
DOI: 10.1093/oso/9780192862525.003.0006

(Sugiyama and Hunter 2013, 43–44). To date, there has been limited empirical work on how social transfers are delivered at the local level in Kenya, with the exception of Kramon's (2019) findings that the formal guidelines for programme implementation limit the ability of politicians to influence and claim credit for distribution. This chapter contributes to the burgeoning literature on the distributive politics of social transfers, emphasizing that policy implementation is not simply a top-down administrative process that uniformly follows official rules and guidelines, but a highly political negotiation involving both state and societal actors (Migdal 2001; Paudel 2009).

The chapter focuses primarily on two social transfer programmes, the CT-OVC and OPCT, the two largest programmes with national coverage, with some attention to the recently introduced Inua Jamii pension, which will eventually replace the OPCT.[2] While the implementation of social transfers encompasses a range of activities, this chapter primarily focuses on targeting and registration. The chapter employs case studies of four diverse counties across Kenya, which vary in their levels of political competition and their historic incorporation into the central state. In each county, researchers conducted 45 key informant interviews with government officials, local and customary authorities, political appointees, members of social transfer committees and health workers, as well as 16 focus group discussions with both beneficiaries and non-beneficiaries of the CT-OVC and OPCT.

The chapter presents two key findings. First, variations in state infrastructural power impact bureaucratic adherence to rules and implementation guidelines. In areas where there is more central state oversight, greater access to human, material, and financial resources, and where the state has a greater territorial reach and is more embedded within the society, implementation of social transfers closely follows official guidelines. However, where state capacity and oversight are relatively limited, local authorities compensate for weak state infrastructural power and thus play a more prominent role in implementation. The second key finding is that state patronage and party politics are less prominent in the distribution of social transfers than has been predicted by existing literature. While MPs frequently claim credit for the expansion of social transfers in their constituencies, they are rarely able to impact the allocation of social transfers to locations or households in practice.

The chapter proceeds in Section 2 with an overview of the historic foundations of state formation in Kenya, and a justification of case selection. Section 3 provides an overview of the targeting procedures in the social transfer programmes, while Section 4 explores the variations in state infrastructural power across the four cases. Section 5 then analyses how these variations have shaped the targeting of social transfers in the selected cases, before Section 6 concludes.

2. Patterns of state formation in Kenya

In Kenya, legacies of colonialism and state formation have had lasting impacts on the balance of political power, incorporation into the central state, and variations in state infrastructural power. The result is that state infrastructural power and party-political allegiances vary markedly across the country.

In the Rift Valley, removal of indigenous populations to allow white settlers to access the fertile highlands during the colonial period resulted in overcrowding in 'native reserves' and an influx of migrants, frequently of Kikuyu ethnicity, in search of agricultural work. After independence, the ruling Kenya African National Union (KANU) supported the resettlement of ethnic Kikuyu into the Rift Valley as white settlers departed. However, the shifting balance of power in national politics between the Kikuyu, Luo, and Kalenjin has had major ramifications for the treatment of these 'indigenous' and 'outsider' populations in the Rift Valley, leading to inter-ethnic conflict over land, one of the main causes of electoral violence in 2007–8 (Kanyinga 2009; Boone 2012).

In contrast, a long history of marginalization from the central state resulted in relatively low levels of state infrastructural power and state legitimacy in arid pastoralist areas of northern Kenya (Achiba 2019, p. 5). The colonial government saw pastoralism as 'primitive, backward and to be discouraged', implementing policies that impeded mobility and limited access to common property (Zwanenberg quoted in Amutabi 2015 p. 126). Post-independence governments have maintained retrogressive policies (Waller 2012; Achiba 2019) and, despite recent investment in infrastructure (Kochore 2020), roads, electricity, schools, and health centres remain limited (Arero 2017). The result of this marginalization is that customary systems of local governance, such as clan leaders, are afforded greater importance than in other parts of the country (Schlee 1989; Bassi 2005).

The balance of political power and ethnicity in the post-independence era also have significant ramifications for access to state resources. Colonial divide-and-rule polices resulted in divisions between major ethnic groups, which deepened in the post-colonial era (Branch 2011; Khisa and Oesterdiekhoff 2012). The political elite controls access to state resources, which are distributed to supporters through a network of patron–client relationships that serve as the basis for continued power. Thus, incumbent areas in central Kenya have historically had greater access to state resources and closer ties to the central state, while opposition areas have been marginalized (Hassan 2020b). Political tensions have aggravated ethnic cleavages. Following independence, divisions between the first president, Jomo Kenyatta, and the vice-president, Oginga Odinga, led to Odinga's abdication and later detention. These events contributed to the continued marginalization of Luo Nyanza under Kenyatta and his successor, Daniel arap Moi.

More recently, multi-party elections from 1992 have been highly competitive and closely contested (Lynch 2011; Muhula 2020). In 1992, the government was accused of inciting ethnic violence, which led to an estimated 1,500 dead and 300,000 displaced in the 14 months prior to the election (Human Rights Watch 1993; Mulli 1999; Klopp 2001; Branch 2011). In 2007, post-election violence erupted following the announcement of Kibaki as president, leading to 1,000 deaths and over 500,000 people displaced (Branch 2011; Mueller 2020). These events were underpinned by patterns of political violence structured along ethnic lines, established under Moi's regime (Kanyinga 2009). Ultimately, a power-sharing agreement led by Kibaki was established and a new constitution outlined social, economic, and political rights for all Kenyans and proposed a new devolved political system that would decentralize some power to newly created counties. Implemented in 2013, devolution created an entirely new level of government, with separate executive and legislative powers (Cornell and D'Arcy 2014). While devolution brought some state systems closer to the people, particularly salient for those living in northern Kenya (Bulle and Ombui 2016; Scott-Villiers 2017; Wagana 2017), it also decentralized patronage networks to the local level (D'Arcy and Cornell 2016).

The election of Uhuru Kenyatta in 2013 and his contested re-election in 2017 did little to alter existing networks of clientelism (Wanyama and McCord 2017; Wanyama and Nyambedha 2017). Rather it saw the continuation of a political system that rewards loyal supporters and ethno-regional allies, and provides the incumbent government 'with opportunities to accumulate private resources and (mis)use public ones' (Pommerolle 2020, p. 16). These histories of marginalization and bitterly contested elections, linked to struggles for control over state power and resources, have implications for the implementation of social transfers. The politically driven expansion of social transfers as a means of providing highly visible forms of distribution suggests that the programmes could represent opportunities for the government to gain support during elections.

Case selection

Sub-national cases were selected to include counties with variation in state infrastructural power, levels of ethnic diversity, and party politics (see Table 6.1 and Fig. 6.1). Nyeri county is a stronghold of the current national government and home primarily to inhabitants from the Kikuyu ethnic group. The county lies in the agriculturally rich central highlands where the state possesses a high level of infrastructural power. Nakuru county in the Rift Valley is likewise an area in which state infrastructural power is strong. In contrast to Nyeri, however, it is ethnically diverse, with the largest ethnic communities being the Kikuyu and Kalenjin, and the

Table 6.1 Sub-national case selection in Kenya

		Party politics	
		Stronghold	Contested
State infrastructural power	**High**	Nyeri	*Nakuru*
	Low	Homa Bay	*Marsabit*

Note: Italics indicate counties with high levels of ethnic heterogeneity.
Source: KNBS (2019)

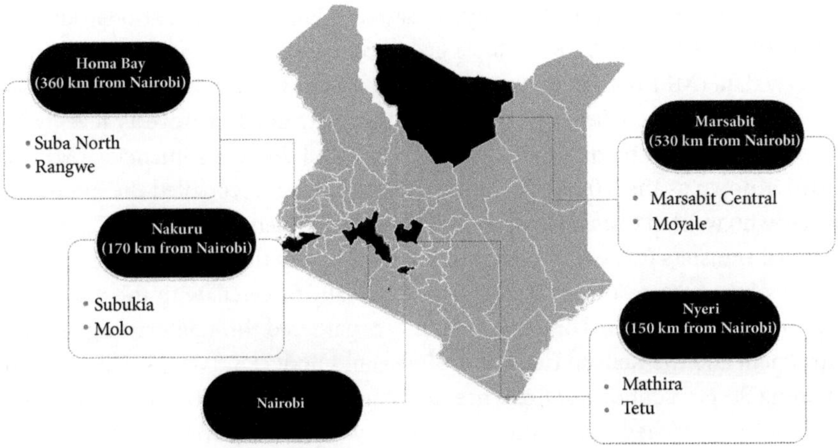

Fig. 6.1 Map of Kenyan case studies
Source: Author, revised from yourfreetemplates.com

county has been hotly contested in national elections. Homa Bay county borders Lake Victoria in western Kenya. It is an opposition stronghold, home primarily to Luo inhabitants. As a result of marginalization under successive political regimes, state infrastructural power is low compared to Nyeri and Nakuru. Finally, Marsabit county is one of four northern counties. It is the largest county in Kenya in terms of land size with a dispersed population, which limits the infrastructural power of the state. Marsabit is also ethnically diverse, with over 14 ethnic communities, and has been highly contested within national political races.

Sub-counties were selected to be representative of each county with respect to state infrastructural power, programme coverage, and duration, using data from the national Management Information System (MIS) and county interviews. Thus, sub-counties with high or low levels of state infrastructural power relative to the county as a whole were excluded, as were sub-counties that were part of pilot programmes.

3. Targeting Kenya's social transfers

Since 2013, all Kenya's social transfer programmes have been coordinated under one umbrella, the National Safety Net Programme, with a new Operations Manual introduced in 2017 to standardize what had been rather diverse implementation structures for the different social transfer programmes. Since 2017, all programmes have, in theory, adopted the same targeting procedures, which comprise four stages: geographic; community-based targeting; a proxy-means test; and community validation.

Programme administration and responsibility for targeting is distributed across the decentralized levels of the Kenyan state (see Fig. 6.2). The national-level Social Assistance Unit (SAU) conducts geographic targeting based on government poverty data (MLEAA 2016). In 2013/14, a decision was made that 70 per cent of the allocation of new beneficiaries would be determined by poverty level, while 30 per cent would be distributed evenly across all 290 constituencies (MLEAA 2016). Known as the '70–30 rule', this political bargain reconciled the interests of MPs—who wanted to ensure coverage of their constituencies—with the expansion of social transfers to areas of high poverty. It stipulates that in any new expansion, 70 per cent of the resources will be geographically targeted, with the SAU determining allocations based on poverty numbers gathered through existing program enrolment and the Kenyan Integrated Household Budget Survey (KHIBS). The remaining 30 per cent of resources are distributed evenly to all constituencies that have not yet reached maximum coverage, regardless of poverty levels, with the

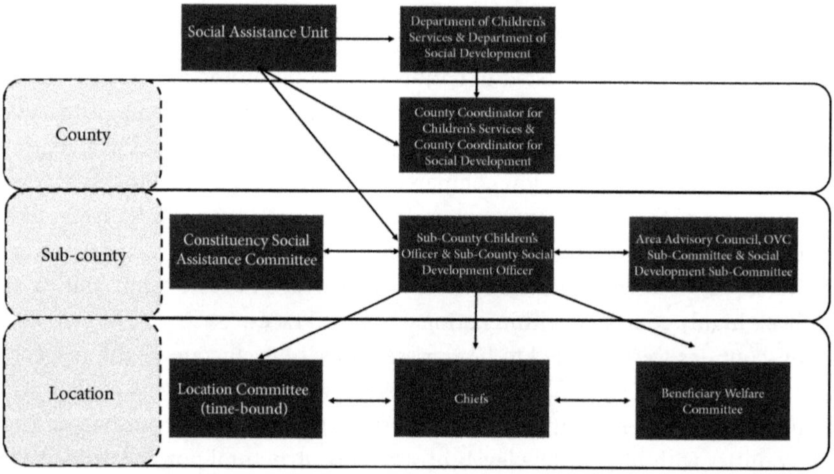

Fig. 6.2 CT-OVC and OPCT administrative structures

Source: Author's representation based on Republic of Kenya (2017) and Government of Kenya (2017).

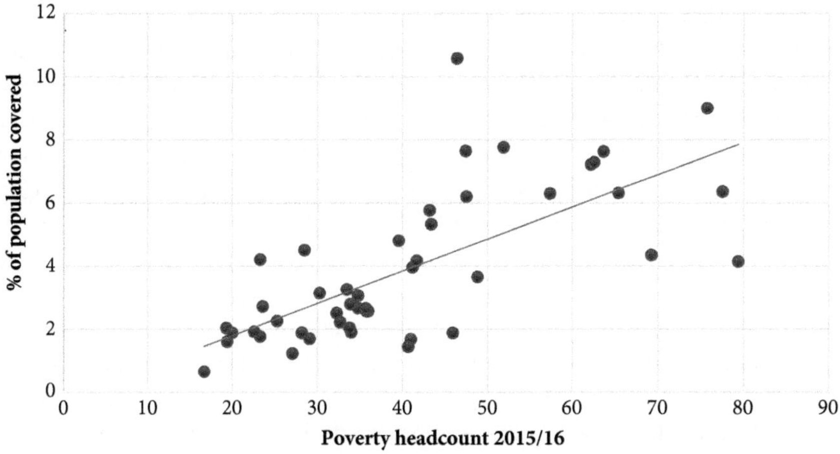

Fig. 6.3 OPCT coverage by county
Source: Author's representation based on Republic of Kenya (2020) and KNBS (2018).

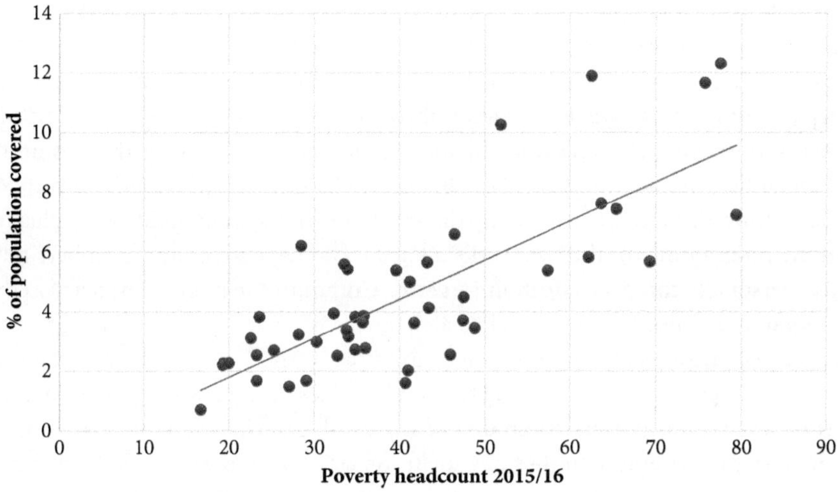

Fig. 6.4 CT-OVC coverage by county
Source: Author's representation based on Republic of Kenya (2020) and KNBS (2018).

SAU generally determining allocations down to the sub-county level. Geographic targeting largely maps onto poverty incidence (Figs 6.3 and 6.4), although northern counties covered by the HSNP have lower coverage of the CT-OVC and OPCT, as households cannot benefit from more than one transfer.

In ethnically heterogeneous counties, the government has sought to use geographical targeting to distribute transfers across ethnic groups. In Nakuru, the history of ethno-political violence created incentives to mobilize state infrastructural power in a fine-grained manner to limit distributional grievances. As such, in areas historically impacted by electoral violence and with high numbers of internally displaced people, the SAU makes geographical targeting decisions right down to the village level. As villages in these areas tend to be ethnically homogeneous, even when locations are ethnically heterogeneous, the SAU allocated numbers to villages based on population, essentially ensuring equitable distribution of the social transfers amongst ethnic groups. In Nakuru, the central state has enough information about local communities to make targeting decisions that are enforceable and viewed as legitimate by beneficiaries and other important local actors. Moreover, there is no opportunity for these numbers to be altered locally. In contrast, in the other ethnically heterogeneous county, Marsabit, the central state lacks the information to make informed decisions about allocations in diffuse pastoral societies and also the legitimacy among local actors to enforce those decisions. The result is that bureaucrats deferred to chiefs and clan leaders to assist with the distribution social transfers within locations, as discussed in Section 5.

The second stage of targeting involves community-based targeting. The new Operations Manual proposes a Location Targeting Committee,[3] comprised of an elected representative from each village in the location, to oversee the process. Targeting procedures begin with sensitization of state officials and committee members, community awareness building through *barazas* (public meetings) within each sub-location and recruitment, and training of Location Targeting Committee members. *Barazas* organized by chiefs and village elders provide the forum for the communities to identify jointly the most vulnerable households for inclusion in the programme. In the two weeks after the *baraza*, community members may also personally contact a Location Targeting Committee member to be listed in the programme. This list of potential participants is provided to the sub-county officers and Constituency Social Action Committee (CSAC) members for review and is posted at churches, schools, and the chiefs' offices for review by the community. After seven days, another community *baraza* will be held, where the community validates the list and identifies any inclusion or exclusion errors. Following this validation process, the list is sent to Nairobi and entered into the MIS.

In the third phase, enumerators—who must be secondary school graduates—are recruited from the community and trained. Enumerators visit all listed households to collect household data, which is subject to a proxy means test (PMT) by the SAU in Nairobi. Using the results of the PMT, potential beneficiary lists for each sub-location are determined per the expansion quota based on the long-list provided by the community. Households with multiple categorical vulnerabilities are given priority. Current rules stipulate that a household can only benefit from one social transfer, and the creation of a single registry for all social transfer recipients has enabled comparison of all participant lists. Finally, in the fourth stage, final beneficiary lists are subject to final community validation.

The main avenue for political involvement in the social transfer programmes has been through the CSACs. CSACs were introduced in 2015 in response to MPs' demands for direct involvement in the programmes. Each CSAC is composed of 15 members, nine of whom are political appointees, and is designed to 'act as a link between the political leaders and the community' (Republic of Kenya 2017, p. 9). The committee's formal roles include participating in validation of potential participants, monitoring targeting procedures, and community awareness raising. Members are expected to attend quarterly meetings, where they receive a 'sitting allowance' of KSH 3,000.[4] Scholars have raised concerns that the CSAC could be used for political manipulation of social transfer distribution (Wanyama and Mc-Cord 2017; Wanyama and Nyambedha 2017). However, as will be explored further in the next section, strong formal rules and guidelines tend to limit the political interference of the CSACs and, where operational, they have been used as an additional tool for monitoring the social transfers.

The new Operations Manual also recognizes the important roles played by chiefs in local implementation. Unlike in Ghana (see Chapter 5), chiefs do not have roots in customary authority, but were creations of colonial authorities that became the lowest level of state administration after independence (Nyamweru and Chidongo 2018). However, the role of chiefs and village elders in the implementation of the social transfers has been a subject of contention. A 2017 survey by the Kenyan Ethics and Anti-Corruption Commission reported that the Chief's Office, composed of the chiefs, sub-chiefs, and village elders, was the most corrupt office in Kenya (Ethics and Anti-Corruption Commission Kenya 2018). Early CT-OVC evaluations indicated that 'the chiefs handpicked [targeting committees] as opposed to community selection' and they frequently acted as the 'chairperson' of the selection committee (Kirera 2012, p. 48), supporting concerns that chiefs could manipulate distribution of the transfers for personal gain. As a result, previous versions of the Operations Manual did not include a role for the chiefs or village elders. However, given the importance of the chiefs in the day-to-day lives of rural villages, and their role in liaising between citizens and higher levels of government (Kirera 2012; Onyango-Ouma and Samuels 2012; Osborn 2020), the 2017 Operations Manual did provide a role for chiefs in 'supporting programme implementation' (Government of Kenya 2017, p. 10). According to the guidelines, chiefs' role in targeting is limited to community mobilization for *barazas*, providing security and, if necessary, assisting potential beneficiaries to acquire the required identification documents.

Furthermore, in each location, Beneficiary Welfare Committees for each social transfer programme provide a link between social transfer participants and local-level bureaucrats and are responsible for informing households of payment dates, following up on non-collection of payments, mobilizing beneficiaries for trainings, updating beneficiary information, and fielding complaints and grievances from beneficiaries. Beneficiary Welfare Committee members are unpaid and elected by social transfer participants, with representatives from each village, to ensure broad representation within each location.

Responsibility for targeting of social transfers is relatively centralized, therefore, with the national SAU conducting geographical targeting and individual targeting through the PMT. Nonetheless, programme administration and the selection of participants depends on the coordination and cooperation of a diverse range of state officials, political and societal actors across the tiers of Kenya's decentralized state administration from the national level down to the village. The following analysis examines how the combination of state infrastructural power and political competition shapes the involvement of these actors in the distribution of social transfers.

4. State infrastructural power in context

This section examines the variation in each of the three dimensions of state infrastructural power—resources, intra-state relations, and state–society relations—across the four research sites.

State resources

While all the bureaucrats interviewed reported resource deficiencies, the extent to which these deficiencies prevented bureaucrats from carrying out their duties varied considerably across counties. Oversight over programme implementation was in part dependent on bureaucrats' capacity to reach communities, which requires human and financial resources, and physical infrastructure, including transportation. Nyeri and Nakuru have a relatively strong network of public transport, through *matatus* (mini-buses) and shared cars. In contrast, in Homa Bay and Marsabit, resource constraints were not only more pronounced than in Nakuru and Nyeri, but they were also exacerbated by poor physical infrastructure, including a lack of public transport. In Marsabit, each sub-county covers a large area of diffuse villages (Table 6.2), while in Homa Bay it is hard to reach interior areas and smaller islands in Lake Victoria. One bureaucrat in Homa Bay reported,

> We don't have vehicles to move, we don't have motorbikes to move, so in most cases we hire and yet what the government is giving in terms of funding is quite limited, so that cannot allow us to carry out all these duties.

Bureaucrats also reported that understaffing frequently forced them to close offices when they were sick or had to attend trainings, and that they relied heavily on local volunteers to support their work. In Marsabit, these structural constraints were even more pronounced and bureaucrats were further challenged by pockets

Table 6.2 County size and population density

	Marsabit	Homa Bay	Nakuru	Nyeri
Area (km^2)	70,944.1	3152.5	7462.4	3325.0
Population density (persons/km^2)	6	359	290	228

of regional instability, low rates of registration for national identity cards, and high rates of seasonal mobility among the transhumant pastoralists. As one officer in Moyale noted,

> We are poorly staffed because we serve seven wards and two districts and the furthest location is 150 km away. Most of the areas are rough and unreachable during rainy season, and some areas are conflict zones we are unable to reach and for the community to get service is hard.

In contrast, bureaucrats in Nakuru and Nyeri were more positive about their ability to meet their targets related to the social transfer programmes, even if they sometimes felt constrained by understaffing and a lack of vehicles. In both counties, bureaucrats frequently solicited help from other local government offices, NGOs, or politicians.

Intra-state relations

Another key component of infrastructural power involves the oversight of the central state over lower-level bureaucrats to ensure that social transfers are uniformly implemented across diverse subnational contexts. In this respect, the physical distance of research sites from central government ministries and offices in Nairobi directly is an important source of variation.

Across all counties, bureaucrats engage in a largely top-down process of goal setting, in line with the broader goals of the ministry and the SAU. These goals are similar across all counties and sub-counties, and relate to payment, management of complaints, and community awareness building. In certain years, bureaucrats are expected to meet goals for targeting and registration, with numbers and timelines 'handed down by SAU', but they are not evaluated on targeting accuracy. Bureaucrats' performance is evaluated annually against these goals, but if goals are not met, bureaucrats are given the opportunity to provide an explanation. Although there is no official incentive structure in place, respondents commonly reported that consistently poor performance might limit opportunities for promotion. Individual performance is rarely rewarded, except through occasional letters of recognition, and high-performing ministries sometimes receive monetary bonuses for all employees. Goal setting and performance monitoring was reported consistently across all counties and sub-counties, but had limited impact on the overall implementation of the social transfers.

All bureaucrats involved in the implementation of the social transfers received training on the Operations Manual and communicated regularly with both their immediate superiors in the ministry and the SAU. The programmes are also subject to additional oversight by the SAU through monitoring visits to the county and sub-county offices, and visits to participant households to assess targeting effectiveness and follow up on complaints. However, there was significant variation between counties in the frequency of SAU monitoring visits, which maps onto both the distance from Nairobi, and the marginalization of distant counties by the central state. SAU visits were most frequent in Nakuru and Nyeri counties, averaging between two and five times per year. In Homa Bay, SAU visits were less predictable, with bureaucrats reporting annual SAU visits to both sub-county offices and participant households. In Marsabit county, SAU visits were even less consistent, with bureaucrats reporting 'occasional' and 'infrequent' visits. One county coordinator reported that SAU visits were 'unusual' and that there was 'limited oversight of the programme by SAU'. The proximity of Nyeri and Nakuru counties to Nairobi also makes it easier for sub-county bureaucrats to travel to Nairobi, with trips being cheaper and requiring less time away from the county offices. Areas close to the centre therefore receive greater oversight from the SAU. Areas that are farther from Nairobi not only receive less direct oversight but also experience greater difficulty following up on programme issues in person, for example around payments and grievances.

State–society relations

Another central component of the state's infrastructural power concerns how societal actors perceive the legitimacy of the institutions of the central state and 'the effects, or weight, of the state on societal power networks' (Soifer 2008, p. 235). The variations in state–society relations in Kenya, shaped by the marginalization and alienation of peripheral communities from the central state, affect the legitimacy of local bureaucrats and perceptions of the transfers by the communities where they are implemented.

All bureaucrats are centrally appointed and rotate postings every few years. However, there are important sub-national differences in the embeddedness of bureaucrats within the communities which they serve. Hassan (2020a) shows that under Kenya's provincial administrations, the percentage of co-ethnic administrators and the length of their tenure were higher in areas aligned with the incumbent president. Therefore, bureaucrats in steadfast opposition areas, such as Homa Bay—which have historically been 'misaligned' with the central government—are less likely to be locally embedded in the communities they serve. Furthermore, bureaucrats generally have a 'strong aversion to assignments in the arid north' with tenure in these 'hardship posts' generally limited to two years (Hassan 2020a, p. 83). Thus, local embeddedness is less likely in the northern counties, reducing bureaucrats' knowledge of and sense of obligation to the communities they serve (Hassan 2020a).

In addition to SAU visits, monitoring at sub-national level is conducted by the county coordinators, the Sub-County Children's Officer, Sub-County Social Development Officer, and the CSAC, mainly focused on payment points. The frequency of monitoring depends partly on the level of oversight from the SAU and the resources available at the sub-county office, as discussed above. However, it also depends on the motivation of CSAC members, and the relationship between the Sub-County Children's Officer, Sub-County Social Development Officer, and local communities. Nyeri and Nakuru counties both had relatively high levels of oversight at this level, which was largely driven by bureaucrats' strong connections with locally embedded actors, including CSAC members, who were willing to conduct informal monitoring and report any issues to bureaucrats who could then follow up. In Homa Bay, while some bureaucrats were from surrounding areas, others lacked either innate or learned embeddedness.[5] Bureaucrats reported that limited resources impeded their ability to monitor programmes effectively at the local level. However, like Nyeri and Nakuru, they compensated for some of these deficiencies through the CSAC members who helped monitor payment points during bi-monthly distribution and chiefs who helped monitor participant households. In Marsabit, meanwhile, bureaucrats often reported feeling removed from the communities in which they worked. Short-term appointments and significant language barriers reduced their ability to build connections with local communities. Bureaucrats often rely on local interpreters, and, as one Sub-County Children's Officer formerly based in Marsabit noted, 'the moment there is an interpreter, and maybe he or she is a local, you could not detect if the community is being given the right information'. Scarce resources and inadequate infrastructure also limited local bureaucrats' ability to visit remote areas, and they often relied on a constrained form of local monitoring by chiefs or community members.

State–society relations also influence community interpretations of the social transfers. Across all counties, participants generally understood that the social transfers were national programmes, implemented by the central government, and not attributable to a specific political party. The OPCT and CT-OVC have survived tumultuous government turnovers and the programmes have been central to both the incumbent and opposition parties' campaigns for many years. However, participant perspectives are also influenced by the transparency of targeting procedures. Participants in Homa Bay and Marsabit were more likely to view the programmes as a 'gift' or a 'favour', while participants in Nyeri and Nakuru were more likely to view the programmes as their 'right'.

Overall, variation in all aspects of state infrastructural power were evident across the four counties. Across all counties, bureaucrats faced resource scarcities and multiple pressures; however, these scarcities were most prevalent in Marsabit, especially relative to the resources required for programme implementation in a vast and sparsely populated county. Bureaucrats in Homa Bay also experienced greater resource deficiencies compared to Nyeri and Nakuru, where bureaucrats felt better able to cope with provided resources. Peripheral areas like Marsabit and Homa Bay had less oversight from the central state over programme implementation than Nyeri and Nakuru, which are proximate to Nairobi. Finally, local bureaucrats in Marsabit and Homa Bay struggled to cultivate trust with local communities, due to political divisions between the central and local government (Homa Bay) and long histories of marginalization from the central state (Marsabit). These dynamics have continued ramifications for policy implementation, as lower levels of state infrastructural power limit bureaucrats' ability to reach remote communities and render populations visible to the central state.

5. Implementation of social transfers at the local level

Despite the consolidation and creation of clear guidelines, in practice targeting is shaped by sub-national variations in infrastructural power and political alignments. The analysis first considers the two sites in which state infrastructural power is relatively high—Nyeri and Nakuru—and where targeting tends to follow formal procedures. The discussion then turns to the sites with lower levels of state infrastructural power—first Homa Bay and then Marsabit—where bureaucrats rely on locally embedded authorities to compensate for limited resources and authority, leading to greater variation in targeting procedures.

Targeting in areas with high infrastructural power: Nyeri and Nakuru

Across Nakuru and Nyeri, the targeting processes for the CT-OVC recounted by bureaucrats, chiefs, committee members, and participants all closely matched the formal guidelines, with only minor limited deviations, and community members generally felt the selection process was transparent.

Among the problems identified, one location in Nakuru reported that beyond their formal role in organizing *barazas*, chiefs would oversee the targeting process by accompanying committee members in the identification and listing of households. Furthermore, in Nyeri, one location reported that committee members were not elected; rather village elders were appointed and trained by the Sub-County Children's Officer. However, in other areas of Nyeri, efforts were made to ensure that neither the chiefs nor village elders were directly involved in identifying households, with one Nyeri-based Sub-County Children's Officer asserting, 'We do not want the chiefs to run this programme, because we want to be as independent as we can.'

In contrast, the OPCT targeting process had changed over time. While donors were heavily involved in the design of the CT-OVC early on, the OPCT was government implemented and financed from the beginning. Initially, OPCT targeting was completed by the chiefs and village elders who identified participants and sent the names to the Sub-County Social Development Officer. OPCT participants frequently reported a lack of transparency during this initial targeting. In an interview, one participant in Nakuru noted that initially,

> the registration was also being done based on personal relationships … we saw scenarios whereby sometimes people would go visit the chief's office and would get registered for the programme [and] you would notice that these people do not deserve to be included in the programmes because they have families that are supporting them.

This was later substantiated by CSAC members and bureaucrats. There were similar reports in Nyeri, with one chief recounting, 'when I was left to do the identification, I would not sensitize the community. I only worked with the village elders.' However, across both counties, respondents noted that these processes had changed over time, as the social transfers were amalgamated under the National Safety Net Programme, which both strengthened the targeting systems and increased central government oversight. During recent OPCT expansions, the targeting processes more closely followed official guidelines, with minor variations. In Nakuru, respondents reported strong oversight from the Social Development Office, noting that the officer 'walked together' with committee members to visit households during the targeting period. In Nyeri, as the programme evolved and targeting procedures were updated, expansions in the OPCT programme involved the community, who were tasked with identifying vulnerable households through *barazas*.

Across both counties and programmes, community involvement through open *barazas* was a priority, providing community members with the opportunity to ask questions and provide feedback on the targeting process and households chosen for inclusion. However, as one Sub-County Social Development Officer noted, verification *barazas* were poorly attended and community members were often reluctant to 'say they reject some of the names, as they might also be in the list and that would increase their chance of also being rejected'. Moreover, across all counties, vulnerable citizens attended *barazas* less frequently, due to the opportunity costs associated with attendance, and were less likely to voice their opinions when they did attend.

In both counties, CSAC members monitored implementation, supported targeting and registration, disseminated information, and sometimes mobilized their networks to supplement central state resources. While CSACs in Nyeri could not influence the initial selection of participants, they reviewed participant lists and would 'remove those who were not deserving' after following up with the identified household. Particularly in Mathira sub-county, politicians had nominated community and religious leaders to the committee. These individuals were active in the community and were widely perceived, by both the community and government officials, to be informed and embedded representatives of their communities. Thus, there was a perception amongst bureaucrats that 'there has been more transparency in the targeting process with CSAC in place' compared to having only the location committees, as it allowed for monitoring across locations.

Similarly, in Nakuru, the CSACs actively supported local bureaucrats by monitoring targeting exercises 'to ensure that transparency is maintained' and using their networks to spread information about the programmes. As one bureaucrat reported, 'the office of the MP or the office of the women's representative may give tents, chairs, facilitate us in terms of venues, among other things'. In this way, politicians would seek to be active representatives of the social transfers and participants in Nyeri and Nakuru noted that politicians used the programmes during their political campaigns, highlighting their involvement in bringing the programmes to their constituents. However, the CSAC had 'no mandate to enrol or remove anyone' from the social transfers.

In general, sub-county offices were able to coordinate politicians, committees, and community members to facilitate targeting exercises that conformed to official guidelines. Strong oversight and high levels of trust between the state and the community facilitated implementation. This was also evident throughout registration for the Inua Jamii pension in both counties. Across the country, Social Development Offices faced significant pressure from coordinators within the SAU to register all eligible beneficiaries in the two months prior to the August election, with little monetary facilitation from the central government. In both Nakuru and Nyeri, Social Development Officers coordinated registration at the sub-county offices with the help of volunteers. Information about the programmes was spread via the radio, chiefs, and village elders. Sub-County Social Development Officers borrowed vehicles from non-governmental organizations (NGOs) and other government offices to travel to more remote locations to register potential participants.

In Nyeri, alignment with the ruling party led to high levels of state infrastructural power, including bureaucratic embeddedness within the communities, which has led to relatively strong oversight of targeting. In Nakuru, histories of ethnic politicization and violence, and the consequent need for neutrality in the distribution of social transfers led to the mobilization of state infrastructural power for effective distribution. This has included high levels of oversight over targeting to ensure equitable distribution amongst ethnic groups.

Targeting in Homa Bay: political misalignment and low infrastructural power

Homa Bay presents a marked contrast with Nyeri and Makuru. Relatively low levels of state infrastructural power, including limited resources and a lack of bureaucratic embeddedness, reduced the level of oversight over targeting procedures, both from the SAU and from centrally appointed bureaucrats. Moreover, Homa Bay is a staunch opposition area, and political divisions meant that centrally appointed bureaucrats sometimes lacked familiarity with the local communities they were meant to serve with the result that politicians and chiefs played a greater role in targeting. Overall, the result was far greater variation in targeting procedures.

Political actors tended to play a greater role in targeting in Homa Bay than in other cases. One Sub-County Social Development Officer explained that the CSAC was a method of legitimizing the involvement of MPs in the social transfers, noting,

> You know this programme has always been used as a campaign tool for everyone who wants to be the area MP. They have always talked about it. When they were not being involved, the MP would visit my office even twice a month to talk about expansion of the programme. So, bringing them on board was a way of sharing the challenges we faced.

CSAC members also understood their role as political. While members helped compensate for limited infrastructural capacity by monitoring *barazas*, mobilizing the community during targeting and disseminating information to the community, they also felt obligated to relay information about the social transfers to politicians, so it could be used during campaigns, when they address 'the *wananchi* [citizens] in any gathering in the community'.

While geographical targeting of counties and sub-counties has been centralized, allocation between locations is the responsibility of the CSAC. In Homa Bay, where trust between opposition politicians and centrally appointed bureaucrats in the CSAC is low, political representatives often influenced the targeting of locations in practice. As one bureaucrat noted,

> If the CSAC committee verifies and decides now that another location was poorer then, and it is a bit better now from other locations, then we could not stop them from amending the locations, as long as the allocation [within the sub-county] remains the same.

Other bureaucrats also noted they were 'just the joint secretary' of the CSAC and that the political appointees had the final decision-making authority. While it was unclear whether decisions made by the CSAC led to the introduction of political priorities in the selection of locations in place of official guidelines, it was evident that CSAC involvement helped bureaucrats compensate for limited state infrastructural power. Bureaucrats noted that because they were not from the area, the connection of political members of the CSAC to local communities was essential, with one bureaucrat claiming that they 'cannot work alone'. The influence of the CSAC, especially politicians' ability to influence geographic distribution within the sub-county, contrasts with how bureaucrats in Nyeri and Nakuru counties portrayed their relationship with the CSAC, where they viewed the SAU, and themselves as bureaucrats, as the final authority.

Divisions between the central state and local political actors were also evident during registration for the Inua Jamii pension. The attempt to register over-70s for the pension in the run-up to national elections was widely viewed as a political tool. This led to distrust between the community and local bureaucrats, both during and after the election period. Rumours circulated that government officials employed at all levels had been directed to campaign for the incumbent. The County Commissioner in the Social Development Office affirmed,

> All the people who were aspiring for political seats were against the programme. We were pushing the programme as the implementers with our stakeholders. Together with the provincial administration, we did a lot of campaigns until we were called 'moles' and that we were campaigning for the government of the day.[6]

Citizens feared that the government was collecting voter information in opposition areas, which would be used to rig the elections. The result was that many eligible citizens refused to register for the pension, while others were unaware of the programme, due to the challenges bureaucrats faced in promoting registration in opposition areas. While the pension registration was seen as a political tool nationwide, bureaucrats and participants in the other study sites believed that Inua Jamii would increase support for the incumbent party.

The association of social transfer programmes with the national government also appears the most likely explanation for the county's efforts to establish its own county cash transfer programme. As Niedzwiecki (2018) shows in Latin America, the association of social transfers with the national incumbent can provide incentives for local administrations run by opposition parties to establish programmes in competition as a means of claiming credit. In Homa Bay, the proposed county programme is part of the governor's 'political agendas'. Although it has not yet been approved by the County Assembly, this has not stopped some county assembly members from using the plan as a campaign tool, even going as far as registering beneficiaries for the non-existent programme.

In addition to the involvement of political actors, centrally appointed bureaucrats, who lacked knowledge of and embeddedness in local communities, sometimes relied on chiefs and village elders to make targeting decisions, contrary to programme guidelines. Across Homa Bay, targeting procedures varied considerably from location to location and programme to programme. In part due to higher levels of oversight, targeting for the CT-OVC programme largely followed the formal procedures laid out in the Operations Manual, with minor variations occurring during recent expansions of ten households or fewer, during which some tasks were relegated to the Beneficiary Welfare Committees in order to compensate for limited resources. In contrast, the OPCT programme experienced wide variations in reported targeting procedures between sub-counties and locations given the historically low levels of oversight over the programme's implementation structures prior to the consolidation of the social transfers under the National Safety Net Programme.

Sub-County Social Development Officers reported that because their office had limited resources, it was necessary to involve the chiefs. They argued that the chiefs helped legitimize the targeting process because they 'are the people who know the challenges, the poverty levels, the deserving cases ... now we leave it to them'. The Sub-County Social Development Officers often noted that they had neither the authority nor the information about the communities to make household targeting decisions alone, and therefore would rely on the chiefs, who are widely seen as powerful local authorities. This was noted widely by both community members and bureaucrats, with one bureaucrat simply stating,

> You cannot engage any community without going through the chief or the sub-chief—those are our eyes on the ground; that is the structure of our governance.

In one sub-county, Social Development Officers asked the chiefs to select a specified number of people from their location for inclusion in the OPCT and only these selected households would be visited by enumerators for household data collection. Thus, while the PMT is intended as a 'check' to ensure households meet the poverty and categorical criteria for the programme, decisions about whom to include in the programme were effectively made by chiefs and sub-chiefs. In another sub-county, half the social transfer participants interviewed identified the chief as the one who directly visited their households, while the other half mentioned that they went to the chief's office to fill in the forms.

While chiefs' involvement was considered necessary, bureaucrats were aware that the chiefs, at times, dominated the process of identifying potential beneficiary households, and that 'at times because of vested interest you find that the chief has given us his mother or at times his cousin who is not deserving or a committee member brings the wife who is not deserving'. One bureaucrat argued that targeting 'transparency is 50 per cent, this because these chiefs are not transparent, as they want to fix their people'. This influence was for personal rather than political gain, as some chiefs took the opportunity either to include friends or family members, or to accept bribes in exchange for entering names on programme lists.

Barazas provided little opportunity for communities to hold chiefs accountable, however. One CSAC member noted that targeting was left to the chiefs, and the Sub-County Social Development Officer did not attend *barazas*, as it would 'generate a lot of unnecessary questions from the community members and so the chiefs were assigned that role'. Furthermore, while a validation *baraza* was held, participants noted that the community was not given the opportunity to make any significant changes in the programme. When asked about the *barazas*, bureaucrats often expressed that, through experience, they had found that the *barazas* were ineffective sites for public discussion. One Sub-County Social Development Officer noted that the community 'don't even say [if there are issues with targeting] because the chief will finish them … they fear they may be attacked when they get back home' for speaking out.

The result was that limited state infrastructural power and party-political divisions between the national government and local opposition resulted in limited oversight over targeting procedures, lack of community engagement, and considerable variation in targeting across Homa Bay.

Targeting in Marsabit: the challenge of low infrastructural power

In Marsabit, low levels of state infrastructural power also impacted targeting procedures for both the OPCT and the CT-OVC. In contrast to the party-political origins of low infrastructural power in Homa Bay, in Marsabit the central challenges were the vast territory covered by the county, the mobile livelihoods of the local population, and the limited capacity of the local state.

The lack of human resources and physical infrastructure was compounded by the vast expanse of the county and the mobile livelihoods of the local population. The design of the social transfer programmes requires households to be visited multiple times to collect household data, register participants, and verify required documentation. This requires the state to have repeated physical access to pastoral populations to collect detailed household and biometric data required for registration and payment. Yet bureaucrats noted difficulties reaching mobile pastoral communities, making it difficult for the state to register and verify vulnerable populations. One bureaucrat explained,

> In Moyale, the community they keep on moving from one area to another, so you could maybe target this community today in sub-location A, then when you go back to that sub-location they have already shifted with their animals to another geographical area. So, there were times we used to carry out the exercise under

the tree. That is when we relied a lot with the local administrators, the chiefs, and assistant chiefs.

The lack of embeddedness of bureaucrats and their difficulty accessing local populations meant that officials frequently compensated for low state infrastructural power by involving chiefs, village elders, and clan leaders in the targeting process.

In both sub-counties, the CT-OVC targeting procedures reported by the Sub-County Children's Officer often differed from reports from other respondents, including the chiefs, village elders, and participants. While the CT-OVC roughly followed the formal steps, with sensitization *barazas*, identification of households, household data collection by enumerators, and validation *barazas*, the chiefs were actively involved in the process of identifying households. The county commissioner noted that they often had to rely on the chiefs because of the geographic expansiveness of the county and because the chiefs were seen by the community as legitimate authorities within the locations. The involvement of chiefs in the targeting process thus compensated for the limited infrastructural power of the state, by providing both additional human resources to help throughout the intensive targeting process, and locally embedded knowledge about communities.

When asked about the efficacy of the targeting system, the county coordinator acknowledged considerable variation:

> sometimes the chiefs do a wonderful job, other times they do a bad job. Overall, I would say that the targeting system is 80 per cent effective in identifying those who are most vulnerable. You see, we do not know these people, so we give them [the chiefs] an opportunity to identify the vulnerable members in their communities.

Reports from the communities varied, with many community members lamenting a lack of information about targeting procedures. Some social transfer participants and members of the Beneficiary Welfare Committees reported that some households without orphans were receiving the CT-OVC and some had even falsified death certificates so they could claim they were caring for orphans. Such reports indicated that some community members felt there was a lack of transparency in the distribution of the CT-OVC, with one Beneficiary Welfare Committee member noting, 'we approached both the children's officer and the chief but our complaints just sleep on their desks'. Moreover, in Marsabit Central, village elders confirmed that there was no community involvement in the targeting, which contributed to what was perceived by the community as a high level of inclusion and exclusion errors. One village elder noted that during registration for the CT-OVC the village elders were simply told to bring the names of ten households with orphans and vulnerable children living in their village, and that the names would be submitted to the chief and Sub-County Children's Officer.

Similarly, targeting for the OPCT did not follow formal procedures and relied heavily on the chiefs, village elders, and clan leaders to organize *barazas* and identify participants. In one sub-county, village elders held open meetings, where the community was given the opportunity to identify participants. In another sub-county, the Social Development Officer reported deferring to the judgement of a committee composed of the chiefs and section heads for each of the clans who selected participants for the programme. One clan elder reported,

> In 2016, the Sub-County Social Development Officer wrote to the chief of my location that he should bring him names of 20 elderly people in his location. The chief called us to his office as the elders from Borana, Kona, and Garre communities to give him names of poor elderly people. As the elders of these ethnic groups, we proportionally shared the number of beneficiaries per ethnic group. As the Garre community, we got six beneficiaries, one from each sub-clan. The rest were shared between seven Borana sub-clans and seven Kona tribes.

The reliance on local authorities is exemplified through the registration for the Inua Jamii pension. Bureaucrats noted that they conducted the registration with 'zero budget' and so had to 'dig in their pockets' to find money to make calls to chiefs in remote locations to mobilize the communities for registration. Another bureaucrat noted that to reach remote locations, they had to involve the county commissioner, who asked the chiefs to forward the names of everyone aged 70 and above to the Social Development Office for registration. Bureaucrats rely on the chiefs to supplement for limited state infrastructural power, but doing so risks the exclusion of eligible beneficiaries who may not receive information about the programmes. Nonetheless, the pension was widely seen as politically advantageous in an electorally competitive county. According to one bureaucrat in Marsabit, he often heard the elders say in the run-up to the election, 'We will keep Uhuru [Kenyatta] no matter what as he brought us the money.'

Across Marsabit county, oversight was limited, as local bureaucrats faced significant resource pressures. Unlike other counties, they were unable to draw on the time and resources of the CSACs to supplement low infrastructural power, as none of the committees were active at the time of fieldwork. In one sub-county, the MP nominated family members and a former campaign manager to the CSAC when it was created in 2013, as a way of rewarding them through the sitting allowance. However, the CSAC stopped meeting when the SAU stopped funding the sitting allowance. A new CSAC had yet to meet, because politicians had not appointed representatives. The CSAC in Moyale was similarly non-functional, due to financial constraints. This contrasts with counties like Nyeri and Nakuru, where many CSAC members would continue to meet and assist with programme implementation, even without compensation. One bureaucrat reported that the

CSAC 'was forced onto the ministry by the MPs, because if the ministry did not approve the CSAC, the MPs would not have approved the ministry's budgets'. They noted that MPs wanted to capitalize on the social transfers, to 'expand their popularity', by making it 'appear as if they were the ones who had brought the programmes to the people'. They noted that this credit claiming was 'more pronounced' in the OPCT than the CT-OVC. Credit claiming may also provide an explanation for the adoption of a county social transfer programme in Marsabit, as is under consideration in Homa Bay. The programme covers participants from the same vulnerable groups—children, those with disabilities, and the elderly—as the national programmes, but restricts participation to those not selected.

Overall in Marsabit low levels of state infrastructural power reduced oversight of the targeting processes and led to greater involvement of local authorities to compensate for state deficiencies. The result was divergence in targeting procedures from official guidelines.

6. Conclusions

Sub-national variations in state infrastructural power have shaped the implementation of social transfer programmes in Kenya in profound ways. Areas with proximity to the capital and close historical ties to the central state have the capacity and oversight to implement programmes according to official state guidelines. Overall, this results in greater transparency at the local level, with implications for how participants view the programmes. However, in areas that have been historically marginalized by the central state, through either political divisions or historical marginalization, bureaucrats compensate for the lack of state infrastructural power by relying on locally embedded actors, including political appointees, chiefs, village elders, and clan leaders. In areas of limited infrastructural power, outcomes are highly variable. In some cases, locally embedded actors have undermined procedures by including family members or friends in the programme, leading to the exclusion of the most vulnerable households. In other cases, the involvement of local actors has resulted in a distribution of social transfers that is perceived as 'fair' according to local understandings of poverty.

The impacts of state infrastructural power on targeting are particularly stark when comparing ethnically diverse areas, where the central state is keen to ensure an equitable distribution of social transfers amongst different ethnic groups to avoid fuelling ethnic tensions. In Nakuru county, the state is embedded in society and has the capacity to allocate social transfers down to the village level and the legitimacy to enforce these decisions. However, in Marsabit county, the state lacks the capacity and legitimacy to make and enforce such decisions, and thus the involvement of a multitude of societal actors in the targeting process is necessary to ensure equitable distribution amongst different ethnic groups.

Variations in political competition and party politics play less of a role in the local implementation of the social transfers than has been predicted by the extant literature. Politicians pushed for the broad expansion of the social transfers to all constituencies and the creation of Constituency Social Assistance Committees headed by the area MP. While this has allowed politicians to put their face on the programmes at the local level, politicians' ability to impact the distribution of the social transfers is limited. Clear formal guidelines in the new Operations Manual and the consolidation of programmes under the National Safety Net Programme have led to stronger oversight of programme design and implementation by the government. This strong central oversight has been motivated in part by concerns over political capture. As noted by Sugiyama and Hunter (2013), the design of policies can help bypass political capture of social programmes. However, where infrastructural capacity is weak, such policy design may be insufficient. In opposition strongholds, where there are significant divisions between central and local governments, there was some evidence that politicians influenced the geographic distribution of social transfers when provided the opportunity. However, given that Homa Bay was the only opposition stronghold included in the study, further research of the influence of the CSAC on local distribution of social transfers in other opposition strongholds would be necessary to draw strong inferences.

Finally, while MPs frequently claimed credit for the social transfer programmes across all counties, this was most likely in incumbent strongholds, where MPs were actively involved in their communities. In opposition strongholds, the framing of the social transfers was aimed at increasing individual credit for the programmes, while minimizing the role of the incumbent party. As Kramon (2019) argues, clearly communicated formal guidelines can minimize political interference in social transfers. However, state infrastructural power is also key to understanding opportunities for local interference in targeting procedures at the local level, for either local or political gain. Where resources are limited and bureaucrats lack embeddedness within the communities they serve, they are more likely to rely on locally embedded actors, such as politicians, chiefs, and clan leaders, to help compensate for limited state infrastructural power, which has a range of implications for the communities where social transfers are implemented.

Notes

1. This study would not have been possible without the research conducted by Waweru Githome, Virginia Kamonji, Patrick Mutinda, Tyson Odoo, Shadrack Okumu, Lydia Oyugi, Tahira Shariff, and Angela Theuri, all of whom also provided valuable insights throughout the analysis of the interviews and focus group discussions. I also wish to

thank Dr Kate Pruce for her beneficial revisions and comments that were essential to shortening this chapter, as well as Tom Lavers and two anonymous reviewers for their helpful comments on previous drafts.

2. The CT-OVC covers 29 per cent of the eligible population, the OPCT and Inua Jamii pension combined cover 78 per cent of the eligible population, whereas the PWSD-CT covers only 3 per cent of the eligible population (KiPPRA 2018).
3. Social transfers had not been expanded in the fieldwork areas since implementation of the new Operations Manual. Before 2017, a Location OVC Committee (for the CT-OVC) and Location Committees (for the OPCT) were responsible for the programmes.
4. There were approximately 145 Kenyan shillings to the British pound at the time of fieldwork in 2018.
5. Embeddedness can either be innate or learned. In other words, either a function of bureaucrats' shared ethnicity with the community or learned through long postings in a single place (Hassan 2020a, p. 50).
6. As D'Arcy (2020) outlines, much of the infrastructure of the provincial administration remained intact after devolution, albeit under new names. Thus 'provincial administration' is still common parlance.

References

Achiba, G. A., 2019. Navigating contested winds: Development visions and anti-politics of wind energy in Northern Kenya. *Land*, 8 (7), 1–29.

Amutabi, M. N., 2015. Pastoralism, social protection and Vision 2030 in Kenya: Possibilities and prospects. *In:* E. Y. Vubo, ed. *Environment, Agriculture and Cross-Border Migrations*. Dakar: Council for the Development of Social Science Research in Africa, 121–138.

Arero, H. W., 2017. Coming to Kenya: Imagining and perceiving a national among the Borana of Kenya. *Journal of Eastern African Studies*, 1 (2), 292–304.

Bassi, M., 2005. *Decisions in the Shade: Political and Juridical Processes among the Oromo-Borana*. New York: Red Sea Press.

Boone, C., 2012. Land conflict and distributive politics in Kenya. *African Studies Review*, 55 (1), 75–103.

Branch, D., 2011. *Kenya: Between Hope and Despair*. New Haven, CT: Yale University Press.

Bulle, S. W. and Ombui, K. A., 2016. Determinants of leadership and governance in Marsabit county, Kenya. *International Journal of Scientific and Research Publications*, 6 (11), 174–181.

Cornell, A. and D'Arcy, M., 2014. Plus ça change? County-level politics in Kenya after devolution. *Journal of Eastern African Studies*, 8 (1), 173–191.

D'Arcy, M., 2020. Devolution and the county government. *In:* N. Cheeseman, K. Kanyinga, and G. Lynch, eds. *The Oxford Handbook of Kenyan Politics*. Oxford: Oxford University Press, 251–267.

D'Arcy, M. and Cornell, A., 2016. Devolution and corruption in Kenya: Everyone's turn to eat? *African Affairs*, 115 (459), 246–273.

Driscoll, B., 2018. Why political competition can increase patronage. *Studies in Comparative International Development*, 53, 404–427.

Ethics and Anti-Corruption Commission, 2018. National Ethics and Corruption Survey, 2017. EACC Research Report No. 6. Nairobi: Ethics and Anti-Corruption Commission.

Government of Kenya, 2017. *Operations Manual for Consolidated Cash Transfer Programmes*. Nairobi: Ministry of East African Community, Labour and Social Protection.

Hassan, M., 2020a. *Regime Threats and State Solutions: Bureaucratic Loyalty and Embeddedness in Kenya*. Cambridge: Cambridge University Press.

Hassan, M., 2020b. The local politics of resource distribution. *In:* N. Cheeseman, K. Kanyinga and G. Lynch (eds.), *The Oxford Handbook of Kenyan Politics*. Oxford: Oxford University Press, 482–497.

Human Rights Watch, 1993. *Divide and Rule: State-Sponsored Ethnic Violence in Kenya*. New York: Human Rights Watch.

Kanyinga, K., 2009. The legacy of the white highlands: Land rights, ethnicity and the post-2007 election violence in Kenya. *Journal of Contemporary African Studies*, 27 (3), 325–344.

Khisa, C. M. and Oesterdiekhoff, P., 2012. *Regional Disparities and Marginalisation in Kenya*. Washington, DC: Friedrich-Ebert-Stiftung.

KiPPRA, 2018. *Social Protection Budget Brief*. Policy Brief No. 7/2018-2019. Nairobi: Kenya Institute for Public Policy Research and Analysis.

Kirera, P. G., 2012. Implications of cash transfer programmes for social relations: Kenya's Cash Transfer for Orphans and Vulnerable Children. Unpublished Master's thesis. International Institute of Social Studies, The Hague.

Klopp, J. M., 2001. 'Ethnic clashes' and winning elections: The case of Kenya's electoral despotism. *Canadian Journal of African Studies*, 35 (2), 473–517.

KNBS, 2018. *Basic Report on Well-Being in Kenya: Based on the 2015/16 Kenya Integrated Household Budget Survey (KIHBS)*. Nairobi: Kenya National Bureau of Statistics. https://www.knbs.or.ke (accessed 1 February 2021).

KNBS, 2019. *2019 Kenya Population and Housing Census, Volume 1: Population by County and Sub-County*. Nairobi: Kenya National Bureau of Statistics. https://www.knbs.or.ke (accessed 1 February 2021).

Kochore, H. H., 2020. North Eastern: From the periphery to the center. *In:* N. Cheeseman, K. Kanyinga, and G. Lynch, eds. *The Oxford Handbook of Kenyan Politics*. Oxford: Oxford University Press, 659–672.

Kramon, E., 2019. *The Local Politics of Social Protection: Programmatic versus Non-programmatic Distributive Politics in Kenya's Cash Transfer Programmes*. London: International Growth Centre.

Lynch, G., 2011. *I Say to You: Ethnic Politics and the Kalenjin in Kenya*. Chicago, IL: University of Chicago Press.

Migdal, J., 2001. *State in Society: Studying How States and Societies Transform and Constitute One Another*. Cambridge: Cambridge University Press.

MLEAA, 2016. *Inua Jamii: Towards a More Effective National Safety Net for Kenya Progress Report*. Nairobi: Ministry of Labour and East African Affairs.

Mueller, S. D., 2020. High-stakes ethnic politics. *In:* N. Cheeseman, K. Kanyinga, and G. Lynch, eds. *The Oxford Handbook of Kenyan Politics*. Oxford: Oxford University Press, 343–355.

Muhula, R., 2020. The limits of multi-partyism (1992–2005). *In:* N. Cheeseman, K. Kanyinga, and G. Lynch, eds. *The Oxford Handbook of Kenyan Politics*. Oxford: Oxford University Press, 69–81.

Mulli, L., 1999. Understanding election clashes in Kenya, 1992 and 1997. *African Security Studies*, 8 (4), 75–80.
Niedzwiecki, S., 2018. *Uneven Social Policies: The Politics of Subnational Variation in Latin America*. Cambridge: Cambridge University Press.
Nyamweru, C. and Chidongo, T. M., 2018. Elders in modern Kenya: 'Dying institutions' or 'reinventing themselves'?. *African Studies*, 77(2), 240–256.
Onyango-Ouma, W. and Samuels, F., 2012. *Transforming Cash Transfers: Beneficiary and Community Perspectives on the Cash Transfer for Orphans and Vulnerable Children Programme in Kenya*. London: Overseas Development Institute.
Osborn, M., 2020. Chiefs, elders, and traditional authority. *In:* N. Cheeseman, K. Kanyinga, and G. Lynch, eds. *The Oxford Handbook of Kenyan Politics*. Oxford: Oxford University Press, 297–309.
Paudel, N. R., 2009. A critical account of policy implementation theories: Status and reconsideration. *Nepalese Journal of Public Policy and Governance*, 25 (2), 36–54.
Pommerolle, M.-E., 2020. The 2017 elections and electoral (in)justice (2015–2017). *In:* N. Cheeseman, K. Kanyinga and G. Lynch, eds. *The Oxford Handbook of Kenyan Politics*. Oxford: Oxford University Press, 109–121.
Porisky, A., *n.d.* The state at the margins: State social assistance and citizenship in rural Kenya and Tanzania. Unpublished doctoral dissertation. University of Toronto.
Republic of Kenya, 2017. *Kenya Social Protection Sector Review*. Nairobi: Government of Kenya.
Republic of Kenya, 2020. *Single Registry for Social Protection*. Nairobi: Social Protection Secretariat. https://www.socialprotection.or.ke/single-registry (accessed 1 February 2021).
Schlee, G., 1989. *Identities on the Move: Clanship and Pastoralism in Northern Kenya*. Manchester: Manchester University Press.
Scott-Villiers, P., 2017. Small wars in Marsabit County: Devolution and political violence in northern Kenya. *Conflict, Security and Development*, 3 (17), 247–264.
Soifer. H., 2008. State infrastructural power: Approaches to conceptualization and measurement. *Studies in Comparative International Development*, 43, 231–251.
Sugiyama, N. B. and Hunter, W., 2013. Whither clientelism? Good governance and Brazil's 'Bolsa Família' program. *Comparative Politics*, 46 (1), 43–62.
Wagana, D. M., 2017. Effect of governance decentralization on service delivery in county governments in Kenya. Ph.D. thesis. University of Nairobi.
Waller, R., 2012. Pastoral production in colonial Kenya: Lessons from the past? *African Studies Review*, 55 (2), 1–27.
Wanyama, F. and McCord, A., 2017. The politics of scaling up social protection in Kenya. *ESID Working Papers*, 87.
Wanyama, F. O. and Nyambedha, E. O., 2017. Political patronage and the expansion of cash transfer programmes in Kenya. *In:* N. Awortwi and E. R. Aiyede, eds. *Politics, Public Policy and Social Protection Policy in Africa: Evidence from Cash Transfer Programmes*. New York: Routledge, 26–44.

PART IV

UNIVERSALISTIC-INCLUSIVE CASES IN SOUTH ASIA

7

The Politics of Distributing Social Transfers in Bangladesh

Insights from the Primary Education Stipends Project

Naomi Hossain[1]

1. Introduction

Bangladesh has had innovative programmes to assist schoolchildren with food or cash since 1993, reflecting the country's longstanding political commitment to social protection and mass education (Rahman et al. 2014; GED 2015). This chapter analyses how politics shapes the implementation of the main national education assistance scheme, the Primary Education Stipend Project (PESP), examining the interaction of state infrastructural power and local power relations in the process of implementation. Bangladesh's education stipends are pioneering (Tietjen 2003; Raynor and Wesson 2006; Baulch 2011) but have in the past been prone to corruption and 'leakage' (Ahmed and del Ninno 2002; Ahmed et al. 2004; Rahman et al. 2011). Reforms to address these implementation problems as part of the National Social Security Strategy mean that, as of 2016, the PESP was disbursing mobile money payments of BDT 100[2] to the 10 million registered mothers of all 13 million of the nation's children attending public primary institutions (roughly 90 per cent of all children) (GED 2015); this amounts to BDT 14 billion per year (USD 165 million), or 3 per cent of the social protection budget (GoB 2017).

This chapter explores the interplay between state capacity, political competition, and local institutions in the implementation of PESP. It compares perceptions of the new politics of PESP implementation since 2016 with older complaints about the ineffectiveness and corruption of local social protection implementation. It explores how a new national, centralized, and digitalized politics is replacing the analogue system of face-to-face patron clientelism and local political competition as the basis for distributional decision making. It also discusses how national and transnational debates and ideas have shaped the development of the programme.

Naomi Hossain, *The Politics of Distributing Social Transfers in Bangladesh*. In: *The Politics of Distributing Social Transfers*. Edited by Tom Lavers, Oxford University Press.
DOI: 10.1093/oso/9780192862525.003.0007

The chapter arrives at two main findings. First, the growing political dominance of the Awami League and a stronger focus on performance legitimacy have reduced incentives for local manipulation of programmes like the PESP, as well as driving programme reforms, including redesign and expansion. The cash is now intended for all children attending publicly supported primary schools who meet basic conditions. The redesign of the programme also introduced technology, through computerized database profiles of eligible pupils, and cash distribution via mobile money services. Universalization and new technology have been crucial to the second finding: that the redesigned PESP has largely bypassed local politics and limited the detrimental effects of weak state infrastructural power on implementation; the PESP is implemented with closer adherence to the official rules than before 2016. However, technology has by no means removed problems of corruption, weak accountability or poor performance. Instead, the research found the redesigned programme suffered from teething problems related to the technology. And the channels that people previously used to demand accountability or complain about the programme no longer worked; there were no functioning mechanisms for grievance redress at all.

Other chapters in this volume show that the local politics of targeting, participant selection, and frontline resource distribution can be direct and powerful influences on who gets what and why. However, the recent reforms of PESP in Bangladesh specifically aimed to reduce the salience of (local) political interests and power in the implementation process, by a) removing or drastically reducing official discretion over participant selection, and b) limiting the scope for 'leakage' and corruption through digital mobile money transfers, replacing the role of local officials and actors with technology. The effort to vacate the space for local politics is itself shaped by the increasing political dominance of the ruling party since a landslide election victory in 2008, with the party seeking to take greater control of the state and a more direct relationship with citizens. Technology is being used here to expand the infrastructural power of the state, with the aim of enabling it to reach more people with less corruption. But while local politics appear less salient in the implementation of the programme, national politics have become more so. This analysis of the reformed PESP provides evidence of the growing infrastructural power of the Bangladeshi state in its current organizational fusion with the ruling party; this has driven a deliberate investment in state capabilities to address poverty reduction and human development.

The chapter addresses these issues as follows. The next section sets out the analytical framework guiding the research and describes its methodology. Section 3 examines the history of the PESP, analysing the political conditions under which the schemes were successively adopted, retained, and expanded, and the changing relationship between the state and citizens. Section 4 looks more closely at how politics and state capacity interact in the implementation of the PESP in the four sites in which primary fieldwork was undertaken. Section 5 draws together the threads of the analysis, arriving at some conclusions about infrastructural power and its interaction with local power relations in the delivery of the PESP transfers.

2. Theory and methodology

For Bangladesh, it is possible to derive a two-part proposition about the relationship between state infrastructural power and local politics in the implementation of the PESP. First, we would expect that the growing dominance of the Awami League within national politics since 2008 would raise its political incentives to expand and improve public service delivery in general, and the performance of the PESP specifically. This may seem counter-intuitive, as education stipend programmes were reformed and expanded with each incoming government during the highly competitive period of multi-party democracy. So why would we expect that a party that lacks credible competition would similarly reform and expand education stipend programmes? Successive governments have expanded and reformed these programmes because they are seen to be politically popular, and an effective way for governments to reach the rural majority. And while the Awami League government faces less political competition since 2008, growing dominance has meant a corresponding loss of procedural or electoral legitimacy, particularly since the 2014 election (Hassan and Nazneen 2017; Riaz 2019). Social service delivery is always important to the legitimacy of the Bangladeshi state, democratic or not (Lewis and van Schendel 2020; Hassan 2013). But it is likely to be more important when the government is perceived to lack democratic legitimacy. We can hypothesize that the Bangladesh government aims to compensate for its procedural legitimacy deficits with the performance legitimacy of shoring up and improving popular pro-poor programmes. The PESP serves this role particularly well because, although the government has a range of social protection instruments available to it, education stipend schemes align with a developmentalist emphasis on investing in human capital (Hossain 2010). So while education stipend schemes started and grew under democratic and competitive politics, we would expect the concentration of political power to further strengthen incentives for the central state to expand the reach of the programme and to improve its performance.

The second part of the proposition follows this logic through: as the ruling party dominates politics to an increasing degree, we would expect it to exercise greater infrastructural power with which to discipline or motivate frontline actors to act in line with central policy aims (Hickey et al. 2015). Political dominance grants the party greater resources and authority with which to command obedience, so it can better afford the political or other costs of enforcing discipline. As a result, efforts to expand or improve the performance of the PESP are likely to involve tighter control of delivery processes, including stronger intra-state accountability mechanisms between the central state and its sub-national actors and institutions. More disciplined policy implementation may take the form of more accurate information about programme progress, stronger sanctions against service delivery failures or corruption, or stronger career motivations for adhering to central policy rules, among others. We have no reason to believe that tighter control by the central state over frontline actors will necessarily work to change state–citizen relations directly. Political dominance is not generally associated with functioning systems of democratic feedback or downward accountability. So while we do expect central governments to be more effective at holding their frontline officials to account, we would not necessarily expect tighter discipline to include requiring those officials to be more accountable to citizens.

Half a century after it won its liberation from Pakistan in 1971, the Bangladeshi state remains weak, with limited capacities to impose its authority, tax, restrain corruption, or control political violence (Khan 2014; Hassan and Prichard 2016). This has been changing since 2009, when the Awami League came to power with a decisive mandate and a weak opposition: a decade of dominant Awami League rule has politicized the administration, and this fusion of party and state is driving through significant economic and social policy changes (Hassan and Nazneen 2017). Despite the state's historically limited capacity, and in contrast to most of the countries covered in this volume, sub-national variations in the infrastructural power of the Bangladeshi state have not been pronounced. A small, accessible landmass, a dense road network, innovative non-state actors, and a common language and culture have enabled broad-based service provision to spread out and scale up fast (Asadullah et al. 2014), even if 'borderlands' and indigenous populations have been incorporated recently, unevenly, and often through repressive means (Van Schendel 2009, 2004). As such, we did not expect to find significant sub-national variations in the implementation of the PESP. If they did exist, we would expect them to be determined by a high degree of social exclusion, marked by ethnicity, language, and geography, as well as wealth and social networks. These considerations shaped our methodological strategy, including our choice of case study sites.

This two-part proposition guided the overall study design, which set out to explore the politics behind the expansion and redesign of PESP, and how the growing power of the Bangladeshi state is shaping its implementation. The research methodology combined a review of the academic and policy research literature, official documentation, media reports, and selected key informant interviews in Dhaka. It should be noted that several key public officials at national and local levels either refused interviews, or granted them off the record, fearful that their superiors would disapprove. To test our initial propositions, the study also analysed implementation of the PESP in four locations. Adopting a comparative case study methodology, two pairs of locations were selected, with a rural and urban site in each of a comparatively central and prosperous (Narayanganj), and a more remote and poor (Mymensingh) district. These were selected with the 'most different systems' design principle in mind (Mills et al. 2010), with the assumption being that if no systematic variation could be found between the poorest rural and the wealthiest urban settings in poorer and less developed regions compared to industrialized and wealthier areas, this would provide affirmation that variations in state infrastructural power were not important. Research in the four locations was based on focus group discussions and key informant interviews in a single school catchment area, each selected as an average performing institution for the area. Interviews with local officials provided an account of the programmes as they operated at the Upazila or sub-district level. Table 7.1 summarizes the key characteristics of the research sites.

Fig. 7.1 shows the location of the research sites. Key informant interviews were undertaken with 26 respondents across the four sites, including local education officials, school officials, teachers, and School Managing Committee (SMC) members. A total of 13 focus group discussions were also conducted, nine with groups of mothers and a further four with fathers, spread across the four sites; each focus group comprised between nine and 12 participants. As Haluaghat is more ethnically diverse than the Mymensingh, we conducted an additional focus group there, to ensure we gave adequate space to the views of indigenous communities.

Fig. 7.2 summarizes differences between the *upazilas* in which the four sites were located. Both are poorer than the national average, but Haluaghat is considerably poorer and more agrarian than Araihazar. Araihazar is well above the national average in terms of access to electricity, while Haluaghat is well below. Educational attainments are less markedly different between the two, and close to the national average. We would expect therefore that any variations in state capacity would favour more the better-connected, wealthier, and more homogenous Araihazar than Haluaghat.

In all four of the study locations, the local elected political representatives belonged to the ruling Awami League. Araihazar is relatively politically competitive compared to Haluaghat, with both inter-party and intra-party political competition. While the opposition Bangladesh Nationalist Party puts up a good fight in Araihazar, the Awami League is dominant in national parliamentary constituencies and in local government. The dominant party is present across the local government positions in ways that are likely to facilitate relationships among those in positions of power.

3. The politics of design and policy making

The third phase of the Primary Education Stipend Project (PESP3, 2016–21) is the latest incarnation of a series of schemes designed to boost mass education. PESP was itself the successor to a Food-For-Education programme that started with the

Table 7.1 Key characteristics of the research sites

Indicators	Araihazar *upazila*	Haluaghat *upazila*
Location	Central Bangladesh; on main river and road networks 40 km/1.5 hours by main Dhaka–Chittagong Highway.	North Bangladesh; on border with Indian state of Meghalaya 200 km/6 hours by road.
Nearest big city	30 km/1 hour by road to Narayanganj city.	50 km/2 hours to Mymensingh city.
Population characteristics	Predominantly Bengali Muslim, some Hindu.	Predominantly Bengali Muslim; Hindu and Garo (indigenous) population around 9 per cent of *upazila* population.
Industry and economy	Very close to Narayanganj port and second biggest industrial centre. Araihazar itself a centre for weaving and textile industries.	Land port for entry to India; located south of the Garo Hills (across the border in India's Meghalaya state).
Political competition	Narayanganj city features intense political competition between main parties (Bangladesh Nationalist Party and Awami League). At present, power (Member of Parliament and mayor) controlled by Awami League, with internal factions. In Araihazar, both parties compete but municipality mayor (Bangladesh Nationalist Party) lost to Awami League candidate.	Political power dominated by Awami League; Member of Parliament and wide support base. Awami League has strong support base in indigenous and religious minority groups, who are comparatively numerous in this area.
Rural site	Excellent road connections to upazila town/*shadar*. Population employed in Narayanganj industries, local textile sector, and farming. Established community; police station since 1921; school since 1919; *upazila* (sub-district) since 1983.	Poor road connections; largely impassable by mechanized vehicle, particularly in wet season. Public school-attending population employed predominantly as agricultural day labourers, often migrating for work. School originally a mission school; nationalized in 1973 but many local Garo children attend Christian schools. Very limited connection between school and education authorities.

Urban site	Two *upazilas* were upgraded to *pourashava*/municipality in 2012; urban facilities and services available. Local school established in 1972. Local municipality politicians are largely aligned with Awami League, but face competition from Bangladesh Nationalist Party. Local politicians closely involved with SMCs. Close to *upazila* town/local government headquarters; interaction with officials. School head teacher chair of *upazila* primary school teachers' association; well connected with education officials.	Formally this union was upgraded to *pourashava*/municipality in 2012; however, remains rural and under-developed. School is close to main highway to Dhaka, and mobile networks etc. very good. At school level, SMC chair and head teacher also support Awami League but SMC also has Bangladesh Nationalist Party members; contention within SMC about how school is run.

return to democratic rule in 1991, later replaced with a cash-based scheme because of concerns about corruption (Hossain and Osman 2007). The PESP has always aimed to widen education by helping poor rural children with the costs of schooling. But which poor children, and where and how they are to be identified, have changed over time. Each successive phase of the PESP has seen geographical or personal eligibility criteria relaxed or abolished to cover an ever-widening section of the child population (see Table 7.2).

While the programme grew, substantially without foreign aid, there were frequent concerns about corruption and misspending. Studies and reports commonly found that a high proportion of the benefits flowed to children from non-poor backgrounds (CAMPE 2005; FMRP 2006; Ahmed et al. 2011; Baulch 2011;), while many eligible children were excluded, particularly in poorer areas (Ahmed and Sharmeen 2004). The lack of geographical targeting and the need to ration benefits gave rise to considerable effective frontline discretion in the selection process (Hossain 2010). The value of the cash stipends was too low to appreciably reduce the costs of schooling (Ahmed and Sharmeen 2004; DPE et al. 2014), and inflation eroded its value further over the 2010s (GoB 2017). Despite such concerns, almost 8 million children were covered by 2016.

A third phase of the PESP began in 2016, as part of a wider National Social Security Strategy. Reforms were undertaken to universalize access across all government-supported primary institutions in rural and urban areas, and to digitalize payments, through a database of service users and mobile money disbursements (GED 2015; GoB 2017). When fieldwork for this study was undertaken

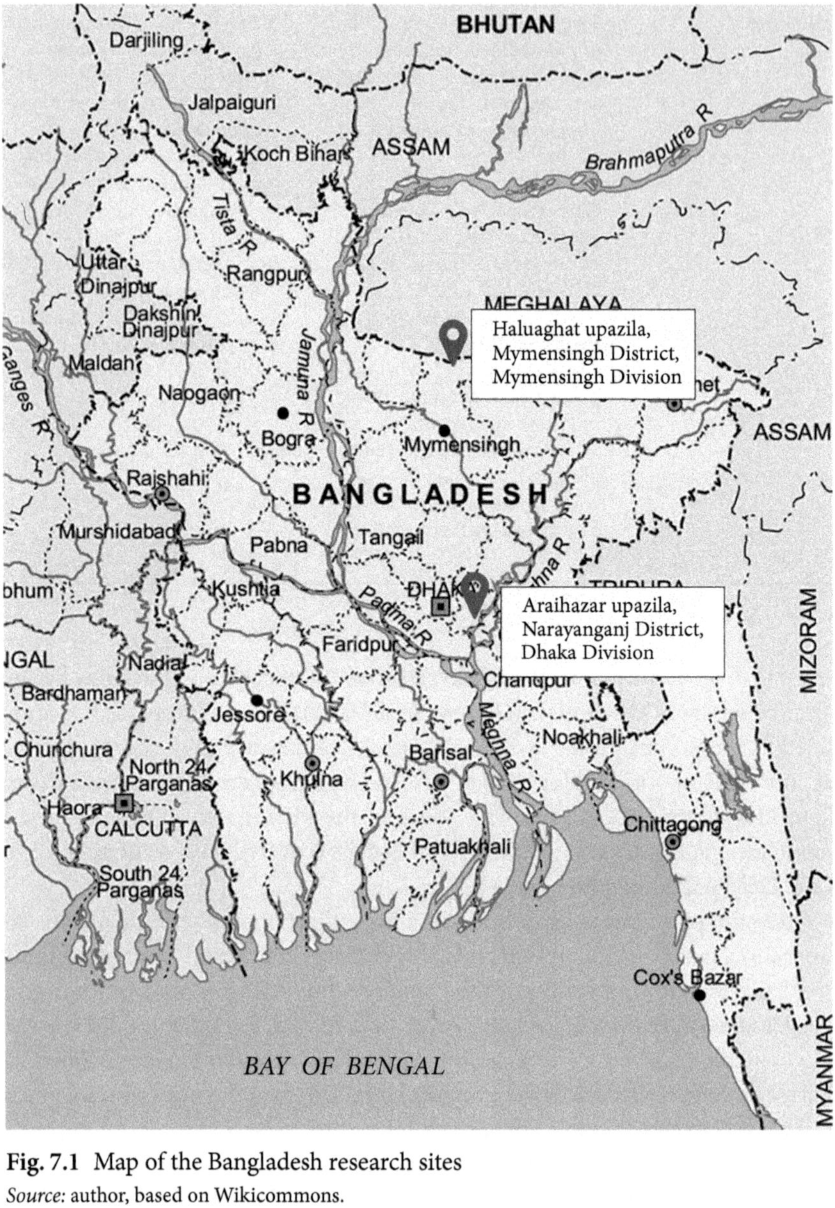

Fig. 7.1 Map of the Bangladesh research sites
Source: author, based on Wikicommons.

in 2018, schools had been receiving benefits for a year and a half, and so the study would have picked up the early adaptation and 'teething problems' of the new system.

As of 2016, the stipend programme was chiefly targeted to children receiving basic education (now extended to include pre-school and Grades VI to VIII)

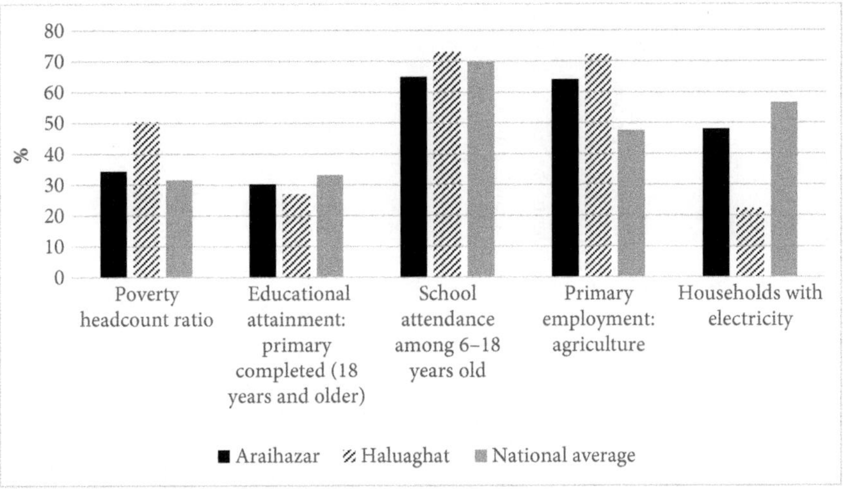

Fig. 7.2 Key social indicators for the research sites

Source: Bangladesh Interactive Poverty Maps, based on selected Bangladesh Bureau of Statistics Sources including BBS (2011); https://www.worldbank.org/en/data/interactive/2016/11/10/bangladesh-poverty-maps; accessed on 31 May 2021.

in schools supported or recognized by the government system. The 13 million children covered comprise around 90 per cent of all primary school children (DPE 2018). Children excluded from the stipend include those from middle-class and rich backgrounds who attend private schools; children who attend non-government organization (NGO) schools, who are often among the poorest, and faith-based schools that are not part of the government system; and the urban poor in informal settlements, where government school places are scarce, to avoid establishing these as permanent settlements (see World Bank 2013).

Stipends are intended, then, for the majority of children who are taught under the official curriculum. While by no means all children in the public system are poor, a rule of thumb is that poorer children tend to be concentrated in public schools. The inclusion of some urban schools under the latest PESP expansion signals recognition of the growing problem of urban poverty, and that Bangladesh's enduring 'rural bias' in social policy is no longer fit for a growing urban population (Banks 2015; World Bank 2016; Alam 2017). Metropolitan and city corporation mayoral and ward elections are more important sites of party competition than in the past, so urban politicians may view school stipend schemes as potential sources of political capital (Banks 2008). Similarly, the inclusion of *ebtedayee* or primary students enrolled in the government-supported Aliya *madrassah* system signals an effort to bring the more religious sections of society into the political fold, as part of the government's accommodation with the religious right (Islam 2018; Riaz 2018).

Table 7.2 Eligibility and targeting in the Food-For-Education and PESP programmes

Eligibility criteria	Food-For-Education (1993–2001)	PESP1 (2002–8)	PESP2 (2009–15)	PESP3 (2015/16–21)
Geographical	Poorest two or three unions in all 460 rural *upazilas* (approximately one-third of rural unions)	All rural unions	All rural unions	Rural and urban areas
Institutional	All rural government and government-supported primary schools and one *madrassah* per union	All rural government and government-supported primary schools, but also government-approved NGO schools	As with PESP1	As with PESP1 + some urban government- and government-supported primary schools + pre-primary students + students of Classes VI–VIII
HH; at least one of the following	Own less than half acre of land Headed by day labourers Female-headed Low-income occupations (fishers, potters, weavers)	As with Food-For-Education	As with Food-For-Education + students with disabilities	All households now eligible
Rationing (selection *within* eligible population)	Poorest 40% of students in each selected union	As with Food-For-Education	Poorest 40% of students across all rural areas + up to 90% of poorest students in targeted areas	No rationing; all eligible students
Conditions	Households not receiving other social safety nets Child attendance rate of 85%	Households not receiving other social safety nets Child attendance rate of 85% 50% marks on annual examination	Child attendance rate of 85% 50% marks on annual examination	85% attendance Pass annual examinations
Total numbers reached	2.1 million (approximately 13% of primary school population)	5.5 million	7.8 million (as of 2015/16)	Up to 13 million
Source	(Ahmed and del Ninno 2002)	(Ahmed et al. 2011; Baulch 2011)	(DPE et al. 2014)	(GoB 2017)

Citizen–state relations in 'Digital Bangladesh'

The stipend schemes expanded gradually through the period of multi-party rule, but rapidly after the Awami League government's decisive return to power in early 2009. The National Social Security Strategy aimed to transform social protection in Bangladesh, 'to streamline and strengthen the existing safety net programmes with a view to achieving better results from money spent'. Accompanying this drive for modernization has been a push for the digitalization of government data and service delivery mechanisms (Zaman 2015). The aim is to bring government closer to the people through 'Government to People' technologies that improve efficiency and shorten the distance between citizen and state. The digitalization of cash social protection payments is part of this strategy (World Bank 2018; a2i 2019).

The expanded PESP3 digitalizes the relationships between parents and their government, making them more direct, if unidirectional. By building a database of the 10 million guardians receiving the stipend, the government has the capacity to communicate with them directly and regularly through their mobile phones. The new PESP has acquired the title *Mayer Hashi* or 'Mothers' Happiness (/Laughter)', framing the government's cash transfers as the fulfilment of mothers' dreams for their children. In her speech inaugurating the mobile money disbursement in 2017, Prime Minister Sheikh Hasina said that in her time as opposition leader,

> Many mothers told me that they would send their children to school if we give them the same amount of money their children earn to support their family ... At that time we had taken a decision to introduce the stipend for poor students if we can come to power.
>
> (Sheik Hasina, cited in the Dhaka Tribune 2017)

Early analysis suggests that women are happier with the new PESP if they are literate and familiar with mobile phone technology (Gelb et al. 2019). In continuity with past versions of PESP, and the tradition of 'empowering' women in the service of the state's poverty reduction agenda (Molyneux 2006), PESP is expected to shape gender relations. From its earliest phases, the PESP was rationalized as both a form of empowerment for stipend mothers, and of efficiency, as women were deemed more likely to ensure the resources were used for educational purposes. One assessment concluded that 'women's empowerment' had been one of the key 'spillover effects' of the scheme (DPE et al. 2014, p. 29).

The reformed PESP3 features a similar emphasis on the roles of mothers as the primary recipients of the cash stipends, identifying positive side effects such as the 'financial inclusion' of women (Ghosh and Bhattacharya 2019). Beneficiaries receive SIM cards (although not phone units themselves) and registered mobile money accounts under the SureCash service provided by the government-owned Rupali Bank (Chiampo and Roest 2018). The creation of a profile database of

10 million regular beneficiaries has potential for direct political engagement by the government and ruling party, but the database has so far remained in the control of the private SureCash mobile money service provider. A recent study recommended that ownership be transferred to the Directorate of Primary Education (DPE) responsible for implementing the PESP (GoB 2017).

The politics of benefits and their distribution

The stipend payment is too small to reduce poverty (Pathmark 2010; DPE et al. 2014; GoB 2017), and inflation has halved its real value since 2000, while the population living in extreme poverty has fallen (BBS 2017). Nevertheless, by universalizing the stipend programme within government schools, the government appears to have two distinct aims beyond providing social protection. The first relates to education. By helping with the costs of schooling, and incentives for children to attend school in order to receive their stipends, PESP aims to improve educational outcomes within the public system. In its old design, the scheme had mixed impacts on education outcomes (Baulch 2011), but the scheme was seen to contribute to improving enrolment, attendance, and survival and progression through primary education (Pathmark 2010; DPE et al. 2014). If the universalized scheme helps strengthen norms about regular school attendance, it could contribute to increasing time-on-task in classrooms, and thereby support reforms intended to improve education outcomes in Bangladesh (Hossain et al. 2017).

The second aim was to remove the need to select beneficiaries, along with the effort and contention involved in that process. It is worth noting which groups are involved and which benefit from the new implementation arrangements. Teachers, a vital constituency for any ruling party, were burdened with the contentious task of selecting beneficiaries and distributing benefits for over a decade. This demoralized teachers and adversely affected their reputations: some parents blamed teachers when their children failed to receive their cash (Hossain 2010; Hossain 2017; DPE et al. 2014). In the redesigned PESP, teachers help register parents and record students' adherence to attendance and performance conditions, but handle no cash. The registration needs updating as children move and new cohorts start school, but this takes far less time than the old manual system. This is a great improvement from the point of view of teachers, who in the past were unfairly suspected of malfeasance when stipends did not arrive, and burdened with additional unpaid responsibilities, which took time away from classroom teaching.

Local community and political leaders were also previously involved in participant selection processes, either through their formal role within SMCs, or informally, using their social and political influence to get favoured names 'on the list' (Hossain 2010). The redesigned PESP has removed the need for participant selection, and therefore eliminated their role in the programme, and with it their interest in it. The removal of this intermediary level of actors between the state and citizen is a sign that the programme is a vehicle for bringing the state and citizens closer.

Key new actors in the reformed PESP are the private mobile money service providers and their agents. The history and policy process that led to the selection of SureCash, a private offshoot of the public Rupali Bank, as the service provider, could not be uncovered, and there is a notable lack of transparency about why the more established mobile money providers were not selected for this role. There are several concerns with the services provided by SureCash: the local contractors who disburse the cash to guardians are reportedly unreliably present, unavailable in some places, and in some cases demand extra payment. The system lacks functioning grievance redress mechanisms when service falls short. It should be noted that respondents thought that errors in the disbursement process were being followed up on by SureCash. However, the research team was unable to uncover any specifics, or to identify any measures put in place after the initial rounds to ensure improved accuracy of disbursement, or to establish or activate grievance redress mechanisms.

4. The politics of implementing the PESP3

Since 2016, all students attending public basic education institutions have been eligible for PESP. This categorical targeting was understood by respondents in the four research sites. According to an assistant teacher in rural Araihazar,

> Those who enrol their children in the private kindergartens have the means to provide for their education, unlike the poor who must opt for public schools.

The rule of thumb is that students in public schools are poor, and need the support of the stipend; students who can afford private school fees do not. By contrast, most respondents were unclear as to whether religious educational institutions were included. Fathers participating in a focus group discussion in the urban area of Haluaghat knew that the stipend program covered government schools, but were uncertain about religious schools. Mothers in the urban Araihazar site were confident (although incorrect) that neither kindergartens nor religious schools were covered. This confusion seems to reflect several facts. *Madrassah* schools in the government-approved *ebtedayee* Aliya *madrassah* institutions were only partially covered in past phases of the programme. Under the expanded scheme, all students in government-supported primary *madrassah* institutions are eligible. At the same time, PESP3 continues to exclude students attending un-approved Quomi *madrassahs*, of which there are many thousands. These tend to be foreign-funded,

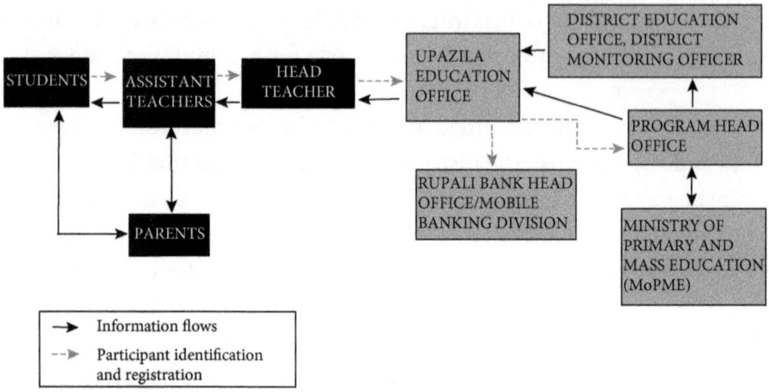

Fig. 7.3 Participant registration process

and they, as well as the small number of Christian mission schools, such as operate in Haluaghat in Mymensingh, are excluded from the programme.

Fig. 7.3 summarizes the process of participant registration. All eligible institutions are instructed to prepare participant lists by the Upazila Education Office. Student and parent details are recorded upon enrolment and in a 'Know Your Customer' form for banking services. Teachers prepare lists of eligible students and the amounts for which they are eligible to the head teacher, who is responsible for verifying information, printing lists, and submitting these to the Upazila Education Office. The Upazila Education Office verifies the lists and sends them to the project head office for approval, from where they are uploaded onto Rupali Bank's server.

The eradication of contentious participant selection

In earlier PESP phases, participant selection was onerous for teachers and contentious within the wider community. Eligible students were supposed to be identified and selected by the SMC through discussions with head teachers. Selected students who were seen to meet the eligibility criteria (or, in areas of greatest poverty, more of the eligibility criteria than other students) were put forward. The list of selected students would then be reviewed and approved by the Upazila Education Officer, and subsequently countersigned by the Upazila Nirbahi Officer.

Since the stipend programme did not cover all students enrolled at the primary school, the parents of the students who did not receive the stipend would try to persuade teachers and the SMC to put their children on the list. As one father in a focus group discussion in urban Haluaghat recalled, 'we'd have to butter up the schoolteachers to ensure our children were eligible'. A rural mother in Araihazar with secondary schooling noted that

> [b]efore the big people used to get most of the money; none used to go to the poor. They used to give it to people whose faces were known.

By implication, now you no longer needed to be a 'familiar face' to get the money. In the past, parents were said to have pressurized and behaved rudely with SMC members in their demands to get their own children on the PESP list, while politically powerful people were said to pressurize schoolteachers and SMC members to award stipends to students who were not technically eligible. For these reasons, highly localized political pressures often led to the selection of better-off students, and the exclusion of those deemed eligible. Some respondents felt supporters of the ruling party tended to have a better chance of getting on the list. The head teacher of a rural Araihazar school had himself faced protests by ruling party-affiliated groups after he had rejected 'suggestions' for inclusion in the programme. The education authorities had rejected demands for his relocation, but the incident illustrated the political energies devoted to participant selection.

This situation had notably improved with the expanded PESP, under which all children within a school were eligible. All teachers, parents, and SMC members noted with approval that this ugly contention was no longer necessary. With reference to the problems faced by teachers, assistant teacher Ms M, at 38 a veteran of previous PESP phases in rural Araihazar, noted that

> now, since all students are eligible for the stipend, we don't face any issues with selection and so we don't have any tension regarding this.

Mr M, a 48-year-old father of children in the urban Araihazar school, contrasted the situation in the past, when the poorest 40 per cent of children were supposed to receive the PESP, with the more harmonious present: 'now that a hundred out of a hundred are getting it, that conflict is no longer there'. In urban Haluaghat, a seasoned SMC chair explained that the old selection process used to lead to a 'whole load of pressures' on the SMC from local influential people and elected representatives, and it was sometimes a struggle 'to manage the whole process peacefully'. With the new 100 per cent coverage, he noted, 'we no longer receive these kinds of requests'.

Previously, local political pressure threw the participant selection process into disrepute, but the system still worked more or less to reach poorer children, with only 6 per cent of children from ineligible groups estimated to have received the stipend (DPE et al. 2014). An assistant teacher in rural Araihazar explained that this was because local political pressure was strenuously resisted by the school authorities, who strove to ensure the benefit went to eligible students from disadvantaged backgrounds, even though they were sometimes overpowered in these struggles. Twenty-nine-year-old Mrs P, a mother of children in the urban Haluaghat community, had completed primary school nearby, and while others had received the stipend, she had not. In her experience the stipend did not usually go to those with connections or money: the community accepted that teachers were mandated to ensure that the stipend went to those who needed it most.

Despite Mrs P's experience, there was a strong consensus among this group of young mothers, most with primary or junior secondary schooling, that the universalization of the scheme was a great improvement. As one Haluaghat mother explained it, 'because everyone is getting it there is no scope for corruption or connections'; in other words, the conditions for such contention were no longer present. Parents in urban areas were less familiar with the politics of targeting in the old stipend programme, because PESP had been suspended a few years earlier when the *upazila* was upgraded to an urban area (making its students ineligible). But in both rural areas, the strength of feeling was powerfully in favour of the new unselective process. This finding was supported by a recent survey of participant mothers, which found that some 79 per cent thought the new system was better overall, and 95 per cent considered it easier to register than in the past (Gelb et al. 2019).

These findings about the social tension associated with targeting, and the pleasing absence of such tension in the present scheme, draw attention to the high local social costs of targeting (MacAuslan and Riemenschneider 2011), in the form of distrust and loss of social harmony. For teachers, in particular, discontent around the preparation of the PESP list and the distribution of stipends has been a source of grave concern and loss of social respect from local communities (see Hossain 2017).

Not all respondents thought universalization would entirely eradicate the problems of corruption, however: one SMC member in urban Haluaghat suspected that teachers might inflate the lists and adjust enrolment sheets to secure more stipends. This seems improbable, given that national identity cards of stipend recipients' guardians are required to prepare these lists. But this baseless suspicion reflects both the broader lack of trust in public agencies and actors with respect to handling cash benefits, and the fact that SMC members no longer play a role in the administration of the stipends scheme.

While there was wide understanding that PESP3 was for 'all' children in eligible institutions, there was less clarity about the conditions of the scheme. In general, there was knowledge that students were expected to attend and pass annual exams, but some parents thought 75 per cent attendance was acceptable, even though the official guidance states 85 per cent. Some parents were unclear that teachers were expected to record attendance and put forward only those children who met all the conditions. This lack of clarity meant that it was often unclear as to whether children who did not receive the stipend did not do so because they failed to meet those conditions or because of some other problem in the system (corruption, for instance).

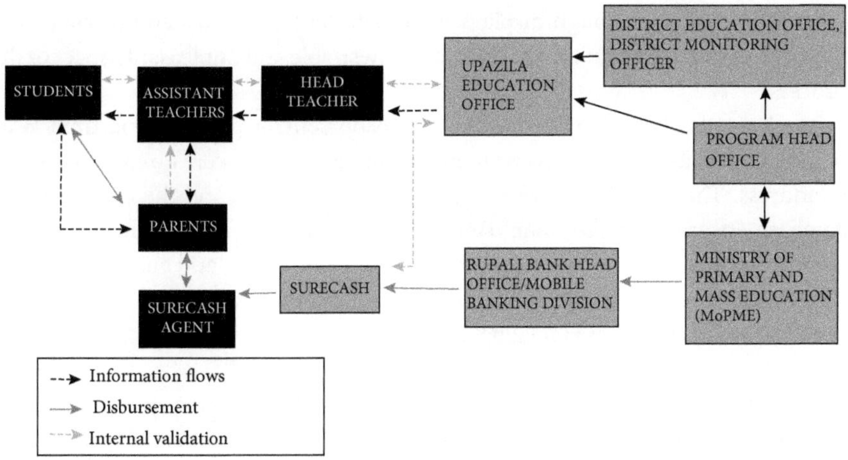

Fig. 7.4 Validation and disbursement processes

Disbursing the stipend

The disbursement system works as outlined in Fig. 7.4. Once the Upazila Education Officers upload student information onto the Rupali Bank server, the Mobile Division of the bank prepares the data and sends the database to SureCash. SureCash then conducts an internal validation of the student records (identifying wrong or missing values), which are returned to the relevant Upazila Education Office for verification. The updated phone numbers are then used by SureCash for disbursement. Mobile text messages are sent to the phone numbers on a particular date, over a period of several hours. Upon receiving the text messages, the parents/custodians of the students can then visit a SureCash agent with the text message and claim the cash.

In previous phases, state-owned banks disbursed the stipends at local branches or disbursement sites near the school. Guardians, mostly mothers, would collect the stipend upon presenting the PESP bank-issued identity card. The old system was notoriously onerous, as mothers had to travel to set locations and queue for hours twice a year. This meant travel costs, time away from domestic labour, and mothers sometimes missed dates or were unable to attend. Disbursement could be fractious. A group of mothers in their thirties in rural Haluaghat described how, when everyone was gathered to collect their payments, 'in the heat, someone would pull someone's clothes or *dupatta* or hair and then a scuffle would start', particularly if someone tried to jump the queue. '[A]nd then when the hair-pulling and clothes-tugging had started, everyone would come from all over to see what the fuss was about', exposing women to the ridicule of the local community. Teachers reported such tussles as common, leading to actual violence on occasion. Local education officials viewed such rough displays with distaste; for officials and teachers, the physical disbursement of the cash was an undesirable and unpleasant aspect of the process.

Teachers also complained that the old disbursement process took time away from teaching, as well as exposing them to complaints they were rarely empowered to address. The 'new system removes most of the hassles', and the computerized database ensures that the same data are not re-collected each year but updated automatically, saving teachers considerable time and effort, and ensuring more of their work time can be devoted to classroom teaching, as the head teacher of an urban primary school in Haluaghat explained. Nonetheless,

> there are sometimes new problems, such as when parents give the wrong number. There might be many reasons why a number is wrong—it might be the typing [i.e. possibly the teachers' fault]. But we don't have the time to check up on each and every number.
>
> (Mr H, 46, head teacher in urban Haluaghat)

Access to mobile phones and the ability to read SMS were important in how parents evaluated the new system. Gelb et al. found that women preferred the mobile transfers when they had easy access to an agent and could understand the SMS. While 60 per cent of women owned telephones, the rest relied on others for their access (Gelb et al. 2019). Access to mobile phones and 'SMS literacy' are evidently important factors in determining how successfully the programme disburses payments (see also GoB 2017).

Gender matters in the adoption of this mobile money disbursement technology. While the programme description emphasizes that mothers receive the cash, there is no actual requirement for schools to register mothers specifically. As women are less likely than men to own phones or visit markets where SureCash agents are present, it is more likely now than in the past that payments will be received in the first instance by men. The programme has attempted to overcome some of the problems, by distributing special SIM cards for registered beneficiaries. But the introduction of technology has introduced a new gender dimension to programme implementation that was previously absent.

Across the sites, there was strong consensus that the money should go to mothers because 'they understand their children's needs best'. This was not presented as a matter of women's empowerment, but of common sense: fathers could receive the money, but it was better for it to go to women. There was one telling point of difference on this: some Bengali Muslim fathers in the rural Haluaghat site queried the benefits of transferring the stipend to mothers, saying that while this was fine for the Garo people of the locality, because of their 'matriarchal' culture, it was different for Muslims. These comments did not indicate actual opposition to the stipends going to mothers, or to the view that mothers were equipped to spend the money correctly. Instead, it drew attention to differences in gender ideology between the majority Bengali Muslim and the Garo population. That such minor reservations were found in the only site with a substantial minority group population highlights its exceptional nature: the general rule is to accept the practice of transferring stipends to mothers.

Despite the improved system, many participating parents had complaints. Some parents queried the amounts they had received, often (as teachers pointed out) without understanding that students are awarded the stipend based on monthly attendance records, so that their payments may be made on a sliding scale. Some reported having to make additional payments to the SureCash agents, amounting to as much as BDT 40 out of the BDT 600 standardly disbursed. These complaints were more common in the rural sites, suggesting that the scarcity of SureCash agents in those areas was enabling them to extract illegal 'taxes' from rural women. In the central and developed setting of rural Araihazar, mothers advocated moving the programme to the bigger mobile money provider, bKash, which disburses the Secondary School Stipends without charge (GoB 2017). The survey by Gelb et al. (2019) similarly found higher support for distribution through bKash, no doubt reflecting its greater recognition as a national brand.

However, some people complained that they had not received the stipend after it had been digitalized. It is not clear what proportion of the total population for 2016/17 (the year it started) was affected, but the diagnostic study noted a 'significant' amount of unspent funds, suggesting that substantial numbers of beneficiaries had not received their disbursements. This may be due to errors a) in registration (administrative or parental); b) in disbursal (via the Rupali Bank-held database and SureCash transfer system); or c) at the point of collection (for instance, the phone number was no longer in operation; the SMS was missed; the SureCash agent claimed there was no such account/has no funds at the time of the claim) (GoB 2017).

It is likely that the errors emanate from high up the system, rather than at registration or disbursement point because complaints about mass exclusions from the stipend were concentrated in a single site, in rural Araihazar. Here, the first time the stipend was distributed electronically, 'around 300' mothers, representing more than half the school's parents, did not receive the cash. Teachers explained that they had verified phone numbers and found few errors; they had taken the issue up to the *upazila* education officials, who were equally unable to determine the problem. One official explained that, while under the old manual disbursement system, the Upazila Education Office was informed about how much money was going to the schools, mobile transfers cut them out of this information flow. As a result, when schoolteachers complain that some of the recipients did not receive the money, the Upazila Education Officer can do little to verify or act. Some officials suggested disbursement information should be shared with the Upazila Education Officer, so the office could follow up on complaints.

Other sites had fewer complaints about funds not being received, and could chiefly explain these through the difficulties of accessing mobiles or networks, understanding messages, and locating agents. This comparatively poor implementation in the rural Araihazar site cannot be explained with reference to political competition or weak state capacity, as this is a centrally located area with good infrastructure, in which local intra- and inter-party political competition has given way to rule by groups linked to the ruling party. As a rural area, people in the community were accustomed to the stipends scheme and well informed about its main features. There were fewer reasons to believe that this site, of all the four sites, would be deprived of the stipend for political reasons. It seems instead that this unfortunate oversight reflected the bigger teething problems with the initial rollout of the mobile transfers. SureCash officials explained that they were aware of such glitches in the initial phases, and were ironing out such problems. In other words, this was more likely to have been a technological problem than an effect of the politics of implementation.

Information, accountability, and grievance mechanisms

The benefits of the new programme were commonly agreed, if challenged on some points in practice. In key respects, the new programme has eased the flow of information, by reducing uncertainty about who is eligible and how payments are to be made. But information flows vary, and in ways that reflect differences in state infrastructural power. Garo parents in the rural Haluaghat site, the site furthest from the administrative centre, and the one most marked by ethnic difference, said they had no information about the programme from the school's head teacher. This may have reflected the dynamics of local conflict, as Garo and some Bengali parents had campaigned for the removal of this head teacher on grounds of incompetence and neglect; his strong relationship with the chair of the SMC continued to insulate him against parental discontent. Nevertheless, when some children did not receive stipends, the parents went to the head teacher. The details were corrected, and they received the next round (whether due to his actions was unknown).

In both urban sites, parents had uneven information about the details of the scheme, but in the towns, this was because of its overall novelty. Whether or not they were interested depended on how much parents cared about the money. As the amounts are small, it was unsurprising that better-off fathers had a more casual knowledge of the scheme than rural mothers, for whom the amounts were more significant. Education administrators at *upazila*- and school-level displayed a clear and consistent grasp of the programme, and referred to the training and guidance they had received. Several complained, nonetheless, that while high-ranking project officials received overseas training, head teachers and *upazila* officials were expected to master computers, database management, and uploading data with inadequate training.

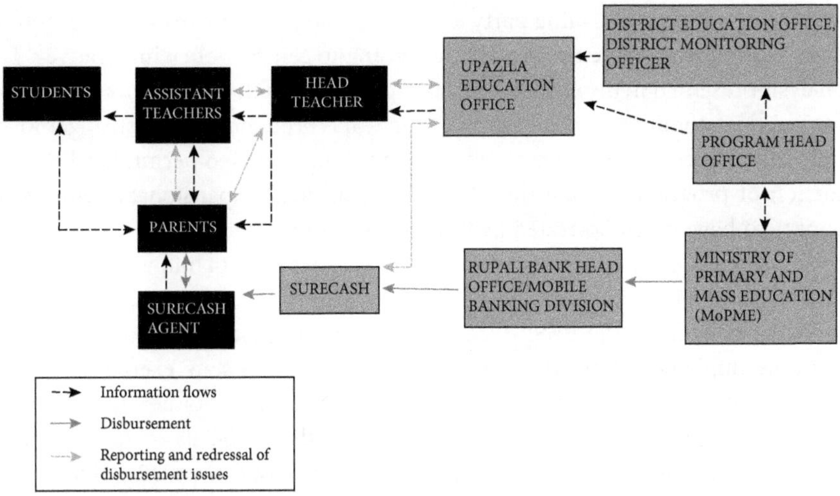

Fig. 7.5 Reporting and redressing disbursement grievances

In addition, the reduction of the role of school and Upazila Education Offices in the programme left these frontline officials with fewer means of addressing grievances or answering complaints. One set of erstwhile stakeholders without knowledge of the reformed process was SMC members. They had previously played a role in helping parents to lodge complaints or make claims. When asked if they helped resolve problems around the stipend, SMC members noted they had no way of helping and no part in, or knowledge of, how it worked under the new system. Teachers also pointed out that their role was now limited to compiling the list, and registering attendance and enrolment; when parents came to them with claims or complaints, at most they could refer them to the Upazila Education Officer. Officials themselves noted that their role was equally limited, and indicated activities at the Rupali Bank and with the SureCash agent as the critical points at which any errors could be addressed.

Fig. 7.5 summarizes the process of reporting complaints and attempting to gain redress. Information flows are established and functioning adequately between students, parents, teachers, *upazila* education officials, and the project staff. By contrast, there are no obvious points of entry for information from the SureCash agents, the SureCash parent entity, or from the various Rupali Bank divisions responsible for delivery on the ground.

5. Conclusion

The study was guided by a two-part proposition about the politics of implementing social protection in Bangladesh: that the growing political dominance of the ruling party provides incentives to expand and improve the performance of the PESP, and that the dominant ruling party exercises greater power to discipline frontline actors to implement the programme according to central policy imperatives. The analysis presented in the chapter affirms the first part of the proposition: the growing political dominance of the Awami League has brought with it a stronger focus on performance legitimacy, which has reduced incentives to permit local manipulation of programmes like the PESP. As such, PESP expansionary reforms do appear to have been motivated by political incentives to reach more of the rural majority with a popular service which serves broader goals of human development and educational attainment.

While reforms to the PESP succeeded in reducing local discretion over programme implementation, this was not the result of the state exercising greater power to discipline or motivate frontline actors, as expected. Rather than strengthening its capacities to discipline or control frontline officials or local political representatives, the reform of PESP has vacated much of the space in which frontline discretion was once exercised and where state infrastructural power was weak by deploying a universal design and new technology. This is in a spirit of bringing the government closer to the people, bypassing mediating groups rather than holding them to account for delivering public policy. This has meant PESP has been implemented in a comparatively rule-based manner, although it also suffers from some apparently technological and quite possibly temporary teething problems.

In its latest phase, the programme involves a bold set of reforms, which substantially eradicate the contentious politics of participant selection and disbursement. The complaints, antagonisms, and lobbying of the past have been replaced with an assumption that all are eligible (unless they do not meet the conditions). The fractious and time-consuming process of queuing on a set day to receive the payments has also disappeared in large part, even though parents still must collect payments once they receive the information that their money has been sent. These are great benefits from the point of view of education officials, teachers, parents, and children. Local elites no longer play a role, even to help parents register or follow up on complaints.

Digitalization is widely considered a boon, for speed, ease of database management, and accuracy. Nevertheless, areas of concern regarding the implementation of PESP3 include, first, that mothers may have less access to mobile phones, or find it difficult to understand or access the mobile money services, and second, that the digitalized process renders the disbursement process opaque to most parents. In the absence of well-functioning grievance redress mechanisms, when the disbursements go wrong because of problems in the registration process or in the SureCash distribution system, it is not clear where the error is, or how it can be rectified. As this study took place in the very early stages of this new phase, it seems likely that many of these errors will be rectified in later phases. Nevertheless, the question of accountability for errors and failures remains unanswered: it is not known how parents can claim their entitlements if SureCash fails to deliver, or its agents fail to pay up in full.

While the reform suggests that the state's infrastructural power has grown, it also suggests that the central state views its local functionaries as an obstacle, rather than an intermediary, in its efforts to reach the citizenry. There is a more limited role for frontline actors than in the past, and no signs that officials at any level are held to account for programme failures. On the other hand, there is clear and consistent information across education officials and teachers about the programme, signalling at least knowledge of the programme's central policy aims. Parents continued to rely on teachers and schools for their information, and received limited direct communication about it from the central state. This may change over time, as parents become accustomed to receiving messages from the government on their mobile phones. But, to date, the old analogue means of face-to-face communication remain important. However, the mechanisms for implementing the programme had become simpler and more manageable for frontline officials. This, rather than formal accountability systems, may help to explain why there is a closer fit between the expressed aims and targets of central policy-making actors, and who benefits and how in practice.

Notes

1. The author thanks Professor Ferdous Jahan, Dr Asif Shahan and Md. Mamun-Ur-Rashid for their valuable guidance and advice with this research, and to the Development Research Initiative team for their excellent research support.
2. There were approximately 120 Bangladeshi taka to the British pound at the time of fieldwork in 2018.

References

a2i, 2019. Accelerating G2P Payment Digitization—A2i. Dhaka: a2i, Government of the People's Republic of Bangladesh. Available online: https://a2i.gov.bd/publication/accelerating-g2p-payment-digitization/ (accessed 3 December 2020).

Ahmed, A. U. and Del Ninno, C., 2002. The Food for Education program in Bangladesh. *FCND Discussion Papers*, 138. Washington, DC: International Food Policy Research Institute (IFPRI).

Ahmed, A. U., Khondkar, M., and Quisumbing, A. R., 2011. Understanding the context of institutions and policy processes for selected anti-poverty interventions in Bangladesh. *Journal of Development Effectiveness*, 3 (2), 175–192.

Ahmed, A. U., Rashid, S., Sharma, M., and Zohir, S., 2004. *Food Aid Distribution in Bangladesh: Leakage and Operational Performance.* Washington, DC: Food Consumption and Nutrition Division, International Food Policy Research Institute.

Ahmed, A. U. and Sharmeen, T., 2004. *Assessing the Performance of Conditional Cash Transfer Programs for Girls and Boys in Primary and Secondary Schools in Bangladesh.* Washington, DC: International Food Policy Research Institute.

Alam, S., ed., 2017. *Exploring the Evidence: Background Research Papers for Preparing the National Social Security Strategy for Bangladesh.* Dhaka: General Economics Division, Planning Commission of the People's Republic of Bangladesh.

Asadullah, M. N., Savoia, A., and Mahmud, W., 2014. Paths to development: Is there a Bangladesh surprise? *World Development*, 62 (October), 138–154.

Banks, N., 2008. A tale of two wards: Political participation and the urban poor in Dhaka City. *Environment and Urbanization*, 20 (2), 361–376.

Banks, N., 2015. Livelihoods limitations: The political economy of urban poverty in Dhaka, Bangladesh: The political economy of urban poverty in Dhaka. *Development and Change*, 47 (2), 266–292.

Baulch, B., 2011. The medium-term impact of the Primary Education Stipend in rural Bangladesh. *Journal of Development Effectiveness*, 3 (2), 243–262.

BBS, 2011. *Household Income and Expenditure Survey (HIES) 2010*. Dhaka: Bangladesh Bureau of Statistics, Statistics Division, Ministry of Planning.

BBS, 2017. *Preliminary Report on Household Income and Expenditure Survey (HIES) 2016*. Dhaka: Bangladesh Bureau of Statistics, Statistics Division, Ministry of Planning.

CAMPE, 2005. *Quality with Equity: The Primary Education Agenda*. Education Watch Report 2003–04. Dhaka: Campaign for Popular Education.

Chiampo, M. and Roest, J., 2018. How Bangladesh digitized education aid for 10 million families. CGAP. Online resource: https://www.cgap.org/blog/how-bangladesh-digitized-education-aid-10-million-families (accessed 3 December 2020).

Dhaka Tribune, 2017. PM launches stipend distribution through mobile banking. *Dhaka Tribune*, 1 March. Available online: https://www.dhakatribune.com/bangladesh/education/2017/03/01/pm-launches-stipend-distribution-mobile-banking (accessed 3 December 2020).

DPE, 2018. *Annual Primary School Census 2018*. Dhaka: Directorate of Primary Education, Ministry of Primary and Mass Education, Government of Bangladesh.

DPE, PPRC, and UNICEF, 2014. *Bangladesh Primary Education Stipends: A Qualitative Assessment*. Dhaka: Directorate of Primary Education, Ministry of Primary and Mass Education, Government of Bangladesh; UNICEF. Available online: https://reliefweb.int/report/bangladesh/bangladesh-primary-education-stipends-qualitative-assessment (accessed 3 December 2020).

FMRP, 2006. *Primary Education in Bangladesh*. Social Sector Performance Surveys. Dhaka: Financial Management Reform Programme, Ministry of Finance, Government of Bangladesh.

GED, 2015. *National Social Security Strategy (NSSS) of Bangladesh*. Dhaka: General Economics Division, Bangladesh Planning Commission, Government of the People's Republic of Bangladesh.

Gelb, A., Mukherjee, A., Navis, K., Akter, M., and Naima, J., 2019. *Primary Education Stipends in Bangladesh: Do Mothers Prefer Digital Payments over Cash?* Washington, DC: Center for Global Development. Available online: https://www.cgdev.org/publication/primary-education-stipends-bangladesh-do-mothers-prefer-digital-payments-over-cash (accessed 3 December 2020).

Ghosh, A. and Bhattacharya, L., 2019. SureCash: Promoting financial inclusion in Bangladesh. *Asian Management Insights*, May, 50–58.

GoB, 2017. *A Diagnostic Study on Stipend Programmes in Bangladesh with Focus on Primary Education Stipend Project (PESP)*. Dhaka: Finance Division, Ministry of Finance, Government of the People's Republic of Bangladesh.

Hassan, M., 2013. Political settlement dynamics in a limited-access order: The case of Bangladesh. *ESID Working Papers*, 23. Manchester: Effective States and Inclusive Development Research Centre, University of Manchester.

Hassan, M. and Nazneen, S., 2017. Violence and the breakdown of the political settlement: An uncertain future for Bangladesh? *Conflict, Security and Development*, 17 (3), 205–223.

Hassan, M. and Prichard, W., 2016. The political economy of domestic tax reform in Bangladesh: Political settlements, informal institutions and the negotiation of reform. *Journal of Development Studies*, 52 (12), 1704–1721.

Hickey, S., Sen, K., and Bukenya, B., 2015. Exploring the politics of inclusive development: Towards a new conceptual approach. *In:* S. Hickey, K. Sen, and B. Bukenya, eds. *The Politics of Inclusive Development: Interrogating the Evidence*. Oxford: Oxford University Press, 3–34.

Hossain, M. A., 2017. Parents', teacher's, and head teacher's perceptions of the Primary Education Stipend Programme (PESP) in improving access and quality of primary education in Bangladesh. Doctoral thesis, University of Sussex.

Hossain, N., 2010. School exclusion as social exclusion: The practices and effects of a conditional cash transfer programme for the poor in Bangladesh. *Journal of Development Studies*, 46 (7), 1264–1282.

Hossain, N., Hassan, M., Rahman, M. A., Ali, K. S., and Islam, M. S., 2017. The problem with teachers: The political settlement and education quality reforms in Bangladesh. *ESID Working Papers*, 86. Manchester: Effective States and Inclusive Development Research Centre, University of Manchester.

Hossain, N. and Osman, F. A., 2007. Politics and governance in the social sectors in Bangladesh, 1991–2006. *BRAC RED Monographs*, 34. Dhaka: Research and Evaluation Division, BRAC.

Islam, M. M., 2018. Secularism in Bangladesh: An unfinished revolution. *South Asia Research*, 38 (1), 20–39.

Khan, M. H., 2014. Aid and governance in vulnerable states: Bangladesh and Pakistan since 1971. *Annals of the American Academy of Political and Social Science*, 656 (1), 59–78.

Lewis, D. and Van Schendel, W., 2020. Rethinking the Bangladesh state. *Contributions to Indian Sociology*, 54 (2), 306–323.

MacAuslan, I. and Riemenschneide, N., 2011. Richer but resented: What do cash transfers do to social relations? *IDS Bulletin*, 42 (6), 60–66.

Mills, A., Durepos, G., and Wiebe, E., 2010. Most different systems design. *In: Encyclopedia of Case Study Research*, Thousand Oaks, CA: SAGE Publications, 571–572.

Molyneux, M., 2006. Mothers at the service of the new poverty agenda: Progresa/Oportunidades, Mexico's conditional transfer programme. *Social Policy and Administration*, 40 (4), 425–449.

Pathmark, 2010. *Evaluation Study of the Primary Education Stipend Project* (first phase). Dhaka: IMED, Ministry of Planning, Government of the People's Republic of Bangladesh.

Rahman, H. Z., Choudhury, L. A., and Ali, K. S., 2011. *Social Safety Nets in Bangladesh, Volume 1: Review of Issues and Analytical Inventory*. Dhaka: PPRC/UNDP.

Rahman, H. Z., Hulme, D., Maitrot, M., and Ragno, L. P., 2014. *Social Protection in Bangladesh: Building Effective Social Safety Nets and Ladders Out of Poverty*. Dhaka: University Press Limited.

Raynor, J. and Wesson, K., 2006. The Girls' Stipend Program in Bangladesh. *Journal of Education for International Development*, 2 (2), 1–12.

Riaz, A., 2018. More than meets the eye: The narratives of secularism and Islam in Bangladesh. *Asian Affairs*, 49 (2), 301–318.

Riaz, A., 2019. *Voting in a Hybrid Regime: Explaining the 2018 Bangladeshi Election*. New York: Springer.

Tietjen, K., 2003. The Bangladesh Primary Education Stipend Project: A Descriptive Analysis. Partnership on Sustainable Strategies for Girls' Education. Available online: http://interactions.eldis.org/sites/interactions.eldis.org/files/database _sp/Bangladesh/Primary%20Education%20Stipend%20Project%20(PESP) /BangladeshStipend.pdf (accessed 3 December 2020).

Van Schendel, W., 2004. *The Bengal Borderland*. London: Anthem Press.

Van Schendel, W., 2009. *A History of Bangladesh*. Cambridge: Cambridge University Press.

World Bank, 2013. Seeding fertile ground: Education that works for Bangladesh. *Education Sector Reviews*, 80613. World Bank. Available online: http://documents.worldbank.org/curated/en/2013/09/18460267/seeding-fertile-ground-education-works-bangladesh (accessed 3 December 2020).

World Bank, 2016. Bangladesh social protection and labor review: Towards smart social protection and jobs for the poor. *Bangladesh Development Series Papers*, 33. Bangladesh Development Series. Dhaka: World Bank.

World Bank, 2018. Cash transfer modernization project (P160819): Project appraisal document. *Project Appraisal Documents*, PAD2224. Washington, DC: World Bank.

Zaman, H., 2015. Service delivery process innovation: Insights from digital Bangladesh. *Innovation and Development* 5 (1), 165–168.

8

The Politics of Social Protection in Nepal

State Infrastructural Power and Implementation of the Scholarship Programme

Uma Pradhan, Deepak Thapa, Jeevan Baniya, Yangchen Gurung, Sanjay Mahato, and Indrajit Roy

1. Introduction

Social protection schemes have emerged in Nepal as a crucial national priority and a means of making the Nepali state both inclusive and effective. Two distinct sets of literatures have emerged to explain the growth of social protection in Nepal. One strand focuses on the adoption of such schemes, affirming that these have emerged as a response to chronic social exclusions in the country (Kabeer 2009) with the intention to foster nation building and political healing (Koehler and Mathers 2017). These studies also affirm the important role played by social and political movements to put pressure on the Nepali state to ensure inclusive programmes (Hangen 2010; Lawoti 2013) and strengthen the democratization process (Drucza 2017). The second strand of the literature focuses on the impact of social protection schemes. This work points to the ways in which these schemes strengthen the relationship between states and citizens (Drucza 2019), have a positive impact on beneficiaries' lives (Sijapati 2017), and offer different avenues for state–citizen engagement (Pradhan 2019).

By drawing attention to the varied capacities, discourses, and interests at different layers of state bureaucracy, this chapter explores the complex dynamics shaping the implementation of education assistance in Nepal, popularly known as the 'Scholarship Programme'. This programme provides cash stipends to primary and secondary students of marginalized communities. The Scholarship Programme exemplifies the 'protective' dimension of social protection, designed as it is to provide recipients with relief from deprivation (Sabates-Wheeler and Devereux 2009). Furthermore, by promoting education among historically oppressed groups, the Scholarship Programme emphasizes the 'transformative' dimension of social protection (Sijapati 2017). Its multi-faceted dimensions make

Uma Pradhan et al., *The Politics of Social Protection in Nepal.* In: *The Politics of Distributing Social Transfers.* Edited by Tom Lavers, Oxford University Press.
DOI: 10.1093/oso/9780192862525.003.0008

the Scholarship Programme a crucial component of social protection in Nepal, and it demands to be studied more extensively than at present. This particularly relates to implementation, since effective implementation at all the stages of the programme is crucial for the realization of the intended objectives and, ultimately, to assess the claims of such programmes as instruments of social inclusion.

The analysis that follows examines the differential interests, ideas, and capacities of three distinct levels of the state bureaucracy: (1) the central state; (2) the local state; and (3) the everyday state. In doing so, it notes the ways in which they have a varied impact on the implementation of the programme, thereby drawing attention to the disaggregated nature of state infrastructural power. Beyond the central state and the districts that comprise the local state, the schools that constitute the everyday state play a vital role in the implementation of the Scholarship Programme and give concrete shape to abstract central policy in their encounters with students. Such everyday actors perform a pivotal role in determining state practices, thus contributing significantly to our understanding of the state (Lipsky 1980). Schools distribute scholarships to the students, thus making them the state agencies that interface with citizens on a daily basis. Schools are thus essential to an understanding of the ways in which the Scholarship Programme operates on an everyday basis.

This chapter makes two distinct arguments. First, it highlights the importance of infrastructural power to the implementation of social transfers. In particular, the main implementation failings of the Scholarship Programme can be attributed to the relations between state agencies and the limited capacity of higher levels of the state to monitor effectively the actions of lower levels. One notable source of divergence between these state agencies is the different ways in which the Scholarship Programme is framed by different state actors, suggesting that different narratives, as well as material interests, of state actors can limit the infrastructural power of the state. Second, the research concludes that programme design can compensate for some of the limitations of state infrastructural power. In particular, the framing of the Scholarship Programme in terms of advancing social justice has resulted in the use of categorical targeting to distribute scholarships to *all* girls and historically marginalized castes. This categorical targeting considerably limits the logistical demands placed on the state in comparison with poverty targeting and, as such, is more in line with the limitations of state infrastructural power in Nepal.

The chapter proceeds by outlining the methodology pursued in the research and the rationale for selection of case studies of implementation. Next, the chapter presents an overview of the political factors shaping the design and origins of the Scholarship Programme, highlighting the use of the scholarships as a means of overcoming social injustice by focusing on marginalized social groups. The main analytical sections examine the process of implementing the Scholarship Programme across the disaggregated levels of the state, focusing on two main issues: first, how the distribution of scholarships and the application of targeting and conditionality criteria are shaped by distinct narratives used to justify the programme; and, second, how the limited infrastructural power of the state contributes to major problems with the disbursement of the scholarships.

2. Research design and methodology

This chapter draws on fieldwork in four districts[1]: (1) Ilam; (2) Saptari; (3) Lalitpur; and (4) Jumla (see Fig. 8.1). The four districts are located in four distinct regions of Nepal, each uniquely situated within the historic process of Nepalese state formation. Lalitpur district abuts the national capital of Kathmandu. Its proximity to Kathmandu, the centre of the high-caste Khas Hindu Nepalese state for over 200 years, has contributed to a relatively high level of state infrastructural power, including a greater presence of state institutions in the district. Likewise, a high level of state infrastructural power in Ilam district, located in Nepal's far east, resulted from a process of increasing state control over the communal lands of the indigenous Limbu community. Distinct from both these processes, state formation in the southern district of Saptari exemplifies neglect by the state and limited infrastructural power, as illustrated by high student–teacher ratios, and appalling levels of poverty and illiteracy. State infrastructural power in the mid-western district of Jumla is impacted by the region's geographic remoteness from Kathmandu. Despite having been the centre of the sprawling twelfth-century 'Khas kingdom', the district rapidly declined in importance once the centre of political gravity shifted to Kathmandu in the eighteenth century. These variations in the infrastructural power of the state find resonance in contemporary socio-economic indices, as demonstrated in Table 8.1.

Case selection also reflected considerable variation in ethnic diversity and the balance of social power in districts across Nepal (see Table 8.2). Members of the historically oppressed Tamang community in Lalitpur, for example, remained largely apathetic to the political churning around them during the ethnic movements of the 1990s (Carter Center 2013). Likewise, members of the Kami, Sarki, Damai, and other oppressed Dalit communities in Jumla remained largely aloof from the Maoist movement whose strongholds lay in the vicinity. By contrast, members of historically oppressed communities, such as the Limbu in Ilam, and the Yadavs and Tharus in Saptari, actively participated in and often led ethnic, linguistic, and caste movements directed against political domination by the 'high caste' Khas leadership of the Nepali state.

In selecting these districts, we expected to find variation in the implementation of the Scholarship Programme between districts, with better implementation in districts with higher levels of infrastructural power, such as Ilam and Lalitpur, and greater politicization of subaltern groups, who would be in a position to hold local officials to account, such as in Ilam and Saptari. However, the analysis that follows

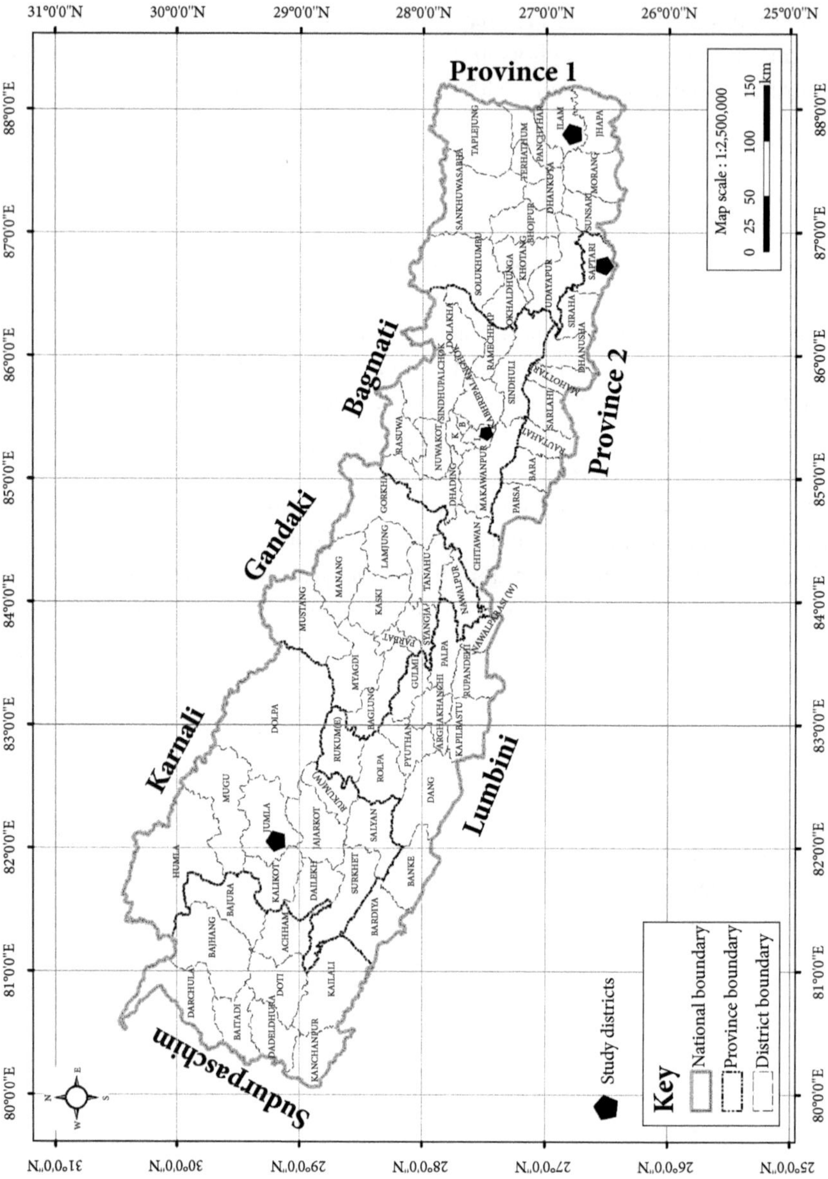

Fig. 8.1 Map of the Nepalese research sites
Source: NAXA for Social Science Baha.

did not suggest significant differences in implementation. Rather, all four districts faced similar challenges in the disbursement of the scholarships.

In all four districts, significant educational budgets were allocated to the school Scholarship Programme. Table 8.3 shows the total budget allocated to the

Table 8.1 Socio-economic indices of research districts

	Ilam	Saptari	Lalitpur	Jumla	National total
Total population	290,254	639,284	468,123	108,921	26,494,504
Total schools	432	449	184	156	29,035
Total students	60,123	129,475	44,157	38,999	6,062,806
Development assistance (USD million)	4.487	8.483	15.787	5.991	–
Child malnutrition (%)	46	34	16	54	41
Poverty rate (%)	7	40	8	49	24
Total teachers	2,352	2,575	1,813	811	152,480
Student–school ratio	139	288	240	250	209
Student–teacher ratio	26	50	24	48	40
Life expectancy (years)	68	71	70	63	
Adult literacy (%)	73	45	80	44	66
Mean years of schooling	5	3	6	3	
Per capita income (NPR)	1,260	801	1,894	1,007	1,160
Human Development Index	0.518	0.437	0.601	0.409	0.574

Source: Adapted from DoE 2018b, MoF 2018, and Sharma et al. 2014.

Table 8.2 Social composition of research districts

	Ilam	Saptari	Lalitpur	Jumla	Nepal
Region	East	East	Central	Mid-west	
Population	290,254	639,284	468,132	108,921	26,494,504
Nepali-speaking population (%)	43	79	48	99	45
Ethnic composition (top three, %)	Rai: 24; Limbu: 16; Brahman: 14	Yadav: 16; Tharu: 12; Muslim: 9	Newar: 33; Chhetri: 19; Tamang: 13	Chettri: 60; Brahman: 11; Thakuri: 7	Chhetri: 17; Brahman: 12; Magar: 7
Ethnic diversity index	86.7	93.0	63.9	58.1	93.4

Source: CBS (2014).

municipalities and rural municipalities for scholarships in the four research districts for the fiscal year 2018/19. The highest amount of budget was allocated to scholarships for girl students. This was followed by scholarships for Dalit students. Comparison of Tables 8.2 and 8.3 suggests that the budgets allocated to the different districts are commensurate to their population.

Table 8.3 Budget allocated by type of scholarship and district (hundreds of Nepalese rupees)

	Ilam	Saptari	Lalitpur	Jumla
Scholarship for girl students (1–8)	8,397	13,674	7,031	4,992
Scholarship for Dalits (1–8)	1,502	14,929	1,762	2,943
Scholarship for Dalits (9–10)	131	729	177	165
Scholarship for student with disability (1–12) non-residential	1,770	3928	169	1,192
Scholarship for student with disability (1–12) residential	2,400	3,480	0	2,600
Feeder hostel	800	0	0	800
Himali residential	0	0	0	2,800

Source: CEHRD (2019).

Table 8.4 Respondent coverage across research districts

Research method	Ilam	Saptari	Lalitpur	Jumla	Total
Key informant interview (KII)	25	24	14	26	89
School stakeholder interview (SSI) (head teachers, teachers, Scholarship Management Committee members)	5	14	3	4	26
Parent survey	100	128	55	84	367

As part of our fieldwork, we gathered existing district-level official statistics on the coverage of the scholarship schemes. This was followed by a survey that entailed in-depth interviews with 367 parents/guardians. The study also interviewed 89 key informants, including bureaucrats, activists, academics, and politicians. In addition, we interviewed 26 school stakeholders, such as head teachers, teachers, and members of School Management Committees (see Table 8.4 for district-wise details).

3. The politics of Nepal's School Scholarship Programme

The Scholarship Programme is a nationwide educational assistance programme that disburses cash stipends to primary and secondary students of marginalized communities in state schools. The Scholarship Programme entails an annual cash stipend of: (1) between NPR 400 and 600 per annum[2] for Dalit and girl scholarships; (2) NPR 1,700 per annum for 'poor and talented' students at secondary level; and (3) NPR 1,000–1,500 per annum for girl students in Karnali zone, including Jumla district. The scholarships also cover students from marginalized communities, students with disabilities, and students from families affected by conflict. The scholarships operate under the School Sector Development Programme. The Ministry of Education disburses the funds to district education offices,[3] from where they are allocated to all state schools in the district. In the schools, the stipends are disbursed to eligible children, preferably in the presence of their parent or legal guardian. This stipend is expected to cover children's education-related costs, over and above the free primary education to which they are entitled. It is estimated that the scholarships reach at least 3 million children, out of a total of 7.4 million children enrolled in grades 1–12[4] (DoE 2017b; DoE 2018b). The School Sector Development Plan (2016/17–2020/1) has budgeted a total of NPR 40,516 million (USD 386 million) for scholarship and incentive programmes. This amounts to 6 per cent of the total education budget for the period (SSDP 2016, p. 110). These scholarship programmes are considered one of the largest social protection programmes in the education sector (GoN 2014).

The Scholarship Programme targets support to multiple groups and categories, reflecting the programme's multiple objectives and framings. Indeed, the dominant framing of the programme has evolved over time, from a limited focus on productive investment in the education and protection of the poorest, to the pursuit of social justice as a means of addressing historical marginalization. The Scholarship Programme was originally introduced under the reign of King Mahendra (1955–72) with the intention of projecting the image of the king as pro-development (*vikas premi*, which literally translates into 'development lover'). The programme aimed to increase literacy, school enrolment, and educational attainment, and was framed as a productive intervention, embedded within narratives of modernization and development. In 1961, King Mahendra formed the Nepal All Round National Education Committee, which eventually led to the Education Act and education regulations of 1971. Nepal's Five-Year Development Plans after 1960 prioritized education, with an emphasis on the Scholarship Programme. For example, the Second Five-Year Development Plan provided for scholarships in higher studies, especially in engineering, agriculture, and medicine (NPC 1962). The Third Five-Year Development Plan emphasized girls' education, teacher training programmes, and hostel facilities for students from remote areas (NPC 1965). In the words of a former National Planning Commission chairperson,

> Education emerged as one of the most important agendas under King Mahendra. He wanted the country to modernize. You could only modernize by eradicating illiteracy. He knew a breakthrough could only be achieved by educating people.[5]

When the western-educated King Birendra ascended the throne in 1972, he continued with his father's liberal education policies (Shakya 1977; Acharya and Bennett 1981; Whelpton 2005). Scholarships were extended as part of the liberalization reforms and introduction of free primary education in the Fifth Five-Year Development Plan (1975/6–1979/80) (Shakya 1977; Acharya and Bennett 1981; Whelpton 2005). Scholarships at this time retained their productive emphasis and were extended to poor but talented students to cover their educational expenses, as well as being extended to some girl students, as part of a residential programme that promoted and trained women as teachers, in part based on the influence of Queen Aishwarya (Dahal 1975). Policies such as girls' scholarship schemes were incorporated within the Equal Access of Women to Education Project (EAWEP). The National Education System Plan (1971–6) included two types of scholarship: (1) to cover educational expenses for poor and talented students; and (2) to cover hostel charges.

The following decade witnessed the gradual shift from the productivist orientation of the scholarship programmes to a greater focus on social justice. Responding to increased opposition movements, as well as democratization of the political system, King Birendra introduced scholarships targeted towards members of marginalized communities. For example, the Sixth Five-Year Development Plan (1980/1–1984/5) included the provision of scholarships to 430 children of marginalized communities, such as Koche, Meche, Chepang, Chhantel, Jirel, and Gaine, among others (NPC 1980). The Seventh Five-Year Plan (1985–90) included the provision of free education to children with disabilities, scholarship provision for female students, and 110 scholarships for students from remote areas (NPC 1985).

The emphasis on social justice deepened considerably in the 1990s (Koehler 2011; Sijapati 2017; Drucza 2019). This shift reflected the democratic transition, the Maoist People's War between 1996 and 2006, and the subsequent reconciliation efforts. The transition resulted in a democratic constitution of 2007 that ensured basic fundamental rights and included a special provision to protect the interests of women, children, people with disabilities, and economically, socially, and educationally backward communities. For example, scholarships were extended to: girl students of 65 districts on a quota basis and to all enrolled girl students of 10 remote districts in 2009; 100 per cent of the girls enrolled in community schools in 2011 (ERDCN 2011); children of families affected by the Maoist insurgency; and, in 2012, to students who had hitherto been bonded labourers (traditionally known as Kamlari and Kamaiya). Fig. 8.2 shows the gradual emergence and expansion of the School Scholarship Programme.

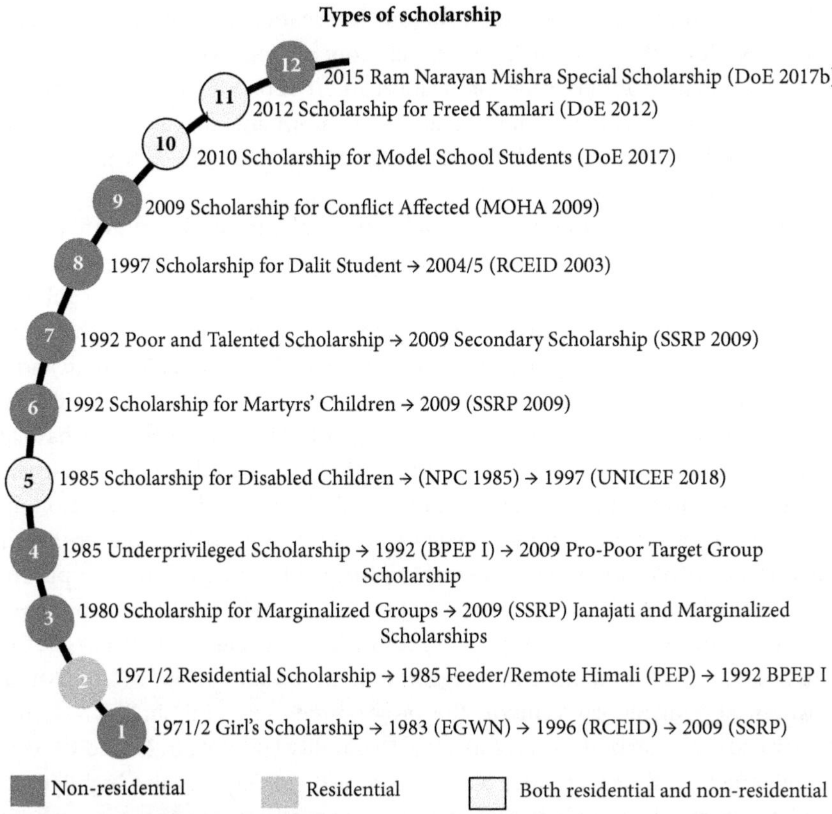

Fig. 8.2 Emergence of different types of scholarship in Nepal
Source: Authors' compilation from Shakya (1977); MoE (1983); NPC (1985); MoE (1984); MoF (1992); MoE (1999); RCEID (2003); MOHA (2009); DoE (2012, 2017a, 2017b, 2017c, 2017d, 2017e, 2018a); EMIS, 2017).

The eventual promulgation of the 2015 Constitution mainstreamed the political discussion on issues of inequitable resource distribution, ethnic/caste discrimination, and demands for greater social inclusion (Thapa and Sijapati 2003; Bennett et al. 2006; Thapa 2017). As one former education minister and CPN (Maoist) party leader said,

> The concept of inclusive scholarship by the state emerged after the Maoist People's War for the *utpidit* (oppressed) groups. After the People's War, the government established constitutional provisions for scholarships.[6]

These movements influenced not only the government's plans and programmes but also those of the donors (Thapa and Sijapati 2003; Murshed and Gates 2005; Bennett et al. 2006; Riaz and Basu 2007; Thapa 2017). The commitment of the central state to the Scholarship Programme was consolidated by the support of donors such as the World Bank, the United Nations International Children's Emergency Fund (UNICEF), the Japanese International Cooperation Agency, the United Nations Development Programme, the Danish International Development Agency and the Asian Development Bank. As such, key informants suggested that the domestic priorities in favour of scholarship programmes were aligned with the social sector focus of donors.[7]

The Scholarship Programme performs both symbolic and instrumental roles. Symbolically, it illustrates the commitment to social inclusion by the central state in Nepal, which, at least rhetorically, distinguishes the central state of republican Nepal from the monarchy. Instrumentally, the programme addresses the political demands made by marginalized groups. Nonetheless, the rapid expansion of the Scholarship Programme, and its shift in emphasis over time from a productive to a social justice framing, raises questions regarding how these changes have affected the process of implementation. The existing literature sheds light on several aspects of the programme's implementation and differential performance on different aspects of the programme. Official reports (DoE 2011, 2017a) aver that the programme enables the state to respond to inequalities in educational opportunities. Indeed, most observers concur that the Scholarship Programme positively impacted educational opportunities, especially for girls and Dalits (Jnawali 2010; DoE 2011, 2017a;), although some suggest that more could be done (DoE 2017a). However, several reports criticize the programme's low and shallow coverage (Drucza 2017), polarized views of its very desirability (Bhusal 2012), and the categorical targeting of social groups (Carter Centre 2013). Reports also highlight the problems of coordination between different state organizations that adversely impact the delivery of the programme. These problems range from limited internal coordination within the educational bureaucracy (DoE 2010) to a mismatch between funds available and number of students eligible for scholarships (DoE 2011). Such commentaries indicate the mixed ability of the state in Nepal to implement and manage the Scholarship Programme.

4. Distributing scholarships: changing frames from productivism to social justice

This section examines the processes by which scholarship recipients are selected for inclusion in the programme in the four case study sites, encompassing both targeting and the application of conditions related to school attendance. A key factor shaping this process is the limit to state infrastructural power and, in particular, the limited ability of higher levels of the state to ensure effective implementation at the district level. One of the key sources of divergence between levels of the disaggregated state concerns the narratives and framings that officials use to justify the Scholarship Programme, and the influence this has on their decision making in the implementation process. As discussed in the previous section, at the national level, the Scholarship Programme is justified in relation to distinct rationales—namely, as a productive intervention and as a means of addressing social marginalization, with the dominant framing of the programme shifting over time from productivism to social justice. With the shift to a social justice framing, the programme design increasingly utilizes categorical targeting to identify the majority of scholarship recipients. As such, all the girl students, Dalit students, and students from Karnali zone received the scholarship, while individual targeting is limited to the 'poor and talented' scholarship, mainly targeting secondary-level students.

Teachers are responsible for identifying eligible students in their schools and, following approval by the Scholarship Management Committee, the school submits the list of recipients to the education officer at the district level. The district then compiles the total number of eligible students in the district and submits this list to the central state for the release of the budget. One important by-product of the shift towards a social justice framing is the lower logistical demands presented by the targeting process. Unlike poverty targeting, which requires the state to generate detailed information regarding the income, consumption, or assets of individuals, categorical targeting of the majority of recipients means that eligible students are easily identifiable by teachers, without any need to submit documentation or generate additional information. Our research in the four districts shows that no specific criteria were followed for the selection of girls and Dalit scholarship. According to the School Scholarship Management Directive 2017, proof of government-recognized Dalit identity and poor economic conditions is required along with an application for Dalit scholarship. However, our study shows that the majority of students submitted no such documents.[8] Teachers and members of School Management Committees informed us that they never asked for documents, since the students lived in the same community as them and they could verify the students' family background and status. Moreover, students' surnames were often taken as a proof of their caste identity. The relative ease of identifying students based on categorical targeting, where the boundaries of the group are relatively clear, made it possible for schools to take such decisions with little controversy or contention. While the focus of the Scholarship Programme and the coverage of particular groups was motivated by the claims of historically marginalized social groups, as discussed above, the design is also well attuned to the limited infrastructural power of the state in Nepal.

While at the national level the social justice framing has attained prominence, as reflected in the programme design, this change in priorities is not uniformly reflected across the levels of the state. Indeed, despite the dominant emphasis of the Scholarship Programme on social justice, the previous emphasis on the use of scholarships as a productive intervention remains, most visibly in the Scholarship Directive 2017, which mandates a minimum attendance criterion. As discussed above, scholarships were first introduced in the education sector with an overall objective to increase education enrolment and attendance. On paper, this emphasis on school attendance still continues as a condition for scholarship transfers.

Despite the central state's commitment to social inclusion, and its continued assurance of the Scholarship Programme, the central state was unable to enforce its framing of the programme as a commitment to social inclusion upon the local state. In particular, district- and local-level actors continued to emphasize the productive potential of the scholarships as a means of enhancing literacy rates, attainment of schooling, and developing a productive labour force. As such, a district education officer[9] in Saptari district claimed that the scholarship boosted the enrolment rate among Dalits and girls, as per the government policy and goals. A bureaucrat[10] in Ilam, emphasizing the need to expand the Scholarship Programme, mentioned, 'Our leaders are educated and know that our country will not develop without education. So they give special importance to education.' At the local level, therefore, scholarships continue to be seen as an important intervention to encourage all children to complete school education, so that they may become productive citizens. Such a productive focus frames students from marginalized groups as a 'problem' to be addressed and social programmes as a way to transform them 'into better, more productive members of society' (Hickey 2008, p. 353). Therefore, in all four districts, resource persons[11] are deployed by the district education officer to ensure that schools follow the scholarship guidelines on attendance.[12]

The focus on the productive contribution of the programme at the district level did not, however, translate into decisions taken at the level of the everyday state. In particular, school officials ignored official criteria requiring attendance requirements that might exclude significant members of these communities from obtaining scholarships. To do so, they took advantage of ambiguity in the programme guidelines. Both the School Scholarship Management Directives 2017 and Programme Implementation Guidelines of 2015 and 2016 stipulated that 80 per cent attendance is required of scholarship recipients (DoE 2015; DoE 2016). However, no such criterion is mentioned in the 2017 Programme Implementation Guidelines, which the schools had chosen to follow. As such, the schools utilized contradictory policy directives to the advantage of students, by using the most inclusive criteria possible. According to a head teacher in Saptari,

> [the] government tells us to give it to those with 75 per cent attendance but it is not possible for us. No student would ever meet the criteria. We are compelled to give it to those (students) who come for 15–20 days but also to those who do not come at all.[13]

The decision to ignore the condition of school attendance—and with it the productive framing favoured by district officials—was, in part, based on a competing framing of the programme at the level of the everyday state. Here, schools prioritized the care and support of programme recipients, in order to be as inclusive as possible when it came to disbursing scholarships, ignoring requirements to distribute the scholarships based on attendance. However, the failure to enforce the attendance criterion was also the result of the weak infrastructural power of the everyday state. When some schools in Saptari district did attempt to enforce official criteria regarding attendance, the parents and guardians of students protested, forcing the schools to discontinue the requirement.[14] Thus, the school was unable to enforce the rule in the face of societal opposition. Many of our key informants reported that keeping attendance as a criterion led to disagreements between school authorities and guardians as well as cases of students fighting with each other.[15] As one head teacher told the research team: 'When we do not give scholarship to students with irregular attendance, their guardians quarrel with us.'[16]

While the scholarships are increasingly framed as a means of pursuing social justice and overcoming past marginalization, the size of the transfers raises questions about the ability of the Scholarship Programme to make a meaningful contribution to these objectives. As discussed above, the Scholarship Programme amounts to between NPR 400 and NPR 1,700 per annum for different categories of student. Moreover, the central state's programme criteria mandate that the local state and the school limit each student to one type of scholarship, with no overlap. Our study found that all schools stringently followed this instruction and avoided duplication in the distribution of cash. For example, a Dalit girl student can claim a scholarship under either the Dalit or the girl child criterion, not both.

State bureaucrats and school authorities across the research sites complained that the money provided by the scholarships was too little.[17] For example, a Scholarship Management Committee head in Saptari argued,

> I do not think the money is adequate. Before, clothes could be bought with 200–300 but now it takes about 1,000 and the sewing cost alone is 200–300, so I think it would be adequate if it was 1,000.

Similarly, some school authorities said that the scholarship of NPR 400 was not adequate to buy uniforms or stationery for the year. A head teacher in Ilam and a guardian in South Lalitpur went to the extent of suggesting that students could earn around NPR 800–1,000 a day working as a labourer in construction or in the field, in some cases more than the annual amount they would receive under the scholarship. Since the scholarship amount is small, many view it as a merely symbolic act.

Nevertheless, although the amount is little, it has provided help for very poor families to buy uniforms and stationery. School authorities, state bureaucrats, and elected representatives in all four research sites agreed that the scholarship provided great support to children. In Jumla, the research team found overwhelmingly positive responses towards the programme, as the scholarship amount was higher (due to the region's remoteness) and was sufficient to cover school materials. In Saptari, Ilam, and South Lalitpur districts, parents and school authorities often shared that the poor felt the state was at least giving them something. For example, a teacher in Saptari noted that

> When the students receive money, students are also happy, parents are also happy. They say we could buy copy, pen, and bag with this. The government at least did this much.[18]

A poor Dalit mother in Ilam, whose daughter received the scholarship, explained,

> It is okay. Even if it is not that much, it is enough. It gives relief to poor. It is enough to buy copies for two to four months. It brings smile in difficult times.[19]

In summary, then, the reframing of the Scholarship Programme has resulted in the dominance of categorical targeting which reduces the logistical burdens on a state with limited infrastructural power. Nonetheless, this shift in programme objectives is incomplete, with officials at different levels of the state emphasizing different programme framings in their decision making. Moreover, despite attempts to frame the Scholarship Programme as a means of overcoming historical injustice, the reality of the low level of transfers threatens to undermine the transformative potential of the programme, even if the minuscule payments are appreciated by members of marginalized communities.

5. Distributing scholarships: logistical challenges

The scholarship programme faced a number of additional implementation challenges across the sites. These implementation failings are a reflection of the weak infrastructural power of the state and, in particular, the inability of higher levels of the state to monitor effectively the behaviour of lower levels. This failing was identified as a typical challenge by an education sector expert in Kathmandu:

> Central government creates popular campaigns and declares commitments. By the time the policy reaches the ground level, it hardly remains the same.[20]

Fig. 8.3 shows the range of individuals involved in the administration of the Scholarship Programme. These individuals include not only bureaucrats, such as the district education officer, but also head teachers, resource persons, and members of the school-level Scholarship Management Committees. Information flows from the district education officer to the resource person but scholarships are disbursed

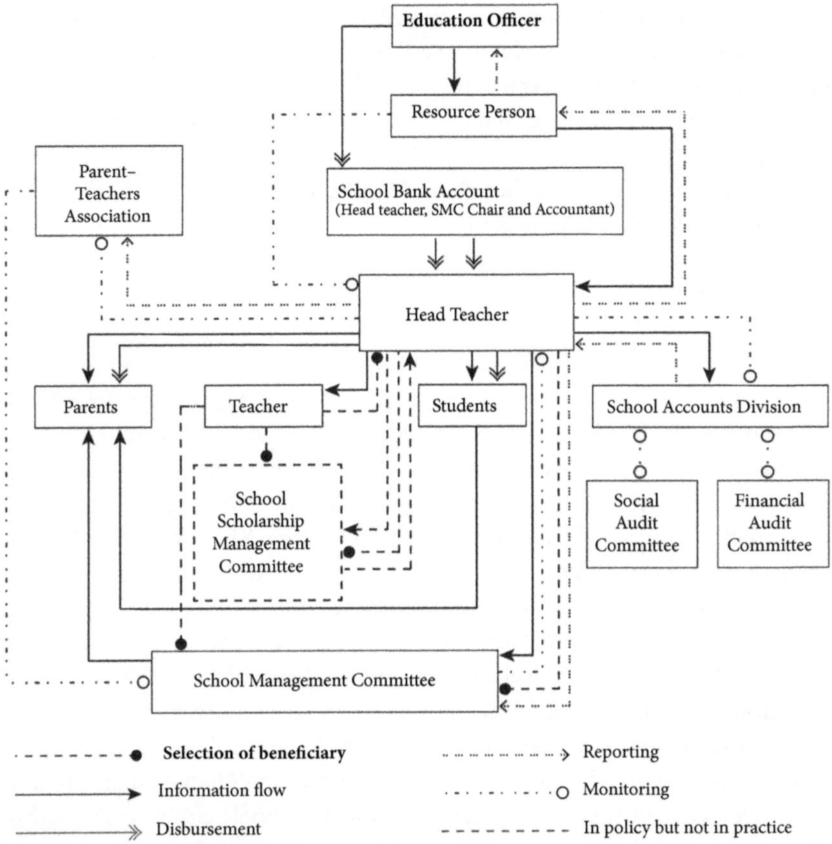

Fig. 8.3 Scholarship distribution process

directly from the district education officer to the school, which then disburses the scholarship to students or parents. The disbursement is monitored by the resource persons, Parent–Teacher Associations, and the school-level Scholarship Management Committees. The school sends reports on scholarship disbursement, via the head teacher, to the district education officer. Crucially, although the district education officer receives reports about the disbursement of the scholarship, s/he does not have any active monitoring role vis-à-vis the schools.

This governance structure to oversee the disbursement of the Scholarship Programme illustrates the weakness of state infrastructural power in Nepal. The district education officer and their team of resource persons were simply not equipped to deal with the volume of monitoring and reports from the schools. On average, it appeared from our interviews that each district education officer was responsible for the supervision of at least 20 resource persons. Each resource person in turn was responsible for a cluster of 20 schools. It was estimated that each district education officer was thus responsible for monitoring and reporting 400 schools, and thousands of students (see Table 8.2 for the total number of scholarships in each district). However, as mentioned above, with the restructuring of the state, this situation is likely to change, with more power being devolved to elected municipalities.

Furthermore, according to the School Scholarship Management Directive 2017, the District Scholarship Management Committee is responsible for monitoring the distribution of scholarships and overseeing the school-level Scholarship Management Committee. However, the school-level committees were not formed (or, if they had been formed, they were not active) in any of the schools studied in the four districts. Similarly, at the district level, the resource persons and school superintendents who were responsible for monitoring the scholarships were not clear about their role. Indeed, head teachers of the study schools in our research sites told us that they rarely saw the school superintendents. When the resource persons did visit schools, they were only interested in collecting school-level data rather than monitoring the distribution of scholarships. The Scholarship Directive mandates that school-level Social Audit Committees submit a report on scholarship distribution to the district education officer. However, our study found that the reporting mechanism is neither clear nor effective at the research sites.

The practice at the local level also provides evidence of a longstanding pattern wherein the state has a more limited presence in more marginalized and remote communities, which are consequently less likely to be regularly monitored. Head teachers reported that the resource persons visited schools based on the proximity and convenience of the school location. As such, schools closer to the highway were more frequently visited than those that were far away. In remote Jumla, the head teachers reported that the resource persons stopped visiting the school once they moved away from the locality.

The implementation of the Scholarship Programme was further impeded by the inability of the state—at both central and local levels—to maintain a database of students. The challenges faced by the district education officers to provide up-to-date information on the number of students in a timely manner hinders the central state's ability to release the full budget to the district in time. This inability reflected the weak logistical capacity of the state. The district education officers were responsible for maintaining the Integrated Educational Management Information System (IEMIS), the electronic software for recording school data.[21] The district education officers struggle to maintain the IEMIS, for various reasons. First, not all schools in their jurisdiction have access to computers, electricity, or staff with adequate computer skills. Second, and as a consequence, schools sometimes submitted their data in print rather than using the software. For example, one primary school head teacher in Ilam told us that he had to walk 40 minutes to the nearby secondary school, which was their closest access to a computer. A similar story was shared by the head teacher of a primary school in Jumla:

> It is challenging to fill IEMIS data for the primary school like ours. We do not have the facility of electricity/solar and computer. Also, there is no person in school who could do such technical work. I go to the cyber in headquarter along with all required document/information to fill IEMIS data every year and pay for it.[22]

The varied formats and timescales in which schools supply their data places an extra burden on district education officers as they struggle to standardize the data. In some cases, like Jumla, even the district education officer does not have reliable electricity and internet connectivity. Connectivity issues prevent district education officers from receiving the most up-to-date data from schools and reporting such data to the central state. This makes it impossible for district education officers to maintain a consistent database for the calculation of target groups for *all* the schools in the district. Given the logistical difficulties, schools were able to share student data only by the end of the first quarter of the academic year. The district education officers managed to collate the data from all the schools within their jurisdiction by the third quarter. Thus, it was often the case that the central state received the data for scholarship recipients almost at the end of the academic year. It was not uncommon for schools to receive the allocated funds towards the *end* of the academic session or even in the following academic year, thus considerably delaying the entire scholarship cycle. These logistical problems meant that there was always a discrepancy between the student data in IEMIS and actual students in the school.

In addition, there is often a mismatch between the number of eligible students and the actual budget that is released to a school. The scholarship amount released to the school account is often up to 50 per cent less than the actual number of students in the schools.[23] Under such circumstances, the head teacher and the school-level Scholarship Management Committee consult with the guardians to distribute a reduced scholarship equally to all eligible students, a practice called *damasahi* in Nepali.[24] Head teachers in Jumla[25] district and Lalitpur[26] district and the school-level Scholarship Management Committee chair in Saptari[27] district confirmed this while distributing the scholarship. Another illustration of this mismatch was provided in Jumla district, where the scholarship amount is sometimes released in two instalments (75 per cent and 25 per cent) over two different academic years.[28] For ease of distribution, the schools distribute the scholarship in one lump sum after they received the second tranche. Such funding inconsistencies often lead to confusion and a lack of trust amongst the recipients. These limitations in the logistical capacity of the state lead to delays and confusions that threaten the social significance of the Scholarship Programme in terms of either inclusion or productivity.

6. Conclusion

Social protection programmes have proliferated across the world as important interventions led by states to promote social inclusion. The case study of Nepal's Scholarship Programme highlights the importance of shifting narratives, competing frames and logistical challenges shaping the implementation of social protection programmes. As this chapter shows, the infrastructural power of the state and its logistical capacity influence the successful implementation of such initiatives. A careful analysis of the emergence of the Scholarship Programme during the 1960s reveals its embeddedness in narratives of modernization and development espoused by the monarch, thus shaping its productive framing. In response to democratization and social movements during and after the 1990s, narratives of social justice permeated the Scholarship Programme. It was during this period that categorical targeting became the characterizing feature of Scholarship Programmes in the country.

Tensions between the productivist and social justice framings continue to mark the implementation of the Scholarship Programme. On the one hand, scholarships are primarily viewed as a productive investment that would enhance the literacy rates and human capability of students in rural areas, with minimum attendance criteria for the disbursement of scholarships. On the other hand, scholarships are also perceived as representing the state's commitment to social inclusion in response to the political demands of historically marginalized groups. Schools navigated these tensions by distributing scholarships irrespective of the attendance conditionalities. The result was to broaden inclusion, rather than use the scholarship as merely an incentive to raise attendance. The reframing of the Scholarship Programme in terms of social justice has led to the programme adopting the use of categorical targeting to distribute scholarships to *all* girls and historically marginalized castes, potentially placing fewer demands on the limited infrastructural capacity of the state.

Nevertheless, limited infrastructural power continues to undermine implementation and particular scholarship disbursement, with relatively uniform problems evident across research sites. The lack of physical infrastructure as well as limited bureaucratic capacity and oversight meant that districts struggled to maintain up-to-date data on eligible recipients in their districts. As such, limited state infrastructural power led to delayed and reduced payments that are likely to undermine the positive contributions of the programme either to address social injustice or to make productive investments.

Notes

1. In should be noted that, during fieldwork, Nepal underwent a major transition in governance, establishing a federal state that transferred responsibility for the Scholarship

Programme from the districts to elected municipalities. The reinstatement of elected local governments, disbanded since 1999, meant that our fieldwork was undertaken at a time of flux, and the situation is likely to have changed by the time this chapter is published.

2. There were approximately 150 Nepalese rupees (NPR) to the British pound at the time of fieldwork in 2018.
3. Since the state restructuring of 2017, the funds are now disbursed to municipalities, which then allocate these to schools under their jurisdiction.
4. According to the *Education Status Report 2016–17*, the scholarship was distributed to 810,700 Dalit students, 31,787 students with disabilities, and 2,205,046 girl students, in addition to other targeted scholarships, such as martyrs' children and Ramnaryan Mishra special scholarships (DoE 2017b, p. xii).
5. KII 111, Kathmandu, 13 August 2018.
6. KII 103, Kathmandu, 20 August 2018.
7. KII 107, Kathmandu, 28 August 2018.
8. The scholarship for students with disabilities constitutes an exception, with students required to provide a disability card authorized by the government.
9. KII 32, Saptari, 26 November 2018.
10. KII 17, Ilam, 23 November 2018.
11. Resource persons are former teachers who are responsible for supervising and providing support to the schools. They were the intermediary between the schools and district office (before transition).
12. KII 87, Lalitpur, 7 December 2018; KII 87, Lalitpur, 7 December 2018; KII 73, Lalitpur, 3 October 2018.
13. SSI 32, Saptari, 26 November 2018.
14. SSI 32, Saptari, 26 November 2018; SSI 39, Saptari, 2 December 2018; KII 64, Saptari, 24 November 2018; KII 65, Saptari, 24 November 2018; informal conversation 27, Saptari, 2 December 2018.
15. SSI 32, Saptari, 26 November 2018; SSI 39, Saptari, 2 December 2018; KII 64, Saptari, 24 November 2018; KII 65, Saptari, 24 November 2018; informal conversation 27, Saptari, 2 December 2018; KII 60, Saptari, 21 November 2018.
16. SSI 32, Saptari, 26 November 2018.
17. KII 60, Saptari, 21 November 2018. Likewise, KII 51, Saptari, 18 November 2018; SSI 30, Saptari, 23 November 2018; KII 63, Saptari, 23 November 2018; KII 66, Saptari, 24 November 2018; SSI 31, Saptari, 25 November 2018; SSI 10, Jumla, 17 November 2018; KII 1, Ilam, 14 November 2018; KII 9, Ilam, 16 November 2018; informal conversation 4, Ilam, 17 November 2018; KII 8, Ilam, 17 November 2018; KII 15, Ilam, 20 November 2018; KII 16, Ilam, 23 November 2018; informal conversation 25, Ilam, 24 November 2018, KII 23, Ilam, 28 November 2018; informal conversation 12, Ilam, 28 November 2018; KII 19, Ilam, 24 November 2018; SSI 35, South Lalitpur, 8 December 2018; KII 91, South Lalitpur, 9 December 2018; KII 97, South Lalitpur, 10 December 2018; KII 88, South Lalitpur, 9 December 2018; KII 93, South Lalitpur, 9 December 2018.
18. KII 63, Saptari, 23 November 2018. Also KII 52, Saptari, 19 November 2018; KII 64, Saptari, 24 November 2018.
19. Informal conversation 10, Ilam, 21 November 2018.
20. KII 112, Kathmandu, 5 July 2018.

21. School data include students' name, ethnicity/caste, date of birth, parents' name, grade, scholarship type received by the student, examination marks, teacher's information, etc.
22. Informal conversation 15, Jumla, 30 November 2018.
23. KII 55, Saptari, 20 November 2018; KII 54, Saptari, 20 November 2018; KII 60, Saptari, 21 November 2018; KII 64, Saptari, 24 November 2018.
24. KII 63, Saptari, 23 November 2018; KII 65, Saptari, 24 November 2018.
25. KII 26, Jumla, 14 November 2018.
26. KII 87, Lalitpur, 7 December 2018; KII 87, Lalitpur, 7 December 2018; KII 73, Lalitpur, 3 October 2018.
27. KII 59, Saptari, 21 November 2018; KII 60, Saptari, 24 November 2018; KII 65, Saptari, 24 November 2018; KII 66, Saptari, 24 November 2018.
28. KII 48, Jumla, 28 November 2018; KII 35, Jumla, 19 November 2018.

References

Acharya, M. and Bennett, L., 1981. *Rural Women of Nepal: An Aggregate Analysis and Summary of 8 Villages Studies*. Kathmandu: Centre for Economic and Development Administration, Tribhuvan University.

Bennett, L., Tamang, S., Onta, P., and Thapa, M., 2006. *Unequal Citizens: Gender Caste and Ethnic Exclusion*. Kathmandu: World Bank and Department for International Development.

Bhusal, L. N., 2012. Poverty estimates and the welfare state: The case of Nepal. *Contemporary South Asia*, 20 (1), 45–59.

Carter Center, 2013. The Carter Center's observations on identity-based political activity and mobilizations in Nepal. 13 March. Available online: https://www.cartercenter.org/resources/pdfs/news/pr/cartercenter-report-idbasedpoliticalactivity-eng.pdf (accessed 26 January 2021).

CBS (2014). *Population Monograph of Nepal, Volume 1*. Kathmandu: Central Bureau of Statistics, Government of Nepal.

CEHRD (2019). *Budget for Grant Disbursable Activities to Local Bodies for Fiscal Year 2074/2075* (*Aa Ba 2074/075 kaa laagi sthaniya nikaema anudan nikasa dina sakine kriyaakalapko baget* (in Nepali). Bhaktapur: Centre for Education and Human Resource Development.

Dahal, Taramani. 1975. 'अन्तराष्ट्रिय महिला वर्ष र नेपाली महिला वर्ग (International Women Year and Nepali Women)'. *महिला बोल्छिन— मासिक पत्रिका (Women Speak—Monthly)*, 13, 17–18.

District Education Office (DEO) 2017. Educational Management Information System (EMIS). Unpublished.

DoE, 2010. *A Study on Scholarship Management and Its Effectiveness in Terms of Enrolment and Retention*. Kathmandu: Department of Education.

DoE, 2011. *A Study on Effectiveness of Girls' Scholarship Program*. Kathmandu: Department of Education, Research and Educational Information Management Section.

DoE, 2012. Education for Freed Kamlari Directive 2012. Sanothimi: Department of Education.

DoE, 2015. Program Implementation Guideline 2015/16. Sanothimi: Department of Education.

DoE, 2016. Program Implementation Guidelines 2016/17. Sanothimi: Department of Education.

DoE, 2017a. Model School Management Directive 2017. Sanothimi: Ministry of Education, Department of Education

DoE, 2017b. Ram Narayan Mishra Scholarship Distribution Directive 2017. Sanothimi: Department of Education.

DoE, 2017c. School Grant Management Directive 2017. Sanothimi: Department of Education.

DoE, 2017d. School Scholarship Management Directive, 2017. Sanothimi: Department of Education.

DoE, 2017e. Program Implementation Guideline F.Y 2017/18. Sanothimi: Department of Education.

DoE, 2018a. Program Implementation Guidelines 2018/19. Sanothimi: Department of Education.

DoE, 2018b. *Flash I Report 2017–18*. Sanothimi: Department of Education.

Drucza, K., 2017. The politics behind social protection in Nepal. *Asian Journal of Comparative Politics*, 3 (4), 311–335.

Drucza, K., 2019. 'At least the government is watching out for us now': Dalit perceptions and experiences of governance and cash transfers in three villages in Sarlahi, Nepal. *Modern Asian Studies*, 53 (6), 2041–2078.

ERDCN, 2011. *A Study on Effectiveness of Girls' Scholarship Program*. Kathmandu: Educational Resource and Development Centre Nepal.

Government of Nepal, 2014. *Consolidated Equity Strategy for School Education Sector in Nepal*. Kathmandu: Ministry of Education.

Hangen, S., 2010. *The Rise of Ethnic Politics in Nepal: Democracy in the Margins*. New York: Routledge.

Hickey, S., 2008. Conceptualising the politics of social protection in Africa. In: A. Barrientos and D. Hulme, eds. *Social Protection for the Poor and Poorest: Concepts, Policies and Politics*. London: Palgrave Macmillan, 247–263.

Jnawali, D., 2010. Rights-based education in Nepal: Existing status and challenges, *The Third Pole*, 8–10, 1–8.

Kabeer, N., 2009. *Social Protection in South Asia: A Review*. Centre for Social Protection: Institute of Development Studies.

Koehler, G., 2011. Social protection and socioeconomic security in Nepal. *IDS Working Papers*, 370. Brighton: Institute of Development Studies.

Koehler, G. and Mathers, N., 2017. Dynamics of social protection in fragile contexts: Nepal and Myanmar. *Global Social Policy*, 17 (3), 347–352.

Lawoti, M., 2013. Varied trajectories of Dalit, indigenous nationalities and Madheshis movement. *In:* M. Lawoti and S. Hangen, eds. *Nationalism and Ethnic Conflict in Nepal: Identities and Mobilization after 1990*. New York: Routledge, 193–225.

Lipsky, M., 1980. *Street-Level Bureaucracy: Dilemmas of the Individual in Public Services*. New York: Russell Sage Foundation.

MoE, 1984. *Primary Education Project (PEP)*. Kathmandu: Ministry of Education.

MoE, 1999. *Basic and Primary Education Project I 1992-1998: A Synthesis of Experiences*. Kathmandu: Ministry of Education

MoE, 2009. *School Sector Reform Plan 2009–2015*. Kathmandu: Ministry of Education.

MoF, 1992. Budget speech 1992. Kathmandu: Ministry of Finance.

MoF, 2018. Budget speech of fiscal year 2018/19. Kathmandu: Ministry of Finance.

MOHA, 2009. Citizen Relief, Compensation and Financial Support Guideline 2009. Kathmandu: Ministry of Home Affairs.

Murshed, S. Mansoob and Gates, S., 2005. Spatial-horizontal inequality and the Maoist insurgency in Nepal. *Review of Development Economics*, 9 (1), 121–134.

NPC, 1962. *Second Five Year Development Plan (1962/63–1964/65)*. Kathmandu: National Planning Commission.

NPC, 1965. *Third Five Year Development Plan (1965/66–1969/70)*. Kathmandu: National Planning Commission.

NPC, 1980. *Sixth Five Year Development Plan (1980/81–1984/85)*. Kathmandu: National Planning Commission.

NPC, 1985. *Seventh Five Year Development Plan (1985/86–1989/90)*. Kathmandu: National Planning Commission.

Pradhan, U., 2019. Multi-ethnic citizens in a multi-ethnic state: Constructing state–citizen relations through 'difference' in Adivasi Janajati scholarship programmes in Nepal. *South Asia: Journal of South Asian Studies*, 42 (5), 937–953.

RCEID, 2003. *Effectiveness of Incentive/Scholarship Programmes for Girls and Disadvantaged Children*. Kathmandu: Research Centre for Educational Innovation and Development.

Riaz, A. and Subho, B., 2007. *Paradise Lost? State Failure in Nepal*. New Delhi: Lexington Books.

Sabates-Wheeler, R. and Devereux, S., 2009. Social protection for social transformation. *IDS Bulletin*, 38 (3), 23–28.

SSDP, 2016. *School Sector Development Plan*. Kathmandu: Ministry of Education.

Shakya, S. K., 1977. Women experimental teaching program. In S. K. Shakya, ed. *Nepal Digest: Nepal Education Special 1977*. Kathmandu: Nepal Digest Publications, 147–154.

Sharma, P., Guha-Khasnobis, B., and Khanal, D. R., 2014. *Nepal Human Development Report 2014. Beyond Geography: Unlocking Human Potential*. Kathmandu: Government of Nepal and United Nations Development Programme.

Sijapati, B., 2017. The quest for achieving universal social protection in Nepal: Challenges and opportunities. *Indian Journal of Human Development*, 11 (1), 17–36.

Thapa, D. and Sijapati, B., 2003. *A Kingdom under Siege: Nepal's Maoist Insurgency, 1996 to 2003*. Kathmandu: The Printhouse.

Thapa, D. 2017. 'Stability or social justice?' *Accord: An International Review of Peace Initiatives*, 26. London: Conciliation Resources, 13–17.

Whelpton, J. 2005. *A History of Nepal*. Cambridge: Cambridge University Press.

PART V
COMPARATIVE ANALYSIS

9

The Intersection of State Infrastructural Power and Political Contestation in the Distribution of Social Transfers

A Comparative Analysis

Tom Lavers

1. Introduction

All of the case studies presented in the preceding chapters underscore the central proposition outlined in Chapter 1 of this book that implementation matters to policy outcomes and that politics is an important factor shaping how social transfer programmes are implemented in practice. In most of the case studies, social transfer programmes differ in substantive ways in their frontline implementation from the original intentions of policymakers, including in the process of selecting districts and participants, the outcome in terms of who gets support and why, and the timeliness of transfers. All of these factors play a vital role in shaping programme impacts on poverty and vulnerability to broader goals of promoting social cohesion and using social transfers as the foundation of emerging social contracts. Moreover, in many instances these factors vary within countries in important ways. As such, the findings highlight the importance of a greater focus on sub-national implementation in research on the politics of social protection.

This final chapter provides a comparative analysis of the six countries and their sub-national cases. In doing so, the analysis links the findings in this volume to the broader theoretical and policy debates raised in Chapters 1 and 2, and reflects on the implications of the research for the evolution of social protection in Africa and South Asia. In particular, the chapter examines the case study findings in relation to the main theoretical debates raised in Chapter 2: first, the relative importance of infrastructural power, rooted in the historical legacy of state formation, as compared to contemporary political dynamics in explaining policy outcomes; and second, the importance of sub-national analysis in comparative

Tom Lavers, *The Intersection of State Infrastructural Power and Political Contestation in the Distribution of Social Transfers.* In: *The Politics of Distributing Social Transfers.* Edited by Tom Lavers, Oxford University Press.
 DOI: 10.1093/oso/9780192862525.003.0009

politics and the politics of development. In addition, the discussion considers the more policy-oriented questions raised in Chapter 1, namely what role do politics and state capacity play in the distribution of social transfers, and under what circumstances are states able to distribute transfers effectively in line with programme objectives?

The wide range of case studies presented in the volume suggests complex and contingent processes shaping distribution through the implementation process in the six countries. Nonetheless, some clear patterns and trends emerge from comparison of the cases. These patterns are considered in three main sections. The next section provides a comparative analysis of the case studies in the light of the analytical framework guiding this volume, which highlights the importance of state infrastructural power and the degree of political contestation for the distribution of social transfers. The analysis then turns to debates about the role of politics in effective implementation and common concerns about the 'political capture' of social transfer programmes. Finally, the chapter reflects on the implications of the research for the future of social protection, including the challenge of targeting, the potential for growth of social transfer programmes, not least in the light of the ongoing Covid-19 pandemic, and the potential for social transfers to form part of a social contract between states and their citizens.

2. State infrastructural power and political contestation in the distribution of social transfers

The approach taken in this book highlights the importance of within country variation in the politics of policy implementation, with sub-national cases selected to explore how variation—or in some cases the absence of variation—in state capacity and power relations shapes the distribution of social transfers. To a significant degree, the cases bear out this approach, with notable variation in key factors of interest and programme implementation in each of Ethiopia, Ghana, and Kenya. The absence of significant variation in the other three countries—Bangladesh, Nepal, and Rwanda—is in itself noteworthy and can largely be attributed to specific political processes, as discussed below.

The importance of state infrastructural power in the distribution of social transfers

Three of the country cases clearly highlight the enduring influence of long-run patterns of state formation—including during the pre-colonial, colonial, and post-independence eras—on variation in state infrastructural power and the contemporary implementation of social transfer programmes. In Ethiopia, Ghana, and Kenya, state infrastructural power is relatively strong in a central core where the state has relatively high levels of implementation capacity and legitimacy, while in the periphery state presence is much more limited. In each case this variation has its roots in the creation of national boundaries and decisions regarding investment in infrastructure and state offices. In Kenya and Ghana, the marginalization of the periphery can be traced to the colonial era, when colonial authorities' infrastructure investments and state-building efforts were shaped by the economic opportunity and potential threat posed by different areas within the territories (Mamdani 1996; Herbst 2000; Boone 2003; Kanyinga 2009). The result was that areas of marginal economic importance—and particularly those utilized by pastoralist populations—were neglected. The unevenness of state infrastructural power was subsequently reinforced by the investment decisions of post-independence administrations, which often made similar calculations to colonial authorities when it came to the challenge of how to project their political authority (Boone 2003). A broadly comparable process took place in Ethiopia also, despite its limited brush with European colonialism. Here, the Ethiopian state expanded its territorial authority massively alongside the nineteenth-century European scramble for Africa, resulting in a highly uneven state-building project that integrated newly incorporated areas to sharply contrasting degrees (Donham and James 2002; Markakis 2011; Lavers 2016).

The result is that state infrastructural power to implement social transfer programmes varies considerably within the three countries across each of the three dimensions identified in Chapter 2. First, infrastructural power varies based on the physical and human resources available to local state administrations. The state in peripheral areas of Afar in Ethiopia, Upper West region in Ghana, and Marsabit in Kenya faces considerably greater challenges in terms of the size of the territories under its jurisdiction, availability of qualified staff, limited road infrastructure, lack of transport and electricity access, and poor communications such as mobile phone networks and internet connections compared to more central locations. The recent trend towards technology-intensive targeting and disbursement modalities in social transfer programmes is sometimes framed as a means of compensating for limited state capacity (Donovan 2015; Seekings 2017). While that can be the case, Ghana's Upper West region suggests that the use of technology can also intensify the disadvantage of these areas as result of the lack of access to electricity and telecommunications. These physical constraints are exacerbated by a shortage of adequately trained staff, with peripheral areas often considered hardship postings that fail to attract sufficient trained officials. The result is that the state in Ethiopia, Ghana, and Kenya continues to face a major challenge just reaching communities in peripheral areas that are often targeted by social transfer programmes.

Second, the case studies underscore the importance of intra-state relations to state infrastructural power. In high-capacity areas of Ethiopia—such as Tigray prior to the recent conflict—and in Rwanda—probably the most infrastructurally powerful state of the six—an important factor underpinning strong state infrastructural power is the system of top-down monitoring and performance assessment. These evaluation systems provide higher levels of the state with control over the activities of frontline officials, ensuring their compliance with central directives. In contrast, in peripheral areas, resource constraints are compounded by the greater difficulty of the central state in monitoring the activities of frontline officials. Distance from administrative centres, communication challenges, and the limited effectiveness of performance evaluation systems all hinder the ability of higher-level officials to monitor their subordinates. The result is that in Afar, Ethiopia, federal and regional officials have little ability to monitor lower-level officials and ensure their compliance with central directives. Marsabit in Kenya also provides a clear example in this respect, with central government inspections and audits much less common in this district located far from Nairobi, compared to more accessible areas. The result of this lack of oversight is that local officials are likely to have much more leeway, with officials' own interests and, as Pradhan et al. argue with respect to Nepal (Chapter 8), competing narratives and framings of programme objectives influencing programme implementation in ways that diverge from the intentions of national policymakers.

Third, state infrastructural power varies within countries based on state–society relations and the ability of the state to penetrate society. Seekings (2017) has argued that one of the benefits of social transfers is the limited demands that these place on state capacity, with the result that many programmes can be implemented on a shoe string. This is certainly true to a degree, with social transfers lowering the logistical challenges compared to some other, more complex initiatives such as the delivery of quality social services or agricultural extension. Indeed, in the core areas of Ethiopia, Ghana, and Kenya, where the state's presence is consolidated and legitimacy is relatively uncontested, the state has been able to mobilize and work with communities to deliver social transfer programmes. Here the state has sufficient capacity to generate knowledge of local communities and utilize this in implementation decisions, including related to targeting. In peripheral areas, however, local officials often lack sufficient embeddedness in and understanding of the communities where they are supposed to work, impeding effective implementation. Unsurprisingly, this is particularly evident in pastoralist areas of Afar, Ethiopia and Marsabit, Kenya where mobile livelihoods impede the state's ability to render society legible (Scott 1998). This lack of embeddedness of state officials is evident in Marsabit, where, as Alesha Porisky (Chapter 6) argues, state officials are centrally appointed on relatively short postings from other parts of Kenya, resulting in significant linguistic and cultural barriers to local integration (see also Hassan 2020). However, related challenges are also evident in Afar where, under Ethiopia's ethnic federal system, most local state officials should be ethnic Afar. Nonetheless, the limited reach of the state still impedes officials' ability to penetrate society. In addition, a lack of state legitimacy can also be an impediment to state infrastructural power. In the sites in Oromiya, Ethiopia, the fused party-state has long lacked legitimacy in the eyes of the local population as a result of the incorporation by conquest of Oromo populations into Ethiopia in the nineteenth century and perceived dominance of the national government by non-Oromo ethnic groups. Thus, while the party-state was able to establish similar administrative structures in Oromiya as in Tigray, these were always less effective in mobilizing the population as a result of the illegitimacy of the party-state.

The common use of community-based targeting procedures in many social transfer programmes, including those in Ethiopia, Ghana, and Kenya, makes state–society relations particularly important. While the intention of community-based targeting is to mobilize the local knowledge of community members and to increase local participation, the role of the state nonetheless remains important in ensuring adherence of selection to programme guidelines. In Afar, Ethiopia and Marsabit, Kenya, however, the limited infrastructural power of the state means that officials have little option but to devolve targeting responsibilities to customary leaders over whom they have little control. Likewise, in the Upper West region of northern Ghana and in Homa Bay, Kenya, the limited reach of the state has impeded the community-based targeting process, often resulting in the mobilization of local party-political officials to fill in the gaps in the reach of the state (see Chapters 5 and 6, and Ibrahim 2021). The result is that the targeting process varies considerably as a result of the involvement of these non-state actors who may introduce divergent social norms or material interests into their decision-making. This sub-national focus therefore highlights considerable variation that is usually obscured by a focus on national programmes. For example, Ethiopia's Productive Safety Net Programme (PSNP) is often highlighted as a success story in terms of effective implementation, including relatively accurate targeting in comparison to similar programmes (e.g. Coll-Black et al. 2012). However, this relative success applies primarily to the highland areas, including Tigray and, to a lesser degree, Oromiya where infrastructural power is strong. In contrast, in both Afar and Somali regions, party-state infrastructural power is much more limited, resulting in more or less arbitrary targeting of participants (see also Sabates-Wheeler et al. 2013).

Importantly, however, the stark sub-national variation in state infrastructural power seen in Ethiopia, Ghana, and Kenya is not evident in some of the other countries. Bangladesh and Rwanda were both selected in the expectation that there would be relatively little sub-national variation in infrastructural power. Both countries are densely populated by a population with common cultural ties and with adequate transport infrastructure covering national territory. Moreover, as discussed below, in Rwanda, national integration has been a central concern of the post-genocide political project carried out by the current government that is dominated by the Rwandan Patriotic Front (RPF). In Rwanda, very high levels of infrastructural power across national territory are based on decentralized state structures that reach down into communities and the *imihigo* system of performance contracts that ensure the compliance of frontline officials with central plans (see also Chemouni 2014). While the Bangladeshi state remains comparatively weak, with frontline officials seen as a barrier to effective policy implementation, Naomi Hossain (Chapter 7) argues that the central state has resorted to bypassing these frontline officials to deliver programmes. As such, the lack of clear variation in infrastructural power and programme implementation in Bangladesh and Rwanda is unsurprising.

In contrast, Nepal presents something of an anomaly in that state infrastructural power clearly does vary across national territory based on the particular pattern of state formation in the country and sharply contrasting state–society relations, leading to the expectation of variation in implementation of social transfers also. According to Uma Pradhan and colleagues (Chapter 8), the absence of significant variation across the four Nepalese sites appears to be the result of two main factors. First is the administrative simplicity of the categorical targeting approach adopted in the Scholarship Programme, with entire categories of easily identifiable caste and gender groups eligible for support. This approach places little burden on limited state infrastructural power in participant selection. Second, the general dysfunction of lower-level state administrations presents similar challenges to the effective disbursement of transfers across all sites, regardless of notable variation in state–society relations.

Political contestation and the deployment of infrastructural power

While the historical legacy of patterns of state formation is clearly important for the contemporary capacity of states to implement social transfer programmes within their territories, the case studies also show that history is by no means deterministic. Rather, more recent political dynamics have the potential to transform state infrastructural power or, at the least, to mediate the deployment of existing infrastructural power.

Tim Williams et al. (Chapter 4) argue that Rwanda provides an example of the possibility of overcoming past variation in infrastructural power through the state-building project carried out by a dominant political party. Here case selection focused on two sites considered most likely to illustrate variation in the reach and capacity of the Rwandan state. Huye is an area that has been integral to Rwanda since pre-colonial times and where the state is embedded in society, whereas Ruvabu was only integrated into Rwanda during the colonial period and the state's presence was more limited even in the independence era. However, the catastrophic effects of the genocide, which particularly affected Huye and other parts of southern Rwanda, and the RPF's intensive state-building efforts to address the past history of regional inequality in the country have changed this picture.

Moreover, Ruvabu has a particularly strategic position on the Congolese border, which provided added incentive to expand the reach of the state as a means of consolidating national security. The result, in line with prior expectations, is relative uniformity of state infrastructural power and the distribution of social transfers across the cases. Indeed, if anything, the state now has greater capacity in Ruvabu as a result of the continuing destructive legacy of the genocide in Huye.

Ethiopia provides a useful comparison here regarding the influence of contemporary politics on state infrastructural power. The Ethiopian People's Revolutionary Democratic Front (EPRDF) government (1991–2019) was able to build on a legacy of a centralized and hierarchical state to extend infrastructural power in Tigray and Oromiya regions, in part through fusion of the state with political party structures and their extension down to the household level. While these structures underpinned relatively impartial policy implementation, including of social transfers, this also left state capacity dependent on party-political control. Tom Lavers (Chapter 3) shows how upheaval within the ruling party in Oromiya from around 2015 led to the collapse of party-state infrastructural power in the region to the detriment of the implementation of social transfers. Subsequent to fieldwork a major conflict broke out in Tigray in 2020 and the forced removal of the once-dominant Tigrayan branch of the EPRDF coalition from office in the region has resulted in the disintegration of what had been the most infrastructurally powerful regional state in the country. As such, while the fusion of the state with powerful political parties can serve to extend infrastructural power (see, for example, Levitsky and Way 2010; Slater 2010), this leaves state capacity dependent, in part, on party structures. Any party-political crisis therefore stands to have major ramifications for state capacity also. Indeed, events in Ethiopia have potential relevance also for Rwanda, where high levels of state capacity are also based on a fusion with the politically dominant RPF. Any future political transition would also have important implications for state infrastructural power and development there.

The initial hypothesis outlined in Chapter 2 was that high levels of state infrastructural power—other things being equal—would result in relatively effective programme implementation. The Ethiopian and Rwandan studies support this to a degree, in that distribution of transfers in areas of high infrastructural power is relatively impartial. However, the cases clearly show that, despite relative impartiality, implementation is not necessarily effective in providing social protection for programme participants as a result of political pressure to limit programme coverage. As Michael Mann and others have noted (Mann 1984; Soifer and vom Hau 2008), infrastructural power is a neutral concept, independent of the purpose to which this power is turned. As such, the power relations shaping how infrastructural power is deployed are of vital importance to the actual implementation of social transfer programmes. For this purpose, Mann (1984) contrasts the despotic power of the state, namely the ability to make decisions without negotiation and consultation with civil society, with its infrastructural power, the ability actually to implement those decisions across national territory.

It is here that the political priorities of national governments are influential. As noted in Chapter 2, the six countries studied in the book were selected as examples of three distinct political rationales for social transfer programmes: a dominant-developmental focus in Ethiopia and Rwanda; a competitive-distributive focus in Ghana and Kenya; and a universalistic-inclusive narrative in Bangladesh and Nepal. First, the party-state in Ethiopia and Rwanda is powerful in terms of not just infrastructural power, but also despotic power, in that policy decisions are generally made by a narrow political elite with minimal negotiation with broader society. For this political elite in each country, a central objective of social transfer programmes is to mobilize people and resources for productive activities in order to contribute to self-reliance and national development, with governments concerned about the potential for receipt of social transfers to lead to welfare dependency (Chemouni 2018; Lavers 2019a, 2019b, 2019c).

While governments' intentions are that the programmes' protective and productive objectives can be complementary, in practice implementation reveals deep tensions between the two, which are generally resolved in favour of productive aspirations. In Ethiopia, a central focus for government has been on graduation from support as an indicator of the PSNP's success. The perverse result of the government's despotic power was the mobilization of party-state infrastructural power to impose graduation targets, knowingly depriving some of the poorest and most vulnerable people of minimal support as a means of demonstrating developmental 'progress', regardless of the actual food security of those graduated from the programme. In Rwanda, meanwhile, the government has mobilized the infrastructural power of the state to pressure participants into taking micro-credit, and has arbitrarily arrested those who fail to repay loans in order to meet top-down quotas in officials' performance evaluations. The emphasis on infrastructure creation through public works also leads local state officials to expand participation in Rwanda's Vision 2020 Umurenge Programme (VUP) beyond the poorest groups that are supposed to be the focus of the programme. Many of the poorest are unable to carry out the heavy labour requirements, forcing officials to recruit able-bodied workers from outside the target group in order to meet ambitious infrastructure development targets.

Ethiopia and Rwanda therefore illustrate both the strengths and limitations of infrastructural power in the light of the despotic power of the state. In each case a politically dominant leadership uses an influential system of top-down performance evaluation to control the activities of state officials and programme participants, both of whom are distrusted by the leadership and suspected of a tendency towards dependency and laziness. As others have argued previously, such forms of top-down monitoring and evaluation are often not conducive to effective policy implementation, since they impose uniform approaches regardless of the context and limit the ability of local officials to innovate and come up with context-specific solutions to adapt national priorities to local settings (Ang 2016; Hassan 2020). Indeed, in both countries, governments have struggled to identify performance targets that accurately capture the range of protective and productive objectives of their social transfer programmes. In both cases, the tendency has been to focus the attention of local state officials on easy-to-measure quantitative targets related to productive rather than protective goals. In Ethiopia and Rwanda, therefore, the government has mobilized party-state infrastructural power in an attempt to limit provision of social transfers, minimizing government financial exposure and attempting to use social transfers as a contribution to and symbol of national progress.

This attempt to direct state infrastructural power to productivist objectives differs sharply from the experience in Ghana and Kenya, with important implications for the distribution of social transfers. In this second group of countries, where elections are extremely competitive, states are not just infrastructurally, but also despotically weaker than their counterparts in Ethiopia and Rwanda. As such, governments have responded to electoral incentives by expanding social transfer programmes as a highly visible means of distribution with a view to winning the support of voters (Wanyama and McCord 2017; Abdulai 2020). Despite this common focus on utilizing social transfers as a means of securing electoral support, this pressure plays out in quite different ways in the process of implementation depending on local patterns of competition and party politics.

In Ghana, electoral pressures have driven significant expansion of the Livelihood Empowerment Against Poverty (LEAP) programme since 2008, which now covers every district in the country, with increases in coverage and payment levels usually taking place in the run-up to national elections (Abdulai 2020). However, LEAP remains a narrowly poverty-targeted programme with modest coverage in each district. Edward Ampratwum's selection of two dominant and two competitive districts clearly illustrates the differing incentives for local political actors to engage in the supposedly technocratic implementation of LEAP. In competitive districts, politicians have infiltrated administrative committees and seek to influence geographic and household targeting to reward supporters of their party and, sometimes, factions within them. In contrast, in dominant settings, these incentives are greatly reduced with the result that party-political affiliation plays less of a role in targeting and, at times, politicians even try to insulate programmes from political influence. The result is that, despite the sharp divergence in the level of infrastructural power between northern and southern Ghana, politically contested Sissala East in the north and Gomoa West in the south have more in common with each other with respect to the distribution of social transfers than they do with politically dominant districts in their own regions. Once again, this shows that, under certain circumstances, contemporary political competition can be more influential than the long-run legacy of state infrastructural power.

In Kenya, in contrast, electoral pressures have driven a more significant expansion of the coverage of social transfers nationally. Indeed, increasingly broad-based programmes are transitioning into universalistic categorical designs with adoption of the social pension in 2017 and current government consideration of a universal child grant.[1] This increasing focus on broad and inclusive coverage partly explains the political incentives supporting largely impartial implementation. The partial exception here is in Homa Bay where, like in competitive districts in Ghana, contemporary political divisions impede the infrastructural power of the state. Rather than competition for power at local level, however, here the challenge relates to the division between the national government and the political opposition, which dominates the district. The result is that local politicians attempted to seize the opportunity for greater involvement in programme administration than in other parts of the country to compensate for the limited capacity and embeddedness of centrally appointed bureaucrats.

The political priorities of national governments differ again in the third set of countries—Bangladesh and Nepal. Here the state is both despotically and infrastructurally weaker than that in Ethiopia and Rwanda, despite the Awami League's growing political dominance in Bangladesh. Both countries have increasingly turned to universalistic approaches in the distribution of social transfers, grounded to some degree in a narrative of social inclusion or social justice. In both countries, a universalistic approach has reduced the logistical barriers to programme implementation, bypassing local political challenges and reducing the pressure on limited state capacity. In Bangladesh, Hossain argues that the universal distribution of stipends to all children attending state primary schools is an intentional effort by the governing Awami League to bypass the limited capacity of the local state that is increasingly seen as an impediment to progress. In contrast, in Nepal, the social justice framing is a response to the political mobilization of historically disadvantaged castes and the Maoist insurrection. However, while this social justice framing dominates nationally, the national government has lacked the control over local officials to impose this emphasis, with many continuing to employ a competing narrative that casts the scholarship in productivist terms.

These political dynamics have therefore been important in the shaping implementation of social transfer programmes across the case studies. However, it is notable that popular engagement and social accountability do not emerge from the case studies as a major factor driving improved service delivery. A central motivation for decentralization reforms has been to increase public participation in service delivery and thereby the accountability of state officials to citizens (World Bank 2004). With respect to social transfers, efforts to promote social accountability in Ghana, Ethiopia, Kenya, and Rwanda include community-based targeting and community 'verification' of centralized targeting decisions, as well as grievance mechanisms that allow community members to make complaints about implementation failings. However, these donor-supported social accountability initiatives do not emerge as a significant factor shaping implementation in any of the case studies. Mirroring findings from the existing literature (Hickey and King 2016), most social accountability measures ignore the reality of local power relations where some combination of state and party officials, and social elites exerts considerable influence over implementation, while weak social accountability measures provide little incentive to take appeals or community input seriously (see Chapters 3–6 and also Ibrahim 2021). Moreover, the turn to proxy means tests in Ghana, Kenya, and Rwanda has tended to reduce community participation and engagement as decision-making is increasingly centralized and lacking in transparency, as discussed below. In Bangladesh, meanwhile, although the centralization of control over the education stipends and the outsourcing of payments to a private provider may have improved implementation in certain respects, Hossain highlights the complete absence of redress mechanisms and lack of accountability for implementation failings. The only clear example amongst the cases studies in which popular mobilization shaped policy implementation was in Saptari, Nepal, where parents of schoolchildren receiving the scholarships protested against a rare attempt by a school to enforce the scholarships' attendance conditions. Rather than a formal social accountability mechanism, this example is closer to the informal processes that Hossain (2010) has previously described as 'rude' accountability, and therefore highlights the limited enforcement capacity of the state.

In sum, then, the country studies clearly demonstrate the influence of both state infrastructural power and political contestation in the distribution of social transfers. Distinct combinations of infrastructural power and political dynamics combine in the case studies to produce significant inter- and intra-country variation in the distribution of social transfers. In general, high levels of infrastructural power are associated with more impartial implementation in the case studies, albeit that the pursuit of productivist objectives in Ethiopia and Rwanda has undermined the programmes' protective function. Meanwhile, political dominance tends to be associated with relative impartiality in Bangladesh, Ethiopia, Ghana, and Rwanda. Indeed, none of the cases provides an example of political contestation driving increased effectiveness, whereas competition—between parties locally or between national and local governments—does sometimes provide incentives for politicians to intervene in the distribution of social transfers to try to secure political advantage. While much research has sought to emphasize the importance of either past critical junctures and the legacy for state capacity *or* contemporary politics for implementation and programme outcomes, this study clearly illustrates that a combination of both is influential in the distributional politics of social transfers. Effective implementation requires both state infrastructural power and its effective deployment through supportive power relations. The studies therefore show the value of this framework for examining the distributional politics of social transfers and its potential for application to other settings also.

3. Distributional politics and the risk of 'political capture'

A widespread concern within the social protection literature is that the expansion of social transfer programmes may lead to the 'political capture' of programmes as political actors seek to use their influence to shape the distribution of social transfers to their advantage. Within the policy literature, this concern can perhaps be attributed to the 'fetish' of poverty targeting and the obsession with limiting inclusion errors (Ravallion 2015). Research on other regions of the world shows the potential for social transfers to be politically manipulated, and research on Africa and South Asia has raised concerns about the potential for social transfers to be distributed based on patron–clientelist rationales (Wanyama and McCord 2017; Hickey and Bukenya 2021; Pruce and Hickey 2019). The studies in this volume certainly show that there have been problems with targeting in many instances and that political motivations are sometimes responsible. However, for the most part clientelism does not provide an adequate explanation for the distribution of social transfers in these cases.

The clearest instances in which political factors have undermined the impartial distribution of social transfers are the two competitive districts in Ghana: Sissala East and Gomoa West. In line with findings regarding the political incentives provided by Ghana's intensely competitive two-party system (Abdulai and Hulme 2015; Abdulai and Hickey 2016; Driscoll 2018; Whitfield 2018), in competitive districts geographic and household targeting has been used to reward party supporters and intra-party factions. Ampratwum argues that local officials do not necessarily disregard official programme criteria entirely, but rather use party affiliation as an additional 'sieve' so that programme participants must meet both poverty *and* political criteria. Nonetheless, the likely result is that poor and vulnerable people who should be eligible for support are omitted due to their lack of political affiliation. It is unclear whether this meets the criteria of a strict definition of clientelism, however. As noted in Chapter 2, clientelism implies an enforceable exchange of resources for political loyalty (Weyland 1996; Van de Walle 2014). Ampratwum provides no evidence that political parties have the capacity or willingness to enforce such an exchange—for example, by withdrawing LEAP access from those who do not turn out to vote the right way at elections. While the distribution of LEAP is certainly politicized, it is perhaps best described as an attempt to secure support through the visible distribution of patronage, rather than an explicit clientelist exchange.

While the competitive districts in Ghana therefore lend some support to the common concerns expressed in the literature, this is not a uniform problem. LEAP implementation experiences far fewer problems in the dominant settings, where the lack of competitive pressures gives more space for bureaucrats to implement the programme impartially. Moreover, the other five country cases provide little evidence for concerns about the dangers of 'political capture'. Kenya represents another country in which one might expect social transfer distribution to be similarly captured within the logic of patron–clientelism. Clientelism is widely considered to be a central feature of Kenyan politics in general (Barkan and Okumu 1979; Kramon 2018; Cheeseman et al. 2020), and the dangers of social transfer distribution being shaped by clientelist relations have been an explicitly stated concern of past research (Wanyama and Nyambedha 2014; Wanyama and McCord 2017). Yet Porisky's contribution suggests that clientelism has not, in practice, been a major factor driving implementation of social transfers. In ethnically homogeneous and politically dominant counties, there is little incentive for politicians to use social transfers in this way. Moreover, in the ethnically heterogeneous and electorally competitive counties in Kenya, thus far, the main political concern has been to distribute social transfers equitably between ethnic groups in order to preserve social peace, rather than using the programmes to reward supporters. Memories of the 2007 election and its violent aftermath are important in this respect. Disputes over the outcome of that election quickly sparked inter-ethnic disputes over the distribution of land and other resources within the Rift Valley, including Nakuru county (Kanyinga 2009; Boone 2014). The result has been strong political pressure to avoid manipulation of the distribution of social transfers. As such, control over targeting has been relatively centralized and, in the most sensitive areas such as Nakuru, the central administration conducts geographic targeting down to the level of ethnically homogeneous villages to limit bias.

Ethiopia and Rwanda present a very different picture again. Here, the governments in power at the time of fieldwork came to power through the military victory of insurgencies associated with ethnic minorities. Given the difficulty of a minority regime maintaining power through competitive elections, the two governments arrived at similar political strategies that aimed at broad-based economic growth and distribution as a means of building popular legitimacy or, at a minimum, acquiescence, backed with repression where required (Booth and Golooba-Mutebi 2012; Gebresenbet 2014; Chemouni 2018; Lavers 2019a). Rhetorically and, to varying degrees, in practice, these regimes have explicitly sought to distance themselves from clientelism and corruption focusing instead on programmatic delivery to deliver developmental success. As such, these dominant parties face little in the way of organized opposition that would provide an electoral threat, reducing the need to manipulate the distribution of social transfers to reward supporters.

Nonetheless, in both Ethiopia and Rwanda, programme implementation is politicized in the sense that political parties are heavily involved in the distribution of social transfers. Contrary to the common concerns about the dangers of 'political capture' in the literature, the intertwinement of the party and state underpins relatively impartial—though, as discussed above, not necessarily effective—implementation. Indeed, as noted in the previous section, the strength of the political party is key to the strong infrastructural power required to deliver social transfers—particularly in terms of the reach of the state into communities, the ability to mobilize community members to participate in programmes, and the systems of top-down accountability that ensure compliance of frontline officials with government initiatives. There are certain similarities here with Naomi Hossain's study of Bangladesh (Chapter 7), which argues that growing political dominance of the Awami League has reduced the government's incentives to politicize the distribution of education stipends. While the Awami League has not initiated the kind of party-state-building effort seen in Ethiopia and Rwanda, the pursuit of performance legitimacy, Hossain argues, underpins efforts to bypass weak local administrative structures, which have in the past been associated with manipulation of programme distribution and are seen as an obstacle to progress, through technology and policy design.

Clientelism is, of course, not the sole means by which party politics can undermine implementation. As Sara Niedzwiecki (2018) argues in her study of Argentina and Brazil, even where implementation is relatively programmatic, political divisions at different levels of the state can undermine programmes. For social transfer programmes, which are usually associated with national governments, the incentives for local governments to support or impede programme implementation depend on their political affiliation. Where local politicians are aligned with national government, they have incentives to support effective implementation that enables their party to claim credit. Where they are in opposition to the national government, they have incentives to impede implementation or even to set up local social transfer programmes in competition, thereby limiting the national government's ability to claim credit.

Kenya's Homa Bay provides a highly relevant illustration in this regard. In a context in which political affiliation is strongly shaped by ethnic identification, social transfers were introduced and expanded under successive governments led by Kikuyu presidents, and research has found highly partisan support for cash transfers in the country (Opalo 2019). In contrast, the dominant Luo population of Homa Bay district provides a stronghold for the political opposition. The result is that local politicians have explored the possibility of establishing a county-run social transfer programme in competition to national programmes. Moreover, the national government's decision to register all over-70s for a new universal social pension in the run-up to the closely contested and controversial 2017 elections led to concerns about the government's use of the programme to secure popular support. The result was that local politicians impeded programme registration, resulting in many people being excluded, at least initially, from access to this nominally universal programme.

In contrast, this dynamic is less evident in Ghana where the pressures resulting from intense electoral competition play out quite differently with respect to the social transfer programme. In Ghana, LEAP was introduced in 2008 under the NPP government shortly before the elections that year. Despite initial criticism of the programme by the opposition NDC, the NDC actually expanded the programme significantly after winning the 2008 elections, while both parties promised further expansion of the programme at the 2016 elections, which were won by the NPP (Abdulai 2020). The result of this alternation of power is that LEAP has lost a strong association with either party. Rather than impeding implementation in an attempt to limit the national government's ability to claim credit, as might be expected, Ampratwum (Chapter 5) as well as Abdulai (2020) rather describe a situation in which politicians at all levels of the state seek to claim credit for expansions and to influence distribution with a view to favouring their supporters and promoting their electoral chances in both party primaries and multi-party elections.[2]

In several instances, policy and administrative reforms have been key means of avoiding past problems or future concerns about political manipulation of social transfer distribution. In Bangladesh and Kenya this has entailed re-centralizing control over the distribution process in order to limit the discretion afforded to local officials. In certain respects this approach echoes what have been described as 'institutional bypasses' (Prado and Trebilcock 2018). From this perspective, rather than directly confronting the reform of an underperforming agency and the barriers in terms of vested interests and entrenched bureaucratic norms, a more successful alternative may be to create a new agency that bypasses the dysfunctional organization entirely and which outperforms the existing one (Prado and Trebilcock 2018). To some degree such a process is evident in the design of social transfer programmes in Latin America also, where new central government agencies staffed with technocrats have been created in Brazil and Mexico to centralize control of targeting through a unified registry and direct payments to programme recipients through ATM cards (Fried 2012; De La O 2013; Sugiyama and Hunter 2013; Nichter 2014).

World Bank influence appears to have been important in driving a series of reforms in African countries that aim similarly to strengthen central control over targeting using a proxy means test, while exploiting new technology to bypass local politics. This approach has been most successful in Kenya. Here a standard targeting procedure has been put in place for all the social transfers under the World Bank-supported National Safety Nets Programme, involving centralized administration of the registry and selection of participants using a proxy means test, direct payments to participants through mobile money, and regular audits of county offices by the national agency. Vitally, national political pressures have been supportive of these attempts to impose impartial implementation, as a result of the pressure for broad-based distribution of transfers and concerns about inter-ethnic conflict, as noted above. The main challenge to effective implementation in Kenya, as a result, is not 'political capture' but rather the territorial reach of the state, with the central administration's oversight of county offices varying enormously depending on their distance from Nairobi and local state offices unable to penetrate local society in peripheral areas.

The World Bank has promoted similar reforms in the other African case studies in this book also, albeit with less successful results. In Rwanda, problems with the Ubedehe's system of community-based targeting led the government to introduce its own proxy means test as an 'objective' check on community selection. However, political criteria do not seem to have been a major factor in targeting decisions, as noted above, and many observers view the survey as poorly designed and unsuitable for the task. In Ethiopia, meanwhile, the government has decided against implementing World Bank proposals to incorporate a proxy means test alongside existing community-based targeting. World Bank promoted reforms have been implemented in Ghana. However, Ampratwum's study underscores the need for alignment between such technical fixes and political dynamics. In contrast to Kenya, where the government generally seems to have supported impartial implementation, similar reforms in Ghana, which aim to limit the role of local political actors by centralizing targeting procedures, have not had the desired effects. Rather, local political figures, enabled by aligned national politicians, have found ways of limiting attempts to bypass their involvement. In the case of geographic targeting, which was centralized to limit the influence of the politically appointed District Chief Executives and elected Members of Parliament, these officials have exploited their connections with the minister and other national politicians, who pressured the national LEAP Management Secretariat to change targeted communities to those favoured by local politicians. Likewise with household targeting, local political actors pre-selected party members and then coached these favoured candidates on how to answer the survey questions to ensure they passed the proxy means test.[3] Indeed, to a lesser degree, similar practices were evident in Homa Bay in Kenya, where local politicians played a greater role in implementation and chiefs in some sub-counties pre-selected people for consideration by the proxy means test.

In Bangladesh and Nepal, the discretionary powers of local state officials have also been limited. However, in these cases local officials were bypassed through universalistic policy designs, rather than the centralization of targeting decisions. In both countries, past research has argued that social programmes have been influenced by clientelism (Galasso and Ravallion 2005; Hossain 2010; Drucza 2019). However, the trend towards universal distribution to entire social groups rather than poverty targeting has limited discretion and the use of these programmes for clientelistic purposes. In Bangladesh, Hossain attributes the decision to distribute stipends to all children attending state schools to the growing political dominance of the Awami League nationally and its pursuit of performance legitimacy, while in Nepal scholarships cover all girls and disadvantaged castes in response to the Maoist insurgency and claims for social inclusion to address past injustice. As a by-product of these changes, however, the reforms have limited the role of frontline officials to registration of easily identifiable participants and removed most of their discretionary powers. The result in both countries has been an absence of politically motivated allocation of the scholarships. A comparable change may be under way also in Kenya. Here, the competitive pressures of the electoral system have favoured increasingly broad-based distribution of social transfers over time, with a universal pension introduced from 2017 and a universal child grant under consideration at the time of writing. This turn to universal distribution would further address concerns about the discretionary power of political actors and, potentially, the limits to the state's capacity to oversee selection processes, as discussed above.

Overall, then, the case studies serve to emphasize the importance of political dynamics to the success of reform efforts. The tendency of the policy literature on social protection has been to seek ways of de-politicizing implementation in order to promote impartiality. Yet, as noted above, in all cases, including where implementation is relatively impartial, politics plays an important role in shaping programme choices and outcomes. This is the case in Bangladesh, Ethiopia, and Rwanda where developmental progress is given priority by the fused party-state, in Kenya where equitable distribution between ethnic groups is prioritized to avoid inter-communal tensions, and in Nepal where the priority is to address social injustice. Ghana's competitive districts, however, show the limits of technical reform processes and the ability of donors to limit political involvement, where political dynamics are not supportive of these efforts. Here local political actors' efforts to utilize political affiliation as a criterion in the allocation of social transfers have been enabled by national politicians seeking to leverage the programme for political gain.

4. The politics of distributing social transfers and the future of social protection

Social transfer programmes have spread rapidly across developing countries in the last two decades, with governments taking steps to institutionalize many such programmes and expand their coverage. The Covid-19 pandemic has accelerated this expansion, at least temporarily, as many governments turned to social transfers from 2020 onwards as a means of cushioning vulnerable groups against the economic shock resulting from the spread of the virus and efforts to contain it. This book makes a significant contribution to the literature through detailed analysis of the political processes shaping the distribution of social transfers. However, the findings have relevance not just to theoretical debates about the drivers of effective implementation, but also to the future direction of social protection policy. This final section considers, first, the implications of the studies for programme design and the challenge of targeting and, second, the potential for social transfers to form the basis of a social contract.

Distributing social transfers and the challenge of targeting

The common focus on narrowly targeted anti-poverty transfers within social protection and the specific mechanisms employed to select programme participants has been subject to considerable debate and critique relating to the political, ethical, and practical challenges of targeting, as discussed in Chapter 1 of this book. Despite much heated debate in this respect, there is a surprising lack of detailed research examining how social transfers are actually distributed in practice, a gap that this book has sought to address by highlighting the importance of both state infrastructural power and political contestation. Effective implementation is not the result of the de-politicization of policy-making, as often seems to be assumed, but rather political dynamics that channel the capacities of the state towards delivery of programme objectives. In diverse ways, all of the case studies support this basic point. What, however, are the implications of this research for the different approaches to distributing social transfers employed in the case studies?

All of the four African cases—Ethiopia, Ghana, Kenya, and Rwanda—as with many other social transfer programmes in Africa, employ some form of community-based targeting to identify participants. The advantages of community-based targeting are generally considered to be that it reduces the burden on the state of generating sufficiently detailed and accurate information with which to select programme participants by mobilizing the local knowledge of community actors. Moreover, by involving members of local communities, this can enhance public participation, transparency, and accountability, potentially leading to more effective and legitimate interventions. Past research has raised valid concerns about the accuracy of community knowledge and ethical questions about the process of assessing the economic status of one's neighbours. Beyond these important issues, the case studies highlight two main points. First, while community-based targeting may reduce the demands placed on the state, to work effectively this form of selection nonetheless requires state infrastructural power, particularly the territorial reach of the state. In both Tigray and Oromiya in Ethiopia, and Rwanda, community-based targeting is something of a misnomer. In these settings, selection would be better described as *party-state targeting*. Targeting decisions are not devolved to community actors, but are made through decentralized party-state structures that penetrate communities and reach down to household level—Ethiopia's development teams and one-to-fives and Rwanda's villages and *Isibo*—mobilizing individuals for participation in government initiatives and serving as structures of control. Where such targeting is relatively effective, it depends on the capacity of the party-state. The importance of state infrastructural power is clearly highlighted when we turn to peripheral areas in Afar, Ethiopia and Marsabit, Kenya. Here, the state lacks sufficient reach and embeddedness within local society to be able to oversee and regulate participant selection. The result in both cases is that the state devolves responsibility for targeting to community actors such as clan leaders, leading to wide variation in targeting processes, which become subject to the authority of social actors over whom the state has little control. The clear implication, therefore, is that community-based targeting is no panacea in areas where state capacity is limited, but rather requires at least minimal degrees of state capacity for relatively effective functioning.

Second, community-based targeting implies an undifferentiated notion of the 'community' where community members are able freely to contribute their knowledge to decision making, ignoring the reality that intra-community relations are shaped by power relations between different social classes, ethnic groups, generations, and genders. The promotion of community-based targeting in this sense reflects common and naïve assumptions about the potential of decentralization and participation to improve implementation (Cooke and Kothari 2001; Hickey and Mohan 2004). In contrast, the case studies show that political parties in all countries, traditional authorities in Ghana, and the clan in Marsabit, Kenya and Afar, Ethiopia are all important power structures shaping community relations. The influence of these factors in targeting decisions has the potential to lead to bias based on party-political affiliation, ethnicity, and gender, contrary to programme guidelines.

The other main mechanism used for poverty targeting in the case studies is a proxy means test. The World Bank, in particular, has pushed governments to introduce proxy means tests alongside community-based targeting with a view to providing an 'objective' check on the inherently subjective nature of community selection and thereby limiting the influence of local political and social actors that might otherwise creep in. The result is that proxy means tests—designed with World Bank support—have been introduced in Ghana and Kenya. In Rwanda, the government designed its own proxy means test, while proposals for such a mechanism in Ethiopia have not, as yet, been implemented. The claimed advantage of proxy means tests is that they provide an objective assessment of eligibility, but lower the vast data requirements facing the state as it seeks to assess the economic condition of its population. Yet, the accuracy of proxy means tests has been questioned, while such surveys require very significant investment to carry out and to keep up to date (Kidd et al. 2017).

The case studies covered here again suggest two main conclusions of relevance to this approach to participant selection. First, the assumption that centralized control over a proxy means test necessarily limits political influence over selection is inaccurate. Centralized control over targeting can contribute to greater impartiality in implementation (whether targeting is accurate or otherwise), as in Kenya (Chapter 6) and in Brazil (Sugiyama and Hunter 2013). However, for this goal to be realized, political dynamics must be supportive of impartial implementation. The competitive districts of Sissala East and Gomoa West in Ghana clearly show that where a centralized proxy means test has been implemented without political support for impartiality, officials can relatively easily find their way around measures designed to insulate selection from political influence. In these districts, pre-selection of potential participants by local political actors and coaching prior to their evaluation by the proxy means test meant that only those affiliated with the right party were selected. Similarly, the lack of state infrastructural power in Marsabit, Kenya meant that pre-selection of participants was deferred to clan leaders, with the result that state officials had no control over the process. Without supportive politics, proxy means tests offer little solution to existing problems.

Second, whatever the merits or otherwise of proxy means tests, attempts to combine the use of community-based targeting and proxy means tests undermine the advantages of the former. A common complaint of community respondents in Ghana, Kenya, and Rwanda was that the centralization of targeting undermines community participation and the legitimacy of the process, which from their perspective is reduced to an arbitrary decision made 'by the computer'. Having put time and effort into making an initial selection, which—accurate or otherwise—is often considered legitimate, community members were understandably frustrated when the centralized process produced a quite different allocation. The common result is disengagement from the process and a lack of transparency.

Another common concern associated with targeted programmes relates to the stigma often attached to programme participation. As discussed in Chapter 1, anti-poverty interventions have a long history of distinguishing between the deserving and undeserving poor, and stigmatizing participants with a view to discouraging reliance on programme support. In extreme cases, such as the English workhouses of the nineteenth century, participants exchanged a loss of civil rights in order to qualify for the minimal support provided. The main example in this respect among the six cases is Rwanda, where the lowest Ubudehe category that qualifies households for the VUP is associated with considerable stigma. Indeed, several respondents expressed apparently unfounded concerns that they might even be branded with an earring or other marking as a symbol of their poverty status. Moreover, for those living in Rubavu, classification in the lowest Ubudehe category meant a loss of civic rights, with participants denied a passport—required to access the nearby Democratic Republic of the Congo—and, on occasion, arbitrary arrests for failure to repay micro-credit. On a much lesser scale, some participants in Ethiopia's PSNP also reported embarrassment at their dependence on support and pride for those who graduate into self-reliance. In the other country cases, however, the expansionary pressures driving social transfer programmes and the use of programmes as a visible means of distribution aimed at winning popular support appear to have largely negated problematic associations with the programmes.

In sharp contrast to the problems associated with poverty targeting, the move to more universalistic categorical targeting in Bangladesh, Kenya, and Nepal offers significant advantages. First, categorical targeting significantly reduces the informational challenge and data requirements facing states in selecting participants. Initial registration of all elderly individuals in Marsabit, Kenya in a compressed period leading up to national elections did pose a challenge for state infrastructural power. However, there is no sign that this is anything more than a temporary challenge to the roll out of the social pension. In Bangladesh and Nepal, selection of participants has posed little challenge to state infrastructural power. Likewise, this universalistic design has limited or eliminated the discretionary power of local officials that previously provided opportunities for the politicization of distribution. This is most clearly demonstrated in Hossain's study of Bangladesh where the targeting of primary education stipends created major headaches for teachers responsible for selection, who were often accused—rightly or wrongly—of bias. Universal registration has removed this challenge. The attempt by local political opposition to impede registration for Kenya's universal pension in Homa Bay county shows that universalism is not without political challenges. However, it seems likely that the problems will be short term, rather than a long-standing barrier to implementation.

The case studies therefore suggest that household targeting remains a major challenge and one that is dependent on the capacity of the state and political dynamics that support impartial implementation. While universalistic programmes of the sort pursued in Bangladesh, Kenya, and Nepal offer significant advantages in simplifying the implementation process and bypassing these political challenges, it is important to note that policy choices are to a significant degree path dependent, with major barriers to policy change. In all of the cases covered in this volume, social protection systems are at a formative stage and future trajectories are not set in stone. However, there are, nonetheless, signs of divergent pathways emerging among the cases. The preceding chapters suggest that Bangladesh, Kenya, and Nepal appear to be on a path towards increasingly broad-based and universalistic distribution of social transfers as a means of competing for electoral support, responding to past social injustice or building the performance legitimacy of the ruling party. This is likely to minimize the challenge that implementation poses to state capacity and reduce the discretion of local political actors in distribution. The future of Ghana's LEAP is rather hard to predict. Like Kenya, Ghanaian politicians have used social transfers as a campaign tool in tightly fought elections, with political actors claiming credit for expansion and using the programme as a visible form of distribution. One possibility, therefore, is that LEAP follows the pattern of social transfers in Kenya where programmes have continuously expanded, eventually transitioning into universalistic programmes. Nonetheless, at present this seems a remote prospect; LEAP remains a relatively small programme with limited population coverage. For the time being, Ghana will continue to face the challenges that variation in infrastructural power and highly competitive politics pose for impartial distribution of social transfers. The possibility of universalism is an even more distant prospect in the final two countries: Ethiopia and Rwanda. Here, social transfers remain embedded within ideological commitments to self-reliance, productivist social protection, and concerns about welfare dependency. The result is that political actors continue to prioritize targeting the poorest and the promotion of graduation out of social protection and into self-reliance.

The Covid-19 pandemic is, of course, of great significance to future trends in social protection. The lockdowns aimed at controlling the spread of the virus, and the disruption of economic activity and international trade, have resulted in a widespread economic shock whose impacts goes well beyond the standard focus of social transfer programmes on the poorest in society. Indeed, the pandemic has led to some recognition of the limits of existing approaches to social protection, which largely exclude those of working age and those working in the informal sector, many of whom have been hit particularly hard. Early indications are that governments have responded to the pandemic by increasing social protection provision in terms of payment levels and coverage of existing programmes and, in some circumstances, also extended them to additional groups such as those of working age (Gentilini et al. 2020; Devereux 2021). Thus far, however, most such responses have been temporary only, rather than signalling a fundamental rethink of the role of social protection. For example, Bangladesh, Ethiopia, Kenya, and Rwanda have all expanded coverage of existing social transfer programmes on a temporary basis; Ethiopia and Rwanda temporarily waived public works obligations in their programmes to avoid contributing to transmission of the virus; and Ethiopia, Rwanda, Bangladesh, and Nepal have all distributed food for the poorest during stay-at-home orders (Gentilini et al. 2020). In a few instances—notably Ghana and Nepal—new programmes have been established to provide support to informal-sector workers whose main activities have been disrupted by the pandemic, albeit on a rather small scale. The limited and temporary expansion of these programmes will also be forced to confront the economic fallout of the pandemic, with any pressure for expansion of programme coverage likely to face significant fiscal constraints and pressure to reduce government and, in some cases, donor expenditure.

Of the common responses to the pandemic, increasing payments to existing participants and waiving associated conditions are relatively straightforward to implement. In contrast, extending programmes to cover previously excluded groups such as informal-sector workers is more problematic and presents particular challenges with respect to targeting. Existing social registries only contain information on candidates assessed for eligibility for past poverty-focused programmes and therefore provide no means of identifying broader sections of the population who may be in need of support as a result of the pandemic. As such, a rapid expansion of programme coverage is subject to many of the informational challenges to state capacity common to targeted programmes in general and discussed at length in this book.

Overall, then, targeting of social transfers is deeply problematic in many ways and, as argued in this volume, the practical challenge of implementation can be added to the ethical and political questions that have frequently been raised in policy debates. Governments' ability to implement targeted social transfer programmes effectively depends to a considerable degree on state infrastructural power and supportive political dynamics. In many instances, where capacity is lacking and political contestation is likely to undermine impartial implementation, universalistic policy designs offer considerable advantages in terms of simplifying the political and administrative challenges of implementation.

Social transfers as the foundation of a social contract?

The introduction and expansion of social transfers across the developing world has led some observers of southern Africa and Latin America to suggest that these programmes could form the foundation of new 'welfare regimes' and emergent social contracts linking states and their citizens (Filgueira et al. 2005; Koehler and Chopra 2014; Ferguson 2015; Garay 2016). To what extent can such claims also be extended to the countries covered in this volume?

A social contract is often invoked in a rather loose way in social protection debates, with this contractarian framing seen as a means of embedding social protection by consolidating political support for programmes, pushing governments to commit to financing programmes in response to the demands of rights-bearing citizens. However, different philosophical traditions have quite different implications for the social contract and the forms of social transfers that would be considered legitimate (Hickey 2011, 2014). From a liberal perspective, a social contract takes the form of an exchange of rights and obligations, with individuals carrying the obligation to work and be a productive member of society, as well as complying with conditions demanded by a particular programme, in exchange for support. Such a framing provides the philosophical justification for poverty-targeting conditional cash transfers, for example. In contrast, from a social rights perspective, social protection is a right of citizenship, providing justification for a universal basic income or perhaps universal grants for children, the elderly, and other vulnerable groups.

To date, most of the debate about social contracts and social transfers has focused on policy choices and programme adoption, with little explicit consideration of implementation. Yet the actual implementation of a programme is vital to developing the kinds of state–society relations that are central to social contract theory. For social transfers to form part of a social contract, they would need to be, at a minimum, implemented in a fair and transparent way so as to ensure that they reached the intended recipients and that those affected by the programme had the ability to appeal where the state does not deliver. As the cases in this volume have clearly shown, however, implementation in most instances falls short of this. Moreover, given the uneven nature of the implementation of social transfers within countries, it therefore seems likely that any move to embed social transfers within a social contract will also be uneven. Once again, sub-national work in political science is relevant here, with past research demonstrating—contrary to standard assumptions—that democratization is a territorially uneven process, and national-level democratization is sometimes dependent on sub-national authoritarianism (O'Donnell 1999; Schedler 2014; Giraudy 2015). Likewise with respect to social protection in Latin America, implementation remains highly uneven within territories (Niedzwiecki 2018). The result is to problematize concepts such as democracies and welfare states, which imply homogeneity within any one country. As Giraudy et al. argue,

> Conceptually, full democracy and welfare state universalism both rest on the idea that all citizens, regardless of where they reside in a country, will have an equal opportunity to exercise their political and social rights. In other words, a full democracy and a universal welfare state can be said to exist only if all citizens across all the national territory can vote, engage in civic activities, express their thoughts freely, and have access to health care and education as well as other forms of social protection. Although a territorially even distribution of political and social rights is implicitly a core attribute of democracy and welfare universalism, it has not been incorporated explicitly into national-level measures of these concepts. Empirically, because existing national-level measures of democracy and welfare state universalism do not account for the uneven territorial extension of rights, they provide limited, and potentially misleading, information for assessing whether countries are fully democratic and universalistic in the provision of welfare benefits.
>
> (Giraudy et al. 2019, pp. 356–7)

If such territorial unevenness applies to democracy and the welfare state, then it surely must also apply to the social contract, given the variation within countries in relations between states and their citizens, the framing of social transfer programmes, the rights and responsibilities of programme participants, and their potential to form the basis of a social contract. Indeed, the case studies in this volume exhibit considerable variation in this respect.

Social transfer programmes in parts of South Asia are increasingly framed within a logic of rights and social justice (Koehler and Chopra 2014) in a way that is not so common in most of Africa. This is the case in Nepal, where Pradhan et al. (Chapter 8) argue that education scholarships are framed as a means of promoting social inclusion and overcoming historical injustice by providing support to all girls and students from disadvantaged castes. Likewise, the universalistic turn in education stipends in Bangladesh, which now cover all primary school students rather than just those in need of support, builds on a longstanding and widely accepted role for the state in preventing crises of subsistence in the wake of the devastating 1974 famine (Hossain 2017). Despite this framing, however, the case studies suggest that social transfers remain limited in important ways. In Nepal, though the Scholarship Programme is framed as a means of addressing social justice, its value thus far is largely symbolic, with minuscule payments making little material difference to the deep-rooted inequalities that persist, while implementation challenges mean that disbursement is slow and unreliable, further diminishing the contribution of the programme. In Bangladesh, meanwhile, the universal turn in the stipend programme is driven not by greater rights and accountability to citizens, but rather by an attempt to secure performance legitimacy to substitute for the lack of procedural legitimacy, as the Awami League consolidates its political dominance in what was previously a highly competitive political system. Any emerging social contract in Bangladesh and Nepal remains very much work in progress.

Kenya provides another instance in which the expansion of social transfers has potential to form part of a social contract. Kenya's social transfer programmes originate in a tiny donor-dominated pilot scheme in the early 2000s (Ouma and Adésínà 2018). However, driven largely by competitive electoral pressures, social transfer programmes have steadily expanded in coverage over the last 20 years and are now transitioning into increasingly universal provision through the adoption of a universal pension and a universal child grant, which is under consideration by the government at the time of writing. This broad-based distribution has the potential to be framed in terms of citizens' rights to support at key stages of the life-cycle, while the 2010 constitutional right to social security has been interpreted by some as providing a legal basis for the ongoing expansion of social protection. The experience in Kenya is noteworthy for several reasons. First, it is significant that a programme that was initially narrowly targeted at the poorest has gradually expanded through competitive electoral pressures—that many have feared would lead to political influence on distribution—into a relatively programmatic and broad-based scheme. This suggests that fears of 'political capture' may not always be well founded, and that politicians' self-interest can drive progressive change. Second, it is notable that the implementation of the social transfer programmes and, consequently, the implications of these programmes for social contracts are territorially uneven. In Chapter 6, Porisky argues that in Nyeri and Nakuru, where implementation is relatively effective as a result of high levels of state infrastructural power, recipients increasingly consider social transfers as a right. In contrast, in Homa Bay, where political party divisions undermine implementation, and in Marsabit, where the lack of state infrastructural power means that state–society relations are mediated by clan leaders, the programmes continue to be seen as a mere gift from national politicians. The findings suggest that the emergence of a social contract in Kenya is likely to be highly uneven.

Beyond Bangladesh, Kenya, and Nepal, there is little sign that social transfers might provide the basis for an emerging social contract. In Ghana, as Ampratwum argues, LEAP remains a narrowly targeted programme and distribution is highly contingent on relations between would-be participants and state officials, political parties, and traditional authorities. Indeed, recent research on Ghana's LEAP shows that the programme has yet to generate the political feedback effects in terms of citizenship and claims-making that might underpin a social contract (Ibrahim 2021). In addition, the Ethiopian and Rwandan cases show that there is little sign of social transfers forming the basis of a social contract. In each case, politics is dominated by a single party with little space for political opposition or a vibrant civil society that could hold the government to account. Moreover, the social transfer programmes in question remain embedded within a productivist framing, whereby participants are expected to work for support, while a central objective of the programmes in each case is to reduce coverage by graduating participants into self-reliance, removing the need for social protection entirely. As discussed above, this has translated in Rwanda into the curtailment of civic rights for programme participants. Clearly there is no space here for the development of a social contract founded on the PSNP or VUP.

The result is that claims made about the potential for social protection to form the basis of a social contract in South Asia (Koehler and Chopra 2014) and southern Africa (Ferguson 2015) feel somewhat optimistic based on the six countries examined in this volume. To date, in the study countries, social transfers have often been of symbolic rather than substantive value, and have often been implemented in highly uneven ways that undermine their potential. Kenya's experience does, perhaps, provide some indications that even small-scale initiatives vulnerable to political interference can, in the right circumstances, expand into substantive programmes that are increasingly consistent with social contract thinking. However, thus far, governments in Africa and South Asia employ social transfers as a means of maintaining political control and securing political advantage just as frequently as they use them to strengthen social rights and build contracts between states and their citizens.

Notes

1. See: https://www.jointsdgfund.org/article/update-progressive-pathway-towards-universal-social-protection-system-kenya-accelerate
2. Niedzwiecki (2018) focuses on electorally competitive contexts where political office is often divided between parties. Unsurprisingly, her theory provides little analytical purchase on the incentives for local state officials to support implementation in the dominant party settings of Bangladesh, Ethiopia, and Rwanda, where one party dominates elected positions at all levels of the state.
3. Mohammed Ibrahim's (2021) research finds similar coaching of potential participants in other parts of Ghana.

References

Abdulai, A.-G., 2020. Competitive clientelism, donors and the politics of social protection uptake in Ghana. *Critical Social Policy*, https://doi.org/10.1177/0261018320945605.

Abdulai, A.-G. and Hickey, S., 2016. The politics of development under competitive clientelism: Insights from Ghana's education sector. *African Affairs*, 115 (458), 44–72.

Abdulai, A.-G. and Hulme, D., 2015. The politics of regional inequality in Ghana: State elites, donors and PRSPs. *Development Policy Review*, 33 (5), 529–553.

Ang, Y. Y., 2016. *How China Escaped the Poverty Trap*. Ithaca, NY: Cornell University Press.

Barkan, J. D. and Okumu, J., 1979. *Politics and Public Policy in Kenya and Tanzania*. New York: Praeger.

Boone, C., 2003. *Political Topographies of the African State: Territorial Authority and Institutional Choice*. Cambridge: Cambridge University Press.

Boone, C., 2014. *Property and Political Order in Africa: Land Rights and the Structure of Conflict*. Cambridge: Cambridge University Press.

Booth, D. and Golooba-Mutebi, F., 2012. Developmental patrimonialism? The case of Rwanda. *African Affairs*, 111 (444), 379–403.

Cheeseman, N., Kanyinga, K., and Lynch, G., 2020. *The Oxford Handbook of Kenyan Politics*. Oxford: Oxford University Press.

Chemouni, B., 2014. Explaining the design of the Rwandan decentralization: Elite vulnerability and the territorial repartition of power. *Journal of Eastern African Studies*, 8 (2), 246–262.

Chemouni, B., 2018. The political path to universal health coverage: Elite commitment to community-based health insurance in Rwanda. *World Development*, 106, 87–98.

Coll-Black, S., Gilligan, D. O., Hoddinott, J., Kumar, N., Taffesse, A. S., and Wiseman, W., 2012. Targeting food security interventions in Ethiopia: The Productive Safety Net Programme. *In:* P. Dorosh and S. Rashid, eds. *Food and Agriculture in Ethiopia: Progress and Policy Challenges*. Philadelphia, PA: University of Pennsylvania Press, 280–317.

Cooke, B. and Kothari, U., 2001. *Participation: The New Tyranny?* London: Zed Books.

De La O, A. L., 2013. Do conditional cash transfers affect electoral behavior? Evidence from a randomized experiment in Mexico. *American Journal of Political Science*, 57 (1), 1–14.

Devereux, S., 2021. Social protection responses to COVID-19 in Africa. *Global Social Policy*, https://doi.org/10.1177/14680181211021260.

Donham, D. L. and James, W., eds., 2002. *The Southern Marches of Imperial Ethiopia*, 2nd edition. London: James Currey.

Donovan, K. P., 2015. Infrastructuring aid: Materializing humanitarianism in northern Kenya. *Environment and Planning D: Society and Space*, 33 (4), 732–748.

Driscoll, B., 2018. Why political competition can increase patronage. *Studies in Comparative International Development*, 53 (4), 404–427.

Drucza, K., 2019. 'At least the government is watching out for us now': Dalit perceptions and experiences of governance and cash transfers in three villages in Sarlahi, Nepal. *Modern Asian Studies*, 53 (6), 2041–2078.

Ferguson, J., 2015. *Give a Man a Fish: Reflections on the New Politics of Distribution*. Durham, NC: Duke University Press.

Filgueira, F., Molina, C. G., Papadópulos, J., and Tobar, F., 2005. Universalismo básico: Una alternativa posible y necesaria para mejorar las condiciones de vida en América Latina. *Documentos de Trabajo del INDES*, I (57).

Fried, B. J., 2012. Distributive politics and conditional cash transfers: The case of Brazil's Bolsa Família. *World Development*, 40 (5), 1042–1053.

Galasso, E. and Ravallion, M., 2005. Decentralized targeting of an antipoverty program. *Journal of Public Economics*, 89 (4), 705–727.

Garay, C., 2016. *Social Policy Expansion in Latin America*. Cambridge: Cambridge University Press.

Gebresenbet, F., 2014. Securitisation of development in Ethiopia: The discourse and politics of developmentalism. *Review of African Political Economy*, 41 (sup1), S64–S74.

Gentilini, U., Almenfi, M., Orton, I., and Dale, P., 2020. *Social Protection and Jobs Responses to COVID-19: A Real-Time Review of Country Measures*. Washington, DC: ILO, UNICEF, World Bank.

Giraudy, A., 2015. *Democrats and Autocrats: Pathways of Subnational Undemocratic Regime Continuity within Democratic Countries*. Oxford: Oxford University Press.

Giraudy, A., Moncada, E., and Snyder, R., 2019. Empirical and theoretical frontiers of subnational research in comparative politics. *In:* A. Giraudy, E. Moncada, and R. Snyder, eds. *Inside Countries: Subnational Research in Comparative Politics*. Cambridge: Cambridge University Press, 353–367.

Hassan, M., 2020. *Regime Threats and State Solutions: Bureaucratic Loyalty and Embeddedness in Kenya*. Cambridge: Cambridge University Press.

Herbst, J., 2000. *States and Power in Africa: Comparative Lessons in Authority and Control*. Princeton, NJ: Princeton University Press.

Hickey, S., 2011. The politics of social protection: What do we get from a 'social contract' approach? *Canadian Journal of Development Studies*, 32 (4), 426–438.

Hickey, S., 2014. Relocating social protection within a radical project of social justice. *European Journal of Development Research*, 26 (3), 322–337.

Hickey, S. and Bukenya, B., 2021. The politics of promoting social cash transfers in Uganda: The potential and pitfalls of 'thinking and working politically'. *Development Policy Review*, 39 (S1), 1–20.

Hickey, S. and King, S., 2016. Understanding social accountability: Politics, power and building new social contracts. *Journal of Development Studies*, 52 (8), 1225–1240.

Hickey, S. and Mohan, G., 2004. *Participation—From Tyranny to Transformation? Exploring New Approaches to Participation in Development*. London: Zed Books.

Hossain, N., 2010. Rude accountability: Informal pressures on frontline bureaucrats in Bangladesh. *Development and Change*, 41 (5), 907–928.

Hossain, N., 2017. *The Aid Lab: Understanding Bangladesh's Unexpected Success*. Oxford: Oxford University Press.

Ibrahim, M., 2021. Social protection, state capacity and citizenship building in Ghana: Do quasi-universal insurance and targeted social assistance policies generate different feedback effects? Ph.D. thesis. University of Manchester.

Kanyinga, K., 2009. The legacy of the white highlands: Land rights, ethnicity and the post-2007 election violence in Kenya. *Journal of Contemporary African Studies*, 27 (3), 325–344.

Kidd, S., Gelders, B., and Bailey-Athias, D., 2017. Exclusion by design: An assessment of the effectiveness of the proxy means test poverty targeting mechanism. ESS Working Papers, 56.

Koehler, G. and Chopra, D., eds., 2014. *Development and Welfare Policy in South Asia*. London: Routledge.
Kramon, E., 2018. *Money for Votes: The Causes and Consequences of Electoral Clientelism in Africa*. Cambridge: Cambridge University Press.
Lavers, T., 2016. Agricultural investment in Ethiopia: Undermining national sovereignty or tool for state building? *Development and Change*, 47 (5), 1078–1101.
Lavers, T., 2019a. Social protection in an aspiring 'developmental state': The political drivers of Ethiopia's PSNP. *African Affairs*, 118 (473), 646–671.
Lavers, T., 2019b. Understanding elite commitment to social protection: Rwanda's Vision 2020 Umurenge Programme. *In:* S. Hickey, T. Lavers, M. Niño-Zarazúa, and J. Seekings, eds. *The Politics of Social Protection in Eastern and Southern Africa*. Oxford: Oxford University Press, 95–121.
Lavers, T., 2019c. Towards universal health coverage in Ethiopia's 'developmental state'? The political drivers of health insurance. *Social Science and Medicine*, 228, 60–67.
Levitsky, S. and Way, L. A., 2010. *Competitive Authoritarianism: Hybrid Regimes after the Cold War*. Cambridge: Cambridge University Press.
Mamdani, M., 1996. *Citizen and Subject: Contemporary Africa and the Legacy of Late Colonialism*. Princeton, NJ: Princeton University Press.
Mann, M., 1984. The autonomous power of the state: Its origins, mechanisms and results. *European Journal of Sociology*, 25 (2), 185–213.
Markakis, J., 2011. *Ethiopia: The Last Two Frontiers*. Oxford: James Currey.
Nichter, S., 2014. Political clientelism and social policy in Brazil. *In:* D. Abente Brun and L. Diamond, eds. *Clientelism, Social Policy and the Quality of Democracy*. Baltimore, MD: Johns Hopkins University Press, 130–151.
Niedzwiecki, S., 2018. *Uneven Social Policies: The Politics of Subnational Variation in Latin America*. Cambridge: Cambridge University Press.
O'Donnell, G. A., 1999. *Counterpoints: Selected Essays on Authoritarianism and Democratization*. Notre Dame, IN: University of Notre Dame Press.
Opalo, K. O., 2019. *The Politics of Social Protection in Africa: Public Opinion Evidence from Kenya on Cash Transfers*. Mimeo. Washington, DC.
Ouma, M. and Adésínà, J., 2018. Solutions, exclusion and influence: Exploring power relations in the adoption of social protection policies in Kenya. *Critical Social Policy*, https://doi.org/10.1177/0261018318817482.
Prado, M. M. and Trebilcock, M. J., 2018. *Institutional Bypasses: A Strategy to Promote Reforms for Development*. Cambridge: Cambridge University Press.
Pruce, K. and Hickey, S., 2019. The politics of promoting social cash transfers in Zambia. *In:* S. Hickey, T. Lavers, M. Niño-Zarazúa, and J. Seekings, eds. *The Politics of Social Protection in Eastern and Southern Africa*. Oxford: Oxford University Press, 176–201.
Ravallion, M., 2015. The Economics of Poverty: History, Measurement, and Policy. Oxford: Oxford University Press.
Sabates-Wheeler, R., Lind, J., and Hoddinott, J., 2013. Implementing social protection in agro-pastoralist and pastoralist areas: How local distribution structures moderate PSNP outcomes in Ethiopia. *World Development*, 50, 1–12.
Schedler, A., 2014. The criminal subversion of Mexican democracy. *Journal of Democracy*, 25 (1), 5–18.
Scott, J. C., 1998. *Seeing Like a State: How Certain Schemes to Improve the Human Condition Have Failed*. London: Yale University Press.

Seekings, J., 2017. State capacity and the construction of pro-poor welfare states in the 'developing' world. *In:* M. Centeno, A. Kohli, and D. J. Yashar, eds. *States in the Developing World*. Cambridge: Cambridge University Press, 363–379.

Slater, D., 2010. *Ordering Power: Contentious Politics and Authoritarian Leviathans in Southeast Asia*. Cambridge: Cambridge University Press.

Soifer, H. and Vom Hau, M., 2008. Unpacking the strength of the state: The utility of state infrastructural power. *Studies in Comparative International Development*, 43 (3–4), 219–230.

Sugiyama, N. B. and Hunter, W., 2013. Whither clientelism? Good governance and Brazil's 'Bolsa Família' program. *Comparative Politics*, 46 (1), 43–62.

Van De Walle, N., 2014. The democratization of clientelism in sub-Saharan Africa. *In:* D. Abente Brun and L. Diamond, eds. *Clientelism, Social Policy and the Quality of Democracy*. Baltimore, MD: Johns Hopkins University Press, 230–252.

Wanyama, F. O. and McCord, A., 2017. The politics of scaling up social protection in Kenya. ESID Working Papers, 87.

Wanyama, F. O. and Nyambedha, E. O., 2014. *The Political Economy of Social Protection Policy Uptake in Kenya*. Nairobi: Partnership for African Social and Governance Research.

Weyland, K., 1996. *Democracy without Equity: Failures of Reform in Brazil*. Pittsburgh, PA: University of Pittsburgh Press.

Whitfield, L., 2018. *Economies after Colonialism: Ghana and the Struggle for Power*. Cambridge: Cambridge University Press.

World Bank, 2004. *World Development Report 2004: Making Services Work for the Poor*. Washington, DC: Oxford University Press/World Bank.

Index

Tables and figures are indicated by an italic *t* and *f* following the page number; 'n.' after a page number indicates the endnote number.